Explaining the Gospels

An Illustrated Introduction

Explaining the Gospels

USA edition published by
David C. Cook Publishing Co.
Elgin, Illinois—Weston, Ontario
ISBN 0 89191 742 X

03905/A3364

Published in Great Britain by
Scripture Union
130 City Road
London EC1V 2NJ
© Scripture Union 1981
ISBN 0 85421 954 4

Produced by Three's Company
Designer Peter M Wyart MSIAD
Organizing Editor Tim Dowley
BA PhD
Scripture Union Executive Editor
Paul Marsh BD

Printed and bound in Great Britain

Foreword

Foreword

When I first saw the plates of this book two years ago in London, I was excited by the creative artistry and biblical scholarship revealed.

Now as I hold the completed volume open before me, that feeling of excitement is only increased. Photographs, three-dimensional maps, diagrams and charts present with exceptional clarity the world in which our Lord Jesus lived and taught. Here are the wildflowers He held up as object lessons, here the coinage of His day, His carpenter's tools, a calendar of the farming year.

I have not visited the Holy Land. The photographs in this book give many answers to my questions that such a trip would have provided: What does Bethlehem look like? Nazareth? the desert region where Jesus was tempted? Galilee, Gethsemane?

Reproductions of paintings by Durer, Raphael, El Greco, Rembrandt and others give artistic depth, while line drawings and even contemporary cartoons give the information so necessary in a commentary.

And commentary this is, with articles by such world-class scholars as FF Bruce and EM Blaiklock. Reading their comments on the text of the four Gospels (Matthew, Mark, Luke, John) I'm impressed with the depth of understanding and simplicity of expression. This is a book that can rest on the coffee table beside the family Bible, to be used in making family devotions come alive.

Family devotions aren't the only thing that will be enlivened by this book. I'm sure Sunday school classes will perk up as teachers use it in lesson preparation and presentation. And preachers will find the book a goldmine of information.

We learn about Jesus Christ in the four Gospels, which makes them supremely important. But the Gospels were also written so that we could encounter Him in a personal way: 'These are written that you may believe that Jesus is the Christ, the Son of God, and that by believing you may have life in his name' (John 20:31, NIV).

That is the purpose of this book. We are indebted to designer Peter Wyart and editor Tim Dowley that the purpose is so splendidly fulfilled.

Joseph Bayly

Contents

Contents

	Page
Foreword	5
Contents	6,7
Contributors	8
Introduction	9
The main ideas of the New Testament	10-15
Books of the Old and New Testament	12,13
The land	16,17

Matthew

	Page
Introduction to Matthew's Gospel	20-22
Outline to Matthew's Gospel	23
Commentary	**24-106**
Mary	25
The Herods	29
Bethlehem	30
Kingdom of God	33
Commandments	40
Matthew	45
Power	50
Qumran and the Dead Sea scrolls	52,53
Law	63
After-life	70
Jerusalem	77-81
Religious and political parties	89
The Temple	96-99
Gethsemane	102
Resurrection	107

Mark

	Page
Introduction to Mark's Gospel	110
Outline to Mark's Gospel	111
The farming year	112,13
Commentary	**115-79**
The home	120
Tax-collectors	121
Disciple	123
Peter	124
Galilee	126-28
Parables	130,31
Capernaum	136,37
John the Baptist	139
Healing	143
Caesarea Philippi	146,47
Unbelief	149
Crime and punishment	156
Messiah	163
The Roman Emperors	167
Mark	174
Blasphemy	175
Pilate	177

Luke

Page

Introduction to Luke's Gospel 182
Outline to Luke's Gospel   183

Commentary   **184-261**

Betrothal   185
Luke   186
Angel   187
Joseph   189
Nazareth   193
Jewish dress in the
time of Jesus   196,97
The Synagogue   200
Demons   202
Jesus in the Four Gospels   205
Languages   206
Bread   214
Weddings   218
Joy   221
The prophets and
the Messiah   224
Forgiveness   237
Humility   240
Jericho   242,43
Judas Iscariot   250
High Priest   254
Funerals   258
Ascension   260

John

Page

Introduction to John's Gospel   264
Outline to John's Gospel   265
The land Jesus knew   266,67

Commentary   **268-343**

Word   268
Life   270
John   271
Regeneration   275
Measures in New
Testament times   278
Samaritans   280
Scribes   281
Authority   283
Temptation   284
Love   285
Exodus   286
Miracles   288,89
Incarnation   292
Trinity   305
Bethany   307
Glory   312
Nicodemus   315
Revelation   317
Counsellor   318
Truth   320
Nazirite   322
Prayer   324
Death   337
Mary of Magdala   338
Thomas   339

Index   344-52

Contributors

Contributors

Matthew: FF Bruce DD, Emeritus Professor of Biblical Criticism and Exegesis, University of Manchester

Mark: Michael Wilcock BA, Dean of Pastoral Studies, Trinity College, Bristol

Luke: EM Blaiklock OBE DLitt, Emeritus Professor of Classics, Auckland University

John: AE Cundall BA BD, (with material by the late RE Nixon)

People: Canon J Stafford Wright MA, former Principal, Tyndale Hall, Bristol

Places: FF Bruce DD

Words: John Eddison MA

Introduction

For the first time this book presents visually a carefully prepared commentary on the four Gospels. It will prove invaluable to a whole range of readers.

The new Christian who wants to come to grips with the Gospel will find *Explaining the Gospels* a source of inspiration.

The church member and his family will find that the photography, maps, diagrams and line illustrations all help communicate the life and times of Jesus of Nazareth.

The clear explanation of the biblical text and special feature articles provide additional background information and insights into the social and physical conditions of the time. Bible study leaders, ministers, Sunday school teachers, pastors and teachers will find a wealth of material here.

Day school teachers will find *Explaining the Gospels* an invaluable reference book for students studying the Gospels.

The commentary text itself, written by dependable and well-known biblical scholars, is fresh and straightforward, and sets out to show how the teaching of the Bible relates to the individual Christian life.

The editorial aim of this major new work of reference has been to explain the scriptural text where difficult or obscure. Both in the commentary, and with specially-commissioned diagrams, maps, photographs, and illustrations, we have attempted to draw out the central teaching of the biblical text.

The main ideas of the New Testament

Main ideas

One way of setting out the main ideas of the New Testament would be to examine the distinctive emphases of the various authors of its twenty-seven books. But here we consider those themes which are not unique to one particular author, but characterize the New Testament as a whole.

The note of fulfilment

Common to nearly all the New Testament writings is the note of fulfilment. This is expressed in various ways: 'The time has come' (Mark 1:15); 'God has come to help his people' (Luke 7:16); 'This is what was spoken by the prophet' (Acts 2:16).

The Old Testament contains much more than promise; but this theme is outstanding in it. The New Testament emphasizes that what was promised by God in Old Testament times is now being fulfilled. It emphasizes, too, that Jesus is the person through whom the promise is fulfilled.

One New Testament writer pictures the ancient prophets as anxious to discover the meaning of what they foretold (1 Peter 1:11). But those who lived in the age of fulfilment had no need to inquire, for they knew. The person was Jesus; the time was now. This is the unanimous verdict of the New Testament.

Jesus congratulated his disciples because in his ministry they saw and heard what 'many prophets and righteous men longed to see . . . and to hear' (Matthew 13:17). Paul says that 'when the time had fully come, God sent his Son' (Galatians 4:4). The writer to the Hebrews begins his letter saying that God, who had spoken 'in various ways' to people in earlier generations, 'in these last days . . . has spoken to us by his son' (Hebrews 1:1,2).

John sums this up by saying that in Jesus Christ 'the Word became flesh' (John 1:14). The 'Word' was God's self-revelation which had existed in the beginning, his agent in creating the universe and in communicating his light and truth to humanity, who was now perfectly revealed in human life.

'The kingdom of heaven is near' (Matthew 10:5).

Jesus' message of the kingdom

Jesus began his public ministry in Galilee with the announcement that the kingdom of God was at hand. Indeed, the kingdom of God was the dominant theme of his teaching. Others in his day spoke of the coming of this kingdom, but not necessarily in the same sense. Jesus' message of the kingdom was proclaimed not only in his spoken words – the parables, beatitudes and so forth – but also in his works of mercy and power. Many of those who saw Jesus' works and listened to his teaching recognized that in his ministry God was drawing near to them, revealing his character and will.

Nothing, in fact, shows what Jesus meant by the kingdom of God more than his teaching about God himself. He called God by the affectionate family name '*Abba*', which children used to their fathers at home. And he taught his followers to follow his example in this as in other ways. The kingdom of God was present where the Father's will was done. His will was done when his children reproduced his character, being merciful as he was merciful and holy as he was holy.

In the circumstances of Jesus' ministry, the kingdom of God was beset by limitations. But one day these limitations would be removed and people would then see it come 'with power'. In order fully to unleash it, it was necessary for the Son of Man to suffer rejection and death. But the powerful progress and coming in power of the kingdom would vindicate the Son of Man.

It became increasingly clear that Jesus himself was the Son of Man. Perhaps he used this title in preference to others such as Messiah because it was not linked in people's minds with ideas or hopes which would have to be given up and replaced.

Events showed the truth of Jesus' words. By his death and resurrection the cause to which his life was devoted advanced more rapidly – and on a much wider scale – than it had done before. The Son of Man, he said, 'did not come to be served, but to serve, and to give his life as a ransom for many' (Mark 10:45). In his own person and work Jesus embodied his message of the kingdom of God. For never was its essence more clearly displayed than when he said to his Father, 'Not my will, but yours be done' (Luke 22:42), and accepted the cross in this spirit.

The apostles' preaching

Jesus presented his message of the kingdom as good news. He said that before the kingdom finally came, the good news would be proclaimed 'to all nations' (Mark 13:10). This task was entrusted to his followers. The account of his ministry in Palestine tells of 'all that Jesus began to do and to teach' (Acts 1:1). Much of the rest of the New Testament is concerned with what he continued to do and teach –

no longer in visible form on earth, but working with and through his followers.

Differences of emphasis may be detected among the various New Testament preachers. But they agreed on the fundamental facts of their message. Of these facts Paul, the apostle to the Gentiles, could say (referring to Peter and other leaders of the mission to Jews), 'Whether, then, it was I or they, this is what we preach' (1 Corinthians 15:11).

The apostles stated that in Jesus Christ God had acted decisively and effectively for the world's salvation. This salvation includes deliverance from all the forces that hold the minds of human beings in bondage – especially from the power of sin, the fear of death and the end-time judgement. The positive side of this salvation is indicated by the closely related word 'life' – the new life of the age to come, presented for enjoyment here and now as God's gift; a participation in Christ's own resurrection life.

1 The author of salvation is Christ. 'Salvation is found in no one else, for there is no other name under heaven given to men by which we must be saved' (Acts 4:12). He has made it available by his death and resurrection. He sustains it by his living power. He will consummate it at his coming in glory.

2 The time of salvation is now. 'Now is the time of God's favour, now is the day of salvation' (2 Corinthians 6:2). The note of urgency with which God addressed his people in Old Testament times is heard again in the gospel age. 'Today, if you hear his voice, do not harden your hearts . . .' (Hebrews 3:7,8). The future climax of Christ's saving work will indeed bring world-wide blessing. But that does not excuse those people to whom the saving message comes from responding to its challenge today.

3 The way of salvation is faith; faith in God as he draws near to men and women in Christ. The repeated assurance of Christ to those he helped during his ministry, 'Your faith has saved you' (Luke 7:50), is the keynote of New Testament preaching. An Old Testament precedent is found in Abraham, who 'believed God, and it was credited to him as righteousness' (Romans 4:3). Salvation offered by God's grace can be received only by grateful faith. But this salvation, though not based on works, produces the harvest of 'good works, which God prepared in advance for us to do' (Ephesians 2:10). True faith, more concisely, is 'faith expressing itself through love' (Galatians 5:6).

4 The heirs of salvation are believers in Christ. They are united in faith with him and with one another. They are called to be

Main ideas

'So Joseph got up, took the child and his mother during the night and left for Egypt' (Matthew 2:14).

The books of the Bible

Old Testament

Old Testament
Books

History, biography	Prophecy	Law	Proverb, epigram	Poetry, drama

The Law

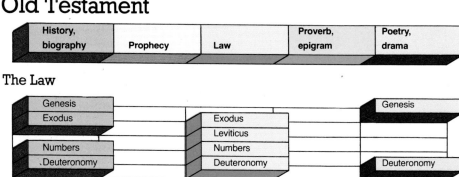

History, biography	Prophecy	Law	Proverb, epigram	Poetry, drama
Genesis				Genesis
Exodus		Exodus		
		Leviticus		
Numbers		Numbers		
Deuteronomy		Deuteronomy		Deuteronomy

History

History, biography	Prophecy	Law	Proverb, epigram	Poetry, drama
Joshua				
Judges				
Ruth				
1 Samuel				
2 Samuel				
1 Kings				
2 Kings				
1 Chronicles				
2 Chronicles				
Ezra				
Nehemiah				
Esther				

Wisdom

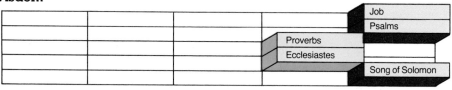

History, biography	Prophecy	Law	Proverb, epigram	Poetry, drama
				Job
				Psalms
			Proverbs	
			Ecclesiastes	
				Song of Solomon

The Prophets

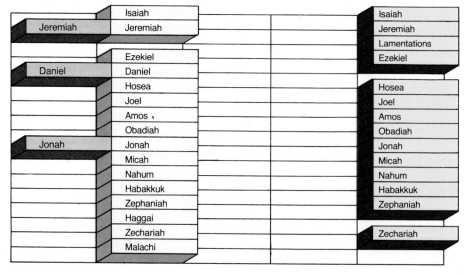

History, biography	Prophecy	Law	Proverb, epigram	Poetry, drama
	Isaiah			Isaiah
Jeremiah	Jeremiah			Jeremiah
				Lamentations
	Ezekiel			Ezekiel
Daniel	Daniel			
	Hosea			Hosea
	Joel			Joel
	Amos			Amos
	Obadiah			Obadiah
Jonah	Jonah			Jonah
	Micah			Micah
	Nahum			Nahum
	Habakkuk			Habakkuk
	Zephaniah			Zephaniah
	Haggai			
	Zechariah			Zechariah
	Malachi			

New Testament

History	Prophecy	Letters	Proverb, epigram	Poetry, drama

New Testament history

				Matthew	
Matthew				Mark	
Mark				Luke	
Luke					
John					
Acts					

The letters

		Romans	
		1 Corinthians	
		2 Corinthians	
		Galatians	
		Ephesians	
		Philippians	
		Colossians	
		1 Thessalonians	
		2 Thessalonians	
		1 Timothy	
		2 Timothy	
		Titus	
		Philemon	
		Hebrews	
		James	
		1 Peter	
		2 Peter	
		1 John	
		2 John	
		3 John	
		Jude	

Apocalyptic

	Revelation			Revelation

New Testament Books

his associates in spreading his salvation. Reconciled through Christ to God and one another, they are a community of reconciliation. They serve as God's pilot scheme for the reconciled universe which 'he purposed in Christ . . . to bring all things in heaven and on earth together under one head, even Christ' (Ephesians 1:9,10).

Main ideas

It is the will of God (as Paul puts it again) that every knee shall bow in Jesus' name 'and every tongue confess that Jesus Christ is Lord' (Philippians 2:10,11). Those who have already learned to acknowledge Christ as Lord have an important part to play as God's agents speeding this longed-for climax. Or, as James (whose idiom is quite different from Paul's) puts it, 'He chose to give us birth through the word of truth, that we might be a kind of first fruits of all he created' (James 1:18).

But heirs of salvation must not reproduce the social, cultural, religious and racial divisions which divide the world. If they do, they deny their distinctiveness and become mere obstacles.

The age of the Spirit

The Christians of New Testament times knew themselves to be living (as Christians today still live) in the interval between the inauguration of the world's redemption by the finished work of Christ in his death and resurrection and the climax of the world's redemption by his final coming in glory. Paul pictures the whole creation eagerly longing for this final redemption, in sympathy with 'ourselves, who have the first-fruits of the Spirit' and who 'groan inwardly as we wait eagerly for our adoption as sons' (Romans 8:22,23).

These words indicate that the present interval is the age of the Spirit. Before his death, Jesus promised that his Spirit would be given to his followers to prevent them from feeling orphaned by his leaving. Luke's vivid account of the first Christian Pentecost describes how the Holy Spirit was sent to fulfil Jesus' promise (Acts 2). The New Testament writers express a consciousness that the Spirit of Christ (or the Spirit of God, or the Holy Spirit) has possessed their personal and corporate lives.

By the Spirit, Jesus' presence and power remained real to them after he himself was removed from their sight. By the Spirit, the benefits of Jesus' saving work were made effective in their lives. By the Spirit, too, they were brought into an unprecedented unity of heart and soul. This enriched their worship and was also reflected in the ready – and increasing – response of others to their witness in the world. The Spirit's guidance was so real to them that they instinctively spoke of it.

Paul makes an important additional point. Not only does the Spirit make the past and present life and power of Christ real; he makes the future real too. That is why Paul speaks of the Spirit as the firstfruits. The Spirit is the initial down-payment of the inheritance of glory which awaits the people of Christ.

The Spirit not only keeps alive in them the hope of resurrection. He actually imparts resurrection life to them by anticipation here and now. This life is 'the common life in the body of Christ'. Those who possess it are united or 'baptized' by the Spirit into one body, which derives its life from the risen Christ.

The members of this body may be known by the spontaneity with which they call God 'Father' (as Jesus did) and acknowledge Jesus as Lord. Their way of life is not careful conformity to a code of rules. It is marked by the growth and ripening of 'the fruit of the Spirit' within them, and by the responsible freedom which is their birthright as the sons of God. 'Where the Spirit of the Lord is, there is freedom' (2 Corinthians 3:17).

The glory of the inheritance which awaits believers is a sharing in the glory of Christ – Christlikeness. The Holy Spirit who prepares them does so mainly by

'Then Jesus took the cup, gave thanks and offered it to them, saying, "Drink from it, all of you. This is my blood of the covenant, which is poured out for many for the forgiveness of sins"' (Matthew 26:27,28).

Main ideas

'Hosanna!
  'Blessed is he who comes in the name of the Lord!
  'Blessed is the coming kingdom of our father David!
  'Hosanna in the highest!'
(Mark 11:9,10).

reproducing Christlikeness in their lives now. They are being transformed into his likeness with ever-increasing glory which comes from the Lord, who is the Spirit' (2 Corinthians 3:18). The Holy Spirit is the Spirit of holiness, creating holiness in those in whom he lives. Present holiness is coming glory begun; coming glory is present holiness completed.

Jesus is Lord

We have already seen the frequency throughout the New Testament of the confession 'Jesus is Lord'. Perhaps if one short sentence could sum up the message of the New Testament, it would be this.

When the early Christians confessed Jesus as Lord, they intended the title 'Lord' to bear the highest possible meaning. This was 'the name that is above every name' given to him by God when

he 'exalted him to the highest place' (Philippians 2:9).

The God who in the Old Testament says, 'I am the LORD; that is my name! I will not give my glory to another' (Isaiah 42:8), now bestows that name on the crucified Jesus. His glory is not lessened but increased thereby. Those who 'confess that Jesus Christ is Lord' do so 'to the glory of God the Father' (Philippians 2:11).

Obviously this confession declares Jesus to be Lord of his

people. But he is also Lord of the universe. All its 'principalities and powers' are under his control. The whole world is subject to the power and empire of Christ. He is Lord of life and Lord of history. Because he triumphed by submitting to death the future belongs to him. Above all, this is the lordship of perfect, self-giving love. God is love. He has given universal power to the one who was sent into the world to reveal God's love.

'What was said through the prophet was fulfilled . . .'

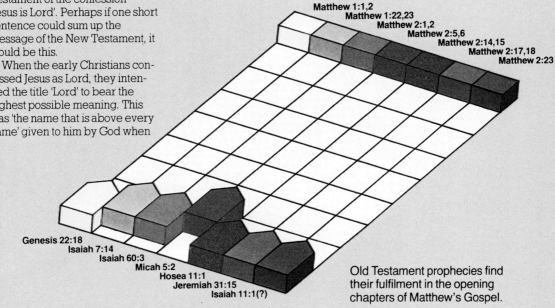

Matthew 1:1,2
Matthew 1:22,23
Matthew 2:1,2
Matthew 2:5,6
Matthew 2:14,15
Matthew 2:17,18
Matthew 2:23

Genesis 22:18
Isaiah 7:14
Isaiah 60:3
Micah 5:2
Hosea 11:1
Jeremiah 31:15
Isaiah 11:1(?)

Old Testament prophecies find their fulfilment in the opening chapters of Matthew's Gospel.

The land

The rift valley is an area of great seismological activity. More than fifty major earthquakes are known to have occurred in Palestine since the time of Christ.

Along the Mediterranean coast there stretches a low coastal plain, and between this area and the Jordan valley rise the West Jordan highlands, merging with the Galilee hills in the north. The East Jordan highlands climb from the Jordan valley to the east.

Although much of this area was once thickly forested, the trees were cleared at an early date, leaving much of the land arid and infertile.

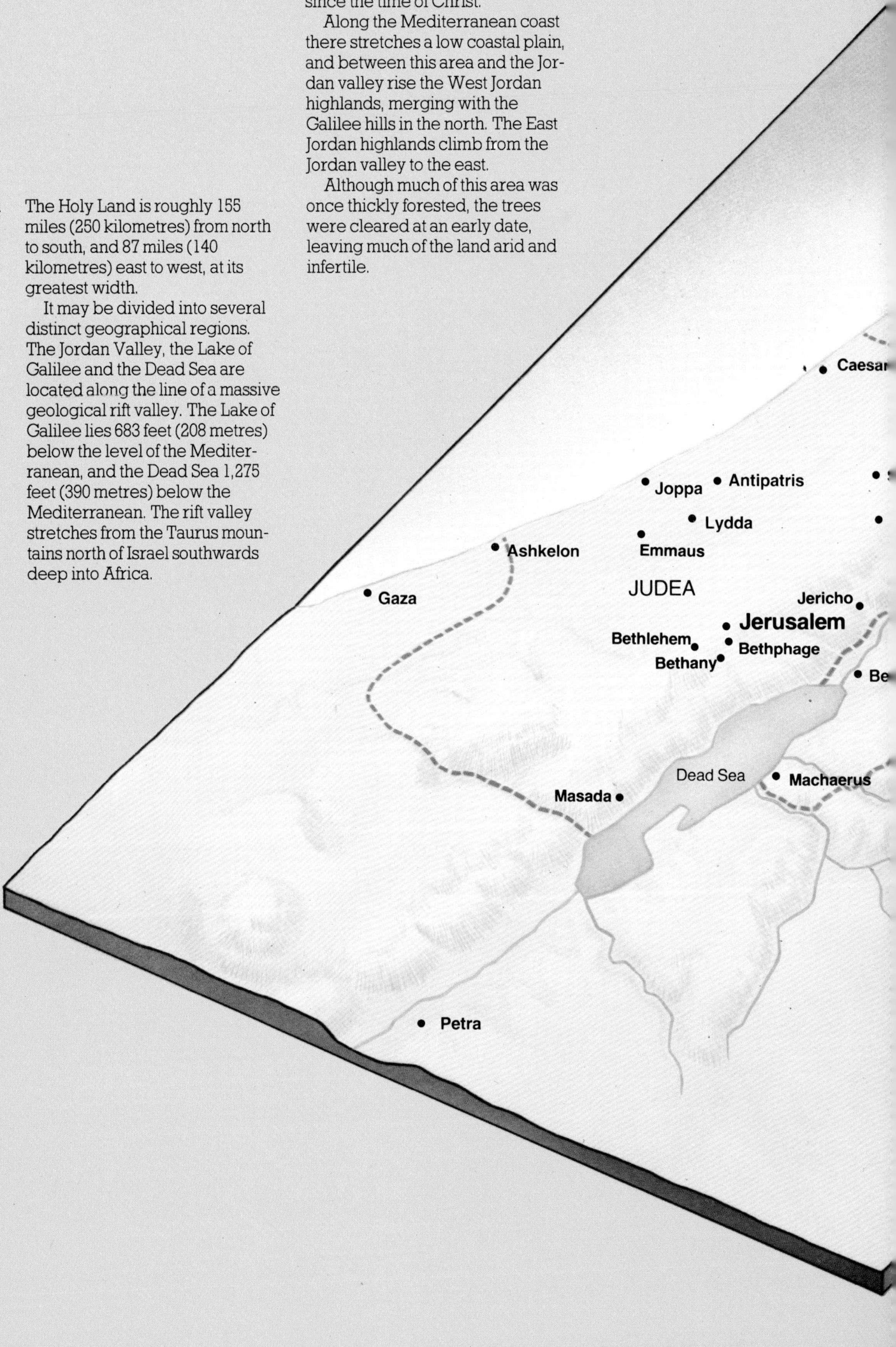

The land The Holy Land is roughly 155 miles (250 kilometres) from north to south, and 87 miles (140 kilometres) east to west, at its greatest width.

It may be divided into several distinct geographical regions. The Jordan Valley, the Lake of Galilee and the Dead Sea are located along the line of a massive geological rift valley. The Lake of Galilee lies 683 feet (208 metres) below the level of the Mediterranean, and the Dead Sea 1,275 feet (390 metres) below the Mediterranean. The rift valley stretches from the Taurus mountains north of Israel southwards deep into Africa.

Caesar

Joppa • Antipatris

Lydda

Ashkelon Emmaus

Gaza JUDEA

Jericho

Jerusalem

Bethlehem Bethphage

Bethany

Be

Dead Sea Machaerus

Masada •

Petra

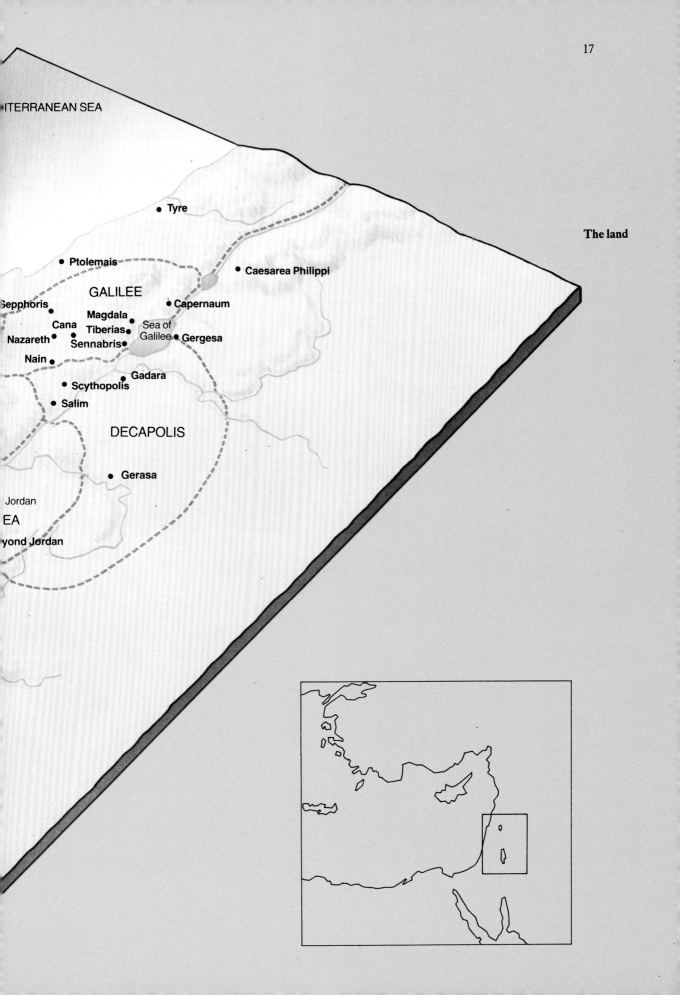

MEDITERRANEAN SEA

The land

• Tyre

• Ptolemais

• Caesarea Philippi

GALILEE

Sepphoris •

• Capernaum

Magdala

Cana • Tiberias •

Nazareth •

Sennabris •

Sea of Galilee • Gergesa

Nain •

• Gadara

• Scythopolis

• Salim

DECAPOLIS

• Gerasa

Jordan

EA

yond Jordan

¹⁸ Contents

Matthew
Contents

		Page
People		
	Mary	25
	The Herods	29
	Matthew	45
Places		
	Bethlehem	30
	Qumran	52, 53
	Jerusalem	77–81
	The Temple	96–99
	Gethsemane	102
Words		
	Kingdom of God	33
	Commandments	40
	Power	50
	Law	63
	After-life	70
	Resurrection	107
Life		
	Religious and political parties	89

Matthew

Introduction to Matthew's Gospel

Matthew's Roots

The writers of the three Synoptic Gospels did not personally autograph the books they wrote. The names we know have been attached to the Gospels since at the latest the first half of the second century; but they do not appear in the original text of the Gospels themselves.

Our earliest evidence for associating Matthew with Gospel-making is a fragment from a lost work of Papias, bishop of Hierapolis in Phrygia about AD130. Papias lovingly collected and recorded what those who had seen and heard Jesus in person remembered. His work, which is not known to have survived, was quoted by Christian writers in the following centuries. Among such writers Eusebius, in his *Ecclesiastical History*, credits bishop Papias with saying that 'Matthew com-piled the sayings in Hebrew, and everyone interpreted them as best he could'.

Later writers who name Matthew as author of the First Gospel apparently based this on what Papias said. But Papias did not actually say Matthew wrote the First Gospel, which is in Greek, but that he compiled the sayings in Hebrew. The laws of Moses and the sayings of the prophets were recognized as divine

sayings; no wonder Jesus' sayings, coming from one to whom Moses and the prophets bore witness, were also recognized as divine.

A collection of sayings

Most scholars believe that Matthew used Mark's Gospel as one of his sources in his writing, for over 600 of Mark's 661 verses are found in Matthew's Gospel.

Still other portions of Matthew's account overlap with some of Luke's Gospel. This common area of agreement has caused scholars to ask if Matthew and Luke were not looking at some common written document of a collection of Jesus' sayings. (We know from Luke 1:1 that there were accounts about Jesus already existing prior to our Gospels.) Such a written document may have circulated at an early date in the church, especially among the Hellenists and Gentile Christians.

Its contents may be summarized:
1 Jesus and John the Baptist
2 Jesus and his disciples
3 Jesus and his opponents
4 Jesus and the future

Who was Matthew?

Who then was the 'Matthew' who is said to have compiled the 'sayings'? Papias was understood by Eusebius to mean Matthew the apostle. What interested Papias was the witness of the apostles, and he gladly recorded anything that came his way on this.

Matthew's material

Matthew's narrative covers the story from the preaching of John the Baptist to the passion and resurrection of Jesus. As in the other Gospels, the story of the passion and resurrection is the goal to which everything leads. The account of the nativity is unique to Matthew. It is quite independent of Luke's account, although it agrees in theology: Jesus' virginal conception by the power of the Holy Spirit; geography: he was born in Bethlehem of Judea, but

Matthew Introduction

Jerusalem, the 'Holy City'.

brought up in Nazareth; and dates: his birth occurred in the reign of King Herod.

It is all too easy, when considering the sources of information on which the Gospel-writers might have drawn, to overlook Matthew's personal contribution. He was a man of literary ability, and possessed the necessary spiritual gifts.

The main themes of Matthew

The teaching of Jesus is arranged into 'five discourses' according to subject: 5:1-7:27; 10:5-42; 13:1-52; 18:1-35; 24:1-25:46; and dominate the Gospel's structure.

Matthew tends to group his material into threes and sevens, wherever it comes from. This is illustrated by the seven parables of the kingdom in chapter 13, and the three in chapter 25. He writes 'to show what the Old Testament meant', and quotations from Old Testament books appear throughout his work.

Matthew is the only Gospel-writer who so much as mentions the word 'church'. He shows an interest in the life, growth and witness of the Christian fellowship.

What is its purpose?

In the first three chapters of the Gospel, Jesus is introduced as King of the Jews, heir to David's throne, acclaimed as such by Gentiles and anointed by God. The words over his head on the cross, 'This is Jesus the King of the Jews', are shown in advance to be no false claim.

Yet in the greater part of the book, Jesus is mainly presented as Teacher. It is his teaching that features most prominently in this Gospel. Indeed, the Gospel has been seen as possibly the 'manual of discipline' of a distinct Christian school; we can easily see how useful it would have been as a handbook for new Christians.

Matthew quickly became the most popular of the Gospels. Once the four records began to circulate as a collection, the Gospel of Matthew almost always took the first place, whatever the order of the other three. Its position at the head of the New Testament books has its own fitness, because its opening section dovetails so well into the Old Testament.

Its original setting appears to have been a Greek-speaking Jewish-Christian community. Possibly it originated in a Hellenistic group in Syria, which preserved the ideals of the Hellenists who first brought the Christian message to Gentiles, in the dispersion following Stephen's martyrdom.

The Gospel concludes with the Gentile mission, entrusted to the eleven apostles. It is anticipated earlier, with the including of Gentile women in the genealogy of chapter 1, in the epiphany story of chapter 2, and in the healing of the centurion's servant of chapter 8:5-13; and the Canaanite girl of chapter 15:21-28.

Matthew himself has his own portrait painted in the 'scribe . . . trained for the kingdom of heaven' whom Jesus compares to 'a householder who brings out of his treasure what is new and what is old', Matthew 13:52. He was a man of generous mind and broad outlook, including in his record and weaving together material cherished by Christian groups of varying viewpoints – stricter Jewish Christians and more liberal Gentile Christians, with many in between. All find something congenial here.

Date

The date of the completed Gospel of Matthew is probably quite soon after the destruction of the Temple and of the city of Jerusalem, AD 70. Echoes of the catastrophe, and its sequel, can be discovered here and there. Moreover, the new situation it created was an opportunity for Christians to consolidate and advance, and to this the Gospel of Matthew contributed powerfully.

This Menorah or seven-branched candlestick stands outside the parliament building of the modern state of Israel. It was presented by the British government in 1956.

1:1-17	The family tree	15:1-20	Clean and unclean
1:18-25	The birth of Jesus	15:21-28	A Canaanite woman's faith
2:1-12	The adoration of the magi	15:29-39	Four thousand fed
2:13-23	The journey into Egypt	16:1-12	Pharisees and Sadducees
3:1-12	The ministry of John	16:13-20	Peter's confession
3:13-17	The baptism of Jesus	16:21-28	Jesus predicts his death
4:1-11	Temptation in the wilderness	17:1-8	The transfiguration
4:12-22	Jesus begins to preach	17:9-20	Little faith
4:23-25	Jesus heals the sick	17:22-27	The Temple tax
5:1-12	The Beatitudes	18:1-14	The greatest in the kingdom
5:13-16	Salt and light	18:15-22	Brotherly behaviour
5:17-32	No divorce	18:23-35	The unforgiving servant
5:33-37	Oaths	19:1-12	Divorce
5:38-42	An eye for an eye	19:13-22	The rich young man
5:43-48	Love for enemies	19:23-30	The needle's eye
6:1-4	Giving to the needy	20:1-16	The workers in the vineyard
6:5-18	Prayer and fasting	20:17-28	On the Jerusalem road
6:19-34	Do not worry	20:29-34	Blind men of Jericho
7:1-6	Judging others	21:1-11	The triumphal entry
7:7-12	Ask, seek, knock	21:12-17	Jesus at the Temple
7:13-29	A matter of life and death	21:18-22	The fig tree withers
8:1-4	The man with leprosy	21:23-32	'By what authority?'
8:5-13	The faith of the centurion	21:33-46	Parable of the tenants
8:14-17	Healing the sick	22:1-14	Parable of the wedding banquet
8:18-22	The cost of discipleship	22:15-22	Taxes to Caesar
8:23-27	Jesus calms the storm	22:23-33	How are the dead raised?
8:28-34	Demons cast out	22:34-46	Debating with Pharisees
9:1-8	The Son of Man's authority	23:1-12	An example to be avoided
9:9-17	Controversy grows	23:13-28	Lament for the scribes
9:18-26	A dead girl and a sick woman	23:29-39	Lament for Jerusalem
9:27-34	Jesus heals the blind and dumb	24:1-14	Signs of the End-time
9:35-38	The workers are few	24:15-28	Sacrilege and tribulation
10:1-15	Jesus sends out the Twelve	24:29-35	The sign of the Son of Man
10:16-23	Persecution ahead	24:36-51	Call to vigilance
10:24-42	Words of encouragement	25:1-13	Parable of the ten virgins
11:1-15	Jesus and John the Baptist	25:14-30	Parable of the tenants
11:16-24	Doom of the lakeside towns	25:31-46	The sheep and the goats
11:25-30	Rest for the weary	26:1-13	Jesus anointed at Bethany
12:1-14	Lord of the Sabbath	26:14-25	The Last Supper
12:15-21	God's chosen servant	26:26-35	Jesus predicts Peter's denial
12:22-37	Jesus and Beelzebub	26:36-46	Gethsemane
12:38-50	The sign of Jonah	26:47-56	Jesus arrested
13:1-9	Parable of the sower	26:57-75	Before the Sanhedrin
13:10-17	Hearing, they do not hear	27:1-14	Judas hangs himself
13:18-30	Parable of the weeds	27:15-31	Jesus before Pilate
13:31-43	The mustard seed and the yeast	27:32-44	Christ crucified
13:44-46	The hidden treasure	27:45-54	The death of Jesus
13:47-52	The parable of the net	27:55-66	The burial of Jesus
13:53-58	A prophet without honour	28:1-10	The empty tomb
14:1-12	Death of John the Baptist	28:11-15	The guards' report
14:13-21	Five thousand fed	28:16-20	The great commission
14:22-36	Walking on the water		

**Matthew
Outline**

FF Bruce
Matthew
Commentary

1:1-17 The family tree

The opening words of Matthew bind the story which follows firmly to the Old Testament. Just as Genesis 5:1 introduces 'the written account of Adam's line', the Gospel-writer does the same for Jesus, 'the second Adam'. However he is more concerned to present him as the son of Abraham, and so the fulfiller of God's promises for Abraham's heirs, such as in Genesis 22:18, and particularly as the heir to David's throne.

The line from David to Joseph probably marks the succession in law, rather than biological descent; in some cases 'father' can be used in this sense. In Luke 3:23-31, the line from David to Joseph is completely different, except for Shealtiel and Zerubbabel.

The ancestors of Jesus, from Abraham to David, and from David to Joseph.

Abraham · Isaac · Jacob · Judah and his brothers, and Zerah · Perez · Hezron · Ram · Amminadab · Nahshon · Salmon and Rahab · Boaz and Ruth · Obed · Jesse

David · Solomon · Rehoboam · Abijah · Asa · Jehoshaphat · Joram · Uzziah · Jotham · Ahaz · Hezekiah · Manasseh · Amon · Josiah · Jeconiah

Shealtiel · Zerubbabel · Abiud · Eliakim · Azor · Zadok · Akim · Eliud · Eleazar · Matthan · Jacob · Joseph and Mary · Jesus Christ

From Abraham to Joseph The line from Abraham to Zerubbabel can be constructed from the Old Testament, but evidence for the links between Zerubbabel and Joseph has not survived. But it was not exceptional in those days for a family to keep its family records for many generations.

The arrangement of the genealogy into three groups of fourteen, in verse 17, depends on missing out some names. For example three are missing between Joram and Uzziah, see also 1 Chronicles 3:11-12; and one, Jehoiakim, between Josiah and Jeconiah (verse 11), see also 1 Chronicles 3:15-16.

The four women mentioned are all Gentiles: Tamar the Canaanite (verse 3); Rahab of Jericho (verse 5) (her marriage to Salmon is not recorded anywhere else); Ruth the Moabite (verse 5); and Bathsheba widow of Uriah the Hittite (verse 6). So it is shown that the blessing brought by the Son of David is not restricted to one race (see also Matthew 4:15; 8:5-13; 15:22-28; 28:19).

1:18-25 The birth of Jesus

Matthew's account of the birth of Jesus is completely independent of Luke's. Luke tells the story from Mary's viewpoint, Matthew tells it from Joseph's. But both writers agree that Jesus was conceived by the power of the Holy Spirit. The law as it affected a betrothed woman, pregnant like Mary, is laid down in Deuteronomy 22:20-24. Joseph's decision not to expose her to the grave consequences of public repudiation shows him to be a decent man.

Mary

Most of what we know about Mary comes from the early early chapters of Matthew and Luke. When the angel announced the birth of Jesus to Mary, she was living in Nazareth, and was betrothed to a carpenter named Joseph. Jesus was conceived by the Holy Spirit, and was born in Bethlehem, towards the end of the reign of Herod the Great.

Luke alone records Mary's visit to her cousin Elizabeth, who greeted her, 'Blessed are you among women...' (Luke 1:42). Mary replied with her song of praise, beginning 'My soul praises the Lord'; this song is often known as the Magnificat. Luke and Matthew tell us that the holy family lived in Nazareth, though only Matthew tells of the flight to Egypt to escape Herod's anger.

Luke tells of Mary's anxious search when Jesus got lost in Jerusalem, and his famous question: 'Didn't you know I had to be in my Father's house?' Evidently Mary did not go with Jesus on his travels, although she was with him at the wedding in Cana (John 2:1).

We meet Mary again, briefly, at the foot of Jesus' cross. Jesus entrusted Mary and John to each other's care (John 19:26,27). Finally, in Acts 1:14 we find her with Jesus' disciples ('constantly in prayer'. The Gospels emphasize Mary's humility, obedience and devotion to Jesus.

The traditional site of the birth of Jesus, inside the Church of the Nativity, Bethelehem. A silver star on the floor of the church marks the spot where Jesus' manger is supposed to have stood.

With the birth of Jesus a new dawn broke.

Here it is Joseph who receives an angel's message, and is told to call the child Jesus. The name (the Greek form of Joshua or Jeshua) means 'Yahweh is salvation'; 'because he will save his people from their sins' (verse 21).

Verses 22,23 include the first of several Old Testament quotations in Matthew to be preceded by a form of words indicating that an event took place to fulfil an oracle. This example from Isaiah 7:14 comes from Isaiah's address to King Ahaz, when Judah was threatened with invasion from Syria and Israel.

Isaiah and Ahaz In the name of God, Isaiah told Ahaz to keep calm, and invited him to name any sign he wanted to confirm that the threat would vanish. Ahaz, who had already invited the Assyrian king to intervene, pretended he was too pious to put God to the test by asking for a sign. Isaiah realized what lay behind the king's pretence of piety, and foresaw the disaster that would result from his negotiations with Assyria. The prophet gave him the sign of a royal child to be born soon, who would not be able to tell right from wrong before the two kings Ahaz feared were laid low. But he would grow up to a devastated heritage because of Ahaz's policy.

Isaiah's oracle is in an ancient form of language. Matthew recognizes its final fulfilment in the birth of Jesus, the virgin's son, according to the Greek version of the Old Testament quoted here; Emmanuel, 'God with us', in the fullest sense. See Matthew 28:20.

2:1-12 The adoration of the magi

If Jesus was the fulfilment of the hope of Israel, he was also the answer to Gentile hopes. The 'magi from the East' were Gentiles, whose journey the early Christians saw as a fulfilment of the words of Isaiah 60:3: 'Nations will come to your light, and kings to the brightness of your dawn'.

For this reason the festival of their visit, on January 6, more ancient than Christmas, is called the Epiphany, or 'appearing', of Christ to the Gentiles. The visitors are traditionally described as 'kings of Orient'; 'three' kings probably because of the three gifts they presented (see verse 11).

But in fact they were magi, or students of the stars. By this time,

'The Adoration of the Kings' painted by Gerard David (d. 1523).

The roof-tops of modern Bethlehem.
(Inset) A shepherd minds his sheep in the countryside near Bethlehem.

the orbits and conjunctions of the planets could be worked out in advance. It has been suggested that the star whose rising they observed was the conjunction of the planet Jupiter, the star of the world ruler, and Saturn, the star of Palestine, in the constellation Pisces, the sign of the last days, in the summer and autumn of 7BC. But this is not certain; other attractive suggestions have been made.

At any rate, their quest naturally brought them to Herod's palace, where it caused great alarm. Herod's reign, 37-4BC, was approaching its end, and he grew more suspicious with each year that passed. A new king of the Jews was a threat to his throne and dynasty, and must be eliminated immediately. Discovering from the chief priests and scribes that, according to Micah 5:2, Bethlehem, David's birthplace, was to be the birthplace of the Messiah, 'great David's greater son', he sent the visitors there to pay homage to the child king.

The magi and the star The reappearance of the star convinced the magi that they were on the right road. How it led them to the right house we can only guess. Did they see it reflected in the well?

It is easy, with Origen and other early writers, to find special meaning in the magi's gifts, 'gold and frankincense and myrrh'. But the Gospel-writer gives us no encouragement to do so. He simply tells us in verse 12 that the magi, after a divine warning, 'returned to their country by another route', so depriving Herod of the information which would have enabled him to pay homage to the new king,

The flight into Egypt

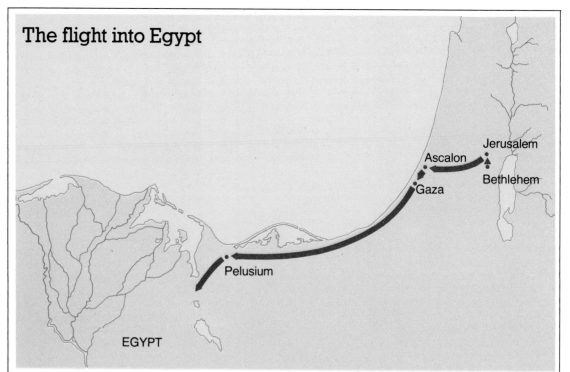

or to take what other action he saw fit.

The mention of 'two years' in verse 16 suggests that the magi arrived in Bethlehem quite a time after the birth of Jesus. We can assume from this that they first saw the star at the time of his birth, and that their journey was lengthy.

2:13-23 The journey into Egypt

The massacre of the Jewish boy children by Herod is not found elsewhere. There is only a possible reference in a contemporary Jewish book comparing Herod's actions with Pharaoh's plot against the Hebrew children, but it fits Herod's character in the closing years of his life.

The holy family's flight into Egypt was remembered in some Jewish circles. A tradition of the rabbis tells of Jesus' stay in Egypt, with the distortions due to memory.

Herod died in March 4BC. His kingdom was divided between three of his sons, of whom Archelaus became ruler of Judea. Archelaus inherited his father's vices without his statesmanship. His misrule led to his being deposed in AD6. Joseph was wise, on returning from Egypt, to settle in Galilee, where another of Herod's sons, Herod Antipas, ruled. Compare Matthew 14:1 onwards.

These verses feature three Old Testament quotations with an introductory form of words like those of Matthew 1:22-23. The first, in verse 15, from Hosea 11:1, refers to God's calling of Israel, his firstborn son, out of Egypt at the time of the Exodus; compare with Exodus 4:22. The Gospel-writer portrays Jesus as repeating in his personal experience the experience of his people, and suffering in all their suffering; notice the parallel in Isaiah 63:9.

The mother of Israel The second quotation, in verses 17, 18, from Jeremiah 31:15, pictures Rachel, the mother of Israel, sitting by the frontier town of Ramah, near which was her tomb, according to 1 Samuel 10:2, weeping for her children as they were driven off into captivity. Now Rachel, perhaps standing for the bereaved mothers of all ages, mourns again, as more of her children fall victims to a new tyrant. Matthew may have in mind the alternative siting of her tomb near Bethlehem (see Genesis 35:19).

The Herods

Herod was the name of a line of kings of Idumean, or Edomite, stock. Herod the Great (40-4BC) followed his father, Antipater, who was appointed procurator of Judea by Julius Caesar. Both before and after he succeeded to the throne, Herod proved an effective general against brigands and invading Parthians. He earned himself the title 'King of the Jews' from the Roman senate.

In 19BC, Herod began to rebuild the Jerusalem Temple in magnificent style; additions were still being made forty-six years later. He also rebuilt Samaria.

Herod fatally attempted to please everyone. He was kind and brutal by turns. Before he died in 4 BC, he was breaking down physically and mentally. His massacre of the babies of Bethlehem was typical of his paranoia about personal attack, and of his unpredictable cruelties.

Archelaus

Archelaus is mentioned only in Matthew 2:22, as Herod the Great's successor. In his will, Herod divided his kingdom; Archelaus, his eldest son by Malthace, a Samaritan wife, had Judea and Perea.

Archelaus is said to have inherited his father's vices without his ability. His cruelty produced revolutions in Jerusalem. It was his reputation that made Joseph and Mary go to the quiet town of Nazareth when they returned from Egypt.

Archelaus' race to Rome to get Caesar to confirm him as king is possibly referred to in Jesus' parable in Luke 19:12; Jesus and his disciples would have just seen the palace Archelaus built in Jericho. Jewish pressure finally achieved his banishment to Gaul (France) in AD6.

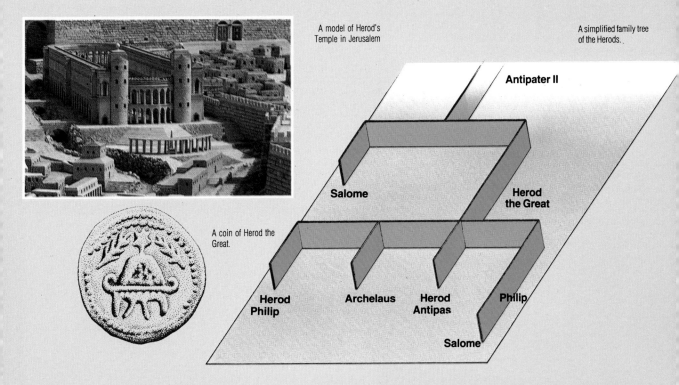

A model of Herod's Temple in Jerusalem

A simplified family tree of the Herods.

A coin of Herod the Great.

Antipater II

Salome

Herod the Great

Herod Philip

Archelaus

Herod Antipas

Philip

Salome

Bethlehem

A view of Bethlehem from the Shepherds Fields. It is here that the shepherds are supposed to have been watching their flocks when the angel told them of the birth of Christ. Set upon a mountain ridge to the south of Jerusalem, Bethlehem is today still surrounded by fields.

Bethlehem is first mentioned in the Bible in the story of Jacob's return to his homeland from Mesopotamia. According to Genesis 35:19, Rachel died and was buried 'on the way to Ephrath; that is, Bethlehem', where her tomb is still shown.

The name of the town originally meant 'house of Lahmu', evidently a Canaanite god. To the Jews it came to mean 'house of bread'. After the Israelites settled in Canaan, it was allocated to the tribe of Judah. It was the home of the Levite who figures in the story of Micah in Judges 17:7, and the home of the ill-fated concubine of another Levite in Judges 19:1. Bethlehem plays a happier part in the story of Ruth, as the home of Elimelech and Naomi, and later as the home of Boaz and Ruth.

The book of Ruth ends with a family tree, showing how King David was the great-grandson of Boaz and Ruth. It was the fact that David was born and brought up there that gave Bethlehem its fame in Old Testament times. Otherwise it was unimportant.

But in the years when the fortunes of the kingdom of Judah were at a low ebb, the prophet Micah foretold that a ruler would arise from Bethlehem and restore his people's fortunes.

Bethlehem in Judea

This oracle from Micah 5:2 is quoted in Matthew's nativity narrative, in his account of the visit of the magi. When they arrived in Jerusalem asking the whereabouts of the new-born king of the Jews, and were directed to Herod's palace, Herod summoned the leading rabbis and asked them where the Messiah was to be born. 'In Bethlehem in Judea' they said, for this was the place indicated by the prophet.

Luke, in his nativity narrative, brings Joseph and Mary to Beth-

The Church of the Nativity, Bethlehem. Opposite: The Shepherds' Fields, Bethlehem.

lehem immediately before the birth of Jesus, because the Roman Emperor Augustus had decreed an Empire-wide census. The census regulations required that everyone to be enrolled should return to his family home: especially, we suppose, if he or his family owned property there. Joseph, being a member of the family of David, returned to Bethlehem with his newly-wedded wife. There is an impressive contrast in Luke 2:1-7, no doubt deliberate, between the most powerful ruler in the world issuing his edict from Rome, and the child born as an incidental result of the edict in an obscure corner of his Empire; a child destined for greater sovereignty than Augustus ever commanded.

In the middle of the second century AD, the Christian writer Justin Martyr reported that, since Joseph found nowhere to lodge in Bethlehem itself, he put up in a 'cave' near the village. Justin, a native of Palestine, may well have known a local tradition that Jesus' birthplace was a cave used as a stable.

Probably in recognition of the local tradition, the Emperor Constantine built over the cave the basilica which was the first Church of the Nativity, dedicated in AD339, two years after his death. The present Church of the Nativity, on the same site, is basically the work of the Emperor Justinian,

AD527-65. During excavations in 1934, the mosaic floor of Constantine's basilica came to light, together with its foundations.

The angel's announcement to the shepherds of the Saviour's birth in Luke 2:8-18 was earlier commemorated by a Byzantine church in the area east of the town, called the Shepherds' Fields. In the crypt beneath its ruins Orthodox services are still held.

After the holy family left Bethlehem, there is no record of Jesus' ever visiting the place again. His early association with it was not generally known, and when once in Jerusalem some of his hearers thought he must be the Messiah, others said that this was impossible, for this man (as every one knew) was a Galilean, whereas we read in John 7:42: 'the Messiah is descended from David, and comes from Bethlehem, the village where David was'.

Jericho

Jerusalem

Qumran

Bethlehem

Machaerus

Dead Sea

After threshing, the corn had to be winnowed. It was thrown several times in the air with a closely-set pitchfork. In the right wind conditions, the grains would fall to the ground in a heap near the feet of the winnower. The lighter chaff was blown further away.

The third quotation, in verse 23, presents a problem. No such text occurs in any edition of the Old Testament we know. It might refer to Isaiah 11:1, where the Hebrew word translated 'branch', referring to the coming ruler of David's line, is similar to the word 'Nazarene'.

All these quotations are said to have been spoken by the Lord *through* various prophets. They are simply his spokesmen, the basic meaning of 'prophets'.

3:1-12 The ministry of John

Whenever John the Baptist is mentioned in the New Testament we find him preparing for the ministry of Jesus. His particular theme is the urgent need to repent, because the Messiah was about to appear. 'The kingdom of heaven' is a phrase found only in this Gospel; 'the kingdom of God', which has the same meaning, is used in other parts of the Bible and occasionally in this book. It refers particularly to the universal and never-ending kingdom which God was about to build on the ruins of successive pagan empires, according to Daniel 2:44; 7:14,18,22,27. On John's lips, the expression implies the day of judgement (compare Daniel 7:9-10). The judgement is the fiery baptism to be administered by the one who is to come, verses 11, 12; hence the call to repent in time.

John the prophet Baptism may have been one of the ways in which a convert from paganism identified himself with the Jewish nation. John tells his hearers that they can only become the children of God by confessing their sins and being baptized. They could not expect to escape simply because they were descendants of Abraham, verse 9. Here John anticipates Paul in Romans 9:7.

John shows himself as one of the line of prophets, which had lapsed for many years. His dress reminds us of Elijah's: compare verse 4, and 2 Kings 1:8. His preaching had the power to convict people. He publicly denounced the religious leaders of the day, verse 7. Worldly Sadducees and strict Pharisees are both compared to serpents fleeing the path of advancing flames.

3:13-17 The baptism of Jesus

John's humble protest when Jesus asked to be baptized by him

Kingdom of God

Matthew speaks of the kingdom of heaven, rather than the kingdom of God. Since his readers were Jewish, they avoided using the name of God. Mark and Luke use the words 'Kingdom of God', but mean exactly the same thing.

Towards the end of the Old Testament, for example in Zechariah 9:9,10; Malachi chapter 4, the 'kingdom' was looked forward to as the great turning point in Jewish history. God would intervene on behalf of his people, restore their fortunes, and release them from the power of their enemies.

In the teaching of John the Baptist, the kingdom began to take on a more moral character; see Matthew 3:1-12. But Jesus changed it even more radically. While he taught in Matthew 13:33-43 about the future growth of the kingdom, he also showed that it was a present reality. It existed wherever people accepted his rule as king. With his coming, God's invasion of the world had begun; Luke 11:20. Jesus' power was already beginning to reveal itself in a new way.

But the kingdom of God differed from earthly kingdoms, and from what the Jews expected, in three distinct ways:

1 It is spiritual, not political
Jesus said in Luke 17:20,21: 'The kingdom of God does not come visibly . . . because the kingdom of God is within you.' In other words, the kingdom of God is the sphere of Jesus' authority. It exists wherever he is acknowledged as king. It cannot be measured in terms of lands or armies. It is a present experience in the life of the Christian believer, although it will only finally be established in the future.

2 It is eternal, not temporal
The kingdoms of this world rise and fall. But the kingdom of God is based in heaven, and 'Christ . . . will reign for ever and ever', Revelation 11:15. It cannot fail; Daniel chapter 2.

3 It is moral, not material
Romans 14:17 and 1 Corinthians 15:50 show that its strength does not lie in material resources, or standard of living, but in 'righteousness, peace and joy in the Holy Spirit'.

'The Baptism of Christ', by Piero della Francesca (d. 1492).

(verse 14) is understandable. John was baptizing those who had repented. Jesus had no sins to confess, so it seemed to John that he should be baptized by Jesus.

Jesus makes clear his purpose in asking for baptism: 'let it be so now; it is proper for us to do this to fulfil all righteousness' (verse 15). Jesus' constant resolve was to do his Father's will. He also recognizes John's ministry as the work of God. He identifies with sinners at the beginning, throughout, and at the climax of, his ministry.

John agrees to baptize Jesus. Then, in response to Jesus' total self-dedication, the heavens open, the Spirit descends and the Father speaks. Here, in the baptism of Jesus, is a moment of divine revelation. The Spirit must be received before being imparted to others. Isaiah 11:2 said 'the Spirit of the Lord will rest upon him', God says of his chosen servant in Isaiah 42:1 'I will put my Spirit on him'. God speaks also of his Son, echoing Psalm 2:7 'You are my Son' and adding 'on whom my favour rests' (verse 7). The king is anointed, but the circumstances show that his royal power and empire must be won through teaching and healing, as a humble, self-sacrificing servant.

4:1-11 Temptation in the wilderness

The Spirit who descended on Jesus at his baptism leads him into the wilderness to be tempted, as part of his probation. Temptation follows all that has happened in baptism. The Jews spent forty years in the wilderness (Deuteronomy 8:2) 'to humble you and to test you in order to know what was in your heart, whether or not you would

keep his commands'. Jesus, recognizing this as a similar situation, uses words from Deuteronomy to turn away temptation.

By saying to Jesus 'If you are the Son of God' (verse 3 and 6) the devil implies that Jesus should put God to the test, following his statement in verse 17 of the last chapter. 'Very well, you have unlimited power at your disposal. Use it for your own advantage. Turn these flat stones into the cakes of bread that they so much resemble and satisfy your hunger.' Jesus' answer is to quote Deuteronomy 8:3; his response is to his Father's direction and not his own self-interest.

More testing 'You are the son of God', the tempter repeats. 'Do something spectacular and compel him to intervene miraculously on your behalf. Throw yourself down from the Temple roof into the Kidron ravine; no harm will come to you, for *scripture says* "His angels by his command will see to it that you don't even stub your toe against the rock". You can quote scripture, so can I', quoting Psalm 91:11. Jesus replies from Deuteronomy 6:16, refusing to do the very thing Israel did repeatedly whilst in the wilderness 'where your fathers tested me and tried me' (Psalm 95:9).

The third temptation is to have power over the world on the devil's terms and by his well-tested methods. Worship and service of the true God only is the reply of Jesus, from Deuteronomy 6:13. Obedience as a servant meant suffering and death for Jesus, but through this he has achieved more secure and permanent Lordship.

The 'pinnacle' of the Temple. The tempter said: 'Throw yourself down from the Temple roof into the Kidron ravine; no harm will come to you . . .'

'Then Jesus was led by the Spirit into the desert to be tempted by the devil' (Matthew 4:1). This photograph of the Judean wilderness reveals how barren it is.

Fishermen on the Lake of Galilee. At least seven of Jesus' disciples were fishermen, and fishing is often mentioned in the Gospels. There are about twenty-five different species of fish to be found in the lake, though only a few of these are important for fishing.

4:12-22 Jesus begins to preach

'Capernaum by the sea' was a suitable base for Jesus' ministry in Galilee. He could cross the lake by boat and be out of reach of Herod, who had imprisoned John. Matthew quotes Isaiah 9:1-2 – the light will scatter the darkness of defeat, and the Gentiles will have a share in all that the Messiah brings.

Jesus' message in verse 17 is John's call to repentance in Matthew 3:2. But on his lips 'the kingdom of heaven' stood for something else. Jesus was calling people to re-assess all their personal and social values in the light of his ministry. We will look at this in the next section, the Beatitudes.

At the start of his ministry Jesus calls his first four disciples. They are to leave their nets, follow him, and become fishers of men (verse 19). The claims of the kingdom of heaven must come first. No family ties or business interests are to stand in their way (verse 22).

4:23-25 Jesus heals the sick

Jesus' ministry began with public teaching and healing. The synagogues of Galilee were open to him for his message that the Old Testament prophecies were now being fulfilled. The 'good news of the kingdom' was the good news that God was visiting his people as he had promised. The various kinds of affliction mentioned in verse 24 marred God's creation. The power of the kingdom of heaven was shown in the relief which Jesus gave to their victims (compare Matthew 12:28). News of his activity travelled far and wide. Crowds flocked to him from all parts of Palestine and from many parts of the surrounding area.

5:1-12 The Beatitudes

The next three chapters present the rule of life in the kingdom of heaven. It is called the Sermon on the Mount from Matthew 5:1 and 8:1. The mountainside referred to is probably a gentle slope rising above Capernaum, where a ridge parallel with the lakeshore forms a natural amphitheatre. It seems that for Matthew a 'mountain' was a 'place of revelation' (compare Matthew 17:1,9 and 28:16).

The use of a mountain may be to contrast and compare with Mount Sinai, where according to Exodus chapters 19-31 Moses received God's law. Jesus' teaching is addressed to the disciples, verses 1 and 2, in the hearing of larger crowds (Matthew 7:28).

The opening section, verses 3-10, blesses eight types of people. The poor in spirit are those who rely on God's grace, as they know their inadequacy. Although they do not have material wealth, they are inwardly rich. The mourners refuse to close their eyes to human grief; they sympathize with the tragic side of life. The meek are the opposite of the self-assertive. Their reward has already been announced in Psalm 37:11. Those who hunger and thirst for righteousness want to work to see God's will done, both in themselves and in mankind. The merciful, the pure in heart and the peace-makers reflect the character of the God of mercy, purity and peace. In the world, where these values are often reversed, such people are not likely to have an easy time. Indeed they are almost bound to be persecuted for righteousness' sake.

True happiness But, says Jesus, this is no ground for complaint, rather for rejoicing. People such as he describes are truly happy and fortunate. The future is with them, not with the hard-boiled 'pushers' who put their own interests first, and get on in the world. The rewards are not accidental, but the natural fruit of the qualities that are commended. These qualities were seen in harmony in our Lord's character. Just in case the disciples missed the practical point of the beatitudes, Jesus repeats the last one in the second person. They will be persecuted and shamed because they are his disciples.

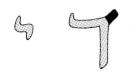

Left: the smallest letter in the Hebrew alphabet, y, ('jot');
right: the 'tittle' is added to the 'r' to mark it off from the 'd' in Hebrew.

Matthew 5

The traditional site of Jesus' Sermon on the Mount. This hill is situated close to the north-east shore of the Lake of Galilee. Since he often taught in the open-air, Jesus used common country scenes and objects to illustrate his message.

They should rejoice in this as a sure sign that they follow in the steps of the prophets.

Because we are so familiar with the beatitudes, we are blind to their revolutionary character. They turn the accepted priorities upside down. They must have presented a more radical challenge to the establishment of the day than even John's fiery condemnation in Matthew 3:7.

5:13-16 Salt and light

Jesus' followers must be like salt, saving their society from corruption. They must be 'the light of the world', scattering the darkness all around (verses 13,14). Salt without its 'saltiness' is good for nothing, and an invisible light useless. Søren Kierkegaard, the Danish thinker, said: 'to be a true Christian in secret . . . is as impossible as firing a cannon in secret'. The teaching of verse 16, 'Let your light shine before men . . .', is echoed in such passages as Philippians 2:15,16 and 1 Peter 3:1,2; 13-16.

5:17-26 Fulfilment of the law

The Sermon on the Mount does not cancel the requirements of the law of the Old Testament. It completes them. People find it impossible to keep the Ten Commandments, so it is naive to say: 'All the world needs is to put the Sermon on the Mount into practice'. Paul knew Jesus' moral teaching well. In Galatians 5:16; 6:2 he claims that those who 'live by the Spirit' will 'fulfil the law of Christ'.

The new standard is higher, but it must be aimed for. The Pharisees' standard was very high, but it could be achieved by such people as the rich young man of Matthew 19:20. But who can keep perfectly the sixth commandment as it is explained here (verses 21,22)? In the heavenly court, not only the act of murder but the angry thought and the despising attitude will be judged (verse 22).

There are two results of this. God cannot be worshipped properly by those who are at odds with their neighbours (verses 23,24). Secondly, since we are all on our way to the heavenly court, where we must account for ourselves, we should settle matters with our neighbours while there is time (verse 25).

5:27-32 No divorce

Jesus continues explaining what the Law of Moses demands. He shows that the seventh commandment, 'Do not commit adultery', also forbids lustful thoughts and glances (verses 27,28). Verses 29,30, like Matthew 18:8, teach that it is better to lose the eye or hand that tempt us to sin than to lose our life by giving way to the sin.

In verses 31,32, Jesus explains the law about divorced people of Deuteronomy 24:1-4. Different parties of rabbis had different causes for divorce. But, as Jesus argued in Matthew 19:3-6, marriage is binding for life. Under Jewish law, a divorced wife could not appeal against her husband's arbitrary act. It was next to impossible for a woman to live singly, so she was bound to re-marry and therefore commit adultery (verse 32).

5:33-37 Oaths

Jesus next explains the law about oaths. Based on the third commandment, it was elaborated in Leviticus 19:12; Numbers 30:2 and Deuteronomy 23:21-23. Jesus lays down a new code for his followers in verses 33-37. They must not swear oaths at all. They should be known as people of their word, so that they will be believed if they use only the simple 'Yes' or 'No'.

The oaths Jesus mentions in verses 34-36 were substitutes for swearing 'by God'. Perhaps people thought that breaking such an oath was not so serious. But Jesus points out the folly of such swearing; 'for you cannot make even one hair white or black'.

'You are the light of the world. A city on a hill cannot be hidden. Neither do people light a lamp and put it under a bowl' (Matthew 5:14,15).

5:38-42 An eye for an eye

A third time Jesus goes further than the Old Testament teachings, using the words 'But I tell you . . .' The prophets long ago said, 'Thus said the Lord . . .'; the rabbis loved to quote a law, using the name of some great teacher from the past. But Jesus emphasizes the 'I'; he appeals to no higher authority than his own.

Originally 'An eye for an eye . . .' (Exodus 21:24,25; Leviticus 24:19,20) marked an advance on barbarous blood-feuds, which could become unlimited. The new rule was 'one eye (and one only) for an eye; one life (and one only) for a life'.

But Jesus' teaching marks a second step forward. His followers should not retaliate at all. On the contrary, they should take the initiative and repay evil with good. If a man volunteered to carry a soldier's pack a second mile, after being forced to carry it for one mile, he showed he was a 'free' person, not just an automaton. But what is important is the way in which these instructions are obeyed. You can even turn the other cheek provocatively (verses 38-42).

5:43-48 Love for enemies

'Love your neighbour as yourself' (Leviticus 19:18) sums up the law of Israel. How it is applied depends on the answer to the question: 'Who is my neighbour?' The additional words '. . . and hate your enemy' are not from the Old Testament. But they are echoed for example in the teaching of the Qumran community, who were encouraged in 'everlasting hatred for all the men of the pit'. There is nothing very special about loving, or doing good to, your friends. But Jesus' followers should be marked out for their kindness to their enemies. This will show that they are true sons of God, since, like him, they do good to all, whether good or evil.

Verse 48, 'Be perfect' recalls Leviticus 19:2, 'Be holy because I, the Lord your God, am holy'. But it refers here particularly to perfect mercy. This is not a law to be enforced, but a pattern to be copied.

6:1-4 Giving to the needy

'Acts of righteousness' in verse 1 covers giving to the poor, praying and fasting, which were all left mainly to the individual's discretion. Jesus shows that people who do such things to get a good public

'When you give to the needy, do not announce it with trumpets . . .' (Matthew 6:2).

Matthew 6

'You are the salt of the earth. But if the salt loses its saltiness, how can it be made salty again? It is no longer good for anything . . .' (Matthew 5:13). The Dead Sea has no outlet and is very rich in salt, which is deposited in salt pans on its shores.

Commandments

In the New Testament we find that Jesus did two things to the Old Testament commandments. First he enlarged on them, giving them a new and deeper meaning. He really added another dimension. For example in Matthew 5:21, 22, 27,28 he shows that they do not merely apply to outward actions, but to the words and thoughts which prompt such actions.

Jesus 'fulfilled' the Old Testament commandments in the sense that you might fill in the bare outline of a map with rivers, mountains and roads, giving it content and substance.

Secondly, Jesus summarized the Old Testament commandments by reducing them from ten to two; see Mark 12:28-34. In doing this, however, he was not substituting love for the commandments.

reputation get exactly that – and nothing more. If they are done from this motive, they do not add up to 'true religion'. What is important is that they are done so that God alone knows about them. He will reward them fittingly.

Giving to the poor comes first here; this is in line with the Old Testament. For example, Proverbs 19:17 reads: 'He who is kind to the poor lends to the Lord, and he will reward him for what he has done'.

6:5-18 Prayer and fasting

As for prayer, there is a place for public prayer. But there is something unpleasant about pretending to pray to God, while actually wanting to be seen by others and get a name for being a person of prayer. The Christian for whom prayer is natural will pray when nobody is about. His or her public prayer will be influenced by this regular secret praying.

Verse 8 reminds us that we do not inform God of what we need when we pray. We recall our needs ourselves, and make ourselves dependent upon him. Having done this, we can receive his mercy in grateful trust.

Jesus gave the Lord's Prayer to his disciples as a pattern to follow. It summarizes in a nutshell his teaching about the kingdom of God. The Lord's Prayer can be repeated in less than half a minute, contains petitions which range from the common bread-and-butter needs of our breakfast tables to the ultimate achievement of the age-long purposes of God; puts God's glory first, our needs second, does not rule out material matters as too trifling to pray about, yet insists on the supremacy of the spiritual and emphasizes the basic condition of the disciples' enjoyment of the Father's forgiveness.

'Hallowed be your name, your kingdom come, your will be done' are probably three ways of making the same request. 'On earth as it is in heaven' can be added to all three requests. The request of verse 11 is content with 'rations' for one day at a time.

In Aramaic, the language that Jesus used, 'debts' and 'debtors' (verse 12) mean 'sins' and 'sinners'. Jesus reminds his followers that only the forgiving can ask for forgiveness (verses 14,15).

'Lead us not into temptation' (verse 13) may mean, 'Don't let us fail in the test' – the ultimate crisis which puts our faith to the test (see also Matthew 26:41).

The words of praise, or doxology, 'for yours is the kingdom and the power and the glory forever. Amen', (verse 13) do not belong to the original Gospel. But this form of words was used by the church at a very early period.

Fasting Like giving and praying, fasting should be private. It should be done voluntarily, and be between the believer and God. It is not a way to impress people. Do we as Christians simply go through religious activities as if they were certain rules to be kept? Do we suppose we can earn God's approval by fulfilling them better than other people?

6:19-34 Do not worry

Jesus commends freedom from anxiety. We can have utter confidence in our heavenly Father's love and care. In the original language, verses 19-21 are a perfect rhyming poem. The parable of Luke 12:15-21 teaches how uncertain is treasure stored up on earth. The 'bad' eye of verse 23 is an envious eye. Such an eye will concentrate on treasures on earth. A good eye is a sign of a generous spirit, like that of God himself (see Matthew 5:45,48).

'Mammon' (verse 24 in some translations) means literally anything in which people put their trust. Here it stands for material gain.

The Father who feeds the birds and adorns the grass can be trusted to provide his children with enough to eat and wear (verses 25-34).

We cannot be sure whether 'a single hour' or 'single cubit to his height' is the better translation.

The Jews thought the Gentiles (verse 32) had little or no spiritual consciousness. Jesus warns his listeners that they are likely to live at the same level as the Gentiles. Verse 33 shows the right order of things. To seek God's kingdom and righteousness first is to take the Sermon on the Mount seriously.

7:1-6 Judging others
The Golden Rule (verse 12) sums up most of what is in these twelve verses. Jesus was not in fact the first teacher in Israel to sum up the 'Law and the Prophets' like this. But most of his predecessors were rather negative. For example a generation earlier Rabbi Hillel said, 'What is hateful to yourself do not do to another. That is the whole law, everything else is a commentary on it.'

'Do not judge . . .' (verse 1); this is not to discourage discernment, but finding fault in others. The picture of a man with a log in his eye volunteering to remove a splinter from his brother's eye (verses 3-5) gives a delightful example of Jesus' sense of humour. A proper sort of discernment is commended in verse 6. If not, the swine will trample the pearls underfoot, and the dogs – pariahs of course – will bite the hand that feeds them. The illustration means that spiritual mysteries are not to be pressed upon people who are unready or unwilling to appreciate them.

7:7-12 Ask, seek, knock
The encouragement to prayer in verses 7-11 emphasizes the teaching of Matthew 6:5-15. Jesus does this by using the 'how much more' argument, which he loved to employ. If even a reluctant and sleepy head of the house will get up at midnight to give his neighbour three loaves for the sake of peace . . . (Luke 11:5-8); if even earthly fathers, sinful men though they are, give their children food when they ask for it, and do not put them off with useless or dangerous substitutes . . . *how much more* will God, the heavenly Father, give his children good things, not harmful things, when they ask him? Therefore 'ask . . ., seek . . ., knock'. For everyone who asks receives. . .'

The flowers mentioned in Matthew 6:28 and Luke 12:27 could refer to any of the beautiful flowers of the Palestine countryside. Among those possible are the anemone (opposite) the corn marigold (left) and the wild corn poppy.

'Do not throw your pearls to pigs. If you do, they may trample them under their feet, and then turn and tear you to pieces' (Matthew 7:6).

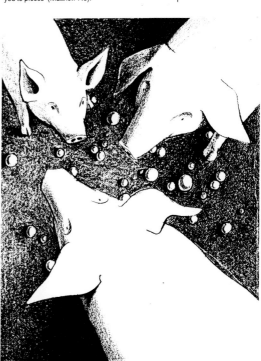

7:13-29 A matter of life and death

There is an urgency and sternness in these verses. It is often overlooked by people who want to underline the ideals of the Sermon on the Mount. Jesus insists that there are two gates, two ways, two destinies (verses 13,14), two kinds of tree and fruit (verses 15-20) and two foundations (verses 24-27). His way is the path of life. Refusal to follow it is the straight road to disaster.

The either/or of Jesus' words cannot be escaped. In the day when all things are shaken, stability and salvation, for both individuals and communities, can be gained only by accepting his way. People who teach differently – however plausible and attractive – are false prophets, wolves in sheep's clothing (verse 15). The principle 'By their fruit you will recognize them' is repeated (verses 16,20).

'Lord, Lord . . .' Only those who obey the Father's will inwardly will enter his kingdom (verses 21-23). It is not enough to claim to be a disciple. It is not enough to call Jesus 'Lord'. It is not enough to

'Watch out for false prophets. They come to you in sheep's clothing, but inwardly they are ferocious wolves' (Matthew 7:15).

preach, drive out demons or even do mighty works in his name. It is some of the most familiar human failings, not outrageous wickedness, that prevent us obeying his will. The teaching of Jesus is difficult and unacceptable because it runs counter to those elements in human nature which the twentieth century has in common with the first – such things as laziness, greed, the love of pleasure, the instinct to hit back and the like. Only those who 'do not live according to the sinful nature but according to the Spirit' (Romans 8:4) can fulfil the requirements of the Sermon on the Mount.

The crowds might well be 'amazed at his teaching' (verses 28,29). But that is not the same as accepting his teaching – nor the same as accepting his authority.

8:1-4 The man with leprosy

Matthew first gives prominence to Jesus' teaching in the Sermon on the Mount. Now he gives detailed accounts of some of the incidents from Jesus' earlier ministry in Galilee (8:1-9:34). The healing of the man with leprosy shows Jesus' compassion. He ignored the isolation that had been forced on a man regarded by the law as 'unclean', by touching him (verse 3). But Jesus did not want to override normal procedures. He told the man to offer the usual sacrifice and so get a priest's statement that he was 'clean' (verse 4; see also Leviticus 13:46; 14:2-32). Jesus soon enough clashed with the religious establishment – but not by his choice.

'Enter through the narrow gate. For wide is the gate and broad is the road that leads to destruction, and many enter through it. But small is the gate and narrow the road that leads to life, and only a few find it' (Matthew 7:13,14). This narrow passage leads through the Jewish quarter of old Jerusalem.

'Everyone who hears these words of mine and does not put them into practice is like a foolish man who built his house on the sand. The rain came down, the streams rose, and the winds blew and beat against that house, and it fell with a great crash' (Matthew 7:26,27).

Some of the types of thistle that grow in Palestine can be up to fifteen feet tall.

8:5-13 The faith of the centurion

The man with leprosy was cured by a healing touch from Jesus' hand. By contrast, the centurion's servant, like the Canaanite girl of Matthew 15:28, was healed from a distance (verses 5-13).

Jesus did not hold back his sympathy from non-Jews. He was prepared to 'go and heal' the centurion's paralyzed servant (verse 7). He did not need to go; the centurion's faith was such as to make the journey unnecessary. Jesus saw in his faith the foreshadowing of the day when many Gentiles would share the blessings of the fathers of Israel, in the new age. The coming of the Gentiles was one sign of the age of fulfilment of what the prophets had foretold (see Psalm 102:15; Isaiah 60:3). Jesus' ministry marked the beginning of this new age. But not till the Son of Man was raised from the dead would it reach its full power and extent.

Unusual faith The centurion recognized that Jesus had invisible powers at his command. He showed a sort of faith Jesus had found in nobody else, and Jesus responded with delight (verse 10).

The 'hard saying' about the 'subjects of the kingdom' (those who were the natural heirs of Abraham, Isaac and Jacob) is not found in the similar account in Luke 7:2-10. But Jesus teaches the same lesson in his sermon in Nazareth (Luke 4:23-27). Those who expect to be at the top of the guest-list find themselves grinding their teeth in vexation outside, because they lack faith.

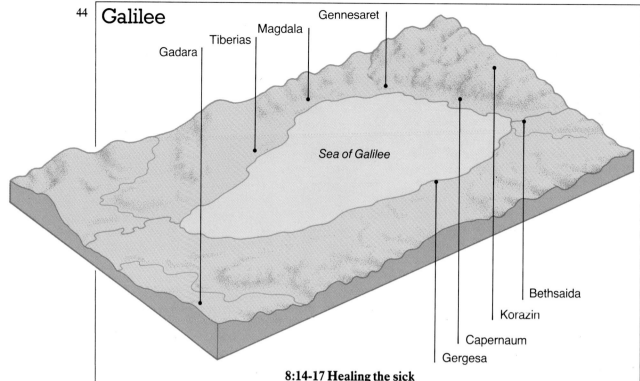

Galilee

Gadara
Tiberias
Magdala
Gennesaret

Sea of Galilee

Bethsaida
Korazin
Capernaum
Gergesa

'He took up our infirmities and carried our diseases' (Matthew 8:17).

8:14-17 Healing the sick

The healing of Peter's mother-in-law from fever by the touch of his hand is just one of many cures done by Jesus that day in Capernaum (verses 14-16). He relieved those possessed by demons with a word of command expressing his authority as Lord of all creation (verse 16). The quotation of Isaiah 53:4 in the context of this healing (verse 17) emphasizes that the Servant takes away the infirmities and diseases which afflict men.

We cannot miss Jesus' note of sympathy, which goes with his powerful action. He is man among men, bone of their bone, flesh of their flesh.

8:18-22 The cost of following Jesus

Verses 18-22 give samples of the tests Jesus set to deter would-be disciples who were half-hearted.

The meaning of the title 'Son of Man' in verse 20 is not totally clear. Perhaps it means 'everybody is at home in Israel's land except the true Israel . . . if you cast your lot with me and mine you join the ranks of the dispossessed, and you must be prepared to serve God under these conditions'.

The second volunteer promised total commitment when he had discharged his last family duty. Jesus replies that he need not fear that his father will be left unburied when he dies. The business of the kingdom of God is urgent. It allows no holding back, no delay.

8:23-27 Jesus calms the storm

Matthew describes this storm on the lake by a very strong word, literally meaning 'earthquake' (verse 24). The stilling of the storm, recorded by all three Synoptic Gospels, pictures Jesus as Lord of the winds and the waves. It recalls the ancient Near Eastern picture of the Creator overcoming the wild sea, standing for the forces of chaos. Matthew chooses the word 'earthquake' to underline this. The upsurge of the deep stands for all the demonic powers which rise to overthrow the kingdom of God, but are overthrown by that kingdom. A similar account is found in Mark 4:36-41, but with a number of differences in detail. Sudden storms can occur even today on the lake of Galilee.

8:28-34 Demons cast out

The lesson taught in nature is now taught again on the human level. The demons' main target is the spirit of man. The Gentile population, more concerned about losing their pigs than the healing of people, have their parallel in our consumer society.

The original manuscripts call the region Gadara, Gerasa and Gergesa in the three different Gospels. Gadara was seven miles southeast of the lake. The best-known Gerasa was modern Jerash, nearly forty miles south-east of the lake. Gerasa and Gergesa are probably forms of the old name for the modern village of Kersa or Kursi, on the east shore of the lake. This is the only point on that coast where the steep hills come down to the shore.

9:1-8 The Son of Man's authority

Matthew here calls Capernaum 'his own town'. Jesus now made the city his headquarters (see Mark 2:1). Matthew shortens the story of the healing of the paralytic. Mark and Luke tell how the man was let down through the roof. But Matthew nevertheless keeps the basic lesson of the incident.

This is not only a miracle story. It is also told for the sake of the statement of Jesus that it leads up to: 'the Son of Man has authority on earth to forgive sins' (verse 6). It is as easy to *say* 'Your sins are forgiven', as to say 'Get up and walk'. But spectators could immediately see the effectiveness of the second order, while the truth of the first belonged to the inner, spiritual world. The scribes were right to think that Jesus was taking on God's role. But God can delegate some of his rights if he chooses. In Daniel 7:13,14 he delegates his rights of control and judgment to 'one like a son of man'. It is as this Son of Man that Jesus now speaks. Yet as the supreme interpreter of God's will, Jesus claims the power not to judge sins, but to forgive sins (see also John 3:17; 12:47). God has delegated to Jesus the judgement of the world. He can use this authority to acquit or to condemn.

Verse 8 suggests that this authority is to some extent shared with other 'men'. This gives a basis for the Prayer Book statement that God 'hath given power, and commandment, to his Ministers, to declare and pronounce to his people, being penitent, the Absolution and Remission of their sins'. They preach the forgiveness which the Son of Man has obtained.

9:9-17 Controversy grows

The story of the tax-collector raises some interesting questions. Why, for instance, is it only in the Gospel linked with Matthew that this tax-collector (called Levi by Mark and Luke) is called Matthew? Why is it in the list of apostles of this Gospel only that Matthew is labelled 'the tax-collector'? (Matthew 10:3).

It is only from this Gospel-writer that we learn that the Twelve included a former tax-collector. That he should belong to the same group as Simon the Zealot is a near miracle. Admittedly it was not for the Romans, but for the government of Herod the ruler of Galilee, that Matthew collected taxes at Capernaum. But tax-farmers were all seen as unpatriotic. Evading taxes was totally excusable.

The story of verses 10-13 is included for the sake of its final statement. Jesus defends his links with such disreputable people by appealing to a great statement by a prophet in Hosea 6:6. He also argues that it is sick people, not the healthy, who need the care of a doctor. 'I have not come to call the righteous, but sinners' (verse 13) is one of the greatest one-sentence summaries of the gospel.

Matthew was one of the Twelve chosen by Jesus as apostles; see Mark 3:18. His call is described in Matthew 9:9; Mark 2:14 and Luke 5:27. Mark and Luke call him Levi the son of Alphaeus; evidently he had two names.

Matthew was a tax-collector (Matthew 9:9). This was an unpopular job, since the taxes were paid to Rome, the occupying power, and the collectors felt free to overcharge and take as much as they dared for themselves; see Luke 3:12, 13; 19:2,8. Luke 5:29 tells how Matthew invited Jesus and the disciples to a magnificent meal at his home, with other tax-collectors and people who did not mind being associated with them.

Apart from this, the New Testament does not mention Matthew.

Matthew 9

The site of the New Testament city of Capernaum as seen from the Lake of Galilee. Situated on the north-west shore of the lake, Jesus made his headquarters here for a period. It was here that Matthew himself was called by Jesus.

The long rolls of papyrus or parchment on which people wrote could be up to one foot wide, and as long as thirty feet. If the roll was long enough, each end was fastened to a stick or wooden pin around which it could be rolled or unrolled for reading.

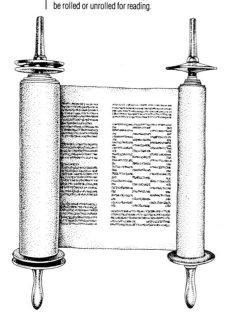

Fasting The fasting story again leads up to a final saying. Regular fasting was a voluntary act of religious devotion; see also Matthew 6:16-18. Although many religious groups in Israel fasted, Jesus' disciples did not fast. Jesus defended their behaviour, revealing something of his own understanding of himself and his role. The second half of verse 15 points forward to the time when the disciples did come to fast.

The disciples' failure to fast underlined the difference made by the proclamation of the kingdom, and the fact that the old and the new orders could not live in harmony.

9:18-26 A dead girl and a sick woman

Like the story of the paralytic, this story is much more compressed here than in Mark (5:22-43) and Luke (8:41-56). From the other Gospels, we know that 'ruler' (verse 18) means 'ruler of the synagogue', and that his name was Jairus. Rulers of the synagogue usually supervised the synagogue building and services. They were often elders of the congregation. Since the synagogue was a sort of community centre, the ruler was an important figure. Only desperate need would have driven such a man to ask Jesus' help, since Jesus was no longer in favour with synagogue leaders.

The woman with continual bleeding had to cope with physical suffering; but according to the law, as stated in Leviticus 15:25, she was permanently defiled ceremonially. This put her at a severe disadvantage socially and in religion. The edge of Jesus' cloak which she touched (verse 20) was one of the tassels laid down by the law of Numbers 15:38 and Deuteronomy 22:12.

The flute players of verse 23 were professional mourners hired for the sad occasion. Some people have argued that when Jesus said, 'The girl is not dead but asleep' (verse 24), she was not really dead. But Matthew is implying that Jesus raised her from death as easily as he might have roused her from sleep; compare John 11:11. Both of these incidents illustrate how ready Jesus was to respond to faith.

9:27-34 Jesus heals the blind and dumb

This story emphasizes there were two blind men (compare Mark 8:22-26) probably emphasizing the note of witness required in

Deuteronomy 19:15. There is a similar duplication in the story of the two demon-possessed men in Matthew 8:28 and the two blind men of Jericho in Matthew 20:30-34. This incident also illustrates the power of faith (verses 28,29). The stern warning of verse 30 is like that given to the man with leprosy in Matthew 8:4, although more strongly put. Jesus conveys indignation, and may be combining anger at the forces afflicting the man with a wish not to let people misunderstand his real mission.

When Jesus expelled the demon and gave its victim the power of speech (verses 32-34) some people suggested mockingly that if he could control demons he must be in league with the prince of the demons. This charge is repeated in Matthew 12:24, and is demolished. This time Jesus cannot silence the healed person, since the cure was seen by crowds of bystanders. The two actions together are a fulfilment of Isaiah 35:5,6: 'Then will the eyes of the blind be opened . . . and the tongue of the dumb shout for joy'.

9:35-38 The workers are few
When the crowds are compared to 'sheep without a shepherd' in verse 35, we should recall 1 Kings 22:17. What is meant is an army without a captain, a leaderless mob, a danger to themselves and everyone else. Jesus knew quite well how easily they could be led to disaster if they found the wrong kind of leader. There were high unemployment and harsh economic problems in Israel at this time, giving rise to severe political unrest. Most people refused to take

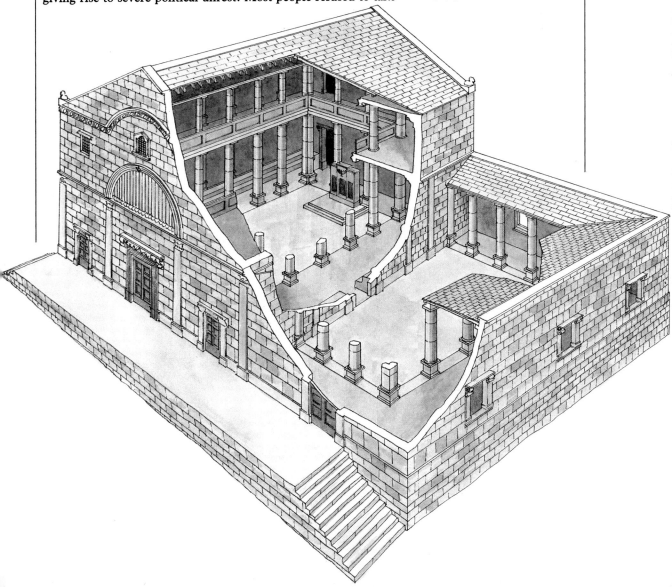

An artist's reconstruction of the synagogue the ruins of which still stand on the site of Capernaum. The building probably dates from the second century AD, but is likely to have been constructed on the same site as the synagogue which Jesus knew.

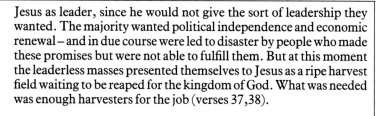

Matthew 10

Jesus as leader, since he would not give the sort of leadership they wanted. The majority wanted political independence and economic renewal – and in due course were led to disaster by people who made these promises but were not able to fulfill them. But at this moment the leaderless masses presented themselves to Jesus as a ripe harvest field waiting to be reaped for the kingdom of God. What was needed was enough harvesters for the job (verses 37,38).

10:1-15 Jesus sends out the Twelve

Into the ripe harvest field, then, the Twelve are sent two by two. The Gospel-writer takes this opportunity to list their names (verses 2-4; see also Mark 3:16-19; Luke 6:14-16; Acts 1:13). The lists given in the different Gospels vary. But if the Twelve are divided into three groups of four, each group always starts with the same name: Simon, Peter, Philip, James the son of Alphaeus. Thaddaeus (also mentioned in Mark 3:18) must be the same as 'Judas the son of James' in Luke 6:16 and Acts 1:13 and 'Judas not Iscariot' of John 14:22. Simon the Zealot, verse 4, evidently was, or had been, a member of the militant resistance movement.

Matthew places here a second section of Jesus' teaching. The Twelve were to speak and act in his name, extending his ministry. Their message is defined in verse 7; compare this with Matthew 4:17. Their time was limited, and they must concentrate on the Jews first. We have already seen that Jesus was willing to help the Gentiles (Matthew 8:5-13), and the other Gospels tell of his friendly contacts with the Samaritans. But as yet his grace was not available to them without restriction, see also John 12:24,32. Matthew himself was not exclusive in his outlook, since he records how Jesus after the resurrection sent his disciples to '. . . make disciples of all nations . . .' (Matthew 28:19,20). Jesus speaks in verse 9 of 'the lost sheep of Israel'. He implies that he is offering himself to them as their true shepherd; compare John 10:1-16, which echoes Ezekiel 34:23, where the son of David takes this role.

The Twelve were to take no provisions for their journey, but to rely on charity. Jesus' saying that 'the worker is worth his keep' (verse 10) is echoed in 1 Corinthians 9:14 and 1 Timothy 5:18. Jesus seemed to rely on 'some worthy person' being found in any town or

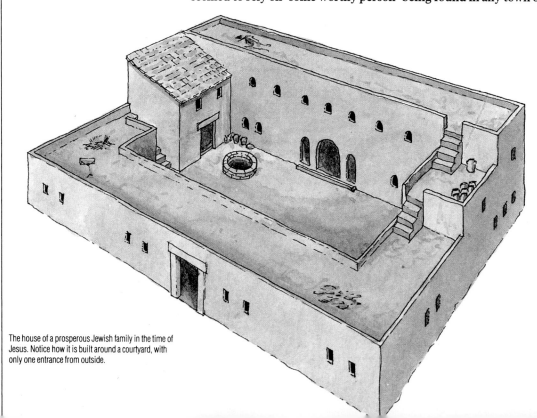

The house of a prosperous Jewish family in the time of Jesus. Notice how it is built around a courtyard, with only one entrance from outside.

village (verse 11). He knew that sympathizers with the message of the kingdom might be found in many places. Some of them would have been influenced by the preaching of John the Baptist (see Matthew 3:5,6).

The 'peace' of verse 13 is the greeting 'Peace be with you'. A terrible judgement will come to the place which refuses the gospel. The Twelve must shake off its dust, to prevent the judgement extending to them; compare Acts 13:51; 18:6.

10:16-23 Persecution ahead

Verses 5-15 relate to the immediate task of the Twelve. But verses 16 onwards look forward to a later period, to the ministry of the Twelve between AD30 and AD70. It partly parallels Matthew 24:9-14, and sheds much light on the disciples' mission to the Jews in Palestine in that period; see also Galatians 2:7-9.

The Twelve were to defend themselves not by force, but in wisdom and innocence; compare Romans 16:19. The 'local councils' of verse 17 were the local sanhedrins. The synagogues could inflict a flogging of 'forty stripes save one'; see also 2 Corinthians 11:24 and Deuteronomy 25:3. The 'governors and kings' of verse 18 might be the Roman governors and Jewish kings.

Verses 18-20 are illustrated by the early Christian martyrs. Christians on trial showed such eloquence that their accusers were astonished (see Acts 4:13; 1 Peter 3:15-16). The warning about households being divided is repeated in verses 35,36 and Mark 13:12. 'When you are persecuted in one place, flee to another'; compare the behaviour of Paul and Barnabas in Acts 14:5,6 and 19,20. The second half of verse 23, 'you will not finish going through the cities of Israel before the Son of Man comes', has long been argued over. It is almost certainly linked with the fall of Jerusalem in AD70 (see the notes on Matthew 16:27,28 and 24:3-5).

10:24-42 Words of enouragement

Further sayings of Jesus are added to encourage his followers. The persecutions in store for them are no greater than what Jesus himself must suffer; see also John 13:16; 15:20; 16:2 and Luke 6:40. But if the servants share their master's sufferings, they will also share his vindication. He himself will put their case before God; he himself will prosecute the faithless (see also Mark 8:38; Luke 12:8,9). They are to be his heralds, proclaiming the 'secrets of the kingdom' without fear or favour (verses 26,27). If they fear God, they need fear nobody else (verse 28). The comparison of men with sparrows is parallelled in Matthew 6:26.

Jesus' warning that his mission would divide families (verses 34-37) echoes Micah 7:5,6. Split families were to be one of the sorrows of the end-time. Jesus may have learned from the lack of sympathy in his own family that 'a man's enemies will be the members of his own household' (verse 36); see also Mark 3:21; John 7:5.

Taking up the cross The Gospels continually underline that the claims of the kingdom of heaven come before all family ties: compare verse 37 with Matthew 8:22; 12:46-50; 19:29. Taking up the cross (verse 38) was not simply a picture for taking on annoying burdens. It meant that Jesus' followers must be prepared to be crucified, as he was; see also Matthew 16:24. But life lost in Jesus' service would be life gained. Life gained at the cost of loyalty to Jesus would be life lost (verse 39); compare Matthew 16:25-27.

Verses 40-42 apply to all followers of Jesus. The treatment meted out to his followers is accepted by Jesus as meted out to himself; see also Matthew 25:40,45; Mark 9:41; Luke 10:16; John 13:20. Compare verse 41 with 1 Kings 17:8-24 and 2 Kings 4:8-37. The reference to 'little ones' in verse 42 is taken up again in Matthew 18:5-14.

Matthew 10

According to the law of Moses, it was permissible to eat sparrows as food. They were caught in nets in the cornfields, and sold very cheaply in the markets.

Power

The Herodion, a fortress south of Jerusalem, built by Herod the Great on the site of one of his greatest military victories.

The Greek word here is the one from which we get our word 'dynamite'. It was used to describe somebody's capacity to do or to afford something.

1 The power of God
God is the source of all power. We read in Psalm 62:11 and 1 Chronicles 29:11,12 that God is strong. It is seen in his creation (Psalm 150:1); in the way he sustains the universe and everything in it (Psalm 65:5-8); and in his mighty acts on behalf of humanity (Psalm 111:6). His power is seen in the life of Jesus, above all in his resurrection (Romans 1:4; Ephesians 1:19,20). It is seen in the power of the gospel to save men and women (Romans 1:16), and in his ability to keep and support all those who put their trust in him (1 Peter 1:5). As Genesis 1:26-28 tells us, any power that humans have over the created world is derived solely from God.

2 The power of Christ
A different word, meaning authority, is used sometimes for Jesus' power. For example in Matthew 7:29 we read of his authority, when it refers to the effect of his teaching; in Matthew 9:6 about his right to forgive sins; in Matthew 28:18-20 about his commission to his disciples. But it is the 'dynamic' power which is expressed in Jesus' miracles, for example in Luke 5:17. It is also this power which will accompany him when he returns in glory, see Luke 21:27; and which is used on behalf of Christians at all times.

3 The power of the Holy Spirit
The coming of the Holy Spirit at Pentecost meant that the power of God was harnessed to the life of the Christian believer in a new way (Acts 1:8; 2:1-3). It enabled the disciples to do miracles, (Acts 3:12), to witness for Christ in a bold, effective way (Acts 4:33), and to have strong, tranquil, inner spiritual life (Ephesians 3:16).

11:1-15 Jesus and John the Baptist
So far we have not been told of the imprisonment of John the Baptist. It is related as a kind of 'flash-back' in Matthew 14:3-12. John had announced that the Coming One would carry out a ministry of judgement. But he heard reports of Jesus' activities while in prison at Machaerus, and they seemed to have little to do with judgement. He wondered whether Jesus was, after all, the Coming One. Had he been mistaken in naming Jesus as the Coming One? When he sent messengers to satisfy himself about these questions, Jesus performed before their eyes many of the signs which the prophets said would mark the new age (see, for example, Isaiah 35:5,6; 61:1). When they told John what they had seen, his faith would be restored. He would stop feeling that Jesus had let him down.

The herald Jesus' witness to John sets John on a pinnacle by himself. People who remembered what he looked like and how he behaved must have laughed when Jesus suggested that people had expected to see a man dressed in fine clothes. Jesus confirmed the widely-held belief that John was a prophet – 'and more than a prophet'; for John, the last prophet of the old order, was the herald of the kingdom which was about to appear. He was the messenger of Malachi 3:1, who would prepare the way of the Lord. He was the returning Elijah foretold in Malachi 4:5,6, whose coming would announce 'the great and terrible day of the Lord'. At the end of the old age of 'the prophets and the law' John stood and announced the dawning of the new age, without himself entering that new age. Although he was unrivalled in his own eminence, he was overtaken by the least person in the new age in terms of privilege (verse 11).

The 'forceful men' of verse 12 may refer to the Zealots or other militant nationalists who were trying to speed up the coming of the new age by violent methods. They turned against Jesus when he refused to exploit his popularity to take up their programme.

11:16-24 Doom of the lakeside towns
People who found fault with John for his harsh way of life were just as ready to criticize Jesus for his very different life-style. (Whatever meaning 'Son of Man' has elsewhere, here it is simply a way of Jesus

saying 'I'.) There was no pleasing such people. They were like children playing out-of-doors, quarrelling because half wanted to play weddings, half funerals. (Verse 17 forms a little jingle, if translated back into Aramaic, the language Jesus probably spoke.) But God's wisdom is proved right both by John's austere life and by Jesus' eating with 'tax collectors and "sinners" ' (verse 19).

Although people got very excited by Jesus' ministry in Galilee, there was little genuine or lasting response from the lakeside towns where he had been most active. Korazin is usually taken as the modern Kerazeh; Capernaum as modern Tell-Hum. Bethsaida may be at either et-Tabgha or Mas 'adiya. In Old Testament times such Gentile cities as Tyre and Sidon had been denounced by the prophets (Ezekiel 26:1-28:23), and Sodom destroyed by God (Genesis 18:20-19:28). But they had been permitted only a fraction of the knowledge of God given to these lakeside towns in the recent months. On the great day, judgement on the lakeside towns would be so much the greater. Their final doom was foreshadowed when the Romans crushed the revolt in Galilee in the spring of AD67. The opening words denouncing Capernaum echo the words addressed to the king of Babylon in Isaiah 14:12-15. The greater the privilege, the greater the responsibility.

11:25-30 Rest for the weary

Jesus deplored the unbelief of most of his hearers. But he warmly commended the minority who did respond to him. Although possibly child-like in intellect, they could recognize the way that Jesus was revealing his heavenly Father to them. This reversing of the world's standard was not new in God's relations with humanity. Jesus saw it as God's way.

Jesus speaks here as the Son and Revealer of the Father (compare John 1:18). He speaks too as the One whose person and purpose are known fully only by the Father. Verses 28-30 are spoken by him as God's Wisdom in person.

'Take my yoke upon you' (verse 29) means 'Enrol yourselves as my disciples'. We may contrast his 'easy' yoke with the unbearable yoke of Acts 15:10. On another man's lips the claim to be 'gentle and humble in heart' would not ring true.

The ruins of the ancient synagogue at Korazin. Situated north-west of the Lake of Galilee, Jesus probably performed miraculous works in this city.
'Then Jesus began to denounce the cities in which most of his miracles had been performed, because they did not repent, "Woe to you, Korazin!" ' (Matthew 11;20,21).

Oxen were used as beasts of burden, pulling ploughs and simple wagons. They were also led round the threshing floor to trample the grain out of the ears of corn at harvest time.

Qumran and the Dead Sea Scrolls

manuscripts are very important, since they narrow the gap between the period of writing and the oldest surviving manuscripts by as much as 1,000 years. One scroll contains all 66 chapters of Isaiah.

Jesus, John and Qumran

Non-biblical manuscripts tell us about the life of this little isolated community. They were strict on Jewish discipline, making even the Pharisees look mild. They expected the End of Time in their period, and believed that their Teacher of Righteousness knew how events would work out.

The Qumran group had fellowship meals together, which some scholars have seen as the pattern for Christian communion. But there is no evidence that Jesus' followers had contact with the desert community. Nor is there any proof that John the Baptist visited Qumran.

Theories that early Christian

The Dead Sea from Qumran

In 1947 and the following years, an important collection of manuscripts was discovered in caves above the Dead Sea area. The most important of these 'Dead Sea Scrolls' were those found in eleven caves near the Wadi Qumran, to the north-west of the Dead Sea.

This group formed the library of a Jewish community centred on Khirbet Qumran. The sect lived here for about two hundred years before they were wiped out in AD 70. The community was probably a group of strict Jews known as the Essenes. Led by 'the Teacher of Righteousness', they withdrew to the isolation of Qumran about 150 BC. They expected God to judge the Jews, and were awaiting the coming of a new age.

The library at Qumran consisted of at least 500 books. Of those surviving, many are from the Old Testament. These Hebrew

Excavations of the buildings in which the Essene community lived at Qumran.

writers borrowed from the teachings of Qumran do not stand up. The Qumran sect saw three different people as fulfilling prophecies about the Prophet, Priest and King of the House of David. But the New Testament sees Jesus fulfilling all three roles. Also, there is no suggestion that the Qumran Teacher of Righteousness would rise from the dead, as Jesus did.

It was probably during the war of AD66-73 that the community left their headquarters. Before leaving, they carefully stored their scrolls in jars hidden in the natural caves nearby.

The caves at Qumran.

The scrolls are featured in a special museum in Jerusalem, shaped like one of the jars in which they were discovered.

One of the jars in which the Dead Sea scrolls were discovered.

12:1-14 Lord of the Sabbath

Jesus finally broke with the synagogue authorities over his freedom to reinterpret the law of the Sabbath in his teaching and behaviour. The wording of the fourth commandment, 'on it (the seventh day) you shall not do any work' (Exodus 20:10; Deuteronomy 5:14), called for a more precise definition of work. The rabbis listed thirty-nine types of activity forbidden on the Sabbath. The disciples' actions were banned under these definitions. Plucking ears of corn was 'reaping'; rubbing them in the hands to extract the kernels was a form of 'threshing'.

David's example Jesus replied to the Pharisees' criticism by appealing to the precedent set by David in 1 Samuel 21:1-6, and by quoting from Hosea 6:6. He argued that the law of God, and so the Sabbath law, were intended to be a blessing to humanity, not a burden. To fulfil to the letter of the law is no fulfilment if the spirit of the law is broken. Human need must always come before religious nit-picking. The Son of Man has the authority to interpret and fulfil the Sabbath law according to God's will.

In their synagogue The second disagreement about the Sabbath takes place in 'their synagogue' (verses 9-14). Perhaps this is to show that Jesus was no longer welcome there. If an act of healing was needed to preserve life, the rabbis allowed it on the Sabbath. But if it was not as urgent as that, it was regarded as proper to wait till after the Sabbath. But Jesus held that the Sabbath was the best day to relieve people from sickness and suffering. Such healing honoured the purpose of this day. Jesus can assume that the Pharisees would rescue an animal in distress on the Sabbath (verse 11); the community at Qumran was so strict that it ruled out such a humane act. The 'priests in the temple desecrate the day' by continuing their work, and even offering more sacrifices than on normal days (verse 5). For Jesus' teaching on the Sabbath see also Luke 6:1-11; Mark 2:23-3:6.

'Jesus went through the cornfields on the Sabbath. His disciples were hungry and began to pick up some ears of corn and eat them' (Matthew 12:1). Harvesting grain in Israel today.

12:15-21 God's chosen servant

The conflict about observing the Sabbath was the cause of the final break between Jesus and the synagogue establishment; see also John

5:9-18. When Jesus withdrew from the synagogue, he was followed by many who needed his help even more than they needed the ministry of the synagogue. And he healed them all. This pattern of withdrawing from the synagogue and taking disciples with him was acted out again and again in the age of the apostles; see for example Acts 13:46-48; Acts 17:4-9; 18:6,7, and especially 19:8,9.

The note of secrecy returns, as in Matthew 8:4 and 9:30. Here Old Testament authority for it is given.

Isaiah quoted The quoting of Isaiah 42:1-4 at this stage is significant. The Jewish religious leaders have rejected Jesus. But what is God's estimate of him? The answer is given in terms of what we know as the first of the four Servant Songs from Isaiah. Its opening words were echoed by the heavenly voice at Jesus' baptism (Matthew 3:17). Jesus is presented by God as his servant. These words show God's approval of the sort of ministry Jesus has been carrying out, including his avoiding publicity.

A quotation from the fourth 'Servant Song' appears earlier in Matthew 8:17 (see also the notes on Matthew 20:28 and 26:28). The final line (verse 21) points forward to the mission to the Gentiles following Jesus' resurrection.

12:22-37 Jesus and Beelzebub

The Jewish authorities had decided that Jesus' attitude towards the Law – and especially towards the Sabbath – ruled out any possibility that he was acting at God's command. But they could not avoid the fact that he did acts of mercy and power, such as casting out the demon from the blind and dumb man of verse 22. The common people saw this as additional proof that Jesus had God's authority; 'Son of David' in verse 23 means Messiah. But the Pharisees felt they had to find the source of his power elsewhere.

The Pharisees claimed that Jesus expelled demons by the power of their prince, Beelzebub. Jesus rejected this as self-contradictory (verses 25-28). Beelzebub was an ancient Canaanite god, whose name means 'lord of the high place' or 'master of the house'; see also Matthew 10:25. Jesus asks the same question of the Pharisees in verse 27. They too expelled demons: where did their power to do this come from?

Two kingdoms The truth was quite different. Jesus expelled demons by the power and 'Spirit of God' (verse 28). This meant, first, that the kingdom of God had come upon them unawares. These actions showed its power at work amongst them, invading the kingdom of evil and releasing its prisoners (verse 29, compare Isaiah 49:24,25; 61:1). Second, the Pharisees, by crediting the work of the Spirit of God to the prince of darkness, and deliberately shutting their eyes against the light, were committing the one sin without a remedy, and therefore without pardon. With clear evidence of the Spirit of God at work before their eyes, they refused to accept it because of their mistaken views. If people have made up their minds not to accept the witness of the Spirit, what can convince them?

Verses 33-37 are made up of a number of sayings, some in the form of proverbs, which drive home the point of verses 25-32.

12:38-50 The sign of Jonah

The 'sign' that the scribes and Pharisees were looking for must have been different from the healings and exorcisms that Jesus did. They could explain these away as done by demons; they wanted some sign that proved beyond doubt that Jesus was sent by God. Perhaps they wanted the sort of sign he refused to give when he was tempted in the wilderness; see Matthew 4:5-7. But a sign like this would leave no room for faith. They would only be given the 'sign of Jonah' (verse

Baal, the most important of the Gods of the Canaanites. Here he is pictured as a storm-god, grasping a club and a thunderbolt.

'Still other seed fell on good ground, where it produced a crop – a hundred, sixty or thirty times what was sown' (Matthew 13:8).

39), which is interpreted here in terms of Jesus' resurrection (verse 40). The people of Nineveh, who repented when Jonah came to them from 'the belly of a huge fish' (Jonah 2:2), would be in a position to condemn the unbelief of the people of Jesus' time at the last judgement (verse 41). So too would the Queen of Sheba (verse 42). The 'one greater' is Jesus' ministry, heralding the kingdom of God.

This wicked generation The parable of verses 43-45 teaches that places which had had the benefit of Jesus' ministry for a time would be in a worse state afterwards because they did not respond to it by repenting and believing wholeheartedly. 'This wicked generation' echoes the words used in the Old Testament about the Israelites as they wandered in the wilderness (Deuteronomy 1:35 and similar passages). They are also called an 'adulterous generation' (verse 39), implying that they were unfaithful to God.

The incident of verses 46-50 emphasizes that earthly relationships must give way to the demands of the kingdom of heaven; see also Matthew 10:37. But it also shows that Jesus' true family is made up of all those who, like him, do God's will. This means, in the first instance, those who abandoned the synagogue in order to form Jesus' new community; compare verse 15. Jesus' brothers are named in Matthew 13:55.

13:1-9 Parable of the sower
This chapter brings together seven 'parables of the kingdom'. Two of them, the sower and the mustard seed, have parallels in Mark and Luke. The parable of the leaven has a parallel in Luke alone. Four, the weeds, the hidden treasure, the pearl and the dragnet, are found only in Matthew.

Matthew opens by saying that Jesus 'went out of the house' (verse 1). He means to show that these parables came after Jesus had been turned out by the synagogue leaders; compare Matthew 12:15. The crowds (verse 2) are more or less uncommitted; they are neither the disciples nor the religious leaders.

Traditional sowing The first parable (verses 3-9) is one of the parables of growth. It describes an experience familiar to anyone from

Galilee. It is usually known as 'the parable of the sower' from verse 18, but it is more concerned with the four sorts of soil on which the seed was sown. Modern readers might think that the sower was particularly wasteful in sowing so carelessly on bad ground. But traditionally sowing came before ploughing in this area. For this reason the sower deliberately scatters his seed on the track beaten by the feet of passers-by and on thorny ground, because it will all be ploughed up. Rocky ground was concealed by a thin covering of soil, and would only be detected when the plough struck it. So the message of the kingdom had been given out to people open to it and people hardened against it. The fact that some hearers did not receive the message did not mean it was pointless proclaiming it, for the fruit it produced in the lives of hearers who received it made it very worthwhile.

The three sets of figures in verse 8 may show the yield in different parts of the good soil. The harvest was plentiful over the whole area, but more plentiful in some parts than others.

13:10-17 Hearing, they do not hear

These verses refer repeatedly to Isaiah 6:9,10, Isaiah's first vision. He is commissioned as a prophet to his people, but warned that they will pay no attention to him. In fact, all his speaking to them will only make them less sensitive and more unresponsive to his message. This situation was happening again in Jesus' time; most of his hearers refused his message. In Aramaic, 'parable' also means 'riddle'. Jesus may have meant that the 'secrets' of the kingdom of heaven were available to faith like that of the disciples, but were only 'riddles' to the crowds who did not believe. It is a common experience that things which are easily understood by people approaching them in the right frame of mind are unintelligible to others. But Matthew, telling the parables against the background of Jesus' rejection, makes the telling of them the result of the crowd's unbelief: 'seeing, they do not see . . .'

The echo of Isaiah 6:9,10 in verse 13 is followed by the quoting of it in verses 14,15, in a version like that of the Greek version of the Old Testament (the Septuagint). The reference to the Old Testament passage in verse 13 is made in the same context in Mark 4:11,12 and

Matthew 13

Wheat and weeds (tares) grow alongside each other in this field. 'Let both grow together until the harvest. At that time I will tell the harvesters: "First collect the weeds and tie them in bundles to be burned, then gather the wheat and bring it into my barn" ' (Matthew 13:30).

The weed that grew in the field together with the wheat was a kind of grass called 'darnel'. Before it grows ears, it cannot be distinguished from wheat. But when both have grown to maturity the darnel can be distinguished. It still cannot be pulled up without disturbing the wheat.

Luke 8:10. It is also quoted in John 12:40 and Acts 28:26,27, to show that the Old Testament testified in advance that Israel would fail to accept the gospel.

13:18-30 Parable of the weeds
The interpretation of the parable of the sower, verses 18-23, is given to the disciples and not to the crowds. The parable is explained in terms of what happens when the message of the kingdom is proclaimed, whether by Jesus during his ministry or by his disciples at a later date.

Some people have their minds diverted from it before they have time to think about it. Some people are attracted to it until they discover it may mean persecution and trouble. Then they are put off, or feel let down (the same word as Matthew 11:6 uses). Yet others let everyday concerns crush the power of the message in their lives. But the people who take it intelligently and hold to it firmly despite hardship or rival attractions produce plenty of the 'fruit' of the kingdom. God's will is fulfilled in their lives.

The enemy The next parable is Matthew's second parable of growth (verses 24-30). He tells of weeds sown by an enemy in a man's wheatfield. The weeds were so similar to wheat that until they both started to ripen the weeds could not be pulled up without threatening the wheat. But when harvest came, there was no problem telling which was which. Harvesters would bundle up the weeds and burn them before reaping the wheat. Jesus is pointing to a time when true 'children of the kingdom' and 'sons of the evil one' could not be told apart.

13:31-43 The mustard seed and the yeast
The parable of the mustard seed is Matthew's third parable of growth. It reminds us that a great enterprise may have tiny beginnings. The 'birds of the air' are probably the Gentiles, as in Daniel 4:12,21, which uses similar words.

The parable of the yeast in verse 33 also points out that great results can come from small beginnings. So Jesus was launching the kingdom of heaven on earth with his ministry. Now let it work!

According to verses 34,35, Jesus now spoke in parables whenever he addressed the crowds. The writer sees this as a fulfilling of Psalm 78:2 where 'parables' has the meaning 'riddles'.

Jesus gave the interpretation of the parable of the weeds, like that of the parable of the sower, to the disciples privately (verses 36-43). While the setting of the parable may be Jesus' ministry, its interpretation may point on to the Christian mission of the Gospel-writer's time.

13:44-46 The hidden treasure

The parables of the hidden treasure (verse 44) and the pearl of great value (verses 45,46) are a pair, both emphasizing the supreme value of the kingdom of heaven. It is probably irrelevant to the main lesson of the parables that the first man hit on the treasure by chance, while the merchant was deliberately making a search for fine pearls.

It is better that a man should let everything else go than miss this. To enter the kingdom of heaven is to possess eternal life. The disciples, who had left everything to follow Jesus (compare Matthew 19:27) had learned the lesson of these parables. Here and now they were initiated into the 'secrets of the kingdom of heaven' (verse 11). And in the new world they would inherit eternal life; compare Matthew 19:28,29. What seemed madness to outsiders was in fact the highest wisdom.

13:47-52 The parable of the net

The parable of the net (verses 47-50) parallels the parable of the weeds (verses 24-30). In both parables the separation of the good from the bad is interpreted as relating to the judgement 'at the end of the age' (verse 49). Many rabbis thought that the present age would give way to the age to come. The transition would be marked by resurrection and judgement. Some schools of thought believed that the Messiah's reign would precede the dawn of the new age. Christians altered this pattern. Jesus' reign as Messiah began with his triumph over death and raising to God's right hand. It would continue until his coming again, which would mark the 'close of the age'; compare Matthew 28:18-20. But even in the earthly ministry of Jesus, and still more after the crucifixion, the powers of the new age were already at work; see Matthew 11:5; 14:2; 15:30,31; 26:64.

It is doubtful whether the disciples understood all this as fully as they imagined (verse 51). It sets out the ideal for anyone who wants to learn or teach in the school of Christ. To them, though not to unbelievers, the parables would put across the teaching they needed about the kingdom of heaven. The source of the instruction was 'old'; it went back to the visions and sayings of prophets of former times. But the way it was communicated was new; it was interpreted in the light of the coming of the kingdom, and the fulfilment of the prophecies in Jesus' ministry.

13:53-58 A prophet without honour

'When Jesus had finished these parables' (verse 53); similar words mark the end of a section of teaching at Matthew 7:28; 11:1; 19:1; and 26:1. 'His home town' (verse 54) means Nazareth; see Matthew 2:23; Luke 4:16. His fellow-townsmen felt no pride in him. Rather, they 'took offence at him' (verse 57, see also Matthew 11:6; 13:21.) They did not see why a member of an undistinguished family should get a reputation for 'wisdom and these miraculous powers' (verse 54). Why was he any better than they? Since 'the carpenter'

Galilee fishermen examine their catch. 'Once again, the kingdom of heaven is like a net that was let down into the lake and caught all kinds of fish. When it was full, the fishermen pulled it up on the shore' (Matthew 13:47,48). The drag-net mentioned here is probably a 'seine' net, which can be several hundred yards in length. A net of this kind catches fish of all shapes and sizes, which are then sorted into those which can – and those which cannot – be eaten.

MIRACLES OF JESUS

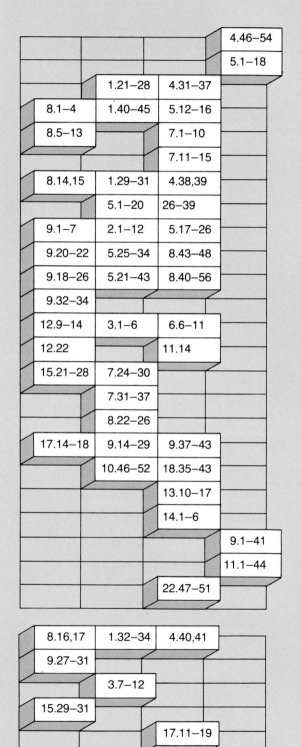

	Matthew	Mark	Luke	John
Healing of individuals				
Son of government official				4.46–54
Sick man at a pool				5.1–18
Man in synagogue		1.21–28	4.31–37	
Man with skin-disease	8.1–4	1.40–45	5.12–16	
Officer's servant	8.5–13		7.1–10	
Dead son of a widow			7.11–15	
Peter's mother-in-law	8.14,15	1.29–31	4.38,39	
An uncontrollable man		5.1–20	26–39	
Paralyzed man	9.1–7	2.1–12	5.17–26	
Woman with severe bleeding	9.20–22	5.25–34	8.43–48	
Dead girl	9.18–26	5.21–43	8.40–56	
Dumb man	9.32–34			
Man with paralyzed hand	12.9–14	3.1–6	6.6–11	
Blind and dumb man	12.22		11.14	
Canaanite woman's daughter	15.21–28	7.24–30		
Deaf and dumb man		7.31–37		
Blind man at Bethsaida		8.22–26		
Boy with epilepsy	17.14–18	9.14–29	9.37–43	
Blind Bartimaeus		10.46–52	18.35–43	
Woman with a bad back			13.10–17	
Sick man			14.1–6	
Man born blind				9.1–41
Dead friend named Lazarus				11.1–44
Slave's ear			22.47–51	
Healing of groups				
Crowd in Capernaum	8.16,17	1.32–34	4.40,41	
Two blind men	9.27–31			
Crowd by Lake Galilee		3.7–12		
Crowd on the hillside	15.29–31			
Ten men			17.11–19	

Control over laws of nature

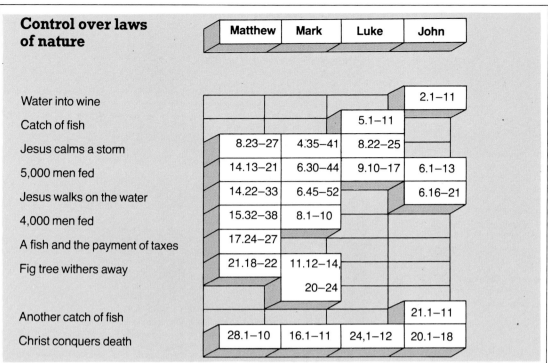

	Matthew	Mark	Luke	John
Water into wine				2.1–11
Catch of fish			5.1–11	
Jesus calms a storm	8.23–27	4.35–41	8.22–25	
5,000 men fed	14.13–21	6.30–44	9.10–17	6.1–13
Jesus walks on the water	14.22–33	6.45–52		6.16–21
4,000 men fed	15.32–38	8.1–10		
A fish and the payment of taxes	17.24–27			
Fig tree withers away	21.18–22	11.12–14, 20–24		
Another catch of fish				21.1–11
Christ conquers death	28.1–10	16.1–11	24,1–12	20.1–18

is not named (verse 55), he may no longer have been alive. The proverb of verse 57 appears in the same setting in Mark 6:4 and Luke 4:24. In John 4:44 it seems to refer to Judea rather than Nazareth. Verse 58 seems to mean that, despite their unbelief, Jesus did some miracles there; compare Mark 6:5 'He could not do any miracles there, except lay his hands on a few sick people and heal them'. But Matthew probably wants to show his readers that, with Jesus' unfriendly welcome to Nazareth, the record of his rejection in Galilee is complete.

14:1-12 Death of John the Baptist
'Herod the tetrarch' was Herod Antipas, the youngest and politically ablest of Herod the Great's sons. He was the brother of Archelaus; see Matthew 2:22. After his father's death in 4BC, Herod became ruler of Galilee and Perea, until deposed by the Roman Emperor in AD39. Herodias was not only the wife of Herod's half-brother Philip, but also the daughter of his half-brother Aristobulus. Marriage with a brother's wife was forbidden by Leviticus 18:16; it was even more grave a matter if the brother was still alive, as he was in this case.

John denounced this match in the Old Testament tradition of the prophets. He was so influential with the people that Herodias felt threatened as long as he was alive. Herodias' daughter (verse 6) was probably not Salome, who was by this time wife of Philip the tetrarch, but a younger daughter. John was held at the fortress of Machaerus, east of the Dead Sea.

The events of verses 3-12 took place earlier. They are put here to explain Herod's mention of John's death in verse 2. The account of Jesus' activity and his disciples' mission in Galilee must have made him feel that this was John the Baptist all over again.

14:13-21 Five thousand fed
Because of the news about Herod, Jesus decided to withdraw to 'a solitary place' east of the lake, outside Herod's territories. But even here he was followed by crowds, who urgently pressed him to put himself at their head. They urged him to overthrow their oppressors and bring in a new era of liberty and plenty. He refused; but in his

Located in the southernmost hills of the mountains of Galilee, Nazareth has a fine view across the plain of Esdraelon. Today it is dominated by the Church of the Annunciation, whose tower is in the centre of this picture.

'Taking the five loaves and the two fish and looking up to heaven, Jesus gave thanks and broke the loaves . . . they all ate and were satisfied' (Matthew 14:18,19). A mosaic pavement incorporating a loaves-and-fish motif.

compassion he healed the sick among them. He then did one of his greatest mighty works.

'Can God spread a table in the desert?' asked the unbelieving Israelites in the time of Moses (Psalm 78:19). They received their answer then. Jesus gives a similar answer here. He gives the blessing over the produce of the land and sea. Lifting the eyes to heaven in prayer seems to have been a general habit.

The second Moses The feeding of the five thousand is told by Matthew with great economy. The inner meaning is brought out in the dialogue in John 6:26-58. But even in Matthew we can read between the lines and see Jesus as the second Moses, the prophet of the end-time; see Deuteronomy 18:15-19. He is feeding his people in the desert, giving them at least a sign of the food which sustains the life of the age to come.

The twelve baskets (verse 20) parallel the total number of tribes of Israel – as do the twelve apostles. Only Matthew among the Gospel-writers adds 'besides women and children' (verse 21; compare Matthew 15:38). An army of 5,000 men would not have been contemptible, if Jesus had decided to lead them.

14:22-36 Walking on the water

After the feeding, Jesus made the disciples embark and leave for the other side of the lake. This was probably because they had become so infected by the militancy of the crowds. Jesus withdrew to pray alone; this may have been a new 'temptation in the desert' (compare John 6:15).

Verses 22-33 record a second storm on the lake, similar to the one of Matthew 8:23-27. But the first voyage was from west to east, while this one was from east to west. On the first occasion, Jesus was with the disciples the whole time, while this time he came walking over the water to help them 'during the fourth watch' (that is, the three hours just before dawn).

Peter sinks Matthew adds to his account here with an incident featuring Peter (verses 28-32). This is the first of three or four such passages unique to this Gospel; see also Matthew 16:17-19; 17:24-27; 18:21,22. Peter's sinking through his lack of faith has its parallel in the story of his denial of Jesus; compare Matthew 26:33-35, 69-75).

The disciples' words of worship and witness in verse 33 go beyond their earlier exclamations of amazement (Matthew 8:27). But perhaps they were so relieved here that they hardly knew what they were saying. Matthew does not put the importance to these words that he does to Peter's confession in Matthew 16:16.

Gennesaret, modern Ginossar (verse 34), is the fertile plain northwest of the lake.

15:1-20 Clean and unclean

The split with the scribes in Galilee is followed by a split with the scribes in Jerusalem itself. They evidently came to assess this troublesome movement and its suspect leader. 'The tradition of the elders' (verse 2) was the total body of law passed on by word of mouth, by which the written law of the Old Testament was interpreted, added to and applied to varying situations in Jewish life. It was intended to safeguard the written law. But it could sometimes override some of its fundamental principles. Jesus interpreted the law in a different way – by appealing to the purpose for which this or that commandment was originally given (compare Matthew 12:1-14; 19:3-9).

The deputation from Jerusalem criticized Jesus' disciples for ignoring the ritual hand-washing before they ate; compare Luke

After they crossed the lake, Jesus and his disciples landed at Gennesaret, on the western shore. Sometimes the Lake of Galilee is also known as Gennesaret.

11:38. Jesus criticized them in return. By ruling that the law about vows in Deuteronomy 23:21-23 takes preference over revering one's parents, they were neutralizing the fifth commandment. They ruled that property vowed to God must not be used for other purposes. If, after making such a vow, a man had nothing left to help his parents in need, that was too bad. This blocking of God's intention is said in verse 8 to fulfil Isaiah's attack on his contemporaries for giving only lip-service to God (Isaiah 29:13). Jesus dubs them hypocrites (verse 7) for this, though the Gospels do not suggest that all Pharisees deserved this title; compare Matthew 23:13-36. Verse 13 reminds us of the parable of the weeds (Matthew 13:24-30). Verse 14 should be compared with Luke 6:39 and Matthew 23:16,24.

Cancelling the law But Jesus' teaching in verses 10-20 goes beyond criticizing the oral law. It cancels the written law where it refers to food-regulations. According to Leviticus 11, various kinds of forbidden meat were 'unclean' and 'detestable'. But Jesus claims that defilement is carried not by food but by moral evil in thought, word and deed – including breaking the sixth, seventh, eight and ninth commandments. The defilement that matters is defilement by moral evil, not defilement by ritual uncleanness. Jesus' teaching not only nullified all the Pharisees' ideals about purification, but the whole basis of separation between Jews and Gentiles.

It is not always certain which part of the Old Testament Law the New Testament is referring to when it uses the word 'law'. However for practical purposes we can take it to mean the entire system of legislation set out at different times in the Old Testament, culminating in the Ten Commandments (Exodus 20).

Christ did not come to destroy the Law but to fulfil it, by giving it a new, inner and spiritual dimension (Matthew 5:17). While the Christian no longer tries to keep God's commandments as a way of earning his salvation, he does try to do so as a way of expressing his love and his gratitude towards God. He will want to obey the Law out of love for Christ, and will also find that 'love is the fulfilling of the Law' (Romans 13:10).

The Apostle Paul taught much about the role of the Law.

'If a blind man leads a blind man, both will fall into a pit' (Matthew 15:14).

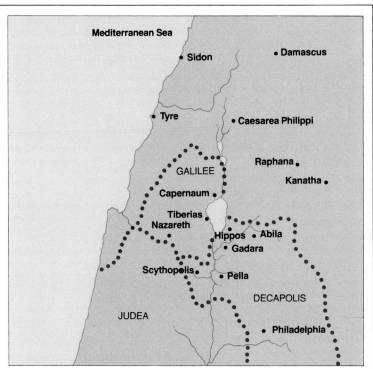

15:21-28 A Canaanite woman's faith

This story is set against the background implying that barriers between Jews and Gentiles were being lowered (verses 10-20). Matthew knew that the mission to the Gentiles could not start properly until after the resurrection; see Matthew 28:19,20; 10:5,6. But he records the healing of this Canaanite woman's daughter as an exceptional happening during the period before Jesus' death, like the healing of the centurion's servant in Matthew 8:5-13. We have previously suggested that there is a symbolic meaning in the fact that both these healings were done at a distance.

The woman is called 'a Greek, born in Syrian Phoenicia' in Mark 7:26. The Tyrians, Sidonians and other Phoenicians were Canaanites who kept their independence for centuries after the other Canaanites lost theirs. Only Matthew records the woman's appeal to Jesus as 'Son of David' (verse 22). The disciples' advice to 'send her away' (verse 23) and Jesus' reply that he was sent 'only to the lost sheep of Israel' are also found only in Matthew; compare Matthew 10:6. The disciples seem to have meant 'Do what she wants and let her go'. Although Jesus did intend to do what she wanted, it was for better motives than getting rid of her noisy clamouring. His questions brought out her exceptionally shrewd and determined faith.

By Jewish standards, Gentiles were 'dogs' – unclean creatures. 'The master's table' (verse 27) may mean that the woman was ready to take a place inferior to the Jews. The cure was immediate (verse 28; see also Matthew 8:13).

15:29-39 Four thousand fed

This incident is a close parallel to Matthew 14:13-22. In both cases great crowds come to Jesus and have their sick healed, and then are miraculously fed. The healings of verses 30,31 may recall the prophecy of the new age in Isaiah 35:5,6; compare Matthew 11:5. They 'praised the God of Israel' (verse 31); this means they were probably Gentiles.

Two feedings are recorded. The first may be seen as Jesus' communication of himself to the Jews; the second as his communication of himself to the Gentiles. If the feeding of the four thousand does symbolize blessing to the Gentiles, it is fitting that it follows the

Matthew 16

teaching of verses 10-20 and the incident of verses 21-28.

The whereabouts of 'Magadan' (verse 39) is uncertain, like that of Dalmanutha (Mark 8:10). It is probably at some point west of the lake of Galilee.

16:1-12 Pharisees and Sadducees

A 'sign' has already been requested in Matthew 12:38. 'A sign from heaven' might have taken the form of a public and conclusive announcement by God. But even an announcement like this could have been explained away by people unwilling to accept it. Jesus answered that as they could forecast tomorrow's weather by today's sky, they ought to be able to see the outcome of trends of their time. For example, they ought to realize the disaster which would follow the increasing rebelliousness against Rome unless the people saw where true peace lay. Compare Matthew 12:39 with verse 4.

Matthew links the Pharisees and Sadducees more frequently than the other New Testament writers; see Matthew 3:7. For instance in verse 1 he adds 'Sadducees' to Mark's 'Pharisees' (Mark 8:11), and in verse 6 has 'the yeast of the . . . Sadducees' instead of 'the yeast . . . of Herod' (Mark 8:15). In this way verses 1-4 and 5-12 are linked more closely.

Beliefs and politics In Jesus' day the Pharisees and Sadducees had little in common. The Sadducees insisted on the literal meaning of the written law. They dismissed the Pharisees' belief in hierarchies of angels and demons, together with their belief in the resurrection of the body; compare Matthew 22:23-28 and Acts 23:8. But both parties opposed Jesus, though for different reasons. The Pharisees opposed him for theological reasons, while the Sadducees objected to him mainly for political reasons. Most of the chief-priests belonged to their party. They were afraid that Jesus' activities might upset their understanding with Rome, and bring about the fall of the Jewish state. 'The teaching of the Pharisees and Sadducees' was not a set of doctrines, but their scoffing demand for a sign (verse 1), and the hostility beneath their demand.

Jesus' reply to the disciples in verses 8-11 confirms that there is a hidden meaning to the feeding incidents (Matthew 14:15-21;

Caesarea Philippi stood near the base of Mount Hermon, and was close to the source of the River Jordan. Herod the Great built an elaborate temple here dedicated to Caesar Augustus. 'When Jesus came to the region of Caesarea Philippi, he asked his disciples, ''Who do people say the Son of Man is?'' ' (Matthew 16:13).

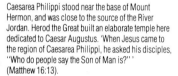

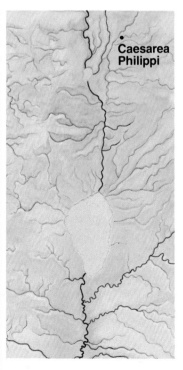

15:32-38). So far they had not seen this deeper significance; but new light was about to dawn.

16:13-20 Peter's confession Caesarea Philippi (modern Banyas) was the capital of Philip's principality, situated at one of the main sources of the Jordan. Jesus and the disciples were coming to the end of their visit to the lands bordering Galilee on the north and east.

The question of verse 13 retains its interest. People's assessment of Jesus may not add to our knowledge of Jesus, but throws much light on them. For Jesus' identification with John the Baptist compare Matthew 14:2; with Elijah compare 11:14; 17:10-12. As for Jeremiah – in Matthew only – we may recall his prophecy of the destruction of the Temple (Jeremiah 7:4, 11-14; 26:2-6; compare Matthew 21:12,13; 24:2; 27:40); and his advice to submit to the Gentiles (Jeremiah 38:17,18; compare Matthew 5:41; 22:21).

But the personal question of verse 15 was the crucial one. The disciples may have thought of him as the Messiah earlier; compare John 1:41. But Jesus had shown himself so unlike the Messiah popularly expected that they could well have changed their minds. Peter declared that he was nevertheless the Messiah. Evidently for him the concept of the Messiah was altering to fit what Jesus actually was and did and taught. At this stage 'the Son of the living God' may have meant little more than that Jesus was the anointed One to whom God says 'You are my Son' (Psalm 2:7).

Peter the rock Jesus was filled with joy. Peter, despite appearance to the contrary, had reached this conviction. Here was proof of God's revealing light (verse 17). Now he could make a beginning and found the new Israel (verse 18).

The similarity of 'Peter' and 'rock' in Greek was even closer in Aramaic, the language in which these words were probably spoken. It is not Peter in his own right, but the recognition that Jesus is the Christ that is the rock. The church to be built on this rock consists of all those who share his belief. 'The gates of Hades'; the realm of the dead is pictured as a prison whose gates will never close on the new community so that it is permanently suppressed. The keys (verse 19) are given to the chief servant as his sign of authority (compare Isaiah 22:22). Binding and loosing may point to the granting of forgiveness in the gospel, and to the use of discipline in the church; compare Matthew 18:18. Later we find Peter opening the 'door of faith' to Jews in Jerusalem (Acts 2:14-21) and to Gentiles in Caesarea (Acts 10:34-43). For keeping the matter secret compare Matthew 8:4; 9:30 and 12:16.

16:21-28 Jesus predicts his death

Peter's confession marks a watershed in Jesus' ministry. 'From that time' he began to speak to the disciples about his approaching death. They had begun to fill the traditional view of the Messiah with new meaning, but were not ready for the radical new look which Jesus now began explaining. A suffering Messiah was a contradiction. Peter rebuked his master for talking like this (verse 22). The disciple who had just been greeted as having received God's revelation was now rebuked as an enemy and a hindrance (verse 23).

Jesus recognized in Peter's well-meant rebuke a repeating of the temptation in the wilderness; the temptation to become Messiah by a way which differed from his Father's will; compare Matthew 4:8-10. Peter's reaction was natural. He saw Jerusalem as the place where the Messiah was to be enthroned, not humiliated. In the event, humiliation and enthronement were bound up together, but this was beyond the understanding of the disciples at this point. The warning of what lay ahead at Jerusalem had to be repeated at frequent intervals; compare Matthew 17:22,23; 20:18,19.

Self-denial If their master was destined for suffering and death, his disciples needed to reassess their own position. They might be involved in his fate. A man who took up his cross (verse 24) was on his way to be crucified. He had 'denied' himself in the sense of bidding a final farewell to all personal interests, hopes and ambitions; compare Matthew 10:38,39. But this should be assessed in the light of the day of final review and reward. In that light, the person who lost his life by following Jesus would gain eternal life. The person who saved his life by turning back would lose everything, even if he gained the whole world meantime.

The Son of Man's coming in judgement (verse 27) is foreseen in Daniel 7:13,14. But verse 28 need not mean that *this* coming would take place in the lifetime of some people standing by. There might be occasions before that when the authority of the Son of Man would be revealed; compare Matthew 24:30; 26:64.

17:1-8 The transfiguration

The transfiguration is not the fulfilment of the promise of Matthew 16:28. One does not say that something due to happen within a week will take place in the lifetime of some hearers. But it looks forward to its fulfilment in the form of a vision. The Son of Man was revealed in glory before the three disciples' eyes. They might not have been able to say whether they were in or out of the body, but they were able to see in advance their master's 'body of glory'; see Philippians 3:21.

'From that time on Jesus began to explain to his disciples that he must go to Jerusalem and suffer many things at the hands of the elders, chief priests and teachers of the law, and that he must be killed and on the third day be raised to life' (Matthew 16:21).

There are some striking similarities between this account and those of Jesus' resurrection appearances. Jesus had told them that his death and resurrection were approaching. This experience was intended to underline his words and show them the nature of the new age these events would usher in. Moses and Elijah represent the law and the prophets; the old order was now replaced by the new; compare Matthew 11:13. The passing of both Moses and Elijah had been clouded in mystery (Deuteronomy 34:5,6; 2 Kings 2:11,12). Some of that mystery still clings to them as they reappear to witness finally to him to whom the law and the prophets pointed forward. Now he has come. In effect they say: 'This is he!' before they recede again into the background.

This is my Son When they have had their say, God says: 'This is my Son, . . . *listen to him*' (verse 5). To the announcement by the heavenly voice at Jesus' baptism (Matthew 3:17) is now added the exhortation about the promised prophet like Moses (Deuteronomy 18:15). All that God has to say is revealed in him.

The 'bright cloud' from which the voice speaks shows that the divine glory is present. Jesus' Father's approval is expressed at the end of his ministry, as it has been at its beginning. With this assurance he will set out for Jerusalem.

For Peter and his companions this was the moment of truth. If only they could hold it, and stop the vision dissolving! But the whole point of the vision was that they could not stay on the mountain, good

Mount Tabor rises 1,800 feet from the Plain of Esdraelon, and has an unmistakeable profile. Although most modern writers believe that the transfiguration took place on Mount Hermon, there is a strong tradition that the site was Mount Tabor.

Matthew
17

Galilee is an area of dry hills and rich, fertile valleys, stretching west and north of the Lake of Galilee. Jesus spent much of his ministry teaching and healing in this region.

as it was to be there. They must descend to the plain and take the Jerusalem road. Only when the Son of Man made his departure there (Luke 9:31) could the kingdom come with power and glory.

17:9-20 Little faith

As on other occasions, Jesus imposed secrecy. Not until the resurrection of the Son of Man would the three disciples understand the vision well enough to speak intelligently about it to other people (verse 9). The question about Elijah (verse 10) was prompted by his appearing in the vision. The fulfilment in John of the prophecy that Elijah would be sent for a special ministry before the great day came (Malachi 4:5,6) has already been mentioned in Matthew 11:14. Here it is explained in more detail. What the first Elijah's enemies failed to do to him (I Kings 19:2) the second Elijah's enemies succeeded in doing to him (Matthew 14:3-12). Jesus saw his own death foreshadowed in John's (verse 12).

An unbelieving generation The group now returned to the suffering and frustration of everyday life. The 'unbelieving and perverse' generation (verse 17) refers to the disciples. Despite their long acquaintance with Jesus, they were still unable to use the authority he had given them (Matthew 10:1).

As with several other healings in Matthew, this account is greatly compressed compared with the account in Mark (Mark 9:14-29). The purpose of this story is to emphasize the importance of faith. The 'little faith' of the disciples has been reproved before, compare Matthew 6:30; 8:26; 14:31. The point about the mustard seed (verse 20) is illuminated by the parable of Matthew 13:31,32. 'This mountain' was the Mount of Transfiguration, by tradition Mount Tabor. When the saying comes again in Matthew 21:21, it refers to the Mount of Olives. Verse 21 is possibly not an original part of this Gospel. It may have been added from a later form of Mark 9:29.

17:22-27 The Temple tax

This additional prediction of Jesus' passion in verses 22,23 was to remind the disciples how serious their situation was. The first prediction, in Matthew 16:21, may well have begun to fade from

This fish, which is found in the Lake of Galilee, is often known as St Peter's Fish, since its mouth is big enough to hold a coin.

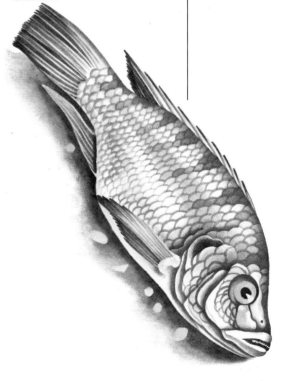

After-life

After-life To understand this subject, we
need to look at four different
words:
1 **Sheol**
This is the word used in the Old
Testament to describe the place
to which people go when they die.
See, for example, Psalm 88:3;
Isaiah 38:18. It means 'the place
of shades', and was seen as a place
of horror. Psalm 16:10 shows that it
was shunned. Physical death itself
was regarded as the penalty of
sin.
2 **Hades**
This is the New Testament
equivalent of Sheol. It is
sometimes translated as 'death' or
'the grave'. In the Apostles' Creed
it is called 'Hell', which has caused
some confusion.
3 **Paradise**
This word means 'garden'. In the
New Testament it is used three
times as a picture of the place to
which God's people go immediately after departing this life.
The most famous instance is Luke
23:43, where Jesus promises the
dying thief that he will join him 'in
paradise' that same day.
4 **Gehenna**
This word comes from the 'Valley
of Hinnom', the refuse dump outside Jerusalem, which had once
been a centre of idol-worship
(Jeremiah 7:31). In the New Testament it is used to describe the
place where the wicked must
suffer the penalty of eternal death,
in Matthew 10:28 and Romans 6:23.
In 2 Thessalonians 1:9 Paul uses it
for what he calls 'the punishment
of eternal destruction and exclusion from the presence of the
Lord'. However much the mind
may shrink from the thought of
such a fate prepared for the
wicked, the Bible refuses to dilute
its teaching on this subject to
accommodate human feelings.

their memories, and especially the memories of the three who had been at the transfiguration (verse 12).

The incident of verses 24-27 is found only in Matthew. It would have been valued by Jewish Christians in the years between AD30 and AD70, when they had to decide whether or not to pay the annual tax of half a shekel, contributed by every male Jew between the ages of twenty and fifty to keep up the Temple in Jerusalem. Jesus' action gave them an example. There was no divine obligation to pay the Temple tax, for with the coming of the kingdom the necessity ceased – 'one greater than the temple is here' (Matthew 12:6). But out of consideration for their fellow Jews, who would be horrorstruck if they did not pay, they continued to pay on a voluntary basis.

The fish is really incidental to the story. It is presumably the 'comb' fish of the Lake of Galilee, which often has glittering objects in its gullet. The coin in its mouth was actually a *stater* or Tyrian tetradrachm, worth the same as a Jewish shekel. It would have paid the Temple tax of two people.

'Unless you change and become like little children, you will never enter the Kingdom of heaven' (Matthew 18:2).

18:1-14 The greatest in the kingdom

This chapter contains a number of Jesus' sayings about fellowship in the kingdom of heaven. The disciples seem to have been concerned on several occasions about being great in the kingdom. Jesus shows that true greatness in the kingdom is a matter of true humility. He takes a child as an example, showing the trustfulness of the very young. Far from being the greatest in the kingdom, the disciples cannot even enter it if they do not completely change their outlook, giving up all self-seeking (verses 1-4).

Jesus identifies the welcome to the child with his own welcome (verse 5; compare Matthew 25:40,45). He couples this with the warning of damnation to anyone teaching a child to sin (verse 6). Then comes another warning against all sources of temptation to sin (verses 7-9; compare Matthew 5:29).

Gehenna The 'fire of hell' (verse 9) is Gehenna, as in Matthew 5:22,29,30. Jesus underlines the dignity of the child; their guardian angels have direct access to God's presence; compare Luke 1:19; Revelation 8:2. Children's helplessness calls forth God's special interest and protection (verse 10).

The lesson is further underlined by the parable of the hundredth sheep (verse 12,13). Here it comes in a different context to the account in Luke 15:3-7.

18:15-22 Brotherly behaviour

Here is a brief 'set of rules' governing the behaviour of Jesus' followers towards each other. It is the duty of a disciple who sees his brother commit a fault to try to put the matter right privately. Failing that, he should put it right in the company of one or two others. To ignore the fault would be unfair both to the offender and to the community as a whole (compare Leviticus 19:17; Galatians 6:1; James 5:19,20; I John 5:16).

If possible, publicity must be avoided. Only if the offender is unbending must the community at large know about it. The 'church' (verse 17) is a local company of disciples. The situation described is one that would arise after Jesus' death and resurrection. To refuse the church's verdict meant excluding yourself from the church. But the church had a duty to win this outsider back into fellowship. The church's verdict, if reached according to Jesus' teaching, had God's approval (verse 18). The authority given to Peter in Matthew 16:19 is here extended to all disciples.

Mention of 'two or three witnesses' in verse 16 is followed by the promise that 'where two or three come together' in Jesus' name, their request will be granted by God. Jesus himself is among them (verses

Women would have used a handmill made from two great mill-stones to grind their flour.

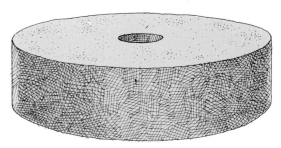

The ruins of Herod's fortress of Herodion stands out prominently from the surrounding countryside.

19,20). This refers to Jesus' unseen presence after Easter.

Peter's question about the limits of forgiveness (verse 21) suggests that to forgive a person seven times would be a mark of extraordinary patience. Jesus advises unlimited forgiveness (verse 22). Disciples must imitate God's all-embracing forgiveness (compare Matthew 5:43-48; 6:12).

18:23-35 The unforgiving servant

A number of parables set their scene in a royal court. Herod Antipas had his palace at Sepphoris, four or five miles from Nazareth, until in AD22 he built himself a new capital at Tiberias, by the lakeside. Happenings at his court would be the common talk among the people of Galilee. This particular parable underlines Jesus' words to Peter about the brotherly duty of unlimited forgiveness.

The first servant, whose debt ran into millions, was probably the king's grand vizier. No other servant could have run up such a colossal debt. His promise to repay in full (verse 26) was merely a form of words. He could never have done it. His master knew this perfectly well, but out of his goodness cancelled the entire debt.

The forgiven servant immediately showed how little he shared his master's mercifulness by enforcing the law against his fellow servant who owed him a tiny amount (verses 28-30). Hearing this, the king cancelled his repudiation of the great debt, and treated him as he had treated his fellow servant. Jesus underlines that God will act in just the same way.

19:1-12 Divorce

Jesus' rulings on divorce have already been recorded in Matthew 5:31,32. He repeats them here in reply to the Pharisees' question. His ruling is clearly based on an appeal to first principles. God's purpose in marriage is implied in the account of creation. Genesis 1:27 and 2:24 are quoted. They are treated as something 'said' by God since they belong to scripture.

From these quotations it is concluded that marriage is instituted by God, is permanent, and is not to be annulled by man. Naturally the question came why divorce was allowed in the law of Moses (Deuteronomy 24:1). Jesus answered that this was as a concession to

'Jesus said, "Let the little children come to me, and to not hinder them, for the kingdom of heaven belongs to such as these"' (Matthew 19:14).

'Christ Blessing Children' by Maes.

'hardness of heart', but departed from the Creator's intention, which Jesus restates. The words 'except for marital unfaithfulness' amount to the same as the exception in Matthew 5:32. In that time and place, Jesus' ruling helped redress the unequal balance in favour of women. The disciples' reaction in verse 10 is a thoroughly male prejudice. They suggest that his ruling was hard on men, since it deprived them of the right to divorce, a right which Jewish women did not have at all.

Those who 'have renounced marriage because of the kingdom' (verse 12) are those who have decided to devote themselves wholly to the service of God.

19:13-22 The rich young man

The incidents about the children and the young man are deliberately placed next to each other, in the setting of 'Judea (on) the other side of the Jordan' (verse 1). They show first, the simple childlike confidence necessary for entering the kingdom of heaven (compare Matthew 18:1-4), and the attachment to material things which keeps people out.

Those who brought the children may have thought that the touch of the prophet from Nazareth would itself give a blessing. Jesus probably wanted to point out that children's readiness to ask and receive is a good example of the attitude his disciples should have towards their heavenly father; compare Matthew 7:7-11.

'It is easier for a camel to go through the eye of a needle than for a rich man to enter the kingdom of God' (Matthew 19:24).

Eternal life In verse 16 eternal life means practically the same as the kingdom of heaven. To enter one is to enter the other; compare Mark 9:43,45 with 47. For the keeping of the commandments as the way to life compare Leviticus 18:5; Deuteronomy 30:15-20. The commandments of verses 18,19 make up the second half of the Ten Commandments, man's duty to his neighbour. These are summed up in the second of the two great commandments (Leviticus 19:18; Matthew 22:39).

A perfect life The young questioner, like Paul, could honestly claim to be blameless according to the law; compare Philippians 3:6. Yet he was still conscious of his need for something more. It is one thing to keep specific, rather negative rules; it is another to fulfil the all-embracing command to love one's neighbour as oneself. For the meaning of 'perfect' (verse 21) see Matthew 5:48. Even selling his goods and giving the money gained to the poor would not totally fulfil the law of love; compare 1 Corinthians 13:3. But it would be a first step, and show that the person involved was serious.

Jesus knew just where this young man's readiness needed to be tested, and he showed himself unequal to the test. The young man's sorrow was genuine. Jesus' probing showed him that his eagerness to be devoted to God's will had its limits.

19:23-30 The needle's eye

Jesus' statement that 'it is hard for a rich man to enter the kingdom of heaven' (verse 23) is rarely taken seriously. Even at the time, he found it necessary to drive it in with a vivid illustration. We must not make it a little easier for the rich man by supposing that the 'needle's eye' is a small gate in a large city gate – or that Jesus meant 'cable' and not 'camel'.

Riches and rewards The disciples were surprised (verse 25). They may have been remembering that in much of the Old Testament riches are a reward for godliness, and a sign of God's blessing (see Deuteronomy 28:1-14; Psalm 128). Entry into the kingdom is difficult for everyone. But it is especially hard for those with material possessions to hinder them. Entry into the kingdom is made only with God's help (verse 26).

A believing community But the apostles had given up all such things to follow Jesus. For them was reserved, not only entry into the kingdom, but also high responsibility. The 'twelve thrones' (verse 28) imply the setting up of the believing community, the 'church' of Matthew 16:18, where the apostles would wield the authority promised in Matthew 16:19; 18:18. For the Son of Man's glorious throne see Matthew 25:31.

But all – not only the apostles – who gave up possessions and earthly ties for Jesus' sake would 'inherit eternal life' and be fully rewarded. However, the reward was not one which on this world's reckoning would make the sacrifice worthwhile. It is implied that the assessment is made in the light of the coming Day, as described in Matthew 16:25-27. Then it will be seen that the first by this world's standards are last, and the last first (compare Matthew 20:16).

20:1-16 The workers in the vineyard

This parable may be put here because it illustrates another side of 'the first will be last, and the last first' (Matthew 19:30; 20:16). It reflects the high unemployment resulting from the desperate economic situation in Israel in New Testament times. In harvest or (as here) vintage time there was always a large pool of casual labourers. Work began immediately after sunrise. The third, sixth, ninth and eleventh hours (verses 3-6) were about 9am; 12 noon; 3pm and 5pm. The wages were paid (verse 8) when work ceased at sunset (about 6pm).

The fact that a denarius, roughly equivalent to 5p or a dime, was the daily wage throws light on other references to money in the Gospels. We can easily understand the raised expectations and later disappointment of the labourers who worked for twelve hours, bearing 'the burden of the work and the heat of the day'.

But the story is introduced as a parable, not to support a principle such as 'to each according to his need'. Its application is not spelt out. Undoubtedly, it emphasizes the householder's generosity. Those hired at daybreak agreed to accept a wage of one denarius. Those hired later agreed to be paid 'whatever is right' (verse 4). It is fortunate for most of us that God does not deal with us on the basis of strict justice and sound economics.

'The kingdom of heaven is like a landowner who went out early in the morning to hire men to work in his vineyard . . .' (Matthew 20:1). The vine is a climbing plant with long, thin branches which need tying to stop them falling to the ground. The vine flowers in May, and the harvest of grapes lasts from August to October. Pruning takes place in December and January.

The workers in the vineyard.

20:17-28 On the Jerusalem road

Jesus' third prophecy of his passion is more detailed than the previous ones (Matthew 16:21; 17:22,23). He mentions for the first time that he will be handed over to the Gentiles – that is the Romans – for execution. They are now on the way to Jerusalem, and Jesus must impress on the twelve that the crisis is near. But the incident of James and John's request follows immediately. The Gospel-writer implies that the disciples' minds were not yet ready to understand the seriousness of Jesus' warning.

The part played by Salome is unique to Matthew's account; see Mark 15:40; Matthew 27:56. The lesson of greatness in the kingdom was hard to learn; see also Matthew 18:1-4. The 'cup' of verse 22 was their master's passion; see also Matthew 26:39. They boasted they were ready to share it, and in a sense they did, but long after Jesus himself endured it; see Acts 12:2.

The Servant Jesus himself was open to God's will for him. So, too, his followers must be ready to accept the places the Father gives them in the kingdom. The ten were indignant, not because they felt that James and John's request was misplaced, but because they had got their request in first. All of them wanted this honour.

Once again the disciples had to be taught the secret of true greatness. Their pattern must not be the Gentile rulers who are served, but the Son of Man who gives humble service. The place of honour is

Jericho's fresh spring-water makes it a oasis in the desert – and it is often called the 'city of palm trees'.

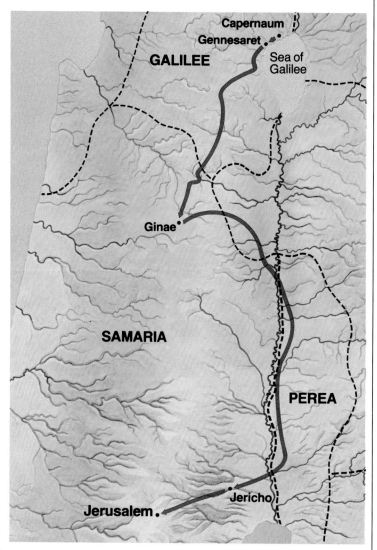

Jerusalem

Except for Luke's account of Jesus being taken there as an infant, and later at the age of twelve (Luke 2:22-50), Matthew, Mark and Luke speak explicitly of only one visit by Jesus to Jerusalem, during which he was arrested, put on trial and crucified. John, on the other hand, tells of several occasions when Jesus visited Jerusalem, especially at some of the great feasts of the Jewish year (John 2:13; 5:1; 7:10; 10:22; 12:12). It would be surprising if he had not paid repeated visits to Jerusalem, and the Synoptic Gospels imply that he did visit it several times. In Luke 13:34 he is reported as addressing the city: 'How often would I have longed to gather your children together . . .'

The Jerusalem that Jesus knew was small, but impressive. Its status as a holy city had been confirmed by successive Gentile overlords – Persian, Greek and Roman. Jesus called it 'the city of

the Great King' in Matthew 5:35, quoting Psalm 48:2. Whether the psalmist was referring to God or to a king of David's line, there is no doubt that on Jesus' lips 'the great king' was God. In Jewish belief, Jerusalem was the city which the God of Israel had chosen 'to put his Name there for his dwelling', Deuteronomy 12:5. By Jesus' day it had changed almost beyond recognition from the city that was hurriedly rebuilt by the impoverished Jews who returned from the exile in Babylon in 539BC and the following years.

City quarters

The main quarters of the city, however, remained much as they had been before; they were shaped largely by natural features. The city was divided into two parts by the north-south line of the Tyropoeon Valley, or Valley of the Cheesemakers. East of this valley stood the Temple and associated

buildings; south of the Temple stood the lower city, the eastern section of which (Ophel) was the original Jerusalem which David captured from the Jebusites and chose as his capital (see 2 Samuel 5:6-9). West of the Tyropoeon Valley was the upper city, which does not appear to have been settled as early as the lower city.

Perhaps eighty years after the return from Exile, an abortive attempt was made to surround the city with a wall (see Ezra 4:12). The building of a wall was actually carried out by Nehemiah, in accordance with the decree of Artaxerxes I, king of Persia in 445 BC. Nehemiah's wall probably enclosed the lower city and the south-western quarter. The Temple was separately enclosed. On the north, the wall probably followed the west-east line of the present King David Street, running north of the south-western quarter and crossing the

Jerusalem

'When Jesus entered Jerusalem, the whole city was stirred and asked, "Who is this?"' (Matthew 21:10). Travellers pass in and out of the Damascus gate to the old city of Jerusalem.

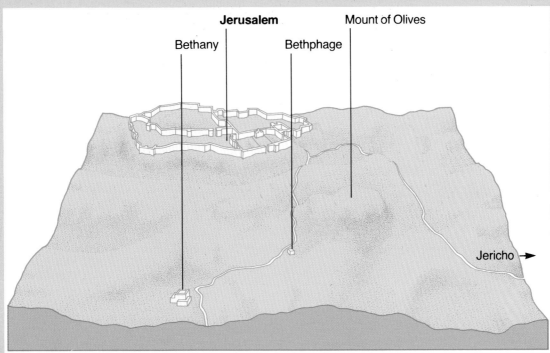

Bethany   **Jerusalem**   Bethphage   Mount of Olives

Jericho →

Tyropoeon Valley to meet the western wall of the Temple.

The walls of Jerusalem were repaired by the high priest Simon II about 200BC. But they were broken down in 167BC by Antiochus Epiphanes, who built a strong citadel in the city of David, south of the Temple. The city was re-fortified by the Hasmoneans, especially John Hyrcanus, who restored the Jewish realm to prosperity.

Herod the Great

Jerusalem was greatly improved by Herod the Great, who erected or restored many fine buildings. Apart from the Temple, the most magnificent of all his buildings, he rebuilt the fortress of Baris, north-west of the Temple area, and renamed it Antonia, after his patron, Mark Antony. He built a palace for himself on the west wall of the city, mentioned in Acts 23:35, and three strong towers

nearby, one of them being incorporated in the present citadel. Herod also built such public buildings as an amphitheatre and a hippodrome. It was under Herod, if not earlier, that a second north wall was erected to enclose the north-western quarter of the city. It began at a point called the Gate Gennath and ran north and then east, passing south of the present Church of the Holy Sepulchre, up to the Antonia fortress.

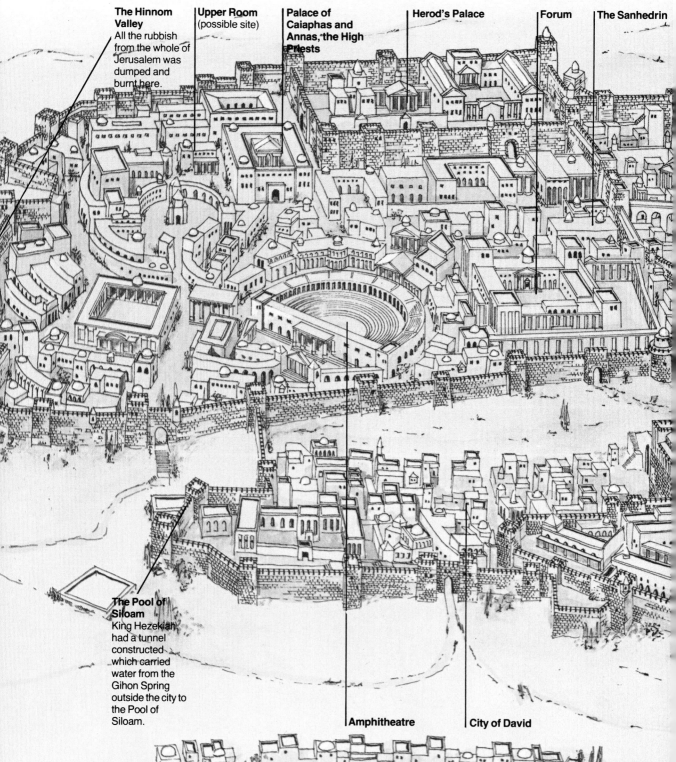

The Hinnom Valley
All the rubbish from the whole of Jerusalem was dumped and burnt here.

Upper Room (possible site)

Palace of Caiaphas and Annas, the High Priests

Herod's Palace

Forum

The Sanhedrin

The Pool of Siloam
King Hezekiah had a tunnel constructed which carried water from the Gihon Spring outside the city to the Pool of Siloam.

Amphitheatre

City of David

The area of the walled city that Jesus knew was about half a square mile (320 acres), and its population may have been as high as 50,000. But already people were beginning to build houses beyond the second north wall, in the section called Bezetha, or 'Newtown'. Ten to fifteen years after the death of Jesus, Herod's grandson Herod Agrippa I began to construct a third north wall to enclose this suburb. After the destruction of the city by Titus in AD70, it lay derelict for over sixty years. Then in AD135 the Roman Emperor Hadrian founded a new, completely Gentile, city on the site, and called it Aelia Capitolina. The walls which enclosed this city are roughly followed by the present walls of the Old City.

Bethesda and Siloam

Some of the sites in Jerusalem mentioned in the Gospels, especially by John, can be identified with confidence; others are more doubtful. The pools of Bethesda and Siloam can be located with certainty. At Bethesda, north of the Temple area, near the present Church of St Anne, there were twin pools which received water from a source nearby. Four porticoes enclosed the area of the two pools, while a fifth stood on the ridge which separated the two. The water, with its reddish tinge,

Jerusalem as Jesus knew it

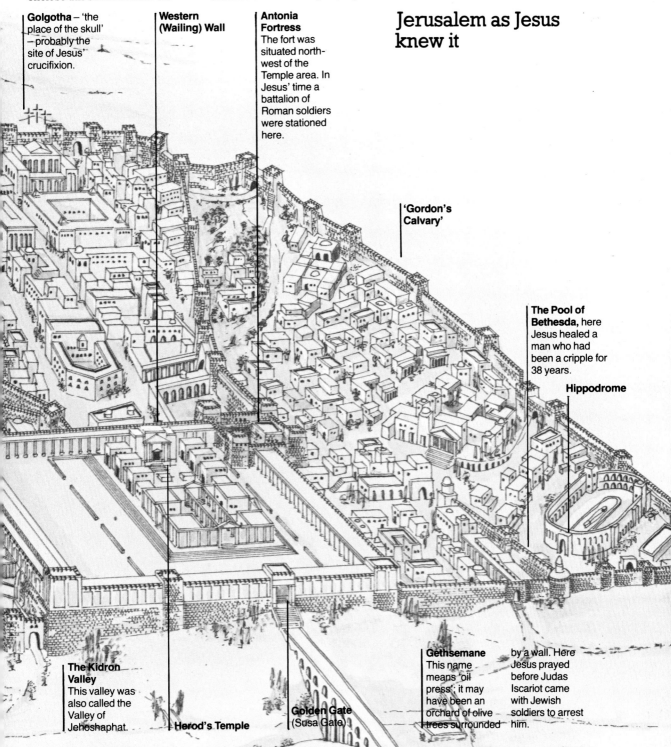

Golgotha – 'the place of the skull' – probably the site of Jesus' crucifixion.

Western (Wailing) Wall

Antonia Fortress
The fort was situated north-west of the Temple area. In Jesus' time a battalion of Roman soldiers were stationed here.

'Gordon's Calvary'

The Pool of Bethesda, here Jesus healed a man who had been a cripple for 38 years.

Hippodrome

The Kidron Valley
This valley was also called the Valley of Jehoshaphat.

Herod's Temple

Golden Gate (Susa Gate)

Gethsemane This name means 'oil press'; it may have been an orchard of olive trees surrounded by a wall. Here Jesus prayed before Judas Iscariot came with Jewish soldiers to arrest him.

Jerusalem

Jews worship at the Western Wall in the old city of Jerusalem. Previously known as the Wailing Wall: its foundations were part of the Temple built by Herod the Great.

A model showing how the Roman Antonia fortress may have appeared in the time of Jesus.

was believed to have healing properties. But the disabled man who had waited his turn for so long in one of the porticoes might have waited the rest of his life if Jesus had not come along and healed him (see John 5:1-9).

The pool of Siloam, at the southern end of the Tyropoeon Valley, near its junction with the Valley of Hinnom (south of the city) and the Kidron Valley (east of the city) receives the water which flows through a tunnel cut through the rock from the Virgin's Fountain (the spring Gihon of the Old Testament) in the Kidron Valley, east of the city of David. The tunnel is a skilled piece of engineering. Its construction was commemorated in a Hebrew inscription cut in the rock near its exit, and it is usually identified with that undertaken at the command of King Hezekiah in 701BC, and mentioned in 2 Kings 20:20; 2 Chronicles 32:4 and Isaiah 22:9. When John reports how Jesus sent the blind man whose eyes he had smeared with clay to the pool of Siloam to wash it off, he mentions in chapter 9:7 that Siloam means 'sent'. This name referred to the 'sending' of the water from the spring Gihon through the tunnel into the pool.

The Mount of Olives, to the east of the city, across the Kidron, is of course an undisputed biblical site. The garden where Jesus had

often met . . . with his disciples', John 18:2, called Gethsemane in the Synoptic Gospels, was on the western slope of Olivet. Its location is not known for sure, but it cannot have been far from the traditional site, marked by the Church of All Nations and other buildings. This was also the first place where the ascension of Jesus was commemorated by Christians from quite an early date.

The passion story

No great certainty attaches to some of the sites recalling episodes in the passion story, such as the house where the Last Supper was eaten, or the church of St Peter in Gallicantu, said to stand where the high priest's palace stood. For the place where Jesus appeared before Pilate there are two rival sites. The place is called the Praetorium in Mark 15:16 and John 18:28, 33, meaning

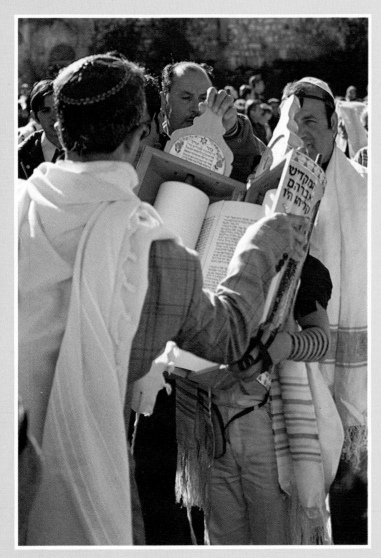

Jerusalem

The Golden Gate in the city walls of old Jerusalem.

The books of the Law are brought to the Western Wall during the Barmitzvah ceremony for a Jewish youth.

the headquarters of the governor or commanding officer. It might refer either to the Antonia fortress or to Herod's palace. Beneath the convent of the Sisters of Zion, which stands more or less on the site of the Antonia fortress, may be seen a Roman pavement which has been identified with the Stone Pavement of John 19:13, where Pilate pronounced judgement on Jesus. The lines of the soldiers' 'game of the king' are traced out on one part of the pavement. It is suggested that this may be the very spot where they dressed Jesus up in mock-royal robes and hailed him as king of the Jews. However, this pavement, like the Ecce Homo arch in the street above, probably dates back only to Hadrian's time. If the Antonia fortress was indeed the Praetorium of the Gospels, then the present line of the Via Dolorosa corresponds more or

less with the road along which Jesus was led to the cross. But if the Praetorium was Herod's palace, then the actual way of the cross must have been quite different from the traditional one.

The place of crucifixion was outside the city gate, see Hebrews 13:12. The Church of the Holy Sepulchre, which tradition- ally marks the site of Jesus' death, burial and resurrection stood just outside the second north wall. It was because of the persistence of the Christian tradition that about AD325 the Emperor Constantine removed pagan buildings to bring to light the holy sepulchre.

It calls for a strong act of imagination for the visitor to the church today to see the site as it was in Jesus' time. Many visitors get a better impression of what it looked like from the Garden Tomb, off the Nablus road. Here we have a garden containing a

tomb, although it cannot be seriously claimed that this is the historical site. The suggestion that it was so goes back to 1883, and formed part of General Gordon's fancy that Jerusalem was laid out on the plan of a human body, with Calvary or Golgotha, 'the place of a skull', forming the head. It is enough to remember that, what- ever place is pointed out as the site of Jesus' tomb, 'he is not here, for he has risen'.

The entrance to an underground tomb in Jerusalem.

not a reward for the service – the service *is* the honour. Is there any greater honour than to be allowed to serve God and our fellow humans? The Son of Man gave the humblest, and at the same time the noblest, service by becoming a ransom for many. It is as his people's Saviour that he receives the highest honour. The shameful cross to which he was fastened has become the object of his people's main glorying (Galatians 6:14).

20:29-34 Blind men of Jericho

The last lap of the journey to Jerusalem was the road from Jericho, leading up the Wadi Qelt. On each side of the lower parts of the wadi stood Jericho of New Testament times – a new city built by Herod the Great as his winter headquarters. It imitated Roman architecture and planning practice. It was sited a mile or so south of Old Testament Jericho.

The incident of verses 29-34 is Matthew's parallel to the healing of blind Bartimaeus in Mark 10:46-52. However this account features two blind men where Mark has one; see also Luke 18:35-43. This incident also closely resembles the earlier one in Matthew 9:27-31. But this healing was carried out in full view of the 'large crowd' of Galilee pilgrims going up to Jerusalem for the Passover; there is no stern warning to keep the healing secret. As before (see also Matthew 15:22) Jesus does not refuse to be called 'Son of David', though he is not recorded as claiming the title himself.

The incident illustrates the blind men's perseverance despite

A striking view of old Jerusalem, with the Mount of Olives standing out clearly on the horizon.

discouragement. It also shows Jesus' compassion and the power of God in his word and his touch. Receiving their sight, the men naturally joined the Jerusalem pilgrims.

21:1-11 The triumphal entry

The steep climb from Jericho to Jerusalem has almost been completed. Jesus and the crowd of pilgrims have reached the Mount of Olives, which lies east of the city. Bethphage – the name means 'the place of young figs' – was a village near Bethany on the east side of the Mount, barely two miles from Jerusalem. Here Jesus had made preparations in advance for his entry into the city.

Matthew mentions two animals (verses 2,7) as opposed to one in the other Gospels (Mark 11:2-7; Luke 19:30-36; John 12:14). This emphasizes that the prophecy of Zechariah 9:9 is fulfilled (verse 5). The other Gospels make it plain that it was on the unbroken colt that Jesus rode into Jerusalem. The introductory form of words in verse 4 implies that Jesus deliberately planned to give effect to the prophet's oracle, probably to see how the people of Jerusalem would respond to his coming in peace. It was not encouraging.

Hosanna! It was the pilgrims thronging around Jesus who made the joyful shouts – perhaps with more enthusiasm than understanding (verse 9). 'Hosanna' – meaning 'save now' or 'give victory now' – is the festival cry of Psalm 118:25. 'Hosanna to the Son of David' amounts to saying 'God save the (messianic) King'. The words of welcome – 'blessed is he who comes in the name of the Lord!' – come similarly from Psalm 118:26. The phrase 'in the highest' is a substitute for the name of God, which was not to be spoken: 'Save now, you who dwell in the highest place'.

But when the people of Jerusalem ask the cause of all the commotion, the crowds claim only that he is the prophet of Nazareth. Would the city recognize him as the Shepherd of Israel? Or would it prefer other shepherds who would involve it in ruin?

21:12-17 Jesus at the Temple

The expelling of the traders from the Temple is best seen as a prophetic act, like those of Old Testament times, where a message is

The ass or donkey was one of the most common animals in Palestine. It was bigger, quicker and stronger than the donkeys used in modern southern Europe. It used to eat grass, hay, thistles and thorn twigs.

driven home vividly. Jesus' attitude to the Temple of his time is like Jeremiah's attitude to Solomon's Temple; compare Matthew 16:14. Jesus' words of rebuke are drawn partly from Jeremiah 7:11: 'Has this house, which bears my name, become a den of robbers to you?' – and partly from Isaiah 56:7: 'My house will be called a house of prayer for all nations'.

The tables and benches may have been installed temporarily as a service to visitors. But they were taking up ground which ought to have been used for the worship of God. The protest was directed against the Temple authorities, and they fully recognized this; see verse 23.

David's greater Son The rule had been laid down since the days of David that 'The blind and lame will not enter the palace' (2 Samuel 5:8). This rule was reversed when 'great David's greater Son' appeared. It is evident from Acts 3:2 that the rule was not enforced for the outer court of the Temple.

The use of the Temple area for healing, and the children's taking up of the Galilean pilgrims' shout of greeting, scandalized the authorities, who invited Jesus' co-operation in moderating what they recorded as disorder. Jesus quoted Psalm 8:1,2 in defence of the children. Verse 17 probably implies that Jesus spent each night with his friends in Bethany during this visit to Jerusalem; see also Matthew 26:6.

An olive press at the village of Bethany.

Jesus' last days in Jerusalem

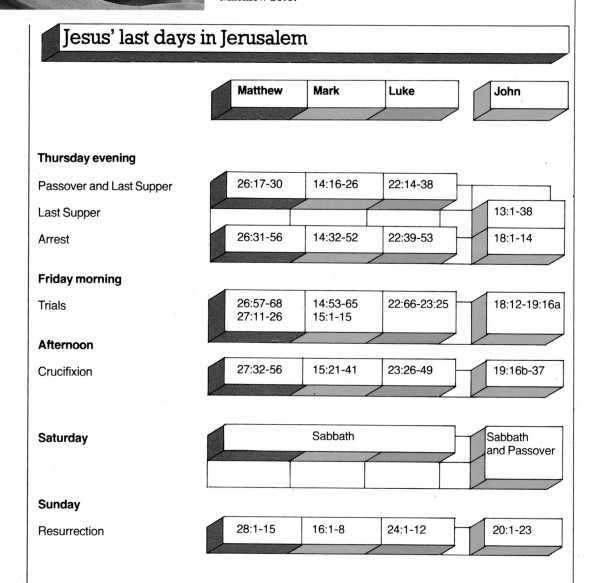

	Matthew	Mark	Luke	John
Thursday evening				
Passover and Last Supper	26:17-30	14:16-26	22:14-38	
Last Supper				13:1-38
Arrest	26:31-56	14:32-52	22:39-53	18:1-14
Friday morning				
Trials	26:57-68 27:11-26	14:53-65 15:1-15	22:66-23:25	18:12-19:16a
Afternoon				
Crucifixion	27:32-56	15:21-41	23:26-49	19:16b-37
Saturday		Sabbath		Sabbath and Passover
Sunday				
Resurrection	28:1-15	16:1-8	24:1-12	20:1-23

21:18-22 The fig tree withers

The withering of the fig tree (verses 18-22) is here telescoped into a short time in comparison with Mark:11:12-14, 20-25. It is a further prophetic action, and the tree may well represent Jerusalem, which was so unresponsive to Jesus' approaches (verse 43; see also Luke 13:6-9). The fact that at this time of year the tree bore only leaves, without any *taqsh*, which precede the figs, showed it was fruitless. The incident is made the basis for a lesson about the power of faith; see also Matthew 17:20. In this setting, 'this mountain' (verse 21) must be Olivet. The fact that Olivet was to be the centre of a major convulsion on the day of the Lord (Zechariah 14:4) stamps this setting as authentic. Perhaps it can be interpreted as: 'If only you have enough faith, the new age will begin sooner than you think'. `

The fig tree was often found near people's houses. The tree has a short trunk with light grey bark, a dense, deep-green crown and branches and leaves that often reach the ground. Figs were used as food, and as a cure for boils and inflammations.

There was often a wall around the vineyard to protect it from foxes, jackals, robbers and other intruders. Sometimes there would be a watch-tower too, to guard the vine harvest.

21:23-32 'By what authority?'

While Jesus spent the nights in Bethany, he spent the days teaching in the Temple area. The 'chief priests and elders of the people' were members of the Sanhedrin, the supreme court of Israel; see also Matthew 26:3,47; 27:1,3,12,20. In particular the final responsibility for keeping order inside the holy precincts lay with the captain of the Temple, who was a member of one of the chief-priestly families, and ranked next to the high priest. So the question of verse 23 related to Jesus' teaching and healing, but perhaps especially to his expelling of the traders.

But what answer would have satisfied these members of the Sanhedrin? If spiritual power and authority is not recognized as self-authenticating, no amount of argument or signs from heaven will confirm it; see also Matthew 12:38; 16:1. Perhaps his questioners suspected that he did these things because he claimed to be the Messiah; but at this stage Jesus does not voice this claim. Instead Jesus asks them what they thought of the authority of John the Baptist – was it from God, or taken by himself? The true answer was, of course, 'from God'; and this was all the more true for Jesus, whose fore-runner John was. But they would not commit themselves to this line of argument, and so their question stayed unanswered.

In the next episode, Jesus asks the opening question, which also involves an appeal to John. John's 'way of righteousness' (verse 32) called for 'fruit in keeping with repentance' (Matthew 3:8). This was produced by those who at first said 'I will not' – the tax collectors and prostitutes – rather than the religious leaders. The latter undertook to do God's will, but did not fulfil their undertaking.

21:33-46 The parable of the tenants

As in Isaiah's parable, 'the vineyard of the LORD Almighty is the house of Israel, and the men of Judah are the garden of his delight', (Isaiah 5:7). The rulers of the people could not miss Jesus' point; they and their predecessors were the tenants (verse 45). The 'servants' are the prophets; see also Matthew 23:37. The significance of the owner sending his own son in the last resort cannot be overlooked (verse 37). Of all the parables in the Gospels, this one comes nearest to being an allegory, where something corresponds to each successive detail of the story.

The son's death The killing of the son after he is thrown out of the vineyard (verse 39) reflects Jesus' being put to death outside Jerusalem. (Contrast the order of events in Mark 12:8.) By 'other tenants' (verse 41) the church, the new Israel, is meant. Its leaders (see also Matthew 19:28) will replace the present rulers in Israel, from whom the kingdom will be taken. The reference to 'fruits' makes the same point as the fig-tree incident of verse 19. The 'wretched end' of the tenants of verse 41 may look forward to the disaster of AD70.

The quotation in verse 42 is from Psalm 118:22-23, the same psalm which provided the shout of verse 9. It is treated as a witness to the Messiah repeatedly in the New Testament; see Acts 4:11; 1 Peter 2:7. What is said of the people's assessment of Jesus in verse 46 echoes their assessment of John according to verse 26. In both places these are probably the crowds of pilgrims. At Passover the visitors to Jerusalem might outnumber the residents by three to one.

22:1-14 Parable of the wedding banquet
Superficially this parable is similar to the parable of the 'great banquet' in Luke 14:16-24. But in meaning it is closer to the parable of the vineyard in Matthew 21:33-43. The proclaiming of the kingdom of heaven is compared to a royal command sent out to people already invited to a wedding banquet at the palace, to come and take their places, as the banquet was now about to start. The command was ignored, and so was repeated. But it was now offensively disregarded – or the servants who called for the guests were beaten up or killed; see also Matthew 21:35,36.

The punishment of the murderers (compare Matthew 21:41) and the burning of the city (verse 7) point to the siege and destruction of Jerusalem in AD70. So the first invited guests stand for the religious leaders in Jerusalem. As in the parable of the vineyard, where the owner let it out to more trustworthy tenants after putting to death the first tenants, so here the king enlists guests who had not previously been invited to come and fill the wedding hall and enjoy the feast. (The punitive action of Verse 7 was not necessarily completed before the second lot of guests were gathered: otherwise the good things provided would have become cold and stale.) These second guests parallel the 'nation' of Matthew 21:43 – the new society of Jewish and Gentile disciples – to whom the kingdom was to be transferred.

The wedding clothes The added incident of verses 11-14 presents a problem. It probably looks forward to the final judgement, when every one will be repaid 'according to what he has done' (Matthew 16:27). The wedding clothes are best interpreted as the way of life that shows how genuine the initial repentance is; see also Matthew 3:8 and Revelation 19:8. For the man's expulsion from the banquet into the darkness outside compare Matthew 8:12 and 25:30. The problem is how to fit some features of this incident into the entire story. Because of the difficulty in doing this, it has been thought that two separate parables have been telescoped together. The moral of verse 14 is that not all invited enjoy the banquet – the blessings of the kingdom. When a limited number of vacancies are to be filled, several candidates are short-listed and interviewed, but not all of them are appointed.

22:15-22 Taxes to Caesar
The tax debated here was the hottest political question of the day in Judea. The question did not crop up in Galilee, which was governed by a Jewish prince, Herod Antipas. But when Judea became a

An aureus coin of Augustus Caesar, who ruled the Empire until AD14.

Roman province in AD6 it had to pay tribute direct to Caesar. Some Jews argued that to pay taxes to a pagan ruler was high treason to God, the true King of Israel; they revolted under Judas the Galilean; see Acts 5:37. Their revolt was crushed, but its spirit lived on among the Zealots; see Matthew 10:4. The Zealots' ideas were very popular, even if their violence was deplored; see Matthew 11:12.

Pharisees and Herodians The Pharisees and the Herodians were strange partners. But if the Herodians claimed that the Herods had the right to rule all Palestine, they too would have objected to the tribute to Caesar. It was hoped that the question would catch Jesus. If he said it was right to pay the tax, he would lose his popularity. If he said it was wrong, he could be reported to the Romans for sedition; see Luke 23:2. But for Jesus, the 'things that are God's' – the interests of his kingdom – come first. They would not be harmed if a pagan ruler got back the denarius which was his own.

Some Jews were so conscientious that they would not touch such a coin, because the portrait of the emperor broke the second commandment. Jesus' words may suggest that such coins were fit only for Gentiles to handle. Caesar's money was best used for paying Caesar's tax. Let them make God's kingdom and his demands their first concern; see Matthew 6:33. Jesus thus avoided the dilemma and turned it to emphasize the central theme of his own teaching.

22:23-33 How are the dead raised?

The Sadducees were the aristocrats, to whom belonged most of the chief-priestly families. They saw themselves as conservative in theology. They rejected the 'tradition of the elders' of the Pharisees, see Matthew 15:2, and stuck to the literal application of the written law. They rejected the idea of the resurrection of the body as something introduced since the Exile; see Acts 23:8. They pictured resurrection as the restoring of the conditions of bodily life on earth. Thus their improbable story with its following question (verses 25-28) was intended to show how absurd such a belief was.

The command of Moses summarized in verse 24 is the law of levirate marriage; see also Deuteronomy 25:5-10; Ruth 3:1-4. Doubtless this problem was often put to the Pharisees to embarrass them. But Jesus told them that their question showed how ignorant they were about resurrection and their own scriptures. Resurrection did not mean returning to the former conditions of biological life and reproduction, but a new level of existence; see also 1 Corinthians 15:35-37. It would be sexless, like the angels (verse 30). The Sadducees saw the first five books of the Bible as their supreme authority. For this reason, Jesus appealed to these books. He grounded the doctrine of resurrection firmly in the being and character of God. The God who could call himself the God of people long since dead (Exodus 3:6) showed that in relation to him they were not dead. 'He is not the God of the dead but of the living' (verse 32).

22:34-46 Debating with Pharisees

The Pharisees could only applaud Jesus' answer to the Sadducees. Now they tested him with the sort of question they debated themselves. Some of them drew a distinction between 'heavy' and 'light' commandments, though they did not treat the latter less seriously. God might assess them differently. Was there one commandment that could be regarded as the greatest, and, if so, how could that commandment be recognized?

In reply, Jesus quoted the command to love God unreservedly (Deuteronomy 6:5). This included obeying all his commandments; see 1 John 5:3. But Jesus coupled with it the command to love one's neighbour unreservedly (Leviticus 19:18). All that God requires is summed up in these two commands.

Religious and political parties

Pharisees

The Pharisees, meaning 'the separated ones', were the most important of the Jewish parties. A Pharisee was expected to live strictly according to the letter of the law of Moses. Most of them were intelligent, highly educated men. There were perhaps 4-5,000 Pharisees in and around Jerusalem in Jesus' time. Some of them were Jesus' most active opponents. Others became Christians at an early date. The Pharisees wanted to keep Judaism pure, but by insisting on strict regulations they denied the spirit of the law.

Sadducees

The Sadducees were much more conservative in their views than the Pharisees. They accepted only the first five books of the Old Testament – the Torah. By contrast, the Pharisees accepted the authority of the 'oral' law, which even included many commentaries on Scripture.

Sadducees did not believe in the resurrection of the dead, or in the existence of angels and spirits. They tried to keep on good terms with the Roman authorities, and to stop the Jews from revolting against Rome.

The influence of the Sadducees was great, since the High Priest and other priests belonged to their party. They virtually controlled the Great Council or Sanhedrin, the highest Jewish court, which was chaired by the High Priest.

Scribes

The Scribes were not so much a party as a professional grouping. They were concerned with the study and teaching of the Jewish law. Many Scribes were in fact Pharisees.

Zealots

The Zealot party was committed to winning Israel's independence. They used violent methods, like today's freedom fighters.

Assassins

The Assassins of Acts 21:38 were the most fanatical Zealots, who would murder for their cause.

Essenes

The Essenes were a disciplined order of men who lived in communities. One such community was at Qumran, near the Dead Sea. There were perhaps 4,000 Essenes in Jesus' time.

Herodians

The Herodians were a Jewish party who supported both King Herod and the Roman authorities. Some Herodians opposed Jesus.

Now Jesus puts a counter-question to the Pharisees. He and they believed that Psalm 110 was composed by David and referred to the Messiah. According to them, the Messiah was to be the son of David; see Matthew 1:1. But in Psalm 110:1, David calls the Messiah 'my Lord'. How can the Messiah be both David's son and David's Lord? Early Christians would see no problem. They knew that Jesus, Son of David, had been lifted up by God and made both Lord and Messiah; see Acts 2:36.

23:1-12 An example to be avoided

Not all Pharisees were willing to debate in a friendly way with Jesus. This chapter brings together a number of criticisms of Pharisaical attitudes. If strict law-keeping is stressed as showing devotedness to God, some people can get a reputation for devotion by copying the outward keeping of the law; see also Matthew 6:1-4.

The Pharisees were well aware of this. Jesus warns his hearers, and especially his disciples, against the temptation to which the Pharisees laid themselves open: setting up a standard of legal goodness which ordinary working people could never achieve.

The phylacteries of verse 5 are parchments containing four extracts from the Old Testament: Exodus 13:1-10; Exodus 13:11-16; Deuteronomy 6:4-9; Deuteronomy 11:13-21. They were placed in a leather container and worn on the forehead and left arm. The fringes or tassels were prescribed in Numbers 15:38-39; Deuteronomy 22:12. Extra-large phylacteries and tassels might be seen by unthinking people as signs of special piety.

Jesus ordered his followers to avoid such displays, and do without titles of honour. He again insists on service and humility as the badge of his disciples (verses 11,12).

23:13-28 Lament for the scribes

The seven woes of verses 13-32 can be read as laments rather than accusations: 'Alas for you!' rather than 'Woe to you!' Jesus is not saying that all scribes and Pharisees are hypocrites. He is talking about the hypocritical, or 'play-acting' scribes and Pharisees, whose piety was merely outward show. This is in contrast to such genuine Pharisees as Nicodemus, Gamaliel and Saul of Tarsus.

Dill is a herb used in cooking and was found in Israel in the time of Jesus.
Mint is a plant with a strong fresh smell. It contains large amounts of scented oil, and has violet flowers. The Jews used mint as a herb with their food.
Cummin (or caraway) is a herb that grows up to two feet tall. It belongs to the carrot family, and has a thin stalk with many branches. It has long, thin seeds with a strong smell and a bitter flavour. It was used to flavour bread.

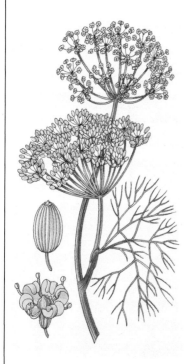

The accusation of verse 13 refers to those who opposed Jesus' preaching of the kingdom, and discouraged others from paying attention to it. Verses 16-22 amplify Matthew 5:33-37. They show how inconsistent it is to distinguish between binding oaths and non-binding oaths.

Scruples The Pharisees were very careful about offering tithes. As well as tithing the main fruits of the earth – grain, wine and olive oil – they interpreted Leviticus 27:30 as covering garden herbs (verse 23). Jesus described this as straining out midges from their drink, while swallowing camels without noticing; see also Matthew 7:3-5. They paid too little attention to 'justice and mercy and faith'.

The two 'woes' of verses 25,26 and 27,28 return to the theme of outer respectability camouflaging inner sin. Tombs were whitewashed to draw attention to them. People who would be ceremonially unclean by accidentally touching them – for example the high priest or a Nazirite – could easily avoid them.

23:29-39 Lament for Jerusalem

We may compare the argument in verses 29-32 with Stephen's charge in Acts 7:51,52. The language of verse 33 is similar to John the Baptist's in Matthew 3:7. 'Hell' is Gehenna, as in verse 15 and Matthew 5:22,29,30. The answer could be simply 'by repentance'; but it is implied that there was no sign of repentance. In verses 34-36 Jesus speaks as God's wisdom. According to the traditional order of Hebrew scripture, Abel (Genesis 4:8) is the first martyr, and Zechariah (2 Chronicles 24:20-22) the last. In the course of transmission, the son of Jehoiada has apparently become confused with the son of Berechiah (Zechariah 1:1).

The horror of the war of AD66-70 was greater than the sins of one generation could have earned as a penalty. In Luke 13:34,35 the lament over Jerusalem follows the remark: 'surely no prophet can die outside Jerusalem!' In both Gospels the lament implies that Jesus made previous visits which are not recorded here. The words 'you will not see me again' in verse 39 apply to the Temple, which Jesus is now leaving for the last time, rather than to the city in general. Verse 38 may recall the gradual departure of God's glory from the earlier

Hens were common domestic animals in the time of Jesus. They came originally from India.

Temple before it was destroyed by the Babylonians; Ezekiel 8:4; 10:4; 11:23. The day foretold in verse 39 would then be linked with the return of the glory to the restored house in Ezekiel 43:1-5, and also identified with the coming of the Son of Man (Matthew 24:27, 30, 31).

24:1-14 Signs of the End-time

The fifth and last 'discourse' begins with the Olivet prophecy, paralleled in Mark 13 and Luke 21:5-38. It deals with the coming of the kingdom, and starts with events linked with the destruction of the Temple (verse 2). In the answer to the disciples' question, we cannot divide neatly the parts referring to the destruction of the Temple from those referring to Jesus' coming and the 'end of the age'.

The Temple was renowned for its splendour. Only the lower courses of masonry of its western wall survive. It was Jesus' prediction of the overthrow in verse 2 that prompted their question as they looked across to the city and the Temple from the Mount of Olives (verse 3). Jesus' reply warns them not to be misled by false Messiahs (verses 4,5). Many such figures attracted enthusiastic devotees between AD44 and 70. He tells them not to be dismayed by wars and natural disasters (verses 6,7; see also Revelation 6:2-8). These are only the birth-pangs of the new age (verse 8).

Next Jesus prepares them for persecution and abandonment of

The Mount of Olives from the old city of Jerusalem. This hill, rising to some 2,700 feet, overlooks the city and the old Temple area. When Jesus rode in triumph into Jerusalem, he came from the Mount of Olives.

the faith in the midst of increasing wickedness (verses 9-12; compare Daniel 11:33-45). But he promises final deliverance for those who stay loyal to the end (verse 13). Verses 9-14 largely repeat Matthew 10:16-23. The assurance that the world-wide proclaiming of the good news of the kingdom must come before the end (verse 14) parallels Matthew 10:23.

24:15-28 Sacrilege and tribulation

The 'desolating sacrilege' of Daniel 8:13; 9:27; 11:31; 12:11 was the installing of an idolatrous object in the Temple of God. The language suggests some colossal blasphemy ushering in unprecedented suffering for the people of God. We may compare what is said of Antichrist in 2 Thessalonians 2:4.

'Let the reader understand' (verse 15) is a challenge today as it was then. There is more in the text than lies on the surface. Instant flight will be necessary, and it will be hard for expectant and nursing mothers (verse 19). Winter would make rapid escape more difficult, and the sabbath would limit the distance that could be covered (verse 20; compare Exodus 16:29).

The 'great tribulation' was already foretold in Daniel 12:1, with the deliverance of the chosen ones. The means of deliverance is stated here as the shortening of its duration; compare Daniel 12:6-12. The deceivers of verse 5 multiplied as the doom of Jerusalem approached, and they promised victory where there was none (verses 23-26).

When the Son of Man comes it will be as sudden and unmistakable as a flash of lightning; verse 27; compare Daniel 7:13. Verse 28 means that where a situation is ripe for judgement – as it was then in Jerusalem – there judgement will fall. The mention of eagles, rather than the expected vultures, may be a reference to the standards of the Roman legions.

24:29-35 The sign of the Son of Man

Cosmic happenings like those of verse 29 appear in the Old Testament as pictures for disasters such as the overthrow of cities. Siege and warfare will be followed by the fall of Jerusalem, and 'all these things' will be completed in the lifetime of 'this generation' (verse 34). Here is the answer to the disciples' first question, 'When will this happen?' (verse 3).

Unlike the coming of the Son of Man (verse 27) the fall of Jerusalem will be heralded by signs that cannot be mistaken by those who have eyes to see. Just as the appearance of leaves on the fig tree is a sign that summer is coming, so the events of verses 5-14, and especially the 'desolating sacrilege' (verse 15) are signs of the approaching destruction of the city and Temple.

On the clouds The coming of the Son of Man, the subject of the disciples' second question (in verse 3) follows the fall of Jerusalem. Only Matthew speaks of the '*sign* of the Son of Man' (verse 30). Since the Son of Man comes without preceding signs (verses 27,37-44) his sign in verse 30 may be himself. Like Jonah, the Son of Man is his own sign; compare Matthew 12:39,40. His coming 'on the clouds' with power and glory (compare Matthew 16:27) is based on Daniel 7:13. The trumpet-call for gathering in the chosen, in verse 31, is based on Isaiah 27:13. The wailing of 'all the nations of the earth' is based on Zechariah 12:10-14. The words of Jesus have the same binding and permanent strength as the words of the law (verse 35; compare Matthew 5:18).

24:36-51 Call to vigilance

The fall of the Temple and city will take place before the passing of 'this generation' (verse 34). But no time can be given for the coming

An 'unclean' bird, the vulture lives by scavenging, mainly on carrion and rubbish from towns and villages.

In Rome, on the Arch of Titus, erected to celebrate the Roman victory over the Jews, there is depicted Roman soldiers carrying off the seven-branched lampstand from Herod's Temple.

'The kingdom of heaven will be like ten virgins who took their lamps and went out to meet the bridegroom' (Matthew 25:1).

of the Son of Man. The Son is subordinate to the Father; he does not know 'that day or hour'. But he is supreme over all created beings, 'even the angels' (verse 36). As no warning signs preceded the flood of Noah's day, so no sign will precede the coming of the Son of Man (verses 37-39). It will overtake people as they carry on their everyday activities, and separate one from the other in judgement (verses 40,41; see also Matthew 25:32,33). No opportunity now for flight!

Two parables The need for readiness is illustrated by two parables, the thief by night (verse 43) and the returning master (verses 45-51). The parable of the thief by night comes several times in the New Testament; see 1 Thessalonians 5:2; 2 Peter 3:10; Revelation 3:3; 16:15. His plan only succeeds when the house is not properly guarded. When the chief steward, whose master leaves him in charge during his absence, has no idea when his master will return, he ought to be on his toes. Only a very foolish steward will neglect his duty in this situation. But if he does misbehave, his master's return will mean not reward (verse 47), but flogging and dismissal (verse 51).

25:1-13 Parable of the ten virgins

Matthew now adds three parables to emphasize the lessons about vigilance, faithfulness and kindness. In the first parable, the ten virgins seem to be the bride's attendants who are to go out to meet the bridegroom when he arrives at her house with his friends. They then escort the couple in a torchlight procession to the groom's house for the marriage feast.

It is best not to allegorize the parable. What matters is that, by the time the foolish virgins bought a fresh supply of oil, they were late for the procession. When they reached the bridegroom's door, the keeper would not let them in. The lesson is: 'Don't be like those foolish girls; keep awake and be prepared'.

25:14-30 Parable of the talents

This parable elaborates the theme of the parable of the returning master (Matthew 24:45-51). It resembles the parable of the pounds in Luke 19:11-27. A talent was not a coin, but a weight roughly equal to half a hundredweight, or twenty-five kilograms, of silver or gold, tied up in bags. It is from this parable that the word has gained its meaning of spiritual gift or ability.

The phrase 'to each according to his ability' (verse 15) means that people are not responsible for talents they have not been given. The third servant probably reckoned that trading was too risky. It was safest to bury his talent. This was a common way of guarding valuables against loss. But nothing venture, nothing win. The kingdom of heaven involves putting everything at risk; compare Matthew 10:39; 16:24-27. The reward for the two faithful servants is the opportunity for more responsible service. The 'master's happiness' is probably the banquet of the resurrection age (verse 21,23). The unprofitable servant excuses his lack of enterprise, blaming it on his master's unreasonableness. His excuses are not accepted; he is thrown out of the merry-making of his master's welcome-home feast, and left in the dark with his remorse and frustration. Verses 28,29 add the lesson that the penalty of a neglected opportunity is the loss of further opportunity.

'Master . . . I knew that you are a hard man, harvesting where you have not sown and gathering where you have not scattered seed' (Matthew 25:24).

25:31-46 The sheep and the goats

The setting of this judgement scene was familiar to the hearers, and probably to the readers. The coming of the Son of Man with his angels (compare Matthew 16:27), the gathering of all nations for

judgement (compare Joel 3:2,11-14), and the allocating of bliss or doom were all derived from the Old Testament. What is distinctive is the criterion on which the verdict is reached. The 'parable' is restricted to the words 'as a shepherd separates the sheep from the goats. He will put the sheep on his right and the goats on his left' (verse 32,33). A mixed flock of sheep and goats is not uncommon in this area. They may look alike superficially, but from time to time must be separated.

Judgement They may be gathered as nations, but are judged as individuals. The principle of judgement, says Jesus, will be: how have they treated me in the person of 'the least of these brothers of mine'? 'These my brothers' suggests that they are present. The followers of the Son of Man are associated with him in the judgement; compare Daniel 7:22; 1 Corinthians 6:2,3. They are to inherit his kingdom (Matthew 21:43); but it has also been prepared for those who have treated them kindly, and so showed kindness to the king himself (compare Matthew 10:40-42; 18:5). Those on the left hand are as surprised by their condemnation (verse 44) as the others are by their acceptance. As elsewhere in the Bible, God's judgement is according to people's actions, whether good or bad. The 'eternal fire' of verse 41 is probably Gehenna; compare Matthew 5:22; 18:8,9. 'Eternal life' (verse 46) is the life of the age to come. Similarly 'eternal punishment' involves exclusion from that life.

'He will separate the people one from another as a shepherd separates the sheep from the goats' (Matthew 25:32). In biblical times, as today, the shepherd would graze the sheep and goats together.

The Temple When Jesus had completed his journey on Palm Sunday, he entered Jerusalem and went to the Temple. He looked around at everything, but since it was already late, he went out to Bethany with the Twelve (Mark 11:11).

The Temple Jesus knew was the Temple renovated, enlarged and beautified by Herod the Great. Architecturally it was new; religiously it was still Zerubbabel's Temple, rebuilt after the Jews returned from the Babylonian exile. The six centuries between the return from exile and the destruction of Jerusalem in AD70 are known in Jewish history as the age of the Second Temple.

The site on which the Temple stood had sacred associations reaching back to ancient times: according to tradition, the rock which crops out on the top of the Temple hill was the place where Abraham built the altar to sacrifice his son Isaac – 'one of the mountains' in 'the region of Moriah' (Genesis 22:2) being identified with 'Mount Moriah' (2 Chronicles 3:1).

Solomon's Temple had stood on the site for over 350 years when it was destroyed by the Babylonians (587BC) beyond the possibility of repair. About seventy years later a completely new Temple was built there, by authorization of the Persian king. When it was dedicated on March 12, 515BC, some very old people who could remember Solomon's Temple reckoned it a poor thing in comparison with its magnificent predecessor. Yet the contemporary prophet Haggai predicted far greater glory for it in days to come (Haggai 2:3-9). The high priesthood in the New Temple remained for nearly 350 years in the family of Zadok, which had supplied the chief priests in Solomon's Temple from its dedication onwards. The Temple was repaired, extended and adorned at various times between Zerubbabel and Herod.

Herod's Temple
None of the restorations or extensions of the second Temple could match, however, with the work initiated by Herod at the beginning of 19BC. Because certain parts of the building could not be entered by the laity, a thousand Levites were specially trained as builders and masons, and carried out their work so efficiently and carefully that at no time was there any interruption in the sacrifices and other services. The Temple platform was extended eastwards on vaulted foundations, with strong retaining walls, so as to increase the area of the precincts, especially of the outer court. The courts were enclosed by magnificent colonnades. Along the east side of the outer court ran what was called Solomon's Colonnade; it was here that Jesus was seen walking during the Feast of the Dedication. Before long it became a habitual meeting-place for the infant church (see Acts 3:11; 5:12).

Wealthy Jews of the dispersion (that is, those living outside Palestine) sent costly offerings to enhance the splendour of the place.

While the main part of Herod's rebuilding was completed before his death in 4BC, the work went on for more than sixty years after that. When Jesus visited the Temple at the first Passover of his ministry it was remarked that the place had by then been forty-six years under construction. The work was not entirely finished until AD63, only seven years before the destruction of the whole fabric.

The whole area was holy, but it became increasingly holy as one

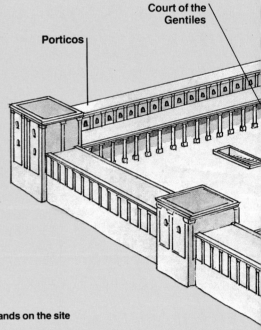

Porticos

Court of the Gentiles

The Dome of the Rock stands on the site of Herod's Temple today.

penetrated farther in, from east to west. The outer court, enclosed by Herod with colonnades, is sometimes referred to as the Court of the Gentiles because non-Jews (like the Greeks of John 12:20) were permitted to enter it and walk about in it. But they were forbidden to go into any of the inner courts: notices in Greek and Latin gave warning that the penalty for such trespass was death. The Romans permitted the Jewish authorities to pass the death-sentence for this offence and to carry it out, even if the offender were a Roman citizen. It was for allegedly aiding and abetting an offence of this kind that Paul was attacked and nearly beaten to death by an angry crowd during his last visit to Jerusalem (Acts 21:27-32).

The inner courts were on a higher level than the outer court: one had to go up several steps to get into them. The easternmost of the inner courts was the Court of the Women – so called because Jewish women were admitted thus far (but no farther). In this court, at the west end, was the 'treasury', the section where there stood thirteen trumpet-shaped containers for voluntary offerings of money. Jesus was sitting 'opposite the treasury' when he saw the widow put into one of the containers the two copper coins which were all that she had (Mark 12:41-44).

Beyond that was the Court of Israel, which was open to Jewish laymen. The innermost court was the Court of the Priests, normally barred to all laymen. In the eastern part of this court, opposite the main gates leading from the other courts and the eastern entrance into the Temple precincts, so that it could be seen from a distance, stood the great altar of burnt-offering. At its west side stood the sanctuary proper, comprising (from east to west) the porch, the holy place, and the cubical holy of holies. Into the holy place the priests entered to discharge various duties, in particular to offer incense on the golden-incense-altar, as Zechariah did on the occasion when an angel appeared to him and announced the forthcoming birth of his son John the Baptist (Luke 1:8-23). No ordinary priest could hope that the lot for offering the incense would fall to him on more than one day in his lifetime (if that); the day when Zechariah received the angelic announcement was in any case the red-letter day of his whole priestly career. Into the holy of holies only the high priest was allowed to go, and that but once a year, on the Day of Atonement in the autumn, when he presented sacrificial blood to expiate his own sins and those of the nation which he represented (Leviticus 16:1-34). In the Letter to the

The Temple

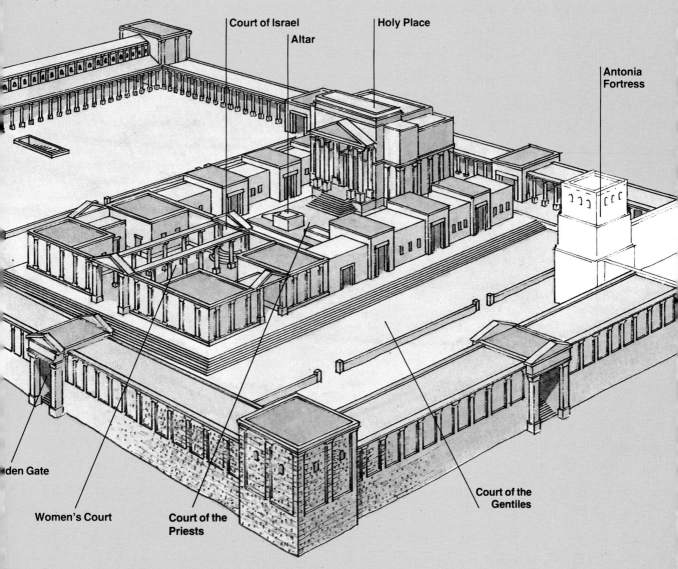

Court of Israel

Altar

Holy Place

Antonia Fortress

den Gate

Women's Court

Court of the Priests

Court of the Gentiles

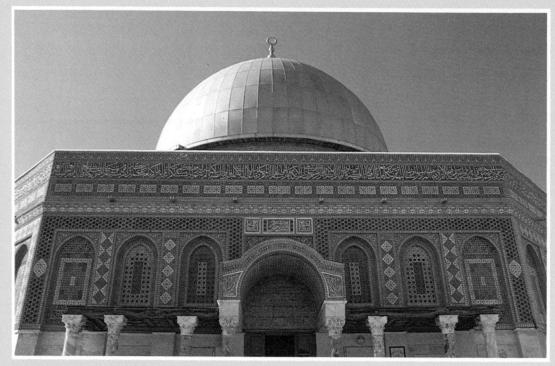

The Dome of the Rock is one of two Muslim shrines which today stand on the site of Herod's Temple. The Temple itself was destroyed in AD70 when the Romans regained Jerusalem from the Jewish forces.

The Temple

Hebrews this ritual is used as a parable (by contrast more than by comparison) of Jesus' atoning death and his present high-priestly ministry in the heavenly sanctuary. But during his Palestinian ministry Jesus, as a layman, could not penetrate beyond the Court of Israel: 'if he were on earth, he would not be a priest' (Hebrews 8:4).

Herod's Temple and its precincts covered an area of twenty-six acres. (The *Haram esh-Sharif*, or 'Noble Enclosure', which occupies the same site today, covers thirty-five acres.) The walls surrounding the area provided it with a system of fortification quite distinct from that of the city. Part of Herod's walls, built of the huge stones which characterized his work, may be seen today: the most famous part is the Western Wall (formerly known as the Wailing Wall), the most sacred place of prayer in the Jewish world. The walls were pierced by several gates: there were four on the Western Wall, leading down into the Tyropoeon Valley. From the Western Wall also a viaduct was carried on arches across the valley to the upper city on the west.

Jesus' first contact with the Temple was in his early infancy, when he was taken there for the ceremony of purification and was

hailed as the coming Deliverer by Simeon and Anna (Luke 2:22-38). His next recorded visit to it was at the age of twelve, when – perhaps to prepare him for his Bar Mitzvah confirmation the following year – he was taken there at Passover-time by Mary and Joseph and was found in conversation with the rabbis who had their 'teaching pitches' in the outer court of the Temple (Luke 2:41-51).

The day was to come when Jesus himself, on successive visits to Jerusalem, would be a familiar figure as he taught in the outer court. Several of his discourses reported in the Gospel of John were delivered there – possibly the discourse on resurrection and judgement which followed the healing of the man at the Pool of Bethesda (John 5:19-47) and certainly the discourses at the Feast of Tabernacles (John 14-8:58), at the Feast of Dedication (John 10:22-39) and during the week before the last Passover (John 12:30-36, 44-50).

It is there that the scene of the adulterous woman is set (John 8:2-11). It was there, too, that a challenge to Jesus' authority was answered with his parable of the vineyard, and that he dealt with the question about paying tribute to Caesar, refuted the Sadducees' objection against the doctrine of resurrection, gave a ruling on the two great commandments of the

law and asked the scribes how the Messiah, being David's lord, could be his son (Mark 11:27-12:37).

Jesus' cleansing of the Temple is recorded in all four Gospels. John, perhaps because its implication for the replacement of the old order by a new one entitled it to a position in the forefront of Jesus' ministry, puts it in the context of an earlier visit to Jerusalem than the Synoptists do (compare John 2:13-22 with Matthew 21:12, 13; Mark 11:15-18; Luke 19:45, 46). It was in a section of the outer court that the vendors of sacrificial animals and the money-changers had set up their stalls and tables, and by doing so they encroached on its proper use. The outer court was the only part of the Temple area where Gentiles could draw near to the God of Israel; Jesus' action made more room for them, and his quotation of Isaiah 56:7, 'My house will be called a house of prayer for all nations' (Mark 11:17), suggests that he had their interests in mind. Those Greeks who had come to Jerusalem to worship God at the last Passover may have asked to see Jesus because they recognized that he had championed their spiritual interests (John 12:21).

The cleansing of the Temple was not the signal for a popular rising, although the Jewish authorities feared it might lead to that. It was rather a symbolical action like those sometimes performed by the Old Testament prophets to confirm their words. It is evident that no breach of the peace was involved, for there was no intervention by the Roman soldiers who were stationed in the adjoining Antonia fortress, northwest of the Temple area, which communicated with the outer court by two flights of steps (compare Acts 21:35, 40).

Jesus' last utterance about the Temple foretold its downfall. His disciples had been impressed by the magnificence of the structure, but as he sat with some of them on the slope of the Mount of Olives, looking across to the Temple area, he spoke of the time, not more than a generation distant, when not one stone would be left standing on another (Mark 13:2-30).

When Jesus was on trial before the High Priest, an attempt was made to convict him of speaking against the Temple, but it failed because the witnesses gave conflicting evidence. Even so, people remembered what he was charged with saying, and when he was on the cross some passers-by mocked him as 'You who are going to destroy the temple and build it in three days' (Mark 15:29). 'But,' says John, the only Gospel-writer who reports him as actually using such language, 'the temple he had spoken of was his body' (John 2:21).

At the moment of Jesus' death, we are told 'the curtain of the temple was torn in two from top to bottom' (Mark 15:38). If this was the curtain that hung before the holy of holies, the throne-room of the invisible presence of God, this seems to show that in the death of Jesus, God is fully revealed.

The Temple

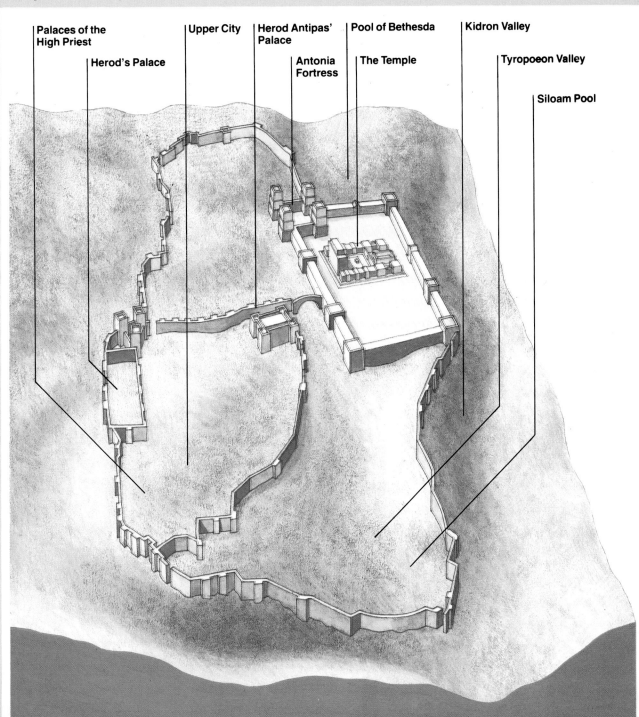

Palaces of the High Priest

Herod's Palace

Upper City

Herod Antipas' Palace

Antonia Fortress

Pool of Bethesda

The Temple

Kidron Valley

Tyropoeon Valley

Siloam Pool

'The Last Supper' by Albrecht Dürer, 1523.

'Then he took the cup, gave thanks and offered it to them, saying, "Drink from it, all of you. This is my blood of the covenant, which is poured out for many for the forgiveness of sins" ' (Matthew 26:27,28). Jesus' words are repeated at the Lord's Supper when the wine is about to be drunk.

26:1-13 Jesus anointed at Bethany

Jesus' teaching ministry is over. His passion is about to begin. The Sanhedrin – or part of it – resolved at a meeting in the high priest's palace to arrange for his arrest and execution. They felt that his popularity, especially with the visiting pilgrims, ruled this out till after the seven days' festival of Unleavened Bread – which began with the Passover meal. But they were given the opportunity to carry it out much sooner.

We cannot be sure why the incident at Bethany, in verses 6-13, stimulated Judas to put Jesus into the chief priests power (verses 14-16). He seems to have voiced the disciples' indignation about the 'waste' of ointment, which would have cost a labourer's wages for a year; compare Mark 14:5; John 12:4-6.

Jesus accepted the woman's anointing as 'a beautiful thing' done in anticipation of his burial. The prediction of verse 13 is fulfilled by the telling of the story in the Gospel.

Simon the leper (perhaps the *former* leper) may have been the father of the well-known family at Bethany.

26:14-25 The Last Supper

Judas immediately made his way from Bethany to see the chief priests. Matthew is the only writer to name the price of betrayal. The last clause of verse 15 is almost a quotation from Zechariah 11:12, where thirty shekels of silver are the derisory wages paid to the prophet for looking after the flock of Israel; compare Matthew 27:9,10. This was the price fixed in Israel's earliest laws as compensation to the owner for a slave gored to death by someone else's ox (Exodus 21:32).

Jesus knew there was a traitor. So he arranged for the Passover meal with his disciples as secretly as possible. The venue had apparently been fixed in advance with the master of the house (verse 18).

During the meal, at which everyone reclined in the proper Passover posture, Jesus revealed that a traitor was present. Only Judas knew what he meant. Each of the others wondered if he had accidentally said or done something to harm his master. The words of verse 23 echo Psalm 41:9. But as they were all dipping their hands in the same dish, the traitor was not unmasked.

Gethsemane, a garden near the Mount of Olives, to the east of Jerusalem. Its name means 'oil press' and it may have been an olive grove with a surrounding wall. Jesus took the disciples here after the Last Supper.

Matthew 26

Jerusalem as seen from part-way up the Mount of Olives.

When Judas repeats the others' question, the responsibility for the answer is thrown back on him (verse 25). He still had time to renounce his plan.

26:26-35 Jesus predicts Peter's denial

The new memorial was initiated in the context of the memorial of the ancient redemption from Egypt. In the course of the Passover meal, unleavened bread was broken and eaten. At the head of the table, Jesus does this, but adds words to give the act new meaning (verse 26). 'Take, eat,' says Jesus. 'This is my body.' As the Passover sacrifice preserved Israel from the angel of death and delivered them from bondage in Egypt, so Jesus devotes himself to death to preserve and deliver his people. The cup (verse 27) seems to have been the 'cup of blessing' drunk at the end of the Passover meal. The wine was usually red, adding point to the new meaning Jesus gave in verse 28. The new covenant is foretold in Jeremiah 31:31-34. It is ratified by the life blood of Jesus, 'poured out for many for the forgiveness of sins' (verse 28). Verse 29 suggests that Jesus himself did not take the cup. He looks forward to renewing fellowship at the table with them the other side of death, in the new age.

The Mount of Olives was, by religious law, inside the city boundaries. Jesus, speaking as the Shepherd of Israel, foretells the imminent fulfilment of Zechariah 13:7. But he promises to return from death, gather his scattered sheep again, and lead them to

Gethsemane

This was a garden near the Mount of Olives, east of Jerusalem (Luke 22:39). The name means 'oil press', and it may have been an orchard of olive trees surrounded by a wall. Jesus went to Gethsemane with the apostles after their last supper, as he had often done before (John 18:1,2). Here he prayed before Judas Iscariot came with the Jewish soldiers to arrest him.

The Golden Gate, Jerusalem, seen from the garden of Gethsemane.

Galilee; compare Matthew 28:7. The disciples, Peter to the fore, stoutly assure him they will not fall away or feel disillusioned because of him. He knows them better than they know themselves; yet his promise remains.

26:36-46 Gethsemane
Gethsemane lay on the west slope of the Mount of Olives. Peter, James and John, who saw him glorified on the Mount of Transfiguration, now witnessed his agony. Jesus nerves himself for the ordeal to come, and dedicates himself to accomplish his father's will. He had to endure the spiritual conflict alone, but he craved companionship. This even his closest friends among the Twelve failed to supply.

'Pray so that you will not fall into temptation' (verse 41) reminds us of the Lord's Prayer, as does 'may your will be done' (verse 42). Jesus rose from his vigil prepared in spirit for the test he had to face. The kingdom of God as proclaimed by Jesus could not have been more fully embodied than in the One who said: 'not as I will, but as you will' (verse 39) and acted accordingly.

26:47-56 Jesus arrested
The 'crowd' which came with Judas consisted of Temple police, whose commander was captain of the Temple. They were at the disposal of the Sanhedrin. Some show of resistance was put up by the disciples; as in Mark, the identity of the swordsman is not given. Then their nerve failed, and they fled. The greater part of Jesus' rebuke in verses 52-54 is found only in Matthew. He submits since the prophecies of scripture point to this hour and must be fulfilled; compare verse 24.

But Jesus points out how incongruous it is that they come to take him by surprise at night, as if he were a leader of bandits, or perhaps a Zealot terrorist.

26:57-75 Before the Sanhedrin
Members of the Sanhedrin waited for Jesus at the high priest's residence. Joseph Caiaphas, son-in-law of Annas (who held the high priesthood AD6-15) was appointed high priest by the Roman governor in AD18. He stayed in office for eighteen years.

When Jesus arrived, Caiaphas and his colleagues were mainly concerned to find evidence against him which the Roman governor would recognize. Since the sanctity of the Temple was protected by Rome, a threat to it would be an offence against Roman provincial law. But their attempt to convict Jesus for uttering such a threat failed, since they could not get Jesus to admit that he had spoken the words alleged.

Challenged to say whether or not he claimed to be the Messiah, Jesus replied in effect that the expression was that of the high priest. He did not necessarily make the claim in the sense intended by the high priest. What he did claim was that from now on the Son of Man would be seen enthroned at the right hand of the Almighty, and coming with the clouds of heaven (verse 64). By combining in this way Daniel 7:13,14 and Psalm 24:30, Jesus was understood (rightly) to be speaking about himself. Vindicated by God, he would come to his people in judgement or in blessing, according to the attitude of their hearts. They would see the kingdom of God set up in power.

Blasphemy Jesus' judges could hardly believe their ears. His voluntary statement amounted to a claim to be equal to the Most High. This was a capital offence in Jewish law – blasphemy – and provided evidence for a capital charge to be put before the Roman governor. The tearing of the clothes was laid down as the way to express horror at hearing blasphemy. The actions of verses 67,68 are probably those of the police who guarded Jesus.

Peter's denial, which is fitted effectively between Jesus' appearance before the high priest and his accusation before Pilate, fulfils the prediction of verse 34. Much to his credit, he follows at a distance and mingles with the crowd in the palace courtyard. If his courage failed in the sudden moment of testing, it was further proof of his master's saying: 'The spirit is willing, but the flesh is weak' (verse 41). His repentance, recorded in verse 75, unlike that of Judas, was the making of him.

27:1-14 Judas hangs himself

The leaders of the Sanhedrin went to Pilate to have Jesus convicted and condemned on a charge of sedition. In whatever sense he claimed to be the Messiah, such a claim could readily be represented to Pilate as political in character, involving rebellion against Rome. In Jewish eyes, the Messiah, the Lord's anointed, was by definition the King of Israel.

From Pilate's question in verse 11, it is plain that Jesus was charged with setting himself up as 'King of the Jews', and it was on this basis that he was executed; see verse 37. He admitted the charge when Pilate put it to him, though 'It is as you say' implies that the form of words is his questioner's, not his own, and that he does not necessarily accept them in the sense intended by the questioner. But Jesus has nothing to say to the charges pressed against him by his accusers; see verses 12,14. It looks as if he resolved to make the question of his kingship the deciding one.

Pilate governed Judea from AD26 to 36, quickly gaining a reputation for ruthless obstinacy.

The Potters field The Judas episode provides a dramatic interlude. Judas had served the chief priests' purpose; now they had no further use for him. But they had to dispose of the thirty shekels which he left in the Temple before taking his life. It is important to realize that in Zechariah 11:13 the same word can be read 'potter' or 'treasury'. It is almost as if the priests said 'Which reading of the prophecy shall we fulfil? Shall we give the money to the treasury or to the potter? We

A denarius coin of the Emperor Tiberius. The denarius was made of silver, and weighed about $\frac{1}{4}$ ounce (8 grams).

'Pilate . . . took the water and washed his hands in front of the crowd. "I am innocent of this man's blood," he said. "It is your responsibility!" ' (Matthew 27:24).

104   'They divided up his clothes by casting lots'
(Matthew 27:35).

Matthew
27

cannot put it in the Temple treasury because it is blood money. Let us give it to the potter in exchange for his field.' So they bought his field as a burial place for foreigners. Because it was bought with blood money, it was called 'Blood Acre' (verse 8), and is traditionally located on the ridge south of the Valley of Hinnom.

27:15-31 Jesus before Pilate
The Barabbas incident is mentioned in all four Gospels. It is linked with a custom not referred to elsewhere. It is strange that the man released had been rightly convicted of the very charge of sedition on which Jesus was wrongly condemned. The episode of verse 19 is recorded by Matthew alone. Pilate's wife's message would have been taken seriously. Every knowledgeable Roman knew that Julius Caesar would not have been assassinated if he had listened to his wife's warning.

Crucifixion was the regular penalty for sedition, except when the accused was a Roman citizen. Scourging (verse 26) was normal before crucifixion. It was so painful that strong men sometimes died under it alone.

This flagstone pavement beneath the Convent of the Sisters of Zion in Jerusalem was probably once part of the Antonia fortress. Scored on the stone are the lines and squares of a Roman game, with one area marked for the 'king'. It was probably here that Jesus stood with the crown of thorns on his head, mocked by the Roman soldiers.

Pilate washes his hands Pilate's hand-washing is found only in Matthew. The people's response (verse 25) is seen by Matthew as fulfilled in the siege and destruction of Jerusalem; compare Luke 19:41-44; 23:28-30. There is no ground for supposing that the call for Jesus' crucifixion came from those who had shouted 'Hosanna' on Palm Sunday.

The soldiers' horse-play, caricaturing his claim to be king (verses 27-31) is often claimed to have taken place on the 'pavement' under the modern Convent of the Sisters of Zion, where the Antonia Fortress then stood.

27:32-44 Christ crucified
The 'cross' carried by the condemned man may have been the cross-beam, to be fixed to the upright post at the place of execution. The 'gall' of verse 34 recalls Psalm 69:21. Possibly the soldiers offered him some of their sour wine. Verse 35 fulfilled Psalm 22:18. What was on the person of the condemned became the booty of the

executioners. Dicing was the normal way of allocating it. In the wording of the charge over Jesus' head, Matthew, like the other Gospel-writers, sees the proclaiming of the truth: Jesus is the Messiah of Israel, the kingliest king of all.

The 'two robbers' crucified with him were probably nationalist terrorists, perhaps Barabbas' supporters. The crosses were planted by the roadside, so that people passing in or out of the city could see the crucified close-up. The derisive words spoken to Jesus by passers-by in verses 40, 42, 43 echo his claims, real or alleged.

27:45-54 The death of Jesus

The cry of verse 46 is quoted in Aramaic. It comes from Psalm 22:1; *Eloi* ('my God') could have been mistaken for 'Elijah'. It was popularly believed that Elijah, who had never died, could help people in desperate trouble. The sour wine may have been to quench his thirst – or to help him speak more clearly. The statement that he 'gave up his spirit' suggests that he stayed in control to the end.

The rent curtain was probably the one separating the inner shrine – the holy of holies – from the outer compartment. Its rending meant that the God who until now was hidden is fully revealed in the death of Christ. Its tearing 'from top to bottom' (verse 51) shows it is God's own act. The statement of verses 51-53, made only by Matthew, is mysterious. It has been suggested that the death of Christ caused a radical disturbance in the realm of the dead.

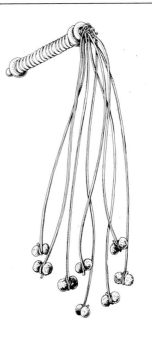

'The Crucified Christ' by Raphael

A Roman scourge would be barbed with pieces of lead or bone that cut into the flesh.

The Church of the Holy Sepulchre is traditionally believed to have been built over the place where Jesus was buried. There is a great outcrop of rock and a nearby tomb to be found inside the church.

'He has risen from the dead and is going ahead of you into Galilee' (Matthew 28:7). Dawn breaks over Galilee.

27:55-66 The burial of Jesus

Of the three women mentioned in verse 56, only the mother of the sons of Zebedee appears earlier in Matthew (chapter 20:20). For Mary of Magdala see Luke 8:2; for 'the other Mary' see John 19:25 and Mark 15:40.

Once Pilate was satisfied that Jesus was in fact dead (see Mark 15:45) he had no objection to letting Joseph of Arimathea take away his body for burial. But the high priest and his party could not forget the words about rising 'after three days'. If they wanted to guard the tomb, said Pilate, they could use their own Temple police. Matthew is the only Gospel to mention the guarding of the tomb and its sequel (Matthew 28:4,11-15).

28:1-10 The empty tomb

The words of the angel and the empty tomb, accessible now the stone was rolled back, testified that Jesus' body was no longer there. The women are invited to inspect the ledge on which his body had been laid on Friday night, and told to report his resurrection to the disciples. 'He . . . is going ahead of you to Galilee' (verse 7) repeats Jesus' own promise of Matthew 26:32.

28:11-15 The guards' report

The incident of verses 11-15 proves that the guards were not Roman soldiers. No intervention by the chief priests would have kept Roman soldiers out of trouble for such dereliction of duty. The tale they were instructed to tell was pretty feeble, but the chief priests knew what they could get away with.

The reason why the early Christians believed in the resurrection was not simply that they could not find his dead body but that they did meet a living Christ.

28:16-20 The great commission

'The mountain where Jesus had told them to go' (verse 16) is traditionally identified with the Mount of Transfiguration; see Matthew 17:1. Jesus reveals himself to them as the exalted Lord, given universal authority by God. In the exercise of that authority, he commissions them to be his ambassadors among 'all nations'; see also Matthew 24:14. All limitations on their mission are now dropped. It includes the task of instruction, making disciples of all the nations and teaching these disciples to keep all the commandments which they themselves had received from their Lord. To 'discharge their commission, the disciples are given the assurance of their Lord's continuance with them, 'to the very end of the age' (verse 20).

'Go and make disciples of all nations, baptizing them in the name of the Father and of the Son and of the Holy Spirit' (Matthew 28:19).

Resurrection

The resurrection is affirmed in the Bible as an historical event. Jesus, having been put to death, rose again from the grave. He had foretold this during his earthly life, for example in Mark 9:9 and John 16:16. Even such passages as Psalm 16:10, in the Old Testament, were later seen to refer to it; see for example Acts 2:27.

It is made absolutely clear that the resurrection of Jesus was quite different from the reviving of Lazarus (in John 11:44), and others whom Jesus raised. Whereas they simply returned from death, Jesus passed right through into another dimension of life. He was the same – and yet different. We see in Luke 24:31,36,37 and John 20:15 that his disciples knew him, and yet they did not always immediately recognize him. He could be seen (Matthew 28:9), heard and touched (Luke 24:39; John 20:17). Yet he could come and go mysteriously, and pass through closed doors as if they were not there (Luke 24:31; John 20:19).

The disciples made little effort to prove that the resurrection had taken place. They felt that it lay with those who did not believe it to prove their case.

There are various possible arguments. If Jesus did not rise, perhaps his friends stole his body to make it appear that he had risen from the dead. But this means we must believe that they escaped detection, deceived the authorities, and spread a lie. Some of them were even martyred. They would hardly have suffered this fate if they had known it was a hoax.

Perhaps Jesus' enemies stole the body. But if so, why does Matthew 28:11-15 show them so agitated when they heard it was missing? And why did they never produce the body to demolish the story of the resurrection when it began to spread?

A third possibility is that Jesus never actually died. Perhaps he swooned, and revived in the tomb. He then escaped, and rallied his disciples. But this stretches our belief too far. In any case, the authorities are shown in Mark 15:44,45 to have been certain that he was dead.

Contents

	Page
People	
Peter	124
John the Baptist	139
Mark	174
Pilate	177
Places	
Galilee	126–28
Capernaum	136, 37
Caesarea Philippi	146, 47
Words	
Disciple	123
Parables	130, 31
Healing	143
Unbelief	149
Messiah	163
Blasphemy	175
Life	
The farming year	112, 113
The home	120
Tax-collectors	121
Crime and punishment	156
The Roman Emperors	167

Mark

Introduction to Mark's Gospel

Mark Introduction

It is generally reckoned that the Gospel of Mark is the oldest of the four. But we would be wrong to assume on that account that it is also the simplest and the least sophisticated. Mark certainly produced the shortest Gospel; it is a ready introduction to the good news of Jesus for those who are unfamiliar with it. But Mark is no naive story-teller. He has his own line and follows it.

Matthew, Mark, Luke and John are often said to portray Christ as respectively king, servant, man and God. The second of these portraits is particularly that of the suffering Servant prophesied by Isaiah. We see on the one hand Jesus suffering on behalf of his people (Mark 10:45). His death is at the heart of the good news which Mark recounts (Mark 1:1). On the other hand Jesus suffers as an example to his people.

Mark's readers were almost certainly Christians facing persecution in Nero's Rome, thirty years after the resurrection. They needed the encouragement of knowing that their suffering was no strange thing, but a trial their Lord had already gone through and emerged from victoriously. This is why Mark's Gospel still speaks especially clearly in times of difficulty and testing.

The Forum in Rome.

Outline to Mark's Gospel

1:1-8	John prepares the way
1:9-13	Jesus is baptized
1:14-20	The first disciples called
1:21-28	Jesus drives out an evil spirit
1:29-39	Jesus heals many
1:40-45	A man with leprosy
2:1-12	Jesus heals a paralytic
2:13-17	Levi is called
2:18-22	Questions about fasting
2:23-3:6	Lord of the Sabbath
3:7-12	Crowds follow Jesus
3:13-19	Twelve apostles appointed
3:20-30	Jesus and Beelzebub
3:31-35	Jesus' mother and brothers
4:1-9	The parable of the sower
4:10-20	Parable-teaching explained
4:21-34	How the 'secret' will work out
4:35-41	The stilling of the storm
5:1-20	The demoniac of Gerasa
5:21-34	The woman with the haemorrhage
5:35-43	Jairus' daughter
6:1-6	Nazareth rejects its greatest Son
6:7-13	The sending of the Twelve
6:14-29	John the Baptist beheaded
6:30-44	The feeding of the five thousand
6:45-56	Jesus walks on the water
7:1-13	Clean and unclean
7:14-23	The heart of the matter
7:24-30	The faith of a Greek woman
7:31-37	A deaf and dumb man healed
8:1-13	Jesus feeds the four thousand
8:14-21	The yeast of the Pharisees
8:22-26	A blind man healed at Bethsaida
8:27-30	Peter's confession
8:31-9:1	Peter predicts his death
9:2-13	The transfiguration
9:14-29	Healing a boy with an evil spirit
9:30-37	Who is the greatest?
9:38-50	Causing to sin
10:1-13	Divorce
10:13-16	Little children and Jesus
10:17-27	The rich young man
10:28-34	Jesus again predicts his death
10:35-45	The request of James and John
10:46-52	Blind Bartimaeus meets the Messiah
11:1-11	The arrival at Jerusalem
11:12-19	Jesus clears the Temple
11:20-25	The withered fig-tree
11:27-33	Jesus' authority questioned
12:1-12	The rebellious tenants
12:13-17	The question about Roman taxes
12:18-27	The question about the resurrection
12:28-37	The two last questions
12:38-44	The widow's offering
13:1-13	What is to come
13:14-27	The end of the Age
13:28-37	The day and hour unknown
14:1-11	Jesus anointed at Bethany
14:12-21	The last supper
14:22-31	The Lord's supper
14:32-42	Gethsemane
14:43-52	The arrest
14:53-65	Before the Sanhedrin
14:66-72	Peter's denial
15:1-15	Jesus condemned
15:16-32	The crucifixion
15:33-39	The death of Jesus
15:40-47	The burial of Jesus
16:1-8	The resurrection
16:9-20	An anonymous postscript

Mark Outline

The farming year

Cold season

Within the cold season November and December were generally recognized as 'seedtime'.

Rainy season

The 'first rains' fell in September and October; the 'latter rains' in March and April.

Farming year

The Israelites learned their agriculture from the Canaanites, who lived in Palestine before they arrived.

The most commonly grown cereals were wheat and barley. Of the fruit trees cultivated, olives, vines and figs were particularly important.

The first rains came in October/November, and were often called the autumn rains, or early rains. They helped break up and soften the hard, dry soil, allowing ploughing to begin.

Once ploughing was completed, sowing began, with the grain subsequently being ploughed in.

It was vital that the winter rains continued for the crop to flourish; otherwise there would be famine.

The grain in the lowland areas ripened in April; first the barley, then the wheat. In May the crops also ripened in the upland areas, and harvesting began. 'Pentecost', or the Feast of Weeks, was originally the festival of harvest, when the people thanked God for the year's produce.

The hot summer is almost rainless, and lasts from May till October. The winters are not cold, however; the temperature falls below freezing point only five or six times a year.

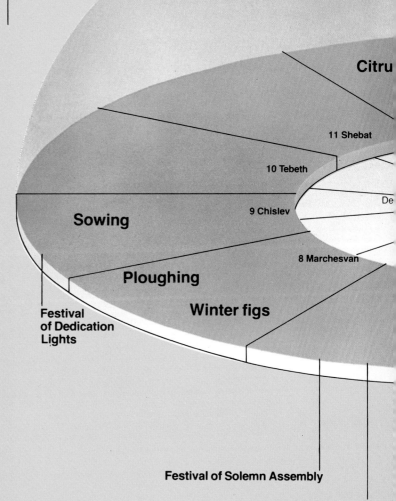

Citru

11 Shebat

10 Tebeth

9 Chislev

8 Marchesvan

De

Sowing

Ploughing

Winter figs

Festival of Dedication Lights

Festival of Solemn Assembly

Festival of Tabernacles Boot

Day o

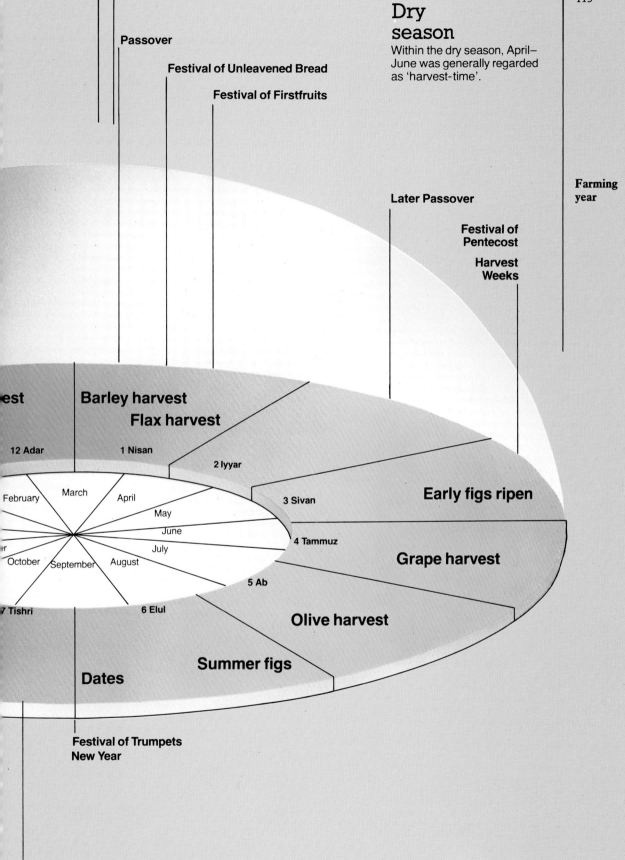

Passover

Festival of Unleavened Bread

Festival of Firstfruits

Dry season

Within the dry season, April–June was generally regarded as 'harvest-time'.

Later Passover

Festival of Pentecost

Harvest Weeks

Farming year

est

Barley harvest

Flax harvest

12 Adar

1 Nisan

2 Iyyar

February

March

April

May

June

July

August

September

October

er

3 Sivan

4 Tammuz

5 Ab

6 Elul

7 Tishri

Early figs ripen

Grape harvest

Olive harvest

Summer figs

Dates

Festival of Trumpets
New Year

ent

Michael Wilcock
Mark
Commentary

1:1-8 John prepares the way

What a resounding start to the Gospel (compare Genesis 1:1; John 1:1). And a strange start, too. The good news concerns a person, Jesus, to be recognized eventually as Christ (Mark 8:29) and Son of God (Mark 15:39). But it began with a place, the desert.

There, first, John appeared. His coming echoes the Old Testament theme of an exodus through the desert out into a new life. As a future hope, this theme is found above all in Isaiah; hence verse 2. But other scriptures are of course bound up with it: Isaiah 40:3; Exodus 23:20; Malachi 3:1.

Whatever baptism may have meant elsewhere, John's was something so special that he actually became known as 'John the Baptizer'. It was a baptism of repentance. All the people needed to confess their rebellion against God, and to go back, as it were, to the 'baptism' of the Red Sea at the Exodus and to the desert encounter with God. In this humiliation lay the hope of a new beginning.

A desert prophet This new start would become possible with the mysterious person who, though John's follower, would be greater than he. For John not only fulfilled the desert scriptures and preached desert baptism. He was also a prophet in the great desert tradition of Elijah. He was even dressed like that historic figure (2 Kings 1:8), thus bringing the lessons of the past into the present with startling clarity. 'The meaning of Moses, Elijah, Isaiah and Malachi comes alive in John the Baptist', Mark tells his readers, as if to say that similarly it is a living message to them too.

John looked back over the past, and forward to the future. He is like the signboard at the approach to a city. Unlike the series of signposts which have pointed us towards our destination, he indicates that we have now reached it. Yet he is not himself that destination, but simply proclaims it, as it looms up immediately beyond him. The directness is Mark's natural style, and also his deliberate object. He wants us to encounter, beyond the servant, the Master (verse 7); beyond water-baptism, Spirit-baptism (verse 8). By the same Spirit who led his people through the original desert experience (Isaiah 63:10-14), Jesus can lead men into a new life today.

1:9-13 Jesus is baptized

As in prophecy (verse 3), so now in fact, the herald was followed by the Lord. Where John the Baptist was, in the desert (verse 4), there Jesus also came.

These verses contain a series of contrasts. First is the contrast between Jesus as baptizer (verse 8) and baptized (verse 9). As John stood between the old age and the new, so Jesus stood between God and man, representing each to the other. As God, he would be baptizer. For the moment, as man, he was baptized. For the moment he accepted that sin (not that he had any of his own) is under God's judgement, and that restoration is only by God's grace.

Another contrast concerns those who came to John's baptism:

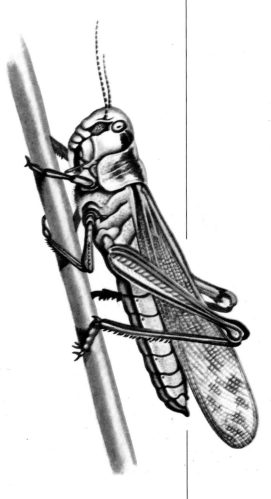

Locusts usually came in great swarms, like clouds, and where they landed devoured all the plants. John the Baptist ate locusts and wild honey in the desert. People still catch locusts and eat them, either dried or fried.

The River Jordan flowing south out of Galilee.

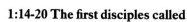
Repent and believe the good news!' (Mark 1:15).

many from pious Judea, only one from irreligious Galilee (verses 5,9). In yet another contrast, with the crowd, man confessed but we do not hear God accept. With Jesus, God accepted though we have not heard the man confess. For Jesus was the one Israelite truly submitted to God's will. So his Father was pleased (verse 11) to appoint him to the task of re-making the broken relationship between him and his people.

Conflict with Satan The wilderness, where they had been made sons (Hosea 11:1) is where they had to be remade. Jesus was already there (verses 4,9), but this corner of it was by now rather crowded. So the Spirit drove him out into solitude. 'At once', implying a close connexion in time and in meaning, is a favourite phrase of Mark's. And so it follows that Jesus had to establish himself, like Moses and Elijah with their forty days (Exodus 24:18; 1 Kings 19:4,8), as a 'desert man'.

Unlike Matthew and Luke, Mark is not concerned with the details of this time. For him, the conflict with Satan continues throughout the Gospel. For sixteen chapters Jesus experiences on the one hand the beasts, and on the other the angels. So in their turn will those for whom Mark writes, in his own age and since – all who (in John Bunyan's words) are travelling 'through the desert of this world' towards their final salvation.

1:14-20 The first disciples called

Once John the Baptist was put in prison (verse 14), the last signboard is passed and we reach our destination. From now on, we are with Jesus himself.

With Jesus's preaching of the gospel, the new age burst in upon humanity. His ministry was in a special sense a Galilean one. If the lower Jordan Valley, the background to Mark 1:1-13, represents the desert, 'Galilee of the Gentiles' (Matthew 4:15) represents the world. In the desert, we see spiritual truth in all its clarity; in the world, human life in all its confusion. Nazareth in Galilee was Jesus' home (verse 9). Bethlehem in Judea had been his birthplace, but Mark is not concerned with that. It was in Galilee that Jesus began to preach (verses 14,15) and to call his disciples (verses 16-18).

Here in the world he announced the good news. 'The time' – the climax of all past times, the goal of Old Testament history and prophecy – had now fully come. 'The kingdom', the rule of God foreshadowed in the past story of Israel, was now with us. Not yet in such irresistible power that it swept all before it, but close enough to confront men with a crisis of decision. Hence the call to repent and believe. What was revolutionary was that Jesus called on the Jews to repent. They as much as the Gentiles were not fit for God's rule.

Fishers of men But there would be an interval between this arrival of the kingdom and its final climax. So here in Galilee, in the world of men, Jesus began to choose those who during that period would follow him in the work of preaching the good news of the kingdom. These disciples would be fishers of men. This is not simply a whimsical pun on their present trade. Against its biblical background, fishing for men is seen to be a matter of judgement (Jeremiah 16:16; Ezekiel 29:4, 5). The net is not conversion, but confrontation with the gospel. This has a double effect (compare 2 Corinthians 2:15-16; 1 Peter 2:6-8); while all the fish come under scrutiny, some were kept and others were rejected (Matthew 13:47-50).

Like the fishermen, we may not understand all that is involved in Jesus' call. But their immediate and wholehearted response is to be imitated by us.

Mark 1

The Lake of Galilee is the lowest fresh-water lake in the world. Measuring roughly thirteen miles by seven, it covers some ninety square miles. The best-known fish is the Cichlid, often known as 'St Peter's fish', and was probably the most common fish in the time of Christ.

Capernaum today, as seen from the Lake of Galilee.

The local Roman centurion helped build the synagogue at Capernaum. These impressive ruins, however, date from a slightly later synagogue. It is interesting to notice the way it combines Roman and Jewish decorations.

1:21-28 Jesus drives out an evil spirit

Back to the Galilean town of Capernaum, home of Simon and Andrew (verse 29) and no doubt also of James and John the 'fishers of men' made their way. The first thing that happened there puts flesh on several of the ideas which Mark introduced at the very start of his Gospel.

Here Jesus combated the power of Satan (see Mark 1:13). In the Gospels, demon-possession is distinct from illness (see also Mark 1:32,34; 6:13). One difference is the way Jesus was addressed in each case; contrast for example Mark 3:11 with 10:47-50. Possession is distinguished by what seems to be a separate personality speaking through the sufferer's mouth – something noted also by modern investigators. The miracle so impressed people that they saw Jesus not simply as the exorcizer of this particular demon, but as the kind of person who surely had authority over demons in general (verse 27).

Jesus' authority Here too Jesus proclaimed the gospel of the kingdom (see Mark 1:14,15), both in word (verses 21,22) and in deed (verse 27). Notice the reaction of the people in each case. Mark often mentions such reactions, and the words he uses suggest not so much surprise as consternation, or even dismay. Jesus had authority not merely greater than one would expect in a village carpenter, but greater even than that of the official teachers of religion. Never before had they heard anything of this kind. He sounded disconcertingly like a prophet of old, with a message direct from God. He declared the rule of God to be something which confronted them, stark, immediate and demanding.

In this way the 'Galilean' and 'fishing' themes also begin to be illustrated (see notes on Mark 1:14,16-18). The net of Jesus' message went forth; it spread out into the world, 'throughout all the surrounding region' (verse 28), reaching out to mankind in all its variety and need. Men were caught and held by it, and drawn into the light.

1:29-39 Jesus heals many

The healing of Simon's mother-in-law perhaps began to teach him and his friends lessons to which Jesus returns in chapter 10. Simon, who had been called to leave his home, was taught that Jesus is no man's debtor. When his mother-in-law had been restored, her response was to serve. The ideal of service was what James and John had to be taught in Mark 10:35-45. Both giving things up and serving turn out to be keynotes of this Gospel.

Jesus had no hesitation in dealing with both demons and disease on the Sabbath. The crowds, inhibited by the rules about Sabbath-breaking, waited till sunset, when the next day officially began. Then they came in droves to seek healing from Jesus. There is a basic lesson they seemed not to have grasped. The 'whole town' wanted his healing; but his preaching was quite another matter – we have already seen how that filled them with consternation. They wanted the benefits, but not the disturbance (compare John 6:26).

Jesus withdraws If we ask whether these twenty-four hours can be reckoned as a successful start to Jesus' ministry, it looks as though the people in general were seeing only what they wanted to see. Disappointment peeps out between the lines of the final paragraph (verses 35-39). Jesus withdrew to a lonely place; the countryside round Capernaum was generally cultivated, but he contrived to find somewhere which early in the morning would do for a 'desert'. Here he could exchange once more the confusion of the town for the clarity of the desert, and see things as they really were. Then it is as though the disciples found him and said, 'Everyone here seeks your *cures*', and he replied, 'Then I must go to the next towns with my *message* – that is what I have come for'. The Galilean ministry had to be preaching as well as healing (verse 39).

The Lake of Galilee viewed from nearby hills.

1:40-45 A man with leprosy

After dealing with demon possession and fever, Jesus next faced leprosy. As with fever, the Bible speaks of a symptom rather than a disease. But whatever might cause the skin condition referred to, its effects were grim. The person with leprosy became an outcast. Jewish law provided both for those suffering from leprosy (Leviticus 13:45,46) and for those who were cured of it (Leviticus 14:1-32); but in practice cures hardly ever happened. Such a complaint well illustrates the power of Satan, and the healing power of Christ.

Two unexpected words stand out in Mark's description of Jesus; his indignation (verse 41 in the *New English Bible* – probably the correct meaning, rather than 'compassion') and his sternness (verse 43). Doubtless Jesus felt pity towards the leper. But really it was Satan, the author of this living death, who was here confronted. Towards him Jesus felt furious indignation. John told of the same anger at the grave of Lazarus (John 11:33).

Jesus speaks sternly But Jesus had stern words for the healed man. Now that the man was cured, he was not 'to talk freely' about it (verse 45), but simply to go through the correct procedure by which the priests would certify the cure. This would be 'a testimony to them' (verse 44). This probably means incriminating evidence against them. When the Jewish authorities came to deny the claims of Christ, they would have to face the fact that they themselves had recognized the cures which backed up those claims, and thus stand condemned (see also John 15:24).

Whether or not the cured man obeyed Jesus by going to the priests, he disobeyed him by spreading the story. The result was that in the towns to which Jesus went as a preacher of the gospel (verse 38), he found himself mobbed as primarily a miracle-worker. Even another retreat to 'lonely places' (verse 45) had crowds pursuing him for the wrong reasons. No wonder he had spoken sternly. His anger was deserved not only by his enemy Satan, but by a well-meaning friend who repaid blessing with disobedience, and thus hindered the work of the kingdom.

The home

The home   The family was very important to the Jews. It was like a little kingdom, where the father was king. He expected everyone to obey him. He saw to it that every member of the family did his or her proper job.

The family assembled in the home, which gave security, shade and coolness. In the evening, the family would gather on the roof of the house to rest or work.

During the day it was quite dark inside the house. The little windows kept out the light as well as the heat. At night wooden shutters covered the unglazed windows. In the middle of the room there was a stone or wooden pillar holding up the roof. An oil lamp rested in a niche in this pillar.

The family would often use the house roof for drying grain, fruit and wood in the sun. Inside the house, what furniture they had was very simple. Household utensils were stored in the family's section of the house, with cupboards and trunks to contain their belongings. During the day, bedclothes were kept rolled up either in a box or in a niche in a wall.

Pots, cups and utensils were made of baked clay, which was cheap. Milk, wine and water might also be stored in leather containers.

Houses

In Jesus' day, ordinary people lived in simple houses made of bricks dried in the sun. In hilly country, the houses were made of limestone. Most houses had only one room, about half of which consisted of a raised platform where the family lived. Domestic animals lived in the other part of the room. There were mangers, as well as containers for stores of corn, fruit, water and oil.

In the family's section of the house there were a few pieces of furniture. Windows were tiny and without glass. Floors were simply clay trodden hard.

Outside, a staircase led up to the flat roof, which had a low wall to stop people from falling.

The roof was made of beams or planks of wood. Across these, twigs and branches were laid, and covered with clay and earth pressed smooth. Sometimes an additional room was built on the flat roof.

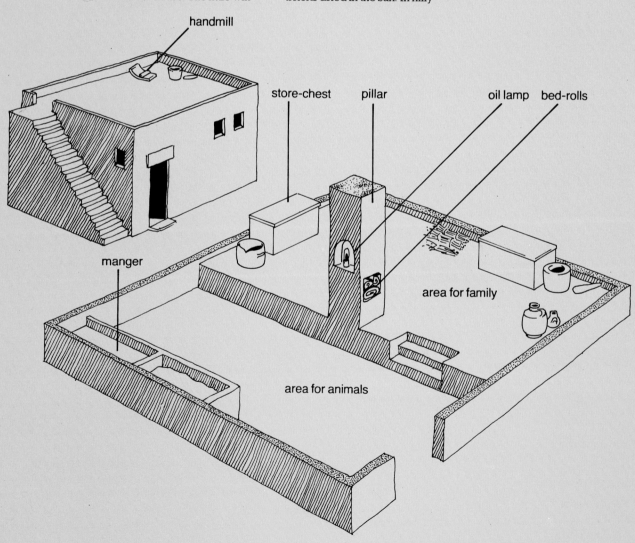

handmill

store-chest   pillar   oil lamp   bed-rolls

manger

area for family

area for animals

2:1-12 Jesus heals a paralytic

When Jesus returned to Capernaum, 'preaching the word' (verse 2) continued to be his prime concern. Doubtless the crowds still wanted the miracles rather than the message. There was a healing – of paralysis – but this incident is the first of several where the Jews' repeated question 'Why?' (verses 7,16,18,24) was dealt with by Jesus' teaching. Here his message concerned the forgiveness of sins.

The miracle involved a man in great need. So helpless was he that it took four friends to carry him, so desperate that they were prepared to climb the outside stairs to the flat roof and remove the tiles to let him through (Luke 5:19). He was perhaps incapable even of believing on his own account ('Jesus saw *their* faith'). His obvious need was to be set free from his paralysis. Many onlookers must have thought the words of Jesus in verse 5 were irrelevant as well as blasphemous.

The general meaning of his two statements to the paralytic (verses 5,11) is clear. Anyone could *say* 'Your sins are forgiven'; so this was linked with words which are immediately verifiable: 'Get up . . . and walk'. The latter works, so presumably the former works too.

The scribes' question The scribes were right to ask 'Who can forgive sins but God alone?' (verse 7). But we may do them an injustice if we say that they ought to have recognized Jesus as God. Both healing and forgiveness could be brought in God's name by a prophet (1 Kings 17:17-23; 2 Samuel 12:13). They may well have thought Jesus was claiming that kind of authority, a direct word from God which was a cut above their own second-hand teaching. To them, this was quite scandalous enough.

But however the scribes took it, Mark expects his readers to draw the deeper conclusion. The beginning of verse 10 may be meant as a footnote, or put in brackets, and translated 'Note that the Son of man . . .'. If so, it was not Jesus proving to the scribes, but Mark pointing out to his Christian readers, that when the gospel of the kingdom confronts the needs of men, it deals with sin as well as sickness, and the sin is the primary problem.

2:13-17 Levi is called

We can approach this passage in several ways. From one point of view, Mark is continuing to unfold the gospel of the kingdom. We have already seen that it confronts men with truth, restores them to wholeness and cleanses them from sin. Now we are shown that it works with the toughest of characters. It can transform even 'tax collectors and sinners'; men willing cynically to collaborate with Romans and rob fellow-Jews, or deliberately flouting accepted standards of decent behaviour. We are further shown that Levi's feast (compare Luke 5:29), rather than the Pharisees', or even John's, fasting, is the right response. Transformations like this are a matter for joy, not mourning.

The feasting of some and the fasting of others provoked the second and third 'Why' (verses 16,18; compare verse 17). To explain why he mixed with bad company, and why his disciples did not fast, Jesus claimed for himself two roles. What sort of people surround a doctor? The sick. And a bridegroom? The cheerful! Joy for sinners, not gloom for saints, is what the gospel brings.

2:18-22 Questions about fasting

It is interesting to notice that Jesus' questioners assumed he was still basically one of them. 'It is because you presumably agree with us about this that we don't understand why you do that.' Not only Jesus' conclusions, however, but also his starting point, differed from theirs. Hence the 'unshrunk cloth' and 'new wine' sayings (verses 21,22). They could not have the new plus the old. If they tried

In Jesus' time, Jews were employed by the Roman government to collect taxes and tolls. These dues were collected on the borders of countries and cities, at bridges, landing-stages and several other places.

Most Jews hated and despised the tax-collectors. They were regarded as polluted by contact with the occupying Romans. In addition, they often demanded higher tolls and taxes than were due.

It surprised and shocked many people that Jesus had anything to do with tax-collectors, and even ate with them. Eating together was a promise of friendship.

A Roman coin of the Emperor Augustus.

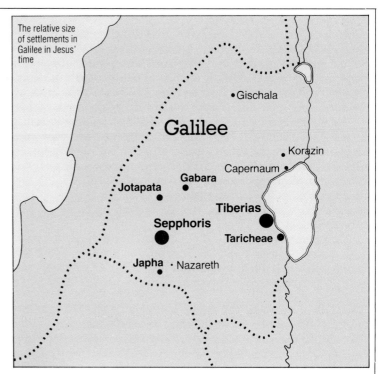

The relative size of settlements in Galilee in Jesus' time

Gischala

Galilee

Korazin

Capernaum

Gabara

Jotapata

Tiberias

Sepphoris

Taricheae

Japha · Nazareth

Skins were used as containers for various liquids. Consisting of the whole skin of a goat or sheep, the neck hole was used as the opening for the container. Water, wine and milk were all carried in such skins.

to have both, the 'wineskin' of traditional beliefs would not survive. The gospel totally replaces the old way of thinking.

The claims of Jesus suggest yet another approach. As with his authority to forgive sins (verses 5-10), they can be taken at more than one level. His hearers would have agreed that a doctor's visit implies sickness in the house, and that a wedding is a joyful occasion. But with hindsight, Mark's readers can see deeper implications. Jesus the 'doctor' was distinct from both the sick and the well, the sinful and the righteous. Jesus the 'bridegroom' linked himself with the biblical teaching about the marriage between God and his people (Isaiah 54:5, compare 2 Corinthians 11:2).

2:23-28, 3:1-6 Lord of the Sabbath

The series of debates between Jesus and the Pharisees which began at Mark 2:1 ends with two Sabbath-day incidents.

In the first, the Jews' objection to the disciples' plucking grain was not that the grain belonged to someone else – the law allowed that (Deuteronomy 23:25) – but that they were 'reaping' on the Sabbath (Exodus 34:21). Jesus' answer was to quote an instance in Old Testament times when a leader and his men infringed similar regulations without being accused of impiety.

The man with the shrivelled hand That is the last of the 'Why?' questions. In the final incident (Mark 3:1-6) the Pharisees' objection was unspoken. Had they replied to verse 4, they would have said: 'Yes, it is lawful to do good on the Sabbath, provided it is indeed a matter of saving life. But in this case it isn't.' Jesus, angry and grieved that they were so insensitive to the purposes of God and to the sufferings of men, sidestepped their accusation by himself saying nothing about healing, but only the unexceptionable words of verse 5.

The cornfield incident illustrated Jesus' general teaching about the Sabbath. The Sabbath rules were for human welfare, which must be the prime consideration (Mark 2:27). The synagogue incident includes the same truth; but its main point was that his enemies were silenced. Realizing there was no common ground between them and Jesus, they began to plot to kill 'on the Sabbath'. This parallels the

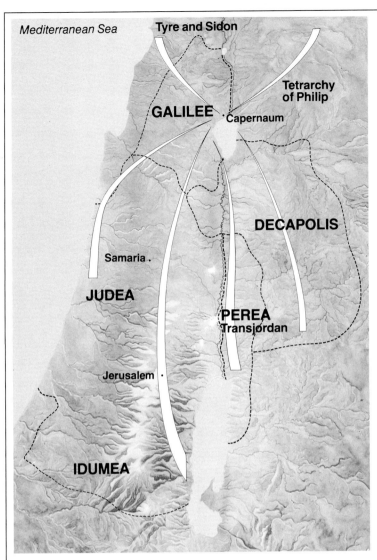

Mediterranean Sea
Tyre and Sidon
Tetrarchy of Philip
GALILEE · Capernaum
DECAPOLIS
Samaria ·
JUDEA
PEREA
Transjordan
Jerusalem ·
IDUMEA

Disciple

The word means 'pupil' or 'student'. It was used for those who attached themselves to a well-known teacher, such as John the Baptist (Matthew 9:14), Moses (John 9:28) or Gamaliel (Acts 22:3). It was therefore natural for it to be used for Jesus' followers. It was applied first to the Twelve (Mark 3:14), and later to those who came to believe in Christ through the ministry of the Twelve (Matthew 28:19; Acts 11:26).

controversies of Mark 12, which also led to the silencing of Jesus' enemies and their plotting to kill him.

3:7-12 Crowds follow Jesus

Mark 3:7-12 begins a new section of the Gospel. Like Mark 1:14,15, it is a 'heading' for the next two or three chapters, summing up the kind of events that Mark would be narrating in them. These verses promise more about the disciples and the crowds, and what they heard and saw of Jesus, particularly his power over the forces of evil.

Jesus's ministry was no longer directed to Galileans alone. The crowds which flocked to him were from southern Israel too (Judea), and even from regions beyond, to the north (Tyre and Sidon), south (Idumea) and east (Transjordan). In due course Jesus himself would visit all these places, except, as far as we know, Idumea. But already it was clear that the spread of the good news had never been intended to be restricted to Israel.

3:13-19 Twelve apostles appointed

The ministry was no longer to be carried on by Jesus alone. Already in Mark 1 Jesus had called his first few disciples and promised to make them fishers of men. Now he 'made' the Twelve – that is the meaning of the word 'appointed' in verse 14. Mark prefers the term 'Twelve' to 'apostles'. The number was to recall the tribes of Israel, as though the people of God was here being formed afresh.

Peter

Peter Peter apparently had four names used regularly. Symeon (Acts 15:14; 2 Peter 1:1) his Jewish name; Simon (Mark 1:16; Matthew 16:17; Luke 22:31) his name in Greek; Peter, a nickname given by Jesus (Mark 3:16) by which he is most commonly known; and Cephas, the Aramaic equivalent of Peter (John 1:42; 1 Corinthians 1:12; Galatians 2:9).

Peter was the son of a man named John (John 1:42) or Jonah.

He was a native of Bethsaida (John 1:44), but evidently married a woman from Capernaum. When the challenge came to follow Jesus, he left his work as a fisherman and obeyed (Mark 1:16-18).

Peter is named in the list of the Twelve (Mark 3:16) and shared several privileged experiences with James and John (Mark 5:37; 9:2; 14:33). He was strong in asserting his loyalty to Jesus (John 6:66-69; Mark 14:27-31), and saw that Jesus was Son of God in a unique sense.

After his confession of Matthew 16:16 Peter was rebuked for trying to turn Jesus from the way of the cross (Matthew 16:21-23). With John, Peter arranged for the final Passover meal (Luke 22:8). After rejecting Christ's warnings that he would deny him (John 13:38) he slept while Jesus prayed in Gethsemane, followed Jesus to the high priest's courtyard, but denied Jesus three times (John 18:15,16; Matthew 26:34; Luke 22:34; John 13:38).

Peter and John were the first to receive news of the empty tomb (John 20:1-10). The risen Christ recommissioned Peter (John 21:15-17).

In the early church, Peter worked many miracles (Acts 3:1-9; 5:12-16; 9:32-43). He was put in prison with others and miraculously released (Acts 5:17-21). He is not mentioned in Acts after the Council in chapter 15, where he stood up for the equality of Gentile converts.

Perhaps Peter visited Corinth with the gospel (1 Corinthians 1:12) as well as Asia Minor (1 Peter 1:1). Tradition tells us that he eventually went to Rome and was executed in the persecutions under the emperor Nero.

The Colosseum, Rome. Here prisoners – some of them Christians – were thrown to lions and bears.

The Twelve's apostleship is described in the simplest words. They were called to 'be with him'. This was their training, which starts between here and Mark 6:6. Then they would be 'sent out to preach', in Mark 6:7-12. Light is shed on their names and nicknames by related passages elsewhere: the lists of Matthew 10:2-4; Luke 6:14-16; Acts 1:13; also Matthew 16:17-18; Mark 9:38; Luke 9:54. Bartholomew is no doubt the Nathanael of John 1:45-51; Matthew is the Levi of Mark 2:14. So Mark's readers can see that the gospel is to be preached to others besides Jews, and by others besides Jesus.

A synagogue school: the boy pupils sit on the floor at their teacher's feet.

'If a house is divided against itself, that house cannot stand' (Mark 3:25).

3:20-30 Jesus and Beelzebub

Three accusations against Jesus are here introduced briefly – he is mad (verses 19-21), or possessed (verse 22) or a sorcerer (verse 22). They are then followed up at greater length in reverse order.

Remembering that Jesus had just appointed the Twelve, we note that he began their training by facing them with their enemy. 'Beelzebub' or 'Prince of demons', the Jews may have called him, but he was in fact the Satan of the desert (Mark 1:13). Jesus' own ministry had begun with a similar confrontation, making plain what the gospel of the kingdom was primarily up against (Mark 1:21-28). Jesus answered the accusation of sorcery, of using Satanic power, by saying that Satan's kingdom showed the strength of a united front rather than the signs of disunity which, on their theory, the scribes should expect (verses 23-26).

Satan's opponent The charge of demon-possession reflected more seriously on those who levelled it at Jesus. It showed that they did not acknowledge the power which really possessed him. For he came as the opponent of the 'strong man' Satan, that is, as the Holy One (Mark 1:24). Jesus came as one stronger than Satan, since he was the one who had the Spirit (Mark 1:7-8).

Persistently to deny ('they kept saying . . .' is the meaning of verse 30) that Jesus' words and deeds have the authority of God's Holy Spirit is the ultimate sin. The man who cannot be forgiven is simply the one who refuses to accept the gospel of forgiveness which Jesus, by the Spirit, brings (verses 28-30).

Galilee

Korazin
Capernaum
Gennesaret
Magdala
Cana
Gergesa
Tiberias
Sepphoris
Nazareth
Nain
Gadara

Galilee The Lake (or Sea) of Galilee is a pear-shaped stretch of fresh water into which the River Jordan flows from the north and out of which it flows towards the south. It is about thirteen miles long from north to south, and nearly eight miles across from west to east at its greatest width; it lies 695 feet below Mediterranean sea-level and reaches a maximum depth of about 200 feet.

In the New Testament it is called not only the Sea of Galilee but the Lake of Gennesaret (Luke 5:1), from the fertile plain on its northwest side (modern Ginossar), and the Sea of Tiberias (John 6:1, 21:1), from the city of that name which Herod Antipas built on its western shore about AD22.

Much of Jesus' public ministry took place around the shores of the lake. One can still be impressed by the acoustic properties of some of the places from which he taught, whether from the slopes of the rising hill-country to the west (the Mount of the Beatitudes) or from a boat pushed a little way out to sea near Capernaum, from which the people on land could hear him as in a natural amphitheatre. Storms such as those described in the Gospel story still blow up suddenly, when currents of air from the west, passing through the Arbel valley, are sucked down in turbulent vortices over the lake.

Herod's territory

In Jesus' time the territory west of the lake was ruled by Herod Antipas, tetrarch of Galilee from 4BC to his deposition in AD39. Herod's new capital of Tiberias (called after his patron, the Roman Emperor Tiberius) is not said to have been visited by Jesus. In fact, for a long time Jews tended to avoid it, regarding it as ceremonially unclean because it was built on the site of a cemetery. It may have

been in his palace at Tiberias that Herod's macabre birthday party was held (Mark 6:21). If so, the messenger who carried the order for John the Baptist's execution had a long way to travel, for Josephus tells us that John was imprisoned and put to death in Herod's Transjordan fortress of Machaerus. Josephus is probably right: John was active in the lower Jordan valley, including Bethany beyond Jordan (John 1:28), which lay in Herod's territory of Perea. Before he built Tiberias, Herod lived in Sepphoris, four miles north-west of Nazareth.

East of the lake the ruler was Herod's brother, Philip (mentioned in Luke 3:1), whose capital was Caesarea Philippi. Philip's territory was untroubled by the tension that made Herod Antipas so suspicious and cunning – it was not for nothing that Jesus called Antipas 'that fox' (Luke 13:32). When Antipas' interest in Jesus became too keen to be healthy, it was easy to avoid his attention by crossing to the opposite side of the lake.

The modern visitor finds it difficult to envisage the thriving towns which surrounded the lake in Jesus' day. The lake teemed with fish, which provided a living for many of the inhabitants of those towns. The fish they caught were not only sent to other parts of Palestine and Transjordan, but salted and exported to other

Galilee

Ruins of the synagogue at Capernaum.

The remains of the synagogue building at Korazin.

The hills near Kersa.

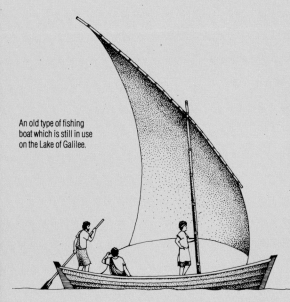

An old type of fishing boat which is still in use on the Lake of Galilee.

lands. Magdala, between Capernaum and Tiberias, was given the Greek name of Tarichaeae, because of the salt fish (*tarichos* in Greek) which it exported. It was the home of Mary Magdalene.

Capernaum

Capernaum, which Jesus chose as his headquarters during his ministry in Galilee, is mentioned alongside Chorazin and Bethsaida in Matthew 11:20-24 and Luke 10:13-15. Doom is pronounced on all three because, although they had witnessed so many of Jesus' mighty works, they refused to repent. (See also page 136.)

Chorazin

Chorazin, two and a half miles north of Capernaum, was destroyed at the time of the second Jewish revolt against Rome (AD132-135) but was rebuilt and remained a flourishing city for some generations, extending to an area of about twelve acres. By about AD330 it lay in ruins. It was well supplied with water. The buildings, including the synagogue, were of the local black basalt. The synagogue, several of whose walls still stand, occupied an area of about seventy by fifty feet. It was supported by pillars and pilasters, whose capitals and cases represented a variety of Greek orders.

Bethsaida

Bethsaida, which simply means 'Fishertown', lay a little way east of the point where the Jordan enters the lake from the north. Philip the tetrarch enlarged it and changed its name to Julias, in honour of Julia, daughter of the Emperor Augustus. It was the original home of Peter and Andrew, and also of Philip the apostle, according to John 1:44. In its neighbourhood the feeding of the five thousand most probably took place. (The traditional site of the feeding, at Tabgha, south-west of Capernaum, is difficult to accept.) Mark also records the healing of a blind man at Bethsaida (Mark 8:22-26).

If one continues round the lake in a clockwise direction, one comes to a place on the east shore called Kursi or Kersa, directly across from Magdala. It is fairly certainly here that the healing of the man possessed by the legion of demons took place. It is the one point on the east side of the lake where the steep hills come right down almost to the water's edge. The modern name preserves the ancient Gerasa or (better) Gergesa. If the region is called 'the region of the Gadarenes' (Matthew 8:28), that may be because the city of Gadara (modern Umm Qeis), nearly seven miles southeast of the lake and separated from it by the deep Yarmuk gorge, had property around here. The presence of a large herd of pigs in the vicinity is sufficient indication that the local people were mainly Gentiles.

When the demon-possessed man was cured, he 'went away and began to tell in the Decapolis how much Jesus had done for him' (Mark 5:20). The Decapolis was a league of ten cities, the most northerly of which was Damascus and the most southerly Philadelphia (Amman); it included Gadara and Gerasa (Jerash). All but one of these cities – Scythopolis (Bethshean) – lay east of the Jordan valley. The term Decapolis may also denote, more generally, the area in which the ten cities lay.

3:31-35 Jesus' mother and brothers

The accusation of madness brings us back to Jesus' family and friends. Of course Jesus upheld what the law said about family loyalty (Mark 7:10; Exodus 20:12; 21:17). But he knew, as the law also knew, that it might be overriden by a higher loyalty (10:28-30; Exodus 32:25-29, Deuteronomy 33:8-9). So when his human family would not recognize his divine authority (compare John 7:5), he contrasted them, 'standing outside', with those who were inside with him, and who accepted the message of God (verses 31-35). Significantly, it was a house belonging to two of his disciples which was now regarded as his home (verse 19; Mark 2:1).

4:1-9 The parable of the sower

Mark devotes most of this chapter to recounting some of the parables which were Jesus' regular method of teaching (verse 34). Most of his hearers were left to work out for themselves what he meant. But occasionally we readers are favoured with the kind of explanation which the disciples were given, and such is the case here.

The parables make homely comparisons with things and events that are known to everyone. At this level his hearers knew exactly what Jesus was talking about. With the passing of time some things seem strange to us (for example, the sowing of seed by hand, to be ploughed in afterwards, so you might not know which ground would be productive).

The 'raven' of the Bible probably includes other large, black, flesh-eating birds such as the crow and the rook.

Mark 4

Some fell on rocky places . . .
some fell among thorns . . .
some fell on good ground.

Parables

About nature and farm life

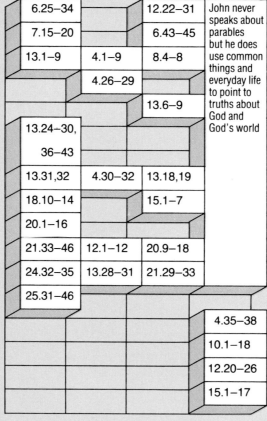

	Matthew	Mark	Luke	John
Birds and flowers	6.25–34		12.22–31	
A tree and its fruit	7.15–20		6.43–45	
The sower	13.1–9	4.1–9	8.4–8	
Growing seed		4.26–29		
Unfruitful fig tree			13.6–9	
Weeds	13.24–30, 36–43			
Mustard seed	13.31,32	4.30–32	13.18,19	
Lost sheep	18.10–14		15.1–7	
Workers in the vineyard	20.1–16			
Tenants in the vineyard	21.33–46	12.1–12	20.9–18	
Fig tree	24.32–35	13.28–31	21.29–33	
Sheep and goats	25.31–46			
Harvest time				4.35–38
The shepherd				10.1–18
Grain of wheat				12.20–26
The vine				15.1–17

John never speaks about parables but he does use common things and everyday life to point to truths about God and God's world

About familiar things in Bible times

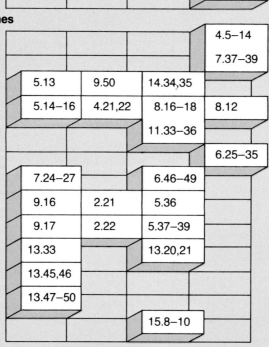

	Matthew	Mark	Luke	John
Water				4.5–14
				7.37–39
Salt	5.13	9.50	14.34,35	
Light	5.14–16	4.21,22	8.16–18	8.12
			11.33–36	
Bread				6.25–35
House builders	7.24–27		6.46–49	
Patching clothes	9.16	2.21	5.36	
New wine	9.17	2.22	5.37–39	
Yeast	13.33		13.20,21	
The pearl	13.45,46			
The fishing net	13.47–50			
Lost coin			15.8–10	

The word 'parable' means 'to lay one thing alongside another' – and thus to make a comparison. It is used in the New Testament for the stories which Jesus told. It covers all sorts of stories from a simple word-picture, such as Mark 13:28, to an elaborate and almost allegorical story such as the Prodigal Son (Luke 15) or the Sower and the Seed (Matthew 13).

The parables are usually meant to teach a few main lessons. Attempts to make every detail bear a meaning are bound to fail. In addition, moral points which are not relevant to the story should be ignored. For instance, the fact that the 'dishonest manager' was commended for his wisdom does not mean that his behaviour was morally justifiable (Luke 16:1-9).

The purpose of Jesus' parables was to make the truth understandable and memorable, by translating it into the language and experience of everyday life. The parables are the major single feature of Jesus' teaching. We read that 'he did not say anything to them without using a parable' (Matthew 13:34).

Mark
4

Parables and illustrations about everyday life

	Matthew	Mark	Luke	John
New truths and old	13.51,52			
Forgiveness	18.21–35			
Two sons	21.28–32			
The wedding feast	22.1–14		14.15–24	
Ten girls at a wedding	25.1–13			
Servants	25.14–30		19.11–27	
Debts and debtors			7.41–43	
Good Samaritan			10.25–37	
Friend in need			11.5–13	
Rich fool			12.16–21	
Watchful servants			12.35–40	
Humility and hospitality			14.7–14	
Counting the cost of discipleship			14.25–33	
Lost son			15.11–32	
Shrewd manager			16.1–13	
Rich man and Lazarus			16.19–31	
A servant's duty			17.7–10	
The persistent widow			18.1–8	
Pharisee and tax-collector			18.9–14	

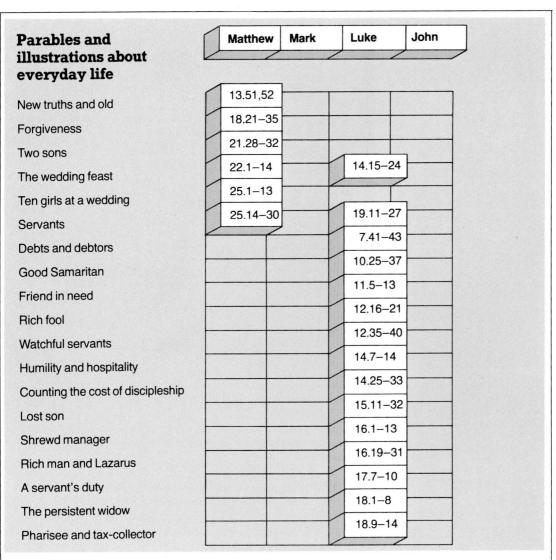

But the audience was exhorted to listen hard. For the parable has an inner meaning which is not obvious. It may have something to do with the many types of soil; or with the large proportion of seed that comes to nothing; or with the enormous harvest that results from the seed that does grow. For often a parable has some startling twist to catch our attention, in this case the hundredfold increase (not of course 100 per cent, but 10,000 per cent!)

Against the background of the surprise, misunderstanding and hostility which Jesus met, his use of parables underlines our need to be attentive, receptive hearers.

4:10-20 Parable-teaching explained

These words of Jesus, spoken when he was away from the crowds and 'alone . . . with the Twelve' and other disciples, answered one question and raised another.

The disciples had apparently asked him about the parable of the sower and about his use of parables in general. With regard to this particular parable, verses 14-20 are sufficiently clear. Note where Jesus laid the emphasis. Nothing at all was said about the identity of the sower. The seed was defined simply as the word, the message of the gospel. It was the soils which were dealt with at length, so presumably the main point is the various kinds of reception given to the message.

But whereas Jesus' words about this parable answered a question,

In May the grain harvest was ripe. The crops were cut with a sickle, which was sometimes saw-toothed, and the stalks were bound up in sheaves to dry.

what he said about his parables generally (in verses 11,12) raised problems rather than answered them. Many readers are offended by his apparent claim to be teaching in this way deliberately to mystify people, and to prevent their understanding. However, we have to accept that this is very nearly what he did say, as he quoted Isaiah 6:9-10.

Believers and unbelievers As some soils are receptive to the seed and others are not, so some people receive the word and others do not. Some are inside the circle of faith and others are outside (like Jesus' unbelieving relations; compare verse 11 with Mark 3:31-32). God's plan is that to the man who has faith, understanding also is given. From the man who has no faith, understanding must be withheld, in order that men may have enough room to make a personal decision. It is never God's intention to make the truth so clear that men have to accept it, even if they don't want to. To those who by faith are inside, 'everything' – the whole gospel – will be explained (verse 34). But to those whose unbelief keeps them outside, 'everything' is spoken in parables, which can be, and are, misunderstood (verse 11).

4:21-34 How the 'secret' will work out
Four short parables are grouped in these verses. Many such sayings of Jesus appear in the first three Gospels, in differing contexts. By recording these four in this setting, Mark seems to be indicating that the message of the kingdom, which many find such a mysterious secret, will not always be so.

A lamp, for example (verses 21,22), might for some reason be hidden temporarily. But it will in the end be brought out where all can see it, and be illuminated by it, for that is its purpose.

As the lamp will ultimately shine out, so the parable of the measure (verses 23-25) tells us that a bountiful return will be given to those who are prepared to heed the gospel. In the terms of verses 10-20, the man who has a believing heart will be given also an understanding mind.

'Jesus got up, rebuked the wind and said to the waves, "Quiet! Be still!" Then the wind died down and it was completely calm' (Mark 4:39).

The growing seed Thirdly, the sown field (verses 26-29) has a power of its own to produce results. Parallel with the day-to-day life of the farmer, the life of the seed is also progressing, much of it under the surface, till the harvest grows up for all to see.

The mustard seed The parable of the mustard ends the series (verses 30-34). As a seed, it is tiny and easily overlooked. As a full-grown shrub, it is so big (perhaps ten feet high) that birds nest in it as in a tree.

Did the disciples think it strange that so important a thing as the message of the kingdom should seem, when it came into the world, so obscure and insignificant? Probably that was one reason why they 'asked him about the parables' (verse 10). Jesus reassured them that one day his message *would* shine out, bring returns, ripen to harvest and spread its branches wide.

4:35-41 The stilling of the storm

Mark's version of the stilling of the storm includes several touches which suggest an account by an eyewitness. (He was presumably Peter; contrast Matthew 8:23-27; Luke 8:22-25.) This vivid story teaches something both about the disciples and about Jesus.

The fact that Jesus explained everything to them (verse 34) did not mean that the disciples understood everything, still less that they could cope with everything. It was in practical difficulties such as the storm described here that their lack of understanding was shown up. They betrayed a curious mixture of reverence and rudeness towards Jesus. They knew him well enough to believe that he could do something about the situation, yet they did not hesitate to say accusingly, 'Don't you care if we drown?' In parables earlier in this chapter he had been assuring them of the eventual triumph of his gospel of salvation, but what use was that if he could not help in their immediate predicament?

Jesus' power But he was of course in control in both realms, the natural as well as the spiritual. Here was a man able to sleep through a storm so violent that it terrified even a crew of experienced sailors. Even more wonderful here was a man able to rebuke and silence

Jesus sailed across the lake to the eastern shores, where he met the demoniac.

the storm (just as he did in cases of demon possession, for example see Mark 1:25).

This was not simply a miracle. It recalled the power which in Old Testament times could control sea and wind (compare for instance Psalm 65:7; 107:28,29). When the Red Sea obeyed such a command (Exodus 14:21), it was the Lord God of Israel whose power was thereby made known. No wonder on this occasion the disciples' 'were terrified, and asked . . . "Who is this?" ' (verse 41).

Here was the Lord whose power had been known and celebrated from the beginnings of his people's history, and the Saviour whose plan of salvation will culminate in the final deliverance from this world to the next. This was the Jesus who was with them in their immediate practical need.

5:1-20 The demoniac of Gerasa
Here is another kind of storm, which like that of the previous paragraph was quelled by Jesus' rebuke.

Why was the demoniac in this state? It was not his own fault; at least, he is not said to be responsible or to need forgiveness. It was partly the fault of the people of Gerasa, whose attitude must have aggravated his suffering. But the real cause of the trouble was the legion of demons that possessed him. It was with them that Jesus was chiefly concerned.

Legion Why their name? A Roman legion was a force of over 6,000 men; the number of demons in the man was certainly exceptionally large. But it may simply mean a horde of spirits all acting as one, like well-drilled soldiers. The actions of Jesus are revealing. If fear was the result of seeing the man seated, clothed and healed, it must have been because Jesus' deed seemed an impossible miracle. This in turn showed the extreme madness to which the demons had already driven their victim. What they would have gone on to do was demonstrated by the fate of the pigs. If we ask why Jesus did not banish the demons altogether, the answer may be partly that it was not yet time for the final defeat of evil. But verse 13 may also be Jesus' way of showing that the object of the powers of evil is not only to spoil, but ultimately also to destroy, the works of God.

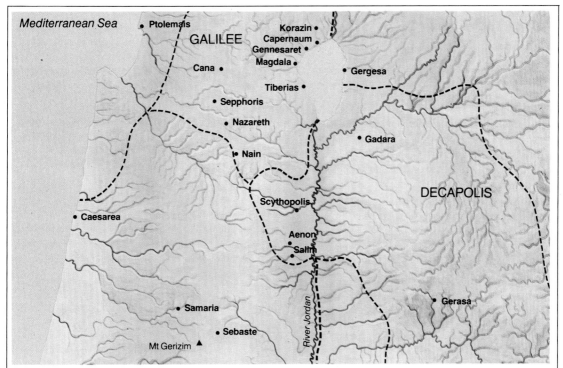

5:21-34 The woman with the haemorrhage

The story of the woman with the haemorrhage is sandwiched between the two halves of the story of Jairus' daughter. At the outset, the child was at the point of death. But though it was an emergency, Jesus' response had to be left till after the woman's need had been dealt with.

The woman's touch Apart from its impertinent tone, the disciples might have been excused their question in verse 31. But the woman's touch was in fact distinguishable in at least three ways from that of the many others who were jostling Jesus. First, it was deliberate, not casual; the woman hoped to obtain a cure by it, in a way that smacks of magic (results guaranteed by what *we* do). Secondly, since we cannot imagine the healing taking place thus automatically, the touch must have been backed by faith in Jesus. Thirdly, it did in fact have a result. 'Power had gone out from him'.

Jesus confronts the woman But Jesus would not let the woman go away under any misapprehension about what had happened. She was made to confront him and to hear his illuminating word (verses 33,34).

Mark gives his readers a yet fuller explanation. For he sets the incident in a series of four (the storm, the demoniac, this woman, Jairus' daughter), so that we may consider the kind of things Jesus was doing. On the one hand, Jesus dealt with human isolation: his disciples alone in the boat, the man driven out from society, the woman 'unclean' and untouchable, the dead child and the bereaved parents. On the other hand, Jesus confronted this as an evil which Satan had done, and showed again that he had come into the world to undo the works of the devil.

But we notice again that to none of these people was attributed any blame for their situation. Nothing was said about sin or forgiveness. All of them might have said with reason, 'Why has this happened to us?' Although as sinners we deserve nothing better, it is encouraging to know that Jesus can deal not only with sin and its consequences, but also with the evils we commonly call undeserved.

Capernaum

Capernaum

Capernaum was the town on the western shore of the Lake of Galilee where Jesus made his headquarters when he came into Galilee preaching the good news of the kingdom of God after John the Baptist's imprisonment. Here Simon Peter and Andrew lived (Mark 1:29) although, according to John 1:44, they originally came from Bethsaida. Jesus preached in the synagogue of Capernaum one sabbath day early in his Galilean ministry and impressed the congregation by the authority with which he expelled a demon from a possessed man. On the same day, 'at even, when the sun did set', he cured a great number of sick people, so that his fame spread throughout the town and into the surrounding countryside (Mark 1:21-45).

It was in Capernaum, too, that he cured the paralyzed man who was let down by his friends through a hole in the roof, and it was on the quayside of the town that he called Matthew to leave the collecting of taxes and follow him as a disciple (Mark 2:1-14).

It was in Capernaum that the centurion lived whose servant was cured by an authoritative word from Jesus spoken at a distance. This centurion is said to have built the local synagogue as a token of his friendship for the Jewish community. He was presumably a non-commissioned officer from the Roman army seconded to the service of Herod Antipas.

The synagogue

John tells us that it was in the Capernaum synagogue that Jesus delivered his discourse on the bread of life after the feeding of the five thousand (John 6:59). But as time went on Jesus was no longer so welcome as a preacher in the synagogue as he was at the beginning of his ministry. In particular, his insistence on healing people there on the sabbath, even while the service was in progress, was felt by the synagogue authorities to be intolerable. So the mountain slope and the lakeside had to serve as his auditoria, but there he was heard by greater crowds than could be accommodated in the synagogue.

It was to Capernaum that Jesus and the disciples repeatedly returned from journeys throughout Galilee. Here, probably, he raised Jairus' daughter from her deathbed (Mark 5:21-43); here he taught his disciples the lesson of humility by the example of the child whom he set in their midst (Mark 9:33-37); here he discussed with Peter the propriety of paying the Temple tax and set him to catch a fish to pay it for both of them (Matthew 17:24-27).

Capernaum, or Kefar Nahum, means 'the village of Nahum' – but it is not known which Nahum is meant. The Jewish historian Josephus says that its hinterland was very fertile; he records how its inhabitants played an active part in the revolt against Rome which broke out in AD66. But later its true location was forgotten for centuries.

The capital of one of the pillars of the second-century synagogue at Capernaum.

Capernaum

The most imposing landmark on the site is the magnificently or-namented two-storey synagogue of white limestone. Its style of architecture and decoration, together with dedicatory inscriptions, suggest that it was built about the beginning of the third century AD. It was not the synagogue in which Jesus taught, though it may have been built on the site of that earlier one.

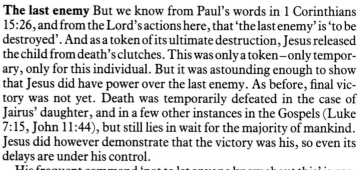

Although Nazareth was Jesus' home town, he did not make it his headquarters when his ministry began. His teaching in the Nazareth synagogue so angered the people that they tried to kill him. The town was located near to several important trade-routes.

A Roman sword of the period.

5:35-43 Jairus' daughter

Jairus' daughter really was dead, whatever Jesus might have meant by saying what he did. The friends by bringing the message, the mourners by their ridicule, and the parents by their amazement, made it plain that she was. All of them presumed that not even Jesus could cope with this situation.

Death is the last evil confronted by Jesus in this sequence of four: storm, demon-possession, sickness and death. Jairus had seen Jesus' victory in the third case, and the disciples had seen all the first three. Jesus could do great things; but could he do the greatest thing?

The last enemy But we know from Paul's words in 1 Corinthians 15:26, and from the Lord's actions here, that 'the last enemy' is 'to be destroyed'. And as a token of its ultimate destruction, Jesus released the child from death's clutches. This was only a token – only temporary, only for this individual. But it was astounding enough to show that Jesus did have power over the last enemy. As before, final victory was not yet. Death was temporarily defeated in the case of Jairus' daughter, and in a few other instances in the Gospels (Luke 7:15, John 11:44), but still lies in wait for the majority of mankind. Jesus did however demonstrate that the victory was his, so even its delays are under his control.

His frequent command 'not to let anyone know about this' is particularly strange in this case. How could such a thing possibly be hushed up? Perhaps he had in mind that while all would see the result, namely the resuscitated child, the details of the actual deed were to be private to parents and disciples – the believers, the 'insiders' (compare again Mark 4:11).

6:1-6 Nazareth rejects its greatest Son

Jesus' visit to 'his home town' could hardly be described as a success. There were no miracles to speak of. When we are told that he could not do such things there, we are to understand, not that he is ever less than all-powerful, but that miracles performed amidst utter unbelief would be mere shows of magic. This could not happen without making a nonsense of what he had come to do. As before (compare notes on Mark 4:11-12), Jesus would not put people in the position of having to acknowledge him even if they did not want to.

On the part of the people of Nazareth, there was no response. This was doubtless a later occasion than the visit described in Luke 4:16-30. The only close parallel is the proverb of verse 4, which Jesus could well have used more than once. There does seem to be a development in Jesus' reputation between Luke 4:22,23 and Mark 6:2-3. Nazareth had now come to disapprove of him. Every phrase used about him in verse 3 could have offensive overtones. What is more, this was the Nazarenes' general attitude: in verse 2 'many' is 'the many'.

But although the whole affair may seem a fiasco, it had its place in Jesus' overall plan. It completed the picture of his friends, his family and now his fellow-citizens 'standing outside' (Mark 3:31; compare Mark 3:21) and not accepting his claims.

The rejection at home resulted in the spreading of the gospel further afield. This incident was to be followed by the sending out of the Twelve. They in turn would be told to leave the unreceptive and to go on to preach to others (verses 10,11). Jesus' own final rejection, on Good Friday, would lead to the sending out of the church at Pentecost. Mark's readers were being taught to view their own troubles in the light of this broader plan.

6:7-13 The sending of the Twelve

The Twelve were sent out as Jesus' representatives. Their mission was an extension of his mission. This is clear first from the way Mark told the story. Jesus' ministry began in Mark 1:14. He preached the gospel by word and deed until opposition to it crystallized in a plan to destroy him (Mark 3:6).

From the start he had called disciples to be with him; and next he chose twelve of them (Mark 3:14), and through a second sequence of words and deeds he set about training the Twelve. Next, ever-increasing opposition culminated in his rejection at Nazareth (Mark 6:1-6). Now a third preaching of the gospel began, but this time the Twelve were doing it.

It is clear from the overall pattern of the story, and from the details, that the Twelve were Jesus' ambassadors. They had the same authority: their being sent in pairs implied that their witness was true, as his was (Deuteronomy 19:15; John 8:13-18). They had the same dependence on the Father.

The slightly different accounts in Matthew 10:9,10 and Luke 9:3 may be making the same point as Mark. They say that the Twelve were to rely on nothing at all except God, and Mark says that, with staff and sandals, the pattern of the Exodus was to be repeated (Exodus 12:11), in its utter trust in God. (We recall the 'desert' theme of Mark 1:12 and elsewhere.) They had the same programme: to preach repentance and restore the suffering, showing that God's plan of salvation dealt with both sin and evil. They caused the same effect: men were divided and judged according to their acceptance or rejection of the message. As Jews would shake off from their shoes the dust of a pagan land when they left it, so the Twelve declared that those who refused the gospel, whether Jews or not, were 'outsiders'.

6:14-29 John the Baptist beheaded

Since the death of his father, the Herod of Matthew 2:1, Herod Antipas had ruled Galilee and Perea. Unofficially, and in his own eyes, a 'king', he was strictly speaking only a tetrarch (ruler of one-quarter of the country). His wife Herodias had been married to his brother Herod Philip. John rebuked him because Philip was still alive (contrast Leviticus 18:16 with Deuteronomy 25:5). The girl, Salome, was their daughter, probably a teenager at the time of this incident, and later to be married to yet another of the Herods. The

Mark 6

The son of old parents (Luke 1) John emerged as a powerful preacher about AD27 (Luke 3:2,3). He knew he was called to be the promised forerunner of the Messiah (Isaiah 40:3-5; John 1:23) in the line of Elijah (Malachi 4:5,6; Luke 1:17). He centred his mission in the Jordan valley, linking his message with a baptism symbolizing repentance, dedication and preparedness for the Messiah's coming (Luke 3:3-17).

His cousin Jesus came to him for baptism; John recognized him as the Messiah (Matthew 3:13-17; John 1:32-34).

John had a few close disciples, several of whom left him to follow Jesus (John 1:35-42). John became puzzled about Jesus' mission, and was himself imprisoned for rebuking Herod over his marriage. (John 3:30; Matthew 11:2-6). John was beheaded in prison through the influence of Herod's wife (Matthew 14:1-12). Josephus says this happened at the fortress of Machaerus, east of the Dead Sea.

Jewish historian Josephus also tells the story, adding such details as the girl's name, the place (the palace of Machaerus, near the Dead Sea), and the political factors which made Herod imprison John.

Herod and Herodias Mark may have at least two reasons for telling this story at this point and at this length. For one thing, it fills in the background to Herod's reaction to the events of verse 13. They had raised the question 'Who is Jesus?' Most said, 'A prophet.' Herod, with his guilty conscience, thought he knew which prophet (this story tells us why). The same question underlies the next two or three chapters, and emerges again to be answered finally at Mark 8:27-29.

In addition, we may compare this passage with chapter 15. We see here, parallel to the passion of Jesus, a 'passion' of John. Herod, unwilling but cornered; malicious Herodias; Salome, prompted to make the actual demand; the soldier who did the deed – all have their counterparts in chapter 15, and lay down the pattern ('They have done to him everything they wished', Mark 9:13) for what was to happen to Jesus. Mark was preparing for the revelation of Jesus' identity and of his destiny. The suffering of the one who was altogether submitted to the Father's will is one of Mark's main themes in the second part of his Gospel.

6:30-44 The feeding of the five thousand

The immediate lesson of this, the only miracle narrated in all four Gospels, is that the Lord can provide for his people when they are in real need, and when their own resources are hopelessly inadequate.

But there is more to be learned than that. For instance, it was the busy ministry of the Twelve (verses 7-13,30,31) which led first to their being given rest, and then to the crowds being given food, in 'a solitary place'. The blessing of the Lord's people in general followed the faithful service of his servants.

The people found themselves out in the pastures ('green grass', verse 39). Men are led out of their old life to a 'desert', where they are alone with the Lord, become his people, and are blessed and fed by him – one of scripture's constant themes. The five thousand illustrated what it meant to be truly Israel, the people of God.

Mark 6

A simple bread oven was made from an inverted clay dish or shallow bowl, which was put on top of the fire, with its rim resting on a few stones. The thin round loaves of bread were placed on top of the dish.

Five loaves and two fish 'Sheep without a shepherd' comes from Numbers 27:17 and Ezekiel 34:5. In the first of those chapters a leader, Joshua, and in the second of them a provider, David, was promised to the wandering sheep. The quotation is apt because in each passage God was caring for them in the desert. Jesus was saying that this care was now to be found by coming into the desert to him.

Even this large-scale demonstration was designed so as not to compel the unwilling to believe. The fare was not exotic, just ordinary bread and fish – you could assume, if you wanted to, that it had come from some quite ordinary source. The sign which the people saw and which prompted them to 'make him king by force' (John 6:15) could have been merely his lavish provision for them. The miracle of how it had been done, which showed him to be not simply prophet (John 6:14) but Lord, was known only to the disciples. You have to believe in him before he will begin to prove himself to you.

6:45-56 Jesus walks on the water

There are two intriguing phrases found only in Mark's account of this miracle. First, the disciples' amazement at it was because 'they had not understood about the loaves' (verse 52). What had the feeding of the five thousand to do with Jesus' walking on the water? Mark implies that if they had understood the one, they would not have been surprised at the other.

Neither was a mere miracle. Both were 'signs'; and in a sense, both signified the same thing. In asking what they meant, we recall the other sea-miracle, when Jesus stilled the storm (Mark 4:35-41). That was one of a series in which the word of Jesus is shown to have power over all kinds of evil. But here it was not so much his word as his identity; less the power he had, than the person he was.

'Don't be afraid' 'Who is he?' is the underlying question from Mark 6:14 to 8:29. The loaves should have taught his disciples that the Lord who in the days of the Exodus had drawn his people into the wilderness, and there looked after them miraculously, was present again, still caring for his people. So they might have expected his care to be shown equally when they were in trouble on the sea.

Mark 6

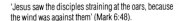

'He had compassion on them, because they were like sheep without a shepherd' (Mark 6:34).

'Jesus saw the disciples straining at the oars, because the wind was against them' (Mark 6:48).

This leads to the other strange phrase: 'he was about to pass by them' (verse 48). Some would translate this 'to pass their way'. But a more attractive suggestion recalls the same phrase where it occurs at two crucial places in the Old Testament. Both Moses and Elijah, those two key men, experienced the Lord's 'passing by'. It was not in the sense that he was going to ignore them and leave them, but as a mighty demonstration that he was present in his greatness and glory. His servants need not fear nor be discouraged, since he is in control (Exodus 33:19-22; 1 Kings 19:11). Faith is the key; verses 55,56 provide further examples.

7:1-13 Clean and unclean

Here is a new development. It was no longer simply that the Pharisees opposed Jesus, but why they opposed him. It was because two quite different systems were in collision, his new one and their old one (not the old original faith of Moses and Isaiah, which Jesus endorsed, but the Judaism that had grown out of it).

First, the new is bigger than the old. Notice the 'footnotes' which Mark attaches to the words 'unclean' and 'Corban' (verses 2-4,11). These are technical terms, understood by the initiated but needing explanation for the wider world for which Mark is writing. Judaism is for an exclusive community, Christianity for everyone.

The tradition of men Secondly, the new is more consistent. The Pharisees' religion was supposed to derive from the original law and the prophets. So Jesus appealed to these origins – to Moses (verse 10; Exodus 20:12; 21:17) and Isaiah (verses 6,7; Isaiah 29:13). He showed how far the Jews had departed from them. The 'tradition of the elders' was the 'tradition of men', and still worse, 'your tradition' (verses 5,8,9), eventually going so far that it actually contradicted God's law. For example, a man who designated his property 'Corban' (not available for normal use) did so on oath. And the rule about keeping oaths (Numbers 30:1,2,) nullified even the rule about caring for parents (Exodus 20:12). But when people make God seem to contradict himself, they show just how far from him they really are (verse 6). Those who truly love him will see that his word is all of a piece.

Most important, the new is deeper than the old. The hand-washing rules which began the dispute were only one example of the whole Pharisaic tradition which reached out through so many areas and down through the generations (verse 13). The trouble was that it dealt with merely the surface cleansing of surface defilement. To the deep need, and the deep answer, Jesus addressed himself in the section which follows.

7:14-23 The heart of the matter

What sparked off the disagreement between Jesus and the Pharisees in this chapter was the disapproval they expressed of his disciples' eating with unwashed hands (verse 2). His actual answer to their question is spoken here in verses 14-23. And he spoke not to them but to the crowds. What Jesus wanted to say should be heard by as wide an audience as possible. We can sense its importance from his solemn command to 'listen', and from the cryptic nature of his 'parable', which was designed to make them think (verses 14,17; in Mark 3:23 also the word 'parable' was used in this sense): 'What defiles a man is not what goes into him, but what goes out of him.'

Though many had heard the 'parable', only the disciples, inside the house with him, began to learn its double lesson. One vital truth concerns how we are to be reckoned clean in God's sight. Jesus shifted the emphasis from right deeds to right desires. Of course 'doing the right thing' is important. But it is no use making sure that we have clean hands – that our activities are properly moral or

Metal vessels were very expensive in Palestine in Jesus' time. Clay pots were cheaper, and were used by most ordinary people for their daily jobs.

Healing

When we look at healing in the New Testament, we find that the spiritual reality behind disease and the physical symptoms are often inseparable. Jesus says to the woman with a haemorrhage, 'Your faith has healed you' (Matthew 9:22). But he does not suggest that her physical ailment resulted from sin. In the case of the paralytic man, Jesus forgave his sins and told him to get up, take up his bed and walk (Mark 2:11).

It seems that illness might result from individual sin, but perhaps in most cases it is a symptom of humanity's fall from a perfect relationship with God.

Jesus' healing practices varied. Normally he used a word of command (Mark 2:11; 5:41) but on two occasions he used saliva as part of his cure for blindness (Mark 8:23; John 9:6). Healings such as the raising of Lazarus from the dead have no natural explanation; they are supernatural. But in the presence of Jesus, what is miraculous is also normal in the kingdom of God.

Demon possession is clearly distinguished from disease (Mark 1:32-34). Similarly, exorcism is distinct from healing (Matthew 10:8). In the Gospels, some people are healed by Jesus at a distance (for instance the nobleman's son of John 4:46-53), some close up, some without physical contact. Others Jesus touched (for example Jairus'

daughter in Mark 5:41) or they touched Jesus (Mark 5:27). Healing is immediate, and often linked with faith.

In John's Gospel, healings are not only mighty works but also signs. They point to the arrival of God's kingdom in Christ. Matthew links Jesus' miraculous healings with the prophecy of Isaiah 53:4 (Matthew 8:17). They show that Jesus was the promised Messiah (Luke 7:22).

Jesus promised his disciples that greater works would follow (John 14:12), namely that Jesus' power would spread through them to a wider waiting world. The book of Acts includes several healing miracles involving the disciples, for instance Paul's snake-bite (Acts 28:3-6).

Doctors or medicine are not invalidated. Jesus used natural means to heal; clay and spittle in Mark 8:23; John 9:6. Prayer and medical aid go together.

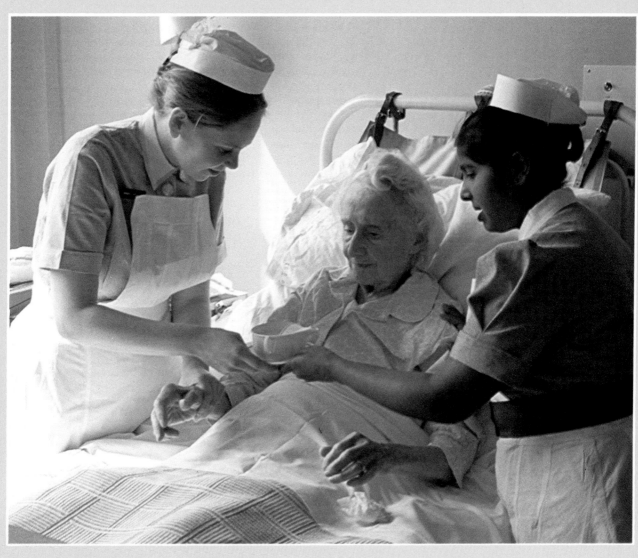

religious – if we do not first have a clean heart.

The second truth was harder. Mark here puts it in a footnote to his readers: 'In saying this, Jesus declared all foods "clean"' (verse 19). But even Peter did not grasp this till long after (Acts 10:9-29, 11:4-10, 15:7-11; Galatians 2:11-16), and Paul was still having to explain it in his letters (Romans 14:14,20; Colossians 2:16, 21-33). Only when it was understood that all Old Testament religious observance had been meant simply as a picture of spiritual realities, to be fulfilled in Christ, could the rightness of an action begin to be determined not by regulations but by principles. We are free to do whatever is in our heart, provided our heart is right.

7:24-30 The faith of a Greek woman

Jesus' reaction to the Syrian Phoenician woman may seem harsh, even rude. But it becomes understandable when we remember how many people had been seeking him merely for the miracles he performed. He needed to know whether this woman understood and trusted him for himself.

The remarkable thing was that she was a Gentile. She provided Jesus with a concrete example of what he had just been teaching (verses 14-23). If we are 'defiled', and therefore rejected by God, is it because we fail to keep the rules or because our hearts are not right? Here was a woman who was outside the rules altogether. Yet in her non-Jewish heart were faith and understanding lacked by most law-abiding Jews.

Outside Israel In this way Mark opens the door on an exciting new view of the gospel. If God was looking for something other than a keeping of the law, and found it in this woman who was right outside the law, then the gospel is available to the most unlikely people. The region Jesus was visiting was outside Israel. But wherever he is, and wherever he finds real confidence like that shown by the woman who accepts his words and follows up their implications, there will be found a blessing which is denied to those people who merely try to live by the rules.

She may possibly have taken 'children and dogs' to mean 'Jews and Gentiles'. On the other hand, she may have taken only the less

The Jews regarded the dog as an unclean animal. To call someone a 'dog' was an insult. When Jesus used the word with the Syrian Phoenician woman, he used a word meaning small pet dogs.

sophisticated point that she, an intruder, could not claim quite the same relationship to Jesus as those who were already 'in the house' with him (compare Mark 3:31-32). But in either case she grasped that both children and pets were dependants in the household. For those who depend wholly on him, the Lord will provide.

On his way back from the vicinity of Tyre, Jesus travelled through the region of the Decapolis.

7:31-37 A deaf and dumb man healed

Taking the handicapped man aside, Jesus 'put his fingers in the man's ears . . . spat, and touched the man's tongue' (verse 33). What was the meaning of the action? Not that Jesus's touch was magic, for it was his word of power which actually healed. Nor that onlookers needed it as a visual aid, for it was done in private. Perhaps it was simply a way of telling the deaf man what Jesus intended to do (particularly as saliva was thought to have healing properties; see also Mark 8:23).

What, more importantly, was the meaning of the miracle? Why does Mark record it – the only Gospel-writer to do so? It added another to the impressive number of Jesus' cures. But it was more than just another miracle. We might say that, like all the signs Jesus did, it had a spiritual significance which paralleled the physical event that had taken place. He himself tells us, for instance, that the healing of a blind man illustrates the fact that true 'sight' is his gift alone (John 9:1-7,39). So here, we learn that he can give the spiritual equivalents of hearing and clear speech.

The people are overwhelmed But the miracle means more than that. We have to account for the reaction of the crowds once the miracle was known, and ask why they were 'overwhelmed with amazement'. The clue lies in the rhythmic words that came to their lips. For these come from the prophecy of Isaiah 35:5,6. That passage, in its Greek version, is the only other place in the Bible where Mark's very unusual word for a speech impediment is found. This suggests a deliberate connection between the miracle and the prophecy. And the prophecy was generally thought to foretell what would happen when the Messiah came. In other words, people took the healing to be a claim that with Jesus the times of the Messiah had arrived. So a chapter and a half of the deeds of Jesus (Mark 6:31-7:37) are

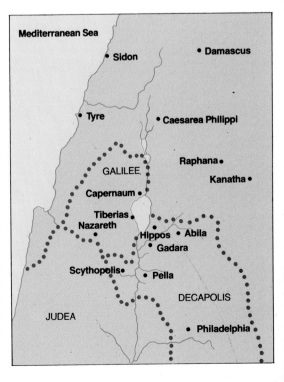

Caesarea Philippi

Over 9,000 feet high and usually capped with snow, Mount Hermon is situated on the border between Syria and Lebanon, close to the site of Caesarea Philippi. It seems probable that the Transfiguration took place here.

Some of the terracotta rock above Caesarea Philippi. Embedded in the cliffs from which the River Jordan emerges is part of the back wall of a temple to Pan.

Caesarea Philippi figures only once in the gospel story. At the end of his Galilean ministry Jesus took his disciples away into the territory east and north of Galilee, and came with them 'to the villages around Caesarea Philippi' (Mark 8:27). He is not said to have visited the city of Caesarea Philippi itself; its 'villages' stood in the surrounding region (Matthew 16:13), which it controlled. It was in this region that he asked his

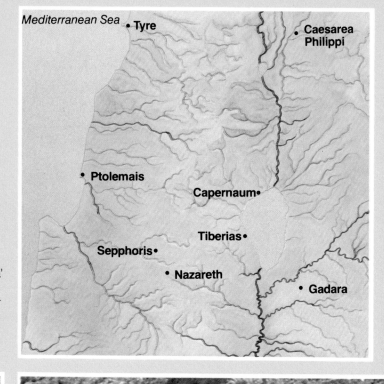

Mediterranean Sea • Tyre
• Caesarea Philippi
• Ptolemais
Capernaum•
Tiberias•
Sepphoris•
• Nazareth
• Gadara

disciples who people said he was and then asked them what account they themselves had to give of him.

Caesarea Philippi is the modern Banyas, standing on a terrace about 1,150 feet high, at the foot of Mount Hermon. Mount Hermon rises on the north-east to a height of 9,100 feet. The Nahr Banyas, one of the principal sources of the Jordan, springs from a cave in the cliff-face here, and waters the whole terrace.

In 64 and 63BC the district of Paneias, with the whole of Syria and Palestine, came under the control of Rome. In due course Paneias was added by the Emperor Augustus to the kingdom of Herod the Great, who acknowledged the gift by erecting a marble temple in honour of Augustus. When Herod died in 4BC, Paneias was included in the territory east and north of the lake of Galilee bequeathed to his son Philip

(mentioned in Luke 3:1). Philip refounded Paneias as the capital of his tetrarchy and, by way of compliment to Augustus, who had confirmed Herod's bequest, renamed the city Caesarea. To distinguish it from Caesarea on the Mediterranean seaboard of Palestine (founded by Herod several years before and named in honour of the same emperor), this was commonly known as 'Philip's Caesarea' – in Latin, 'Caesarea Philippi'. Philip was the most moderate of all Herod's sons who succeeded to parts of his kingdom – partly, no doubt, because his subjects were mainly Gentiles. When tension mounted in Galilee, and it became expedient for Jesus and his disciples to avoid the attention of Herod Antipas, it was easy for them to get into a boat and cross the lake into Philip's territory.

Twenty years after Philip's death (in AD34), his grand-nephew

the younger Agrippa (whom Paul could not altogether persuade to be a Christian) received Caesarea Philippi as the capital of his kingdom (which covered more or less the former tetrarchy of Philip). He gave it the new name Neronias, as a compliment, this time, to the Emperor Nero.

Not much of the ancient architecture of Caesarea Philippi remains intact: hewn stones are scattered all over the site.

The largest of the four sources of the River Jordan is located at Caesarea Philippi.

climaxed by public recognition that with him the promises were coming true.

8:1-13 Jesus feeds the four thousand

The similarities between the feeding of the 4,000 and the feeding of the 5,000 (Mark 6:35-44) are obvious. So too are the differences – the numbers of people, loaves, and fish, and the amount of food left over (seven large baskets instead of twelve small ones). It is perverse to see these as two versions of the same incident.

We can see a development from the first to the second incident. This feeding of a crowd from the mixed population of the Decapolis confirms the trend of chapters 7 and 8 towards an increasing sense of responsibility to the Gentiles.

In any case, Mark himself understood that there were two feedings (compare Mark 8:19-20). Indeed, compare Mark 6:31-7:37 with 8:1-30 and you will see that he reckoned an entire sequence of events to have been repeated: crowds fed, Pharisees rebuffed, bread discussed and infirmity healed. That is, he saw this as part and parcel of Jesus' own teaching method. And since the Lord did teach in this way, then the repetition of such a miracle is very likely, and not a mistake or an invention of Mark.

For not only in the Gospels do we find that the divine teaching covers the same ground again and again. Throughout his revelation God worked in this way. His written word is full of repetitions of the basic lessons concerning holiness and sin, judgement and grace.

The terebinth is a large tree which grows particularly in the north of Israel. It looks rather like the oak tree, and offers shade to people and animals.

8:14-21 The yeast of the Pharisees

Like the earlier feeding of a crowd, the one in Mark 8:1-10 leads on to an exposure of the Pharisees' unbelief and the disciples' lack of understanding (compare Mark 7:6,7; 17,18).

The trouble with the Pharisees was that they would only believe if given a 'sign' – not a miracle such as they had already seen, but something more, which would prove the miracles divine to their own satisfaction. This unbelief is like yeast in dough; it affects the whole of one's life. The trouble with the disciples was that they were preoccupied with their ordinary needs, and so teaching like this often passed them by. They heard what they wanted to hear, and presumably took Jesus' mention of yeast (verse 15) to refer to the bread they had forgotten.

For those with eyes to see, there was a plain message in the two bread-miracles, brought out especially clearly by the amounts left over. On both occasions they should have grasped what it was they were seeing and hearing (verse 18): namely, the abundant grace of God given to the world in his Son the Messiah (see comment above on Mark 6:45-56).

8:22-26 A blind man healed at Bethsaida

Amazing that the Pharisees should remember the facts, but miss the meaning? Not really; it simply highlights the total inability of even the most privileged people to grasp spiritual truth until God works a miracle in them. In the earlier sequence, the Syrian Phoenician

Unbelief

Mark 8

The Bible never finds any excuse for unbelief. We read that Jesus was 'amazed' by the lack of faith he met (Mark 6:6). It was the main sin of which Jesus told his disciples that the Holy Spirit would accuse and convict the world (John 16:9).

The reason for this is that unbelief amounts to making God a liar (John 5:10). It casts doubt on his integrity and character, thus amounting to blasphemy. It is for this reason that we find unbelievers and the faithless so severely judged (Luke 12:46; Revelation 21:8), for 'without faith it is impossible to please God' (Hebrews 11:6).

In the Bible, unbelief is always seen as rebellion, a moral rather than an intellectual problem (Hebrews 3:12). Where there is honest doubt, as in the case of John the Baptist (Luke 7:19-23), or the father of the epileptic boy (Mark 9:24), or Thomas (John 20:24-29), it was always dealt with gently by Jesus. In such instances, there was a great wish to believe, and it was the mind, not the will, that was at fault.

'When Jesus had taken the seven loaves and given thanks, he broke them and gave them to his disciples to set before the people' (Mark 8:6).

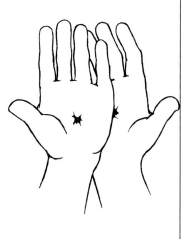

woman was enabled in this way to hear and speak truth. Her experience was vividly embodied in Jesus' healing of the deaf-mute; the result was recognition of Jesus as Messiah (Mark 7:24-37). In this chapter, the healing of the blind man points us back to the other half of the messianic prophecy of Isaiah 35:5,6. The result is similar, the great confession that Jesus is the Messiah which stands at the heart of Mark's Gospel (Mark 8:27-29).

But to acknowledge Jesus as Messiah, the disciples needed not only to see the facts, but to have their eyes opened to the meaning. To illustrate this, the healing of the blind man was, alone among the miracles, a two-stage process. It is only by the touch of Jesus that we come to see anything at all; but we need that extra touch to see things as they really are.

8:27-30 Peter's confession

The whole story so far had been moving towards the crucial event at Caesarea Philippi. Every possible hint had been given as to who Jesus was, and not one had been properly grasped, not even by those closest to him (verse 21). But now Peter's eyes were miraculously opened, as Mark says in one way and Matthew in another (verse 25; Matthew 16:17). The great title, hidden all the way from Mark 1:1 to 8:29, was at last uttered. The second half of the Gospel is concerned with unfolding the meaning of Jesus' messiahship. As the messianic Son of Man he must undergo the fate of the righteous sufferer of the Psalms and of the Servant of Isaiah (Psalm 22;69;118; Isaiah 50:4).

Mount Hermon, the remote mountain which is the most likely site of the Transfiguration.

8:31-9:1 Jesus predicts his death

At once its two chief implications are stated 'plainly' (verse 32). The Hebrew word 'Messiah' and the Greek word 'Christ' both mean 'anointed' – appointed. Whether Jesus was anointed as prophet, priest, king, or all three, is not the first point. Whatever his ultimate glory, first he was to suffer. This was what God had decreed, so to suggest otherwise was the kind of thing Satan would say (verse 33). Perhaps when Jesus told Peter to get behind him, he meant him to return to the humble, teachable position of a disciple.

What Peter had to learn was a second lesson, besides the necessity of Messiah's suffering. For the followers of Jesus, too, the cross must come before the crown. This is for all who would follow him (verse 34). A few of his hearers would be given a glimpse of the glory of the kingdom before they were called to follow the way of the cross. Jesus no doubt referred to the experience Peter, James and John would have in a week's time on the Mount of Transfiguration. Nevertheless the call is to give up one's life for the sake of Messiah, and only afterwards to receive it back again.

9:2-13 The transfiguration

All the disciples' assumptions had been upset by what Jesus said about the path of suffering which both the Messiah and his followers would have to tread. They (and Mark's readers, for whom suffering was a more immediate problem) needed reassurance that things would work out in the end; that there would be a crown after the cross. The transfiguration was a preview of Jesus' return in glory, designed expressly for their benefit (verses 2,4,7).

Mount Tabor, the traditional site of this event, is less likely than Mount Hermon, which is higher, remoter and more in accord with Jesus' withdrawal to the far-north region of Caesarea Philippi. It is a counterpart of Mount Sinai/Horeb, that other mountain of revelation in the far south, where both Moses and Elijah met God (Exodus 24; 1 Kings 19).

We are back in the atmosphere of Mark's earliest chapters, with the theme of the desert. There, far from the distractions of the world, things could be seen as they really were, and the voice of God clearly heard (see especially Mark 1:1-13, and Jesus' baptism).

Jesus carries his cross to Calvary: a carving on the Via Dolorosa in Jerusalem.

Rising from the dead Yet Jesus had said that such mountain-top experiences would be the exception, and that discipleship is normally a hard way. The disciples still found this incomprehensible. They could not square his gloomy talk of suffering, and having to rise from the *dead*, with the glorious Messiah they had just seen, and the prophecy about Elijah putting things right before Messiah comes (Malachi 4:5,6).

To their astonishment, they learned that even their idea of Elijah the great restorer had to be turned upside down. John the Baptist was the one who filled that role, as had been hinted at the time (Mark 1:2-8). The work of restoration was in fact his preaching of repentance. So far from a triumphant progress, even the new Elijah's way had been a way of suffering, with Herod and Herodias taking the roles of Ahab and Jezebel.

9:14-29 Healing a boy with an evil spirit

Another link between Jesus's transfiguration and his baptism was that each great experience of God was followed immediately by conflict with Satan. The conflict which follows is related to the recent mountain-top events also, since they left a group of the disciples temporarily without a leader. The result was that expectations of a miraculous healing were dashed.

The father had expected a cure for his son, who was dumb, deaf and epileptic. These were the symptoms; but the cause was demon

Characteristic red rock-face near Caesarea Philippi.

possession. He had brought the boy to the disciples, assuming that this would be as good as bringing him to Jesus himself (verses 17, 18). What is the point of being a disciple of Jesus if you can't pass on the blessings of Jesus?

Jesus agreed. He too would have expected the disciples to rise to such a challenge. One day they would have to manage without him, and would be left as his representatives in a world full of evil. But for the moment it seemed to him that they were no better than the 'unbelieving generation' around them. He stood alone over against everyone else: 'How long shall I stay with you?'

The disciples themselves had no doubt expected to be able to cure the boy. They had after all done such things before (Mark 6:7, 13). But perhaps that was the trouble. They reckoned that the power had been given them and was now at their disposal. But 'this kind can come out only by prayer'. Where they failed, the father succeeded – that is, in a cry for help out of helplessness, which is the essence of the prayer of faith. That is the way to see Jesus work even when he is not with you, says Mark.

9:30-37 Who is the greatest?

From its turning point at Caesarea Philippi, where the messiahship of Jesus was revealed with both its glory and its suffering, Mark's story begins to move steadily towards the cross. So does the band of disciples, journeying southward through Galilee.

Eight chapters of evidence about Jesus' identity lead up to the confession of Mark 8:29. For the next eight chapters those who have grasped who he is learned what that meant. Both on the road (verse 30) and 'in the house' (verse 33; remember Mark 3:31-35) it was with the disciples that Jesus was now chiefly concerned. Indeed the rest of chapter 9 is a series of loosely-connected lessons for them.

Glory The central lesson? As before, glory to come but humiliation first. To the first prophecy of the cross, at Caesarea Philippi, is now added a second. Verse 31 is plain enough, so the fact that the disciples 'did not understand' means that it was simply too extraordinary for them to take it in. Or it has been suggested that the Aramaic word Jesus used for 'kill' was ambiguous, like the 'lifted up' in John 12:32. If they thought he was foretelling exaltation, not death, that might account for their arguing about precedence in the coming glory.

They had the grace to be ashamed to admit what they had been talking about. But Jesus knew anyway, and based an important lesson on it. What makes a person truly great is humility.

9:38-50 Causing to sin

The rest of the collected sayings which begin with verse 33 are linked together less by logic than by word-association.

The first follows the disciples' complaint about an exorcism by a stranger. They were no doubt sore about their own recent failure in this respect (verse 18), and touchy about their special relationship with Jesus (Mark 3:14, 15). They did have such a relationship, but this did not mean that they were the only people allowed to do such deeds. Jesus permitted this one, called it a mighty work, and recognized it as done in his name.

Out of the incident he brought the great principle of verse 40. How do men show themselves to be 'for him'? Not only spectacular exorcisms, but even so humble a thing as the giving of a cup of water, if done for his sake, shows that the doer cannot be against Jesus. What matters is not whether the deed is great or small, but whether it is done for him. Perhaps verse 42 takes up verse 37. As Jesus there compared the Twelve to children, so here he expressed as much concern for these little ones – the exorcist, the water-giver – as for the self-important 'inner circle'.

'Whoever welcomes one of these little children in my name welcomes me' (Mark 9:37).

Children's concept of hell, as painted on a street hoarding.

Hell So to discipleship in general (verses 43-48). 'Hell' here means unquenchable fire, as Mark's footnote in verse 43 translates 'Gehenna'. Life means eternal life, explained by making 'kingdom of God' its parallel in verse 47. Cutting off your hand and so on means putting a stop to the things your hands do, the ways your feet go, the sights your eyes enjoy, if these betray you into sin.

The fire of hell in the next life (verse 48) leads to the thought of the fire of suffering in this life (verse 49). Some manuscripts explain this saying by adding another: 'Fire, that is suffering, is what "salts" Christians (in the sense that salt "salts" sacrifices, by making them fit to be offered to God).'

Then from the salt of sacrifice we move to salt as a preservative. If Christians, who are meant to affect the world for good, are themselves bad, like second-rate 'salt' which turns out to be full of impurities, which of their worldly neighbours will purify *them*? So, argumentative Christians, behave yourselves!

'Salt is good, but if it loses its saltiness, how can you make it salty again? Have salt in yourselves, and be at peace with each other.' (Mark 9:50). Salt is deposited on the shores of the Dead Sea.

10:1-13 Divorce

Marriage, appropriately followed by children, is the subject of Jesus' teaching here.

The question about divorce was not so much whether, as when, the law of Moses might allow it. Two noted rabbis differed in their interpretation of Deuteronomy 24:1. Shammai restricted the grounds of divorce; Hillel would permit it for numerous reasons, some quite trivial. For Jesus the test (verse 2) was that whichever side he took, he would be discredited with the other party.

Jesus however aimed to make them think about what was originally commanded, not what was subsequently allowed. 'Since you break the law anyway, Moses tells you how best to pick up the pieces. But I remind you not of what follows from the law, but of what lies behind it' (verses 5-9). So Jesus went back to the very start of the 'law of Moses' (Genesis 1:27, 2:24). Indeed his 'let man not separate' had a ring of authority about it, quite unlike the scribes' teaching. It echoed the great 'Let there be' commands of the creation story.

Jesus was, if anything, siding with Shammai, but on such basic principles that no one dared to disagree with him. On these principles he established not only that marriage is indissoluble (verse 9) but that husband and wife have equal responsibility to make it work (verses 11,12).

Something else underlies the discussion on divorce. Jesus was in Perea, Herod's territory (verse 1). His words in verse 12 are a direct comment on the conduct of Herod's wife. For saying the same thing, John had been executed (Mark 6:17-29). But Jesus was in any case on his way to the cross, and in no circumstances now would he mince his words, or teach anything other than plain, fundamental truth.

10:13-16 Little children and Jesus
What Jesus said about children is similar in tone. They, or those who brought them, were regarded by the disciples as simply a nuisance. Again Jesus penetrated this thoughtless attitude to uncover principles. The deepest truth about a child is that it is a model for entry to the kingdom of God. It is mere sentimentality to imagine that he was talking about the child's supposed 'innocence'. What really is true of every child is that it is helplessly dependent. This is the basic qualification for entering the kingdom.

'Anyone who will not receive the kingdom of God like a child will never enter it' (Mark 10:15).

10:17-27 The rich young man

It was very unusual to call someone 'good teacher'. Most Jews would have responded as Jesus did in verse 18. This strange verse is actually a key to the whole passage. Jesus was telling the young man: 'You might use such language less readily if you grasped what real goodness is; and for that you must look to God.'

God's goodness is seen first in the law, which shows us what we ought to do. This the questioner understood (verse 17). But when we discover that such goodness is beyond us, he sends us the gospel. This shows us that goodness is something we have to receive as a gift from him (as in verse 15).

The peril of riches General amazement followed Jesus' words on the peril of riches, because wealth was taken to be a sign of blessing. It showed that you must already have achieved God's favour, and it gave you the wherewithal to be generous and so gain more of his favour. Yet Jesus called it a positive hindrance. No wonder the disciples asked 'Who then can be saved?' The whole basis of acceptance by God was being cut away.

Perhaps the rich man had glimpsed this already. He had achieved something, but it seems to have brought him no assurance. So Jesus said, 'If you want eternal life, you must give up these things, and follow me.'

To be able so to abandon oneself to Jesus is not natural, indeed not possible. We are all incapable of giving up anything. Think of the camel and the needle's eye, and don't tone down the idea by saying that 'camel' should be 'rope', as some say, or that the 'needle's eye' was a narrow gateway. The thing is as impossible as getting the biggest creature in Palestine through the smallest opening you can imagine. But God can, and does, do the impossible.

10:28-34 Jesus again predicts his death

Peter boasted 'Unlike the rich man, we have left everything that might earn us eternal life' – as if that leaving everything would in itself earn them life.

But whatever was in Peter's mind, he had the nub of the matter. The disciples would indeed find life in the age to come, according to

Crime and punishment

Crime and Punishment

When a Jewish law court pronounced its verdict, punishment followed immediately. The judge himself, the witnesses and others in court joined to carry out the sentence.

The death sentence was common. To sentence someone to death, there had to be two or three witnesses (Deuteronomy 17:6; 19:15). Death was normally by stoning; see Exodus 17:4; Acts 7:58.

In Israel, capital punishment was used in cases of:
breaking the sabbath laws (Exodus 31:13-14)
blasphemy against the name of God (Leviticus 24:11-16)
image-worship (Deuteronomy 17:2-7)
to preserve the nation from the bad influence of rebellious sons (Deuteronomy 21:18-21).

In cases of murder or manslaughter, the family or relatives of the dead man used to settle matters with the murderer's family by blood vengeance (Deuteronomy 19:2; 2 Samuel 14:6). Vengeance could not exceed the original injury (Exodus 21:12, 23-25; Leviticus 24:17-20).

Prisons were used mainly for keeping the suspect or criminal under arrest until he was brought for trial. The prisoner might be put in the stocks inside or outside the prison.

Whipping or flogging was a common form of punishment. The Jewish law limited flogging to forty strokes; in practice flogging was thirty-nine strokes, lest the counting was wrong. For flogging, whips, canes or sticks were used.

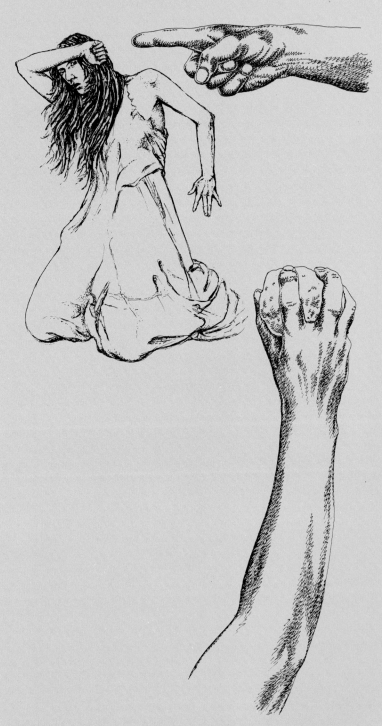

Jesus' words to the rich man (verses 17,21). They had grasped one central truth of the gospel. Now they needed to be reminded of another, the nature of the life of the disciple in this age. On the one hand, there would be renunciation, persecution and suffering, but on the other hand there would be great rewards. We notice that those who have given up houses or brothers or sisters will get back far more – houses and brothers and sisters.

So we are once again shown basic truths: life in this age and what it is like, life in the next age and how it is obtained. It is all upside down by worldly standards (verse 31).

Meanwhile for Jesus too, following his Father's will meant suffering and the loss of all things. For the third time he foretold the cross. Here first Jerusalem is indicated as his goal. Following the pattern set in prophecy for the obedience of God's servant, he set his face like a flint (Isaiah 50:5-7). On his carrying out of his Father's will everything depended. Unless he himself left all and went to the cross, there would be no eternal life for anyone.

10:35-45 The request of James and John
Again, the disciples betrayed their gross misunderstanding of Jesus' teaching, as they had done after the previous prediction of the cross (Mark 9:30-32). We shall not wonder at their dullness when we remember how easily our own thoughts slip from the sublime to the foolish. And the conceited request of James and John did arise from a truth, however garbled: they had at least grasped that they would

'Many who are first will be last, and the last first' (Mark 10:31).

Jesus now led his disciples steadfastly to Jerusalem, by way of the barren road from Jericho, leading through the Judean wilderness.

one day be with him in glory. But they had no more idea what they were saying in verse 39, about the cup and the baptism, than they had in verse 37, as Jesus told them. He was speaking of the judgement which awaited him (the cup) and which would overwhelm him (the baptism). In one sense, the fate of the cross was his alone; in another, it would be the lot of all his disciples. But James and John understood neither meaning.

Back to basics So Jesus gathered the whole group – the rest, indignant because James and John had got in first, were no better – and patiently took them back once more to the principles. For again it was the reversal of worldly values they had to learn. As with dying or living (Mark 8:35), being last or first (Mark 9:35, 10:31), being poor or rich (Mark 10:21,29,30), so now in the matter of greatness or humiliation, the truth is the opposite of what the world thinks. Values 'among you', the people of God, must be the opposite of those held by the Gentiles, meaning all who do not belong to his people.

In this particular reversal the pattern of greatness was to be Jesus himself. Though he was Lord he was also Servant – in fact the latter qualified him to be the former (Philippians 2:7,9,11). Jesus in turn followed the pattern of the Servant in Isaiah 53. The cross has the same double meaning when regarded as Jesus' service as it did when thought of as his cup and his baptism. In one sense it is unique: only he could die 'as a ransom for many'. Yet it is also an example: we are to be prepared for the humiliation of service, because Jesus came to serve (verse 45).

10:46-52 Blind Bartimaeus meets the Messiah

As he left the ancient city of Jericho, Jesus came within earshot of the blind beggar known simply as the son of Timaeus. So it is that Mark translates the Aramaic name 'Bar-Timai' for the benefit of his non-Jewish readers.

But in fact the whole incident has an important Jewish background. Although Bartimaeus' cry 'Son of David' does not necessarily mean that the beggar believed Jesus to be the coming messianic king, Mark's readers will with hindsight certainly read that meaning back into it. Once Jesus is recognized as Messiah, such a title is seen to be altogether apt, and all the circumstances fit meaningfully into place.

'Son of David' The messianic claim was not now to be hushed up, as it was in Mark 8:30, for Jesus was on his way to declare himself publicly at the gates of Jerusalem. Perhaps the throwing aside of Bartimaeus' cloak meant that it had been spread open before him to receive alms. If so, the coming of Messiah will do away with the need to beg. Having shown his faith by his persistence, he was then encouraged to put his desire into words. And he was duly healed.

Both the 'cheering up' and the healing (verses 49,52) figure in prophecies of the coming Messiah (for instance Isaiah 35:4,5). It is as though Mark is putting together the essential parts of the picture. He has already said that there will be glory, but that there must first be a cross. Then he says that while this meant self-sacrifice on Jesus' part, it would require similar sacrifice from the disciples as well. Now he reminds them of what they had earlier seen, but could have forgotten – that Messiah's coming will in the end (and also on the way) bring healing, salvation and joy.

Model disciple So Bartimaeus is in several ways a model disciple. Till Jesus came, he had sat useless beside the way; now he could follow him on it (verses 46,52). That is, he joined the pilgrims as they went up to Jerusalem, praising God for what he had been enabled to see.

'They went and found a colt outside in the street, tied at a doorway' (Mark 11:4).

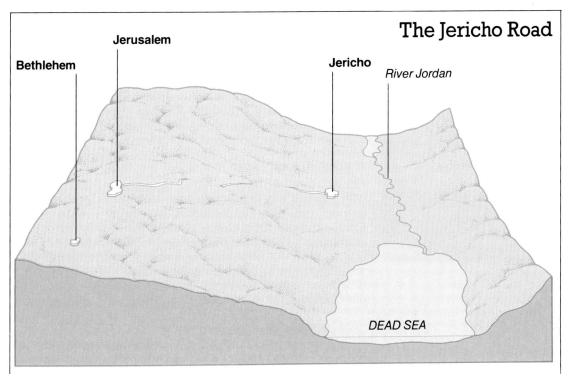

Bethlehem

Jerusalem

Jericho

River Jordan

DEAD SEA

11:1-11 The arrival at Jerusalem

Detailed preparation lies behind the events of Palm Sunday. In the practical sense, arrangements seem to have been made in advance for borrowing the colt. Maybe the disciples were told to say 'The owner needs it and will be returning it at once', the owner being with Jesus' company at the time.

In another sense, prophecy had long ago prepared for this great day. The outstanding reference is Zechariah 9:9, which speaks of the coming of Zion's king, his riding on an ass, and the city's rejoicing. Zechariah had also spoken (14:1-9) of the revealing of Messiah's glory on the Mount of Olives. Although that belongs to the end of the age, this prefigured it.

Blessed is he who comes Other Old Testament scriptures may well have come to the minds of some who witnessed these events. Psalm 118:25,26 was actually quoted: 'Blessed is he who comes in the name of the Lord'. 'He who comes' might also be the mysterious person of Genesis 49:10, especially since that passage goes on to mention his tied colt, and Mark seems at pains to note the untying of the animal. Furthermore, animals which had not been put to ordinary use were especially appropriate for a special use of this kind (compare Deuteronomy 21:3; 1 Samuel 6:7).

In spite of all this, the fulfilling of Scripture was still not so unmistakable that people had to believe it. 'Blessed is he who comes', certainly, and 'Blessed is the kingdom', but the first might mean any pilgrim. Even if it meant Jesus, it did not necessarily mean that Jesus embodied the kingdom. Although Zechariah 9:9 was coming true before their eyes, his enemies were not forced to accept the fact.

11:12-19 Jesus clears the Temple

There is one quotation (Isaiah 56:7) and one allusion (Jeremiah 7:11) in this passage (verse 17). But Jesus' cleansing of the Temple had a great deal more Old Testament background than that. Behind the trading lay the need to provide pilgrims with the right coins for the Temple tax and the right animals for sacrifice.

But it was the Court of the Gentiles that was being used for this. Behind Jesus' anger was the fact that Gentiles were being hindered

Pigeons or doves were used as the poor man's sacrifice at the Temple

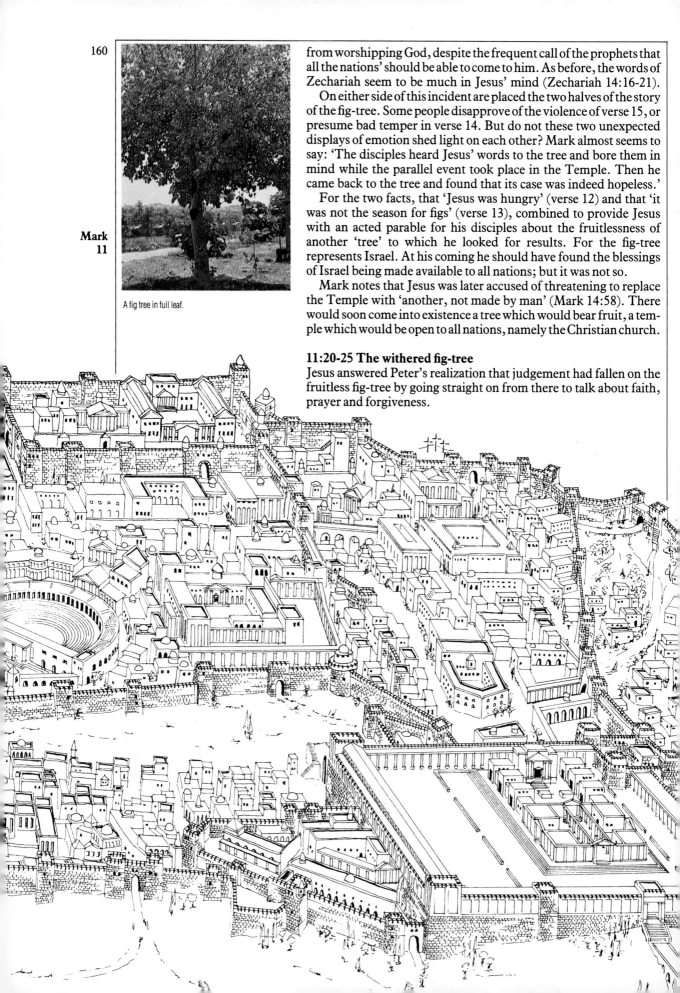

160

Mark 11

A fig tree in full leaf.

from worshipping God, despite the frequent call of the prophets that all the nations' should be able to come to him. As before, the words of Zechariah seem to be much in Jesus' mind (Zechariah 14:16-21).

On either side of this incident are placed the two halves of the story of the fig-tree. Some people disapprove of the violence of verse 15, or presume bad temper in verse 14. But do not these two unexpected displays of emotion shed light on each other? Mark almost seems to say: 'The disciples heard Jesus' words to the tree and bore them in mind while the parallel event took place in the Temple. Then he came back to the tree and found that its case was indeed hopeless.'

For the two facts, that 'Jesus was hungry' (verse 12) and that 'it was not the season for figs' (verse 13), combined to provide Jesus with an acted parable for his disciples about the fruitlessness of another 'tree' to which he looked for results. For the fig-tree represents Israel. At his coming he should have found the blessings of Israel being made available to all nations; but it was not so.

Mark notes that Jesus was later accused of threatening to replace the Temple with 'another, not made by man' (Mark 14:58). There would soon come into existence a tree which would bear fruit, a temple which would be open to all nations, namely the Christian church.

11:20-25 The withered fig-tree
Jesus answered Peter's realization that judgement had fallen on the fruitless fig-tree by going straight on from there to talk about faith, prayer and forgiveness.

Although it is not easy to see, Mark presumably makes a connection between God's judgement on the tree (and Jesus' anger in the Temple) and God's answers to prayer. It was certainly the power and authority of God that the disciples had just witnessed in both incidents. Perhaps the connection is that when we pray with undoubting faith (verse 24) and with forgiving hearts (verse 25), we shall receive not simply answers, but answers which are in some way like those recent happenings.

11:27-33 Jesus' authority questioned

Jesus' actions with regard to the tree and the Temple were clearly linked with the fact that God was visiting his people. Messiah was present and active, as Scripture had said he would be. To pray in faith is to align ourselves with what Scripture tells us is God's purpose and God's plan.

The casting of a mountain into the sea may be more than simply a vivid example of the impossibilities which believing prayer can achieve. The mountain may be Olivet, where they were standing, and the sea may be the Dead Sea, visible from it. The words may be meant to recall once more the words of Zechariah – not just 4:7, but the levelling of that very land, which the prophet spoke of as one of the mighty events of the Day of the Lord (Zechariah 14:4-9;10).

The Jewish leaders, out to trap Jesus yet again, were again hoist with their own petard. They must have known in their hearts that John the Baptist had divine authority. But if they admitted that, they

Mark 11

' "Have faith in God," Jesus answered. "I tell you the truth, if anyone says to this mountain, "Go, throw yourself into the sea," and does not doubt in his heart . . . it will be done for him" ' (Mark 11:22, 23). On a clear day, you can see the Dead Sea from Jerusalem.

The Damascus Gate into old Jerusalem.

162

Grapes were pressed in a special press usually hewn out of the rock. The ripe grapes were put in the tub, and one or more people trod them under their bare feet, to burst the skins and make the grape juice run out. The work was done amid singing and clapping. The juice ran through channels into a vat where it was collected.

The walled vineyard was often guarded by a watchman in a tower. The guardtower might be built of stone, but was usually simpler in construction.

would have had to admit that Jesus had the same authority – that the things they were witnessing were the acts of Messiah. The Day of the Lord had, in a sense, already begun.

12:1-12 The rebellious tenants

Compared with earlier parables, this one has new and disturbing features. For one thing, it looks in some ways more like an allegory. The vineyard's owner is God, the son is Jesus, and the tenants are the Jewish leaders. But the details cannot all fit. The fond hopes of verse 6 may be the owner's, but they are surely not God's. Neither would the chief priests have assumed what the tenants presumably did – that the owner must have died, so that if the son died too, they could legally claim the vineyard.

No; this is a true parable, with one main point. The details simply set the scene, even though more of them than usual turn out in allegorical manner to fit the facts.

The scene they set is a typical Galilean estate, with its absentee landlord requiring rent in kind. But Mark frames the story between two references (verses 1,9) to Isaiah 5:1-7. He shows Jesus departing from his usual custom. Speaking to the Jewish leaders, he uttered the parable explicitly 'against them' (verse 12), since they knew that the vineyard in Isaiah 5 meant Israel.

They drew the obvious conclusion; and this too was a new development. Still Jesus had made no unequivocal claims about himself. Verse 9 might be taken to refer merely to the owner, not to God. The owner's son might be thought to mean simply the last messenger, and not necessarily the Son of God.

But it was increasingly hard even for the wilfully blind enemies of Jesus to miss the meaning of what he was saying, especially when he underlined it with yet another scripture (Psalm 118:22-23). They perceived at last a gleam of the truth, and it strengthened their determination not to accept it. The only person who can understand a parable is one who is willing to accept or reject its message. The parable-teller says bluntly, 'If the cap fits, wear it'.

12:13-17 The question about Roman taxes

By this, the first of a series of questions to Jesus, the plot against him was further advanced. The questioners' hypocrisy (verse 15) was obvious as soon as they opened their mouths. The very compliments they paid were designed to force Jesus to commit himself one way or the other – to forfeit his popular support by approving of Roman taxes, or to risk official condemnation by disapproving of them. Those who supported Herod, who ruled with Roman backing, naturally upheld the system; while the Pharisees, though they accepted it, resented it. But they were prepared to make common cause against Jesus; no longer simply to test him (Mark 8:11; 10:2), but now actually to trap him (verse 13).

By Jesus' answer, however, not only was the plot foiled for the time being, but his reputation was further enhanced. He said in effect: 'The picture and the wording on this coin are Caesar's. Since you are prepared to use it' (they had no difficulty in producing it) 'you are recognizing that the coinage itself belongs to him. Whatever you reckon is due to him, that you must pay to him.' In this way he threw the question back to them, together with the responsibility for working out its implications. Those who had intended to trap him were themselves trapped. His talk, far from betraying him, amazed them (verses 13,17).

But he said more. In his reply, disciples were further instructed. Caesar has a place in God's world, and some things do belong to him. What is due to him, we pay. Here, in embryo, is the doctrine of the state, to be amplified in such passages as Romans 13:1-7. But God has his rights also, and they are paramount.

Messiah

The word 'Messiah' was the title used by the king. It is a Hebrew word meaning 'the anointed one'. When the king was set apart for his office, he was anointed with oil. This symbolized his receiving God's Spirit, wisdom to rule and lead his people, and power to defeat his enemies. Priests and perhaps prophets were also anointed (2 Samuel 2:4; 1 Kings 19:16; Exodus 28:41).

The idea of a Messiah is found quite early in Israel. King David was seen as the greatest of the kings of Israel. The Messiah was to come from his family; so in the first place he would be the Messiah of Israel (Amos 9:11-15; Hosea 3:5).

It was primarily the prophets in the Old Testament who repeatedly reminded the people about the Messiah. They taught Israel that the Messiah one day would come and set up his perfect kingdom (Jeremiah 23:5-8; Ezekiel 23:5-8). The people looked forward eagerly to what they considered to be the nation's golden age, referred to as 'that day' or 'the day of the Lord'. When the nation fell into corruption and evil, the prophets had to remind them that it would also be a day of judgement (Amos 5:18-20). For centuries Israel looked forward to a spiritual or national deliverer; both these ideas were strong when Jesus was born.

One of the most important ideas of the New Testament is that Jesus is the Messiah, fulfilling the Old Testament expectations (John 4:25,26). He is also the Prophet, Priest and King (Hebrews 7-10).

Jesus was of the family of David, and was born in David's city, Bethlehem. Jesus did not speak openly about himself as the Messiah. But when the high priest asked: 'Are you the Christ?' Jesus answered 'I am' (Mark 14:61,62).

At Caesarea Philippi Peter said that he believed Jesus was the Christ (Matthew 16:13-17; John 4:21-26).

Through his death on the cross, Jesus showed that the Messiah had to die at the hands of men, as he had warned his followers (Jeremiah 14:8; 1 John 4:14). This went clean against the political and national hopes of many Jewish people.

Jesus as Messiah/Christ is ruler of the kingdom of God. This kingdom will stretch across the boundaries of Israel and not be tied to any one people or country.

Messiah

'Jerusalem, Jerusalem, you who kill the prophets and stone those sent to you. . . . For I tell you, you will not see me again until you say, "Blessed is he who comes in the name of the Lord" ' (Matthew 23:37, 39).

Roman coin of the Emperor Tiberius.

By adding the second half of his reply (verse 17), Jesus was saying, 'Your question left out the vital matter of ultimate authority'. The rule of the state is there for our benefit, but we are not to regard it uncritically – especially when it begins to direct our lives in ways that deviate from the way of God (verse 14).

12:18-27 The question about the resurrection

Here, for the first time in Mark, the Sadducees appear. Being the 'establishment', a priestly aristocracy which collaborated with the Roman government, they were as concerned as the Pharisees to silence Jesus. Their question seemed designed, however, not to trap him but merely to ridicule him – over a matter in which both the people and the Pharisees would have sided with Jesus. Perhaps we are meant to see less his escape from a series of snares than his supremacy in every encounter, whatever its motive.

Their question has two aspects. It was ostensibly about marriage. The principle of 'levirate' marriage, which the Sadducees' example illustrates, was part of Moses' law (Deuteronomy 25:5-10). But the question was really about resurrection. They sat loose to all Scripture except the law of Moses, and even that they interpreted rationalistically: 'We can't believe the fact of resurrection, and we're sure that Moses didn't either, because levirate marriage (for example) would make it so ridiculous'.

Jesus' answer This leads directly to the two aspects of Jesus' answer. He said they were simply wrong. Wrong about the manner of the resurrection, because they did not know the power of God; and about the fact of it, because they did not know the Scripture.

Beyond this world, God's power has brought into being another, where life is like that of the angels (something else the Sadducees didn't believe in!) – life without end, service without pain, love without limit. Relationships of a depth which for us is limited to marriage will there be known universally, without restriction.

As to the fact of the resurrection, Jesus turned to Moses, whom they had used to discredit the idea, and referred them to 'the account of the bush' (Exodus 3:6). In effect, he said: 'God reminds Moses that he made a covenant with the fathers of Israel. Though they had long been dead, that covenant guaranteed that the ever-living God would never let them down. No enemy, not even the last enemy, death, could break their relationship with him. So he rightly said not "I was", but "I am" their God. Because he is alive now, they also must be.'

12:28-37 The two last questions

The Pharisees' and Herodians' question arose from ill-will, the Sadducees' from unbelief. By contrast, the scribe's question appears to be sincere. In reply, Jesus quoted Deuteronomy 6:5 and Leviticus 19:18. He included the preface to the first of these – 'Hear, O Israel, the Lord' – reminding his hearers that God had spoken to them, loved them and made them his covenant people. That is the meaning of his name YHWH, the Lord. What was asked of them was their devotion to him, in a personal relationship of love, responding to his grace. All other laws are not things we must do to gain his approval, but simply aspects of that response. So the scribe, though he did not ask for it, was given a second commandment, since loving God means that we shall want to regard everything and everyone else as he regards them.

Jesus asks a question Jesus' questioners having been silenced, the remaining question was put to them by him. He raised an issue as central as the one just raised by the scribe. The latter concerned the relationship between God and man. Jesus took the same crucial matter one step further, to the means by which that relationship is made possible. He re-focused attention on himself as Messiah and as Redeemer.

The scripture Jesus now quoted (Psalm 110) was recognized as dealing with the Messiah. In what sense did the scribes speak of Messiah as David's son? Like most Jews, they saw him as a descendant of David, on David's throne, with the same kind of power as David's; in other words, a political king. But in David's prophetic vision, his great descendant was called his lord, *adonai*. He is enthroned not in Jerusalem but at God's right hand on high. Messiah's victories would be greater than David's, primarily spiritual, not political. They would make available to all men the relationship with God spoken of at the start of our passage. No wonder 'the large crowd listened to him with delight' (verse 37).

12:38-44 The widow's offering

Mark did not add these closing verses simply because of a superficial association of ideas (scribes in verse 35 remind him of verse 38, and widows in verse 40 remind him of verse 42). All the questions of this chapter were essentially about God; what he said, and what he really required.

In teaching scripture, the scribes held a key position. This was generally accepted, and they were honoured for it. They were distinguished by their dress, and were the objects of public respect and private generosity.

A Pharisee and a Sadducee in characteristic dress.

The Dome of the Rock now occupies the area once taken up by Herod's Temple. 'As he was leaving the Temple, one of his disciples said to him, "Look, Teacher! What massive stones! What magnificent buildings!"
"Do you see all these great buildings?" replied Jesus. "Not one stone here will be left on another; every one will be thrown down" ' (Mark 13:1,2).

The massive masonry arches forming the undercroft to the Western Wall of the Temple.

Scribes condemned But, with exceptions such as the questioner of verses 28-34, most Jewish scribes fell under the condemnation of Jesus. How easy it was for them to begin to desire respect and distinction, and sponge on the hospitality of poor people. And how ironic that those who were immersed in the teachings of scripture, which are designed to fix the heart upon God, should become so concerned about the praise of men and the satisfaction of self. It was because their calling was so honourable that they merited such severe punishment.

The Temple treasury On his way out of the Temple, Jesus stopped by the great trumpet-shaped collecting boxes. There he saw someone who provided him with a perfect contrast to the scribes, and a summary of all he had been saying. A woman put into the treasury two *lepta* (the equivalent of one *quadrans*, your smallest coin, explains Mark in a footnote to his Roman readers). Somehow, Jesus knew both that she was a widow, and also that this was all the money she possessed.

The lesson for Jesus' disciples was that the amount of one's giving was not the important thing. What mattered far more was how much it represented of one's total wealth; or, if you like, how much one had left. Behind that is the absolutely basic question, which underlies also all the discussions of this chapter, which causes the widow to stand out in such contrast to the scribes, and which we have to ask ourselves: How totally am I devoted and submitted to God, his truth, his word and his demands?

13:1-13 What is to come

The disciples may not have been altogether taken aback at Jesus' prophecy about the Temple's doom. His earlier quotation about its being a den of robbers (Mark 11:17; Jeremiah 7:11) may have reminded them that the prophecy goes on to speak, like many others, of judgement on the city of God.

At any rate, the discourse which takes up this whole chapter, perhaps the most difficult in the Gospel, re-states on the grand scale the now familiar theme of 'tribulation before glory'. Immediately impending was Jesus' passion and at the far end of the vision which he

The Roman Emperors

Octavius Caesar was dubbed 'Augustus' meaning 'majesty' in 2BC, soon after he had defeated Mark Antony and Cleopatra of Egypt at the great sea-battle of Actium. Augustus was the Roman Emperor at the time of the birth of Jesus. His reign, which lasted till AD14, was a period of great strength and stability for the Roman Empire.

Tiberius, Augustus' grandson, reluctantly took over from him in AD14 at the age of 56. He continued Augustus' policies, but without enthusiasm or imagination, and eventually withdrew to retirement on the island of Capri. It is 'Tiberius' who is meant whenever 'Caesar' is mentioned in the Gospels.

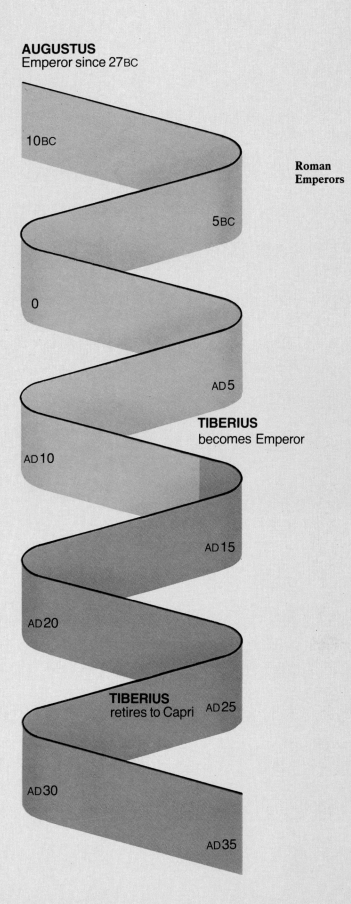

AUGUSTUS
Emperor since 27BC

10BC

Roman Emperors

5BC

0

AD5

TIBERIUS
becomes Emperor

AD10

AD15

AD20

TIBERIUS
retires to Capri AD25

AD30

AD35

The site of Masada, near the Dead Sea. Here, after the great Jewish revolt against the Romans of AD66, about 1,000 Jews held out for nearly three years against a determined Roman siege. Finally, rather than be taken captive, the Jewish survivors committed mass suicide. It was to such future trials that Jesus was in part referring.

opened up for them was his glorious return. As his own earthly ministry was about to end, he prepared to launch his church on its ministry, giving to the four original disciples the encouragement they needed for the troubled times ahead.

This is the object of Mark 13. All the complex and often misunderstood events that it foresees are simply the background to, and the reason for, a series of practical instructions. Here is the concern of the shepherd for his flock. Jesus had a word for his disciples' confused minds (verse 5) and troubled hearts (verse 7). Exhortations and warnings of this kind are the points we find him repeating again and again throughout the chapter.

The end of all things Whatever they meant by 'these things' (verse 4), he shifted the focus of attention away from the destruction of the Temple to 'the end' of all things. His first warning was that events which might look like signs of the end in fact are not. They are only the beginning – that is, if they signify anything, it is 'More to follow'.

As well as wars and famines, there would be suffering, betrayal and death at the hands of authorities, both religious and secular (verses 9-13). But the power of God's Spirit would be with his people. Although what was promised them was not rescue, but only the right words to say, yet the great object – witness for the sake of Jesus – would be achieved. There was a 'must' about the proclamation of the gospel (verse 10), as there was about the troubles of the world (verse 7). However dismaying the prospect, this comforts us with the reminder that God is working his purpose out, and is ultimately in control.

13:14-27 The end of the Age
The disciples' confused picture of what was to come was separated out by Jesus into three main areas: the destruction of Jerusalem, the second coming and the 'church age' as a whole. As we have already seen, his prime concern was with how his church could be prepared for what might happen. He had spoken in this general way from verse 5 to verse 13.

Now Jesus went on to speak particularly of the destruction of Jerusalem, which was the original question. The 'abomination that causes desolation' was a fearful event prophesied in Daniel (for instance Daniel 11:31). Some thought it happened in 168 BC, when Antiochus IV desecrated the Temple by sacrificing a pig to Zeus. Caligula's proposed setting up of an image there in AD 40 would have been a similar outrage. But the real fulfilment came with the war of AD 66-70, and the Temple's desecration by Jewish Zealots and Romans in turn, in the war which ended with the sack of the city.

Many saw in time that Jerusalem, for centuries a refuge to flee to, had become finally a place to flee from. Certainly there were Christians who escaped before the final siege to the city of Pella in Transjordan, heeding Jesus' prophetic warning.

The coming of the Son of Man The events of AD 70 were an unparalleled disaster (verse 19), not only because of the terrible suffering involved, but because in a sense they wrote 'The End' to the story of Israel. The first half of history came to an end. But all this was set in the context of Jesus' loving care for his church. He was concerned that Christians should not sit passively assuming that the second coming was about to happen, but should take practical steps to escape while they could.

Not even this catastrophe, let alone the wars and famines and earthquakes of verses 7,8, would be a sign of the end. That would not come till afterwards. In verse 24 we should stress not 'In those days', that is, the same days as in verse 19, as if Jesus meant the second coming would quickly follow the fall of Jerusalem, but rather 'the days after that tribulation'; that is his return belongs to a later period than the one just described. But whenever it comes, we are to serve him while we may and suffer for him when we must.

Mark 13

Anti-Christian graffiti scratched on a wall in Rome. From earliest times Christians came under persecution and ridicule.

13:28-37 The day and hour unknown

One possible interpretation of this much-debated passage is represented by the following summary of the whole discourse, starting again from the disciples' question in verse 4 about the sign that these things (the destruction of the Temple, verse 2) 'are all about to be accomplished'.

Verses 5-13 add up to: 'I want to tell you about the end of the world, as well as about the destruction of the Temple. Many things will happen which you will be tempted to think are signs of the end. You will be wrong; they are simply constantly-recurring features of the church age'. Verses 14-23: 'Referring to your original question, Jerusalem will indeed be sacked; but even that disaster will not be the end, nor even a sign of it' (verse 21). Verses 24-27: 'By contrast, when the end really does come it will be quite unmistakable (verse 26), a cataclysm beside which even the sack of Jerusalem will seem trivial'.

Watch! In the two remaining paragraphs, Jesus took up in the same order the two topics just dealt with: Jerusalem and the end. Here he tied up the whole matter by finally answering the query about signs (verse 4). Verses 28-31: 'These things (verse 29) – the events relating to the desolating sacrilege – will indicate that it – the destruction of Jerusalem – is near. Think of the fig-tree, which does give signs what is coming. Some of this generation will still be living, will see the sacrilege in the Temple, and will flee, for that will be the sign when these things are all to be fulfilled (verse 4)'. Verses 32-37: 'But *that* day (verse 32), the end of the world, will be different. Think of the householder who goes away and does not give warning of when he is about to return. So with regard to the end, the Master's return, you are to watch not for preliminary signs, but simply for the return itself, and be ready'.

What Jesus stressed throughout was the practical matter of our being prepared for his own second coming, and for whatever may come in the meantime.

'Keep watch because you do not know when the owner of the house will come back – whether in the evening, or at midnight, or when the cock crows, or at dawn' (Mark 13:35).

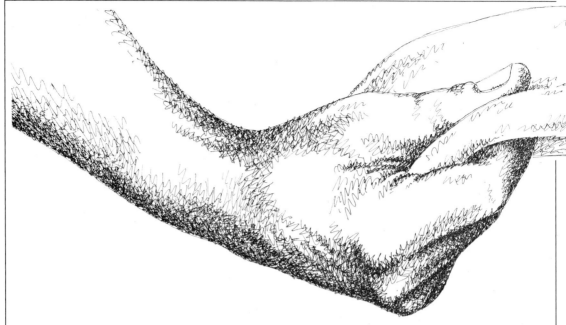

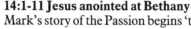

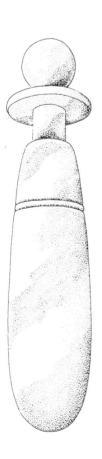

'Jesus took bread, gave thanks and broke it'
(Mark 14:22).

Before glass was commonly available, bottles were
made of alabaster, a kind of stone which is light in
·colour and easily worked. Perfumes and ointments
were kept in them.

14:1-11 Jesus anointed at Bethany

Mark's story of the Passion begins 'two days before the Passover'. It is a sequence of actual historical events which can be anchored in the calendar, filled with meaning by the Jewish festival. The leaders sought to arrest Jesus: no easy matter in view of his fame, the huge crowds in Jerusalem, the Passover's theme of deliverance from oppressors, and thus the risk of popular insurrection and Roman retaliation. Judas sought a chance to betray him, perhaps in response to an official 'Wanted' notice that had been published (John 11:57).

The incident at Bethany was another thing altogether. If it is the same as the one described in John 12:1-8, it had happened a few days earlier. The fact that a denarius was a day's wage (Matthew 20:2) gives us some idea of the value of the ointment which the woman 'wasted' on Jesus.

Judas objects The churlish objection of verse 5 is in John 12 attributed to Judas; contrast the thirty pieces of silver (Matthew 26:15) that he was prepared to *take* for Jesus. But Judas' words were the opportunity for the breathtaking insight of verses 6-9. The cross was as far as the enemies of Jesus could see. But he saw his death, his burial, his resurrection – for how can there be a gospel without a resurrection? – and the universal spread of that gospel.

Scripture sets before us 'the Poor Man' as a picture of one helpless and humiliated, unjustly persecuted, friendless and forsaken, whose hope is in God alone. To see Jesus in that picture, and to honour and love him for it, is to be very near the heart of the gospel. The fact that we always have the poor with us (verse 7) is not an excuse for doing nothing about economic injustice; but neither is it a reason for exalting the second great commandment above the first.

14:12-21 The Last Supper

Whether the supper took place on or before Passover night is an unsolved problem. Matthew, Mark and Luke seem to indicate one thing, John the other. Suffice it to say that we are clearly meant to regard it as a Passover meal.

For once, Mark does not attempt to explain the Jewish technicalities to his Gentile readers, but simply fastens on two or three points in it. The dipping of bread in the dish of sauce turns our

thoughts directly to the cross; for it is at this point that Jesus revealed that there was a traitor among the Twelve. So this passage, like the previous one, ended in the dark shadow of betrayal (verses 11, 21 and on to 42).

Again, the treachery of Judas is set in the wider context of an overriding plan. All had been prepared beforehand. On a simple practical level, plans for the supper had been made in advance (as with the arrival in Jerusalem, in Mark 11:2-6). The unusual sight of a man with a water-jar must have been a pre-arranged sign, and the householder had ready what Jesus knew would be 'a large upper room, furnished'.

The betrayer The betrayal falls into place in a biblical background, too. If Psalm 41:1-2 was in mind, with the woman at Bethany who 'considered' Jesus, and so was 'called blessed in the land,' verses 9,10 are even more apt with regard to Judas: 'Even my close friend, whom I trusted, he who shared my bread, has lifted his heel against me.' Nor is it only individual stages in the whole tragic, yet glorious, process which have been mapped out beforehand. The entire 'going' of the Son of man is taking place 'as it is written' (verse 21).

It is clear that Judas could not claim diminished responsibility on that account. What he did, he did deliberately, or Jesus would not have declared 'woe' to him. Yet the paradox is that nevertheless all is within the plan, and under the controlling hand, of the God who will use even the wrath of man in the redeeming of his people, as he did long before on the first Passover night.

A Sri Lankan artist's impression of the foot-washing during the Last Supper.

14:22-31 The Lord's Supper

After the dipping in the dish, the other point in the Passover meal where Mark lingers is the thanksgiving for, and sharing of, the bread and the cup. He does not explain which bread, or which of the four cups, in the complex ritual.

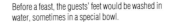

Before a feast, the guests' feet would be washed in water, sometimes in a special bowl.

The shared elements mean first the unity of the Lord's people with him and with one another (1 Corinthians 10:16,17). We may imagine the disciples' astonishment as Jesus introduced startling new words into the time-honoured liturgy. Their minds were torn away from the 'bread of affliction' which related to the old deliverance from Egypt. The cup now represented a covenant of a new kind, which would replace the covenant of Sinai. Through the body and blood of Jesus a new thing was coming into being, of the same kind as, but infinitely greater than, the nation founded at the Exodus. A new Israel was being established.

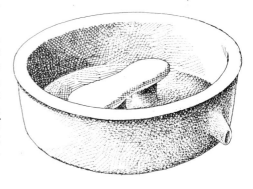

'While they were eating, Jesus took bread, gave thanks and broke it, and gave it to his disciples, saying, "Take it; this is my body" ' (Mark 14:22).

'They went to a place called Gethsemane, and Jesus said to his disciples, "Sit here while I pray" ' (Mark 14:32).

This is my blood The supper means secondly a proclamation of Jesus' death, to be repeated until his second coming (1 Corinthians 11:26). First death then glory: the theme of Mark, the Gospel of the Servant, sounds yet again. The history of the new people of God begins with Jesus' suffering, and will end with his return. This too is here in the original words. The immediate tragedy is the pouring out of the blood (verse 24). The final glory will be when at last the feast of victory reunites him and all his people in heaven (verse 25).

Did the disciples need yet another illustration of this principle? They were given it. Within three days they would experience both the death of their leader and the breaking of their fellowship, and his rising and their reunion (verses 27,28). But it was so hard to grasp! Well, let them remember these words from the last of the six psalms they sang before setting out for Gethsemane: 'I will not die, but live, and will proclaim what the Lord has done' (Psalm 118:17).

14:32-42 Gethsemane

Mark does not bother to translate Gethsemane (oil-press); it is simply the name of an olive garden. '*Abba*' is a different matter. He wants us to know both that *Abba* means Father, and that although most Jews would have thought this is a gross over-familiarity, it was Jesus' word for his Father God. We find we can be equally 'familiar' with God (Romans 8:15-17).

Jesus turned to *Abba* in his extremity. As from the start of his ministry he had felt the need to go out to a lonely place to pray (Mark 1:35), so now at its climax he found a little 'desert' where he could both be away from distraction and also see things clearly by drawing closer to his Father.

Abba, Father It was to *Abba*, and not to his remaining eleven disciples, that he turned for strength. As he had left the city, so Jesus left both the eight, and then even the three, knowing that none of them could be relied on (verse 27). Peter, James and John were taken furthest with him, but that was for their sake, not his. These three self-important men (Mark 10:37; 14:29) needed to learn the way of the suffering servant (Mark 10:45). 'Watch and pray', not to keep him company, but to keep yourselves from temptation (verse 38).

To *Abba* Jesus came at the end of all things, knowing that prayer aligns our wills with our Father's will. Our truest joy lies in this. What then if that will turns out to be the 'cup', the hour of suffering which will not go away (verses 35,36), and which is no ordinary suffering, but the wrath of God against sin? What if at the time of greatest need a son flees for refuge to his dearly-loved father, and finds that *Abba*'s will is this? That the way of the privileged Son has to be the way of the submissive Servant? The only answer Jesus received to his prayer was the hard answer of events, beginning with the failure of the three to watch with him.

14:43-52 The arrest

With the arrival of the party to arrest Jesus, we come to the core of the passion story, the heart of what the early church believed and what it preached.

To his wickedness Judas added the sin of hypocrisy, with a kiss that said 'respect and love', and meant just the opposite. Then he disappeared from Mark's story, having, ironically, set the tone for all that was to follow: 'The one I shall kiss is the man'. For Jesus now dominated the scene, even more than on any earlier occasion. All focused on him.

Jesus is deserted This was the man whom these very guards had known as a teacher of righteousness, preaching constantly in the Temple, unmolested as they themselves patrolled it, one they knew did not deserve arrest. This was the man who was now assailed as if he was a robber, so that the prophetic words of Isaiah 53:12 began to come true in him, 'He . . . was numbered with the transgressors'. This was the man who now stood isolated, again fulfilling both ancient and recent prophecy (verse 27; Zechariah 13:7). Even his friends failed to understand him, thinking to prevent by the sword the fulfilling of his destiny, and then deserted him altogether.

So it was Jesus alone upon whom all this suffering was to fall. As if to stamp as factual truth this central story which all the church of Christ holds to be of prime importance (1 Corinthians 15:3-7), Mark adds a personal signature: I was there. It is very hard to account for verses 51,52 if the young man was not Mark, risen from bed in his

Ancient olive trees in the garden of Gethsemane.

Mark

John Mark is the writer of the second Gospel. He lived in Jerusalem. It is usually thought that he was the young man nearly arrested in Gethsemane (Mark 14:51,52).

It was in the house of his mother, Mary, that the first Christians met (Acts 12:12). Mark travelled with Paul and his cousin Barnabas (Colossians 4:10) to Cyprus on their first mission. Since he deserted them half-way, Paul refused to take him a second time, so Mark went with Barnabas alone (Acts 15:36-41). But later Mark spent time with Paul in prison in Rome, when Paul spoke of him as a loyal helper and friend (Philemon 24; Colossians 4:10). It was probably Peter who told Mark much of the story of Jesus which we now find in his Gospel.

'Christ before the High Priest' by Gerrit van Honthorst (1590-1656).

home in Jerusalem, perhaps the very house where the supper had just taken place (Mark 14:15; Acts 1:13; 12:12), and throwing a sheet or loose garment around himself to follow Jesus and the eleven. 'I was no more courageous than the rest,' Mark says, 'but at least I saw it happen'.

14:53-65 Before the Sanhedrin

What an unlikely scene. At dead of night, in so respectable a house as the high priest's, an upstairs room with a host of eminent people hastily assembled, and a courtyard below with a fire lit, servants still up, a crowd of guards waiting. Mark will tell us later (verses 66-72) what happened to Peter in the courtyard. Upstairs the scene was again dominated by Jesus.

At first Jesus dominated even in his silence. Writers differ about the legality of this trial, indeed about whether it was a trial at all, or simply a preliminary enquiry to find proper grounds for a charge against Jesus. Around him was the ebb and flow of conflicting evidence brought by a whole series of witnesses, which from the point of view of the high priest turned out to be no more than a maddening waste of time.

'Are you the Christ?' Still Jesus stood silent as the damaging report about a threatened destruction of the Temple was brought (compare John 2:19). Perhaps it was the messianic overtones of this charge, the failure of all the others, and the desire to speed things up, which

decided Caiaphas to fasten on Jesus' supposed messiahship and to force him on oath to answer. So at last Jesus spoke; and in none of Mark's scenes is attention so riveted on him as with the sensational 'I am' of verse 62.

His blasphemy (verse 64) was that he dishonoured God by claiming to be God's chosen Messiah, when anyone could see he was not. Whatever people may have thought of his feeding 5,000, or riding into Jerusalem, or teaching masterfully in the Temple, these all counted for nothing now. It was at this point, as a friendless, helpless prisoner, that he at last made the great claim unequivocally. The secret was out.

To the Jewish leaders, his humiliation was the proof that he could not be Messiah. And that was their blasphemy. Mark is the Gospel of the Servant; and it was precisely there, in his humiliation, that the true Servant of God should have been recognized. Mark's readers are to learn from their Lord yet again that to serve and to suffer are the prime characteristics of him, and of those who follow him.

14:66-72 Peter's denial

Increasingly clearly we have seen Jesus as the Servant, submitting to his Father's will. If Peter represents those who follow him in the way of service, we are here warned how easy it is to stray from that path. The account of Peter's denial has a very practical purpose. No one was louder than Peter in his claims of loyalty to Jesus.

But words are not enough. How does the servant actually show his obedience? What came after the big words of verse 29 was failure to keep awake, failure to pray; an instinctive grab for worldly weapons, and a following of Jesus which was neither brave enough to keep right up with him nor wise enough to keep right away from temptation.

Peter's shame So Peter found himself in the courtyard of the high priest's house, in a situation which starkly paralleled the one upstairs. Mark no doubt meant us to see it that way, by planting verse 54 in the previous paragraph, and indicating that the two interrogations were happening at once. The tragedy of course was that Peter turned out to be not on the side of Jesus, but on the side of the Sanhedrin.

We can see Satan's subtlety (Luke 22:31) in the way the temptation is set up. Peter's fears for his own safety, his desire to give an acceptable answer, and the angle of the questions, which might have been deliberately calculated to provoke a denial of Jesus, are just what we might expect the great enemy to use. The only defence against him is precisely that we should expect such methods. Be aware of him, Jesus had said, and keep in touch with your Father – 'Watch and pray, so that you will not fall into temptation' (verse 38).

Awareness of the actual state of affairs came to Peter when it was too late. He remembered not just what Jesus had said, but how he had said it; all the circumstances of Jesus' agony and the disciples' weakness and presumption. He was prepared to have Mark record his shame so that the realities of temptation might not be ignored by others as they had been by him. Even so, true repentance leads to restoration, as Mark will show (Mark 16:7, compare Luke 22:32).

15:1-15 Jesus condemned

What complications beset both the Jews' attempts to have Jesus condemned, and Pilate's to have him released.

Having set up the arrest, the trial and the false witnesses, the chief priests still had to ensure the actual execution. For that they needed Roman authority: hence the dawn meeting to draft the charges on which Jesus would be sent to Pilate (verse 1). Their change of ground at this meeting is ironic. They had condemned him because of his claims to be a prophet, which seemed to them unsubstantiated and blasphemous (Mark 14:64-65). But the claims to kingship, which–

Blasphemy

To blaspheme is to speak against God or in any way to slander or speak evil of him. In the Old Testament it was a sin which was punishable by death (Leviticus 24:10-14). The idolatry of God's own people practically amounted to blasphemy (Romans 2:24).

In the New Testament, the meaning of blasphemy is sometimes extended to include slander against God's representatives, such as Moses (Acts 6:11), Paul (Romans 3:8) and Jesus (Matthew 27:39).

The 'unforgivable sin' is described as 'blasphemy against the Holy Spirit' (Mark 3:28-30). It refers to a state of mind when a person can attribute the works of Christ to the devil. It is obvious that this sin cannot be forgiven, since repentance is impossible to a person who seriously believes that the evil he has done is good. It is a persistent attitude, sometimes described as 'hardness of heart'. Some Christians have become worried that some single sin they have committed may be the 'unforgivable sin'. But the fact that they are so concerned is a sign that it is not unforgivable; the Holy Spirit is convicting them with a view to repentance and forgiveness.

'The cock crowed the second time. Then Peter remembered the word Jesus had spoken to him' (Mark 14:72).

Jesus was mocked with a crown of thorns.

they laid before Pilate, would lead to a condemnation only if Pilate could be persuaded to think there was some substance in them.

Pilate, for his part, first put the straightforward question of verse 2. It arose from the charge – now treason, instead of blasphemy – on which Jesus stood accused (compare Luke 23:2). But for the Roman, too, a series of complications followed. Jesus' reply was not so clear a 'Yes' as to amount to admitting guilt, or else there would have been nothing more to be said.

In any case Pilate surely suspected the Jews of bad faith. They were unlikely to care much about protecting the Roman government against traitors! Further, Pilate knew their real motive was envy (verse 10). But he thought it prudent not simply to release Jesus, as he should have done, but to release him under the terms of the Passover amnesty (verse 6). This move was the mistake which finally ensured that Pilate lost and the chief priests won (verse 15).

15:16-32 The crucifixion

In Mark's account of the crucifixion allusions which he himself does not develop can be filled out by comparison with the other Gospels. (For example the reason for verse 24 is given in John 19:23,24). What Mark does stress is the royalty and the suffering of the crucified one, three times referred to as king, yet each time in mockery.

To the soldiers, the title of king was quite incongruous. In casting Jesus in the role of a vassal-king under Roman rule, complete with purple cloak, crown, salutations, a 'reed' for sceptre and spitting for

'The curtain of the temple was torn in two from top to bottom' (Mark 15:38).

the kiss of homage, they 'mocked' (verse 20). The whole charade was ludicrously out of keeping with what seemed to the soldiers to be the facts about him.

The chief priests mock Jesus The chief priests, however, knew better. They saw Jesus as a powerful and dangerous character, now successfully neutralized. Everything they said about him in verses 31,32 was true, but in ironic senses they did not intend. They could not see truth the right way round, because they demanded proof before faith. They 'mocked' (verse 31) not in ignorance but in unbelief.

Between these two mocking salutations is a much more complex one – the inscription put on the cross by Pilate (see John 19:19-22). It was factual; this was the charge against Jesus. It was also a mockery, contrasting the grandiose title with the helpless victim. It was an insult to the Jews, implying that this poor creature was the kind of king they deserved. Hence their objection in John 19:21. Yet it was in the deepest sense the truth, for Jesus Christ was, and is, the King of the people of God.

In this passage, however, even more important than the kingship is the suffering. In the suffering of the cross, far more important than its cruelty is its place in the scheme of redemption. Jesus refused the cup of drugged wine (verse 23) because consciously and deliberately he was going to drink another cup (Mark 10:38; 14:36). By not sparing himself, he was to save a multitude of others. In that, too, his enemies spoke more truly than they knew (verse 31).

15:33-39 The death of Jesus
Three times called a king in irony (verses 18,26,32), Jesus in his death received an even greater title (verse 39).

Mark's deceptively simple style does not draw attention to the truths which lie beneath these largely unwitting testimonies. But we have already seen that he notes meaningful incidents which his readers are expected to look at with Christian eyes.

So here Jesus' death was preceded by three hours of darkness. Whether a supernatural event or a natural one miraculously timed, this is highly significant. It recalls Exodus 10:21,22 and Amos 8:9,10, and is set side-by-side with the next event, the cry which quotes Psalm 22:1. The Son's (and the world's) separation from the light of the Father's face was expressed first visibly, then audibly. The unity of the Trinity cannot be broken. Yet in whatever sense Isaiah 59:2 was fulfilled in 2 Corinthians 5:21, and Deuteronomy 21:23 in Galatians 3:13, in that sense the Son was at this moment cut off from the Father.

The Temple curtain is torn Just before the moment of death, Jesus uttered another cry, probably the triumphant 'It is finished' of John 19:30. Again Mark sets, without explanation, sign beside word: Jesus' death-cry and the tearing of the Temple curtain. Whether this was the curtain before the Holy Place, or (more likely) the 'second curtain' (Hebrews 9:3) which screened the Holy of Holies, its tearing points to the destruction of the Temple itself, of the whole Old Testament system, and of the barriers which exclude sinners from God's presence and Gentiles from his people (Hebrews 9:1-10:22).

And the reactions of those who stood by the cross? Some, though sympathizing with the suffering man (the 'vinegar' was cheap wine, offered in kindness), could not see what was really happening – another aspect of the darkness. But the centurion, whatever pagan meaning he may have had in mind, saw what he could only describe as the death of 'the Son of God' (verse 39).

Mark surely intends his readers to see that with the centurion's words his Gospel comes full circle (compare Mark 1:1,11), and to

Pilate

Pontius Pilate was the Roman goveror of Judea between AD 26-37. Cruel and unpopular with the Jews, he was afraid that his low esteem might mean his loss of office. Although he recognized that Jesus was innocent, he was afraid that the Jews would cause a riot if he was released. For this reason he condemned Jesus to death.

read them in the full Christian sense. As verses 33,34 dramatize the suffering of the Christ, and verses 37,38 the salvation which is thereby obtained for us, verse 39, with its implications, is the response of worship and service we therefore owe to him.

15:40-47 The burial of Jesus

Both for Jesus' chief enemies and for his chief followers, it was enough to have seen him dying. It was left to lesser characters in the drama to see him dead. A group of women remained, including some who quite possibly were not only friends and followers of Jesus, but also related to him, and to several of the Twelve. But at the last, those you would have thought closest to him were, sadly, far from him (Mark 14:50).

The chief priests seem to have departed too, having achieved their object. As the strange darkness cleared to give three more hours of daylight before sunset and the coming of the Sabbath, officialdom was represented now by three people.

Joseph of Arimathea The emergence of Joseph of Arimathea as a disciple of Jesus testified to a real, if belated, courage. He now did for Jesus what Jews considered ought to be done (the body taken from cross to tomb before the onset of night and of the Sabbath) but what those closer to him would not, or could not, do. Pilate's exercise of his right to grant the body to the relatives for burial, unusual in a case of treason, testified to his suspicions about the whole affair, and perhaps to his sense of guilt over condemning an innocent man. The centurion, having declared that Jesus was truly Son of God, now testified that he was equally truly dead.

From one point of view the whole passage is about testimony. The testimony of all these people concerning Jesus was that he really had died, and was buried in *this* tomb (verse 47). The witnesses either had nothing to gain, or were witnessing to something they wished were not true, or spoke as military men, with authority. So we take their witness to be truthful.

16:1-8 The Resurrection

Mark completes his Gospel with the resurrection. For him it is a fact as real as every other great event he has recounted. This paragraph is bound closely to those that precede. It was the women who saw Jesus dead (Mark 15:40) and buried (Mark 15:47) who now heard his resurrection announced. The tomb earlier occupied and sealed was the one now open and empty. He 'who was crucified . . . has risen' (verse 6). If what went before was historically true, then so (we are meant to understand) was this, although it be the greatest and most incredible miracle of all time.

This final great fact has, for Mark, one overwhelming result (verse 8); and it leads us to consider how he ends the Gospel. After verse 8 there is added, in some manuscripts, a short ending of one or two sentences. In other manuscripts there is a longer ending, often now printed as verses 9-20. These were added presumably because it was thought more fitting that the closing words of the Gospel should express joy, faith or challenge. But if Mark actually meant to end at 16:8, what was in his mind in so doing?

A study of words for amazement, awe and fear will show that these are what he constantly uses to describe reactions to the way God reveals himself in the gospel story. People were astonished and afraid at the deeds, words and appearance of Jesus. Beyond that, they trembled when it was revealed that the Son of God was prepared to be also the suffering Servant (Mark 10:32-34), and still more at the teaching that his followers also would have to tread the way of the cross (Mark 8:34).

From Mark's point of view, then, it is fitting that when his

ends by declaring that the gospel in fact goes on, with Jesus still 'going ahead' (verse 7), the human reaction was trembling, astonishment and fear (verse 8). Yet paradoxically, Mark's ending – as abrupt as his beginning – strikes the note of encouragement for suffering Christians. Their trials were foreknown, allowed for, and in the plan and control of the God who, after Calvary, did raise his Son from the dead.

The Church of the Holy Sepulchre was built in the fourth century as a witness to the resurrection. It was believed to cover the site of the tomb where Jesus was buried.

'Skull Hill', which General Gordon rather fancifully took to be the true site of Jesus' crucifixion.

16:9-20 An anonymous postscript

These additional verses are not in Mark's style, and the join at verse 9 is untidy. But the unknown writer's object is clear enough. Either he knew this Gospel did not originally end at Mark 16:8 (that is, Mark wrote an ending that was later lost), or he knew it did, but felt it should not; so he supplied verses 9-20 to round it off. He might well have believed that a proper Gospel, like the sermons in Acts, ought to include human (not just angelic) witness to the risen Christ.

That at any rate is the content of this postscript. It describes resurrection appearances found in different form, and at much greater length, in the other Gospels (see John 20:11-18, Luke 24:13-35, Matthew 28:16-20 and other passages). The miraculous signs which it says will be seen in the New Testament church are all (except the poison-drinking) found in Acts. It ends with the twin statements of verses 19-20: Jesus goes up to sit on the throne of heaven, while his church goes out, to preach to the people of earth. Jesus' 'sitting' means not the posture of his body, but the majesty of his empire. We know that so far from his ascension separating him from his people, it enabled him now to wield his power universally, as by his Spirit he worked 'with them' (verse 20). All this sums up a good deal of the earliest Christian belief. In fact, its chief value may be to focus our attention on belief and unbelief. First it stresses the latter, in a way found elsewhere only in the Thomas story (John 20:24-29).

This leads up to the crux of the passage: for faith, which the apostles themselves had found so hard, was at the heart of the message they now had to preach (verse 16). Would their hearers believe in Christ, or not? If they did, then the faith which leads to salvation (verse 16) would be followed by action on their own part ('and be baptized'), and confirmation by God ('signs', verses 17,18,20).

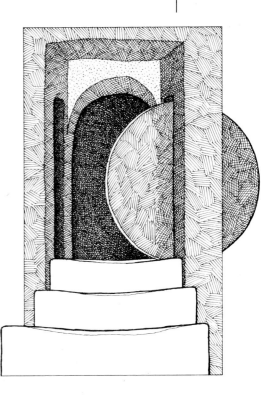

Contents

	Page
People	
Luke	186
Joseph	189
Judas Iscariot	250
Places	
Nazareth	193
Jericho	242, 43
Words	
Angel	186
Demons	202
Jesus in the four Gospels	205
Joy	221
The prophets and the Messiah	224
Forgiveness	237
Humility	240
Ascension	260
Life	
Betrothal	185
Jewish dress	196
The Synagogue	200
Languages	206
Bread	214
Weddings	218
High priest	254
Funeral	258

Luke

Introduction to Luke's Gospel

Luke Introduction

All the evidence supports the view that the third Gospel was written by the physician Luke, friend and fellow-traveller of Paul. He was also the writer of the Book of Acts, and it is clear that he was very familiar with the world of the first century.

Luke was probably the only Gentile author of the New Testament, and was a particularly careful reporter and historian. He begins both his books with a dedication to 'Theophilus', who may have been an official of standing.

While Paul was in Roman custody at Caesarea, Luke would have had the time to find eyewitnesses to Jesus' ministry. He might have been able to meet Mary, and some of John the Baptist's followers, allowing him to cover the early years of Christ in unique detail.

It is not clear when and where the Gospel was written. It is possible it was written in the early 60s in Rome.

The Gospel of Luke has the same general arrangement as Matthew and Mark, but also possesses distinctive features. Luke's narratives of the birth of John and Jesus are different from Matthew's, and also include worship hymns on the lips of Mary, Zechariah and Simeon. At the end of the Gospel, Luke includes another distinctive feature: a detailed description of the ascension. In this respect, his is the most comprehensive Gospel.

Luke includes much material that is common with Matthew and Mark. He shares a block of teaching with Matthew only, and also includes a considerable amount of material of his own. Luke's special material gives his characteristic emphasis to his picture of Jesus. Luke basically has a deep interest in people. In Luke, Jesus is portrayed as having a great concern for social outcasts. His parables centre on the daily concerns of ordinary people. It is interesting, too, to notice how often women are mentioned in Luke's Gospel.

Some aspects of Luke's telling of the passion story are less stark than Mark's or Matthew's. For example, he omits the cry of desolation from the cross. Yet this remains the climax of his account.

In the second part of his Gospel he shows Jesus resolutely setting his face to go to Jerusalem (Luke 9:51).

Outline to Luke's Gospel

1:1-25	The birth of John the Baptist foretold
1:26-45	The birth of Jesus foretold
1:46-56	Mary's song
1:57-80	The birth of John the Baptist
2:1-20	The birth of Jesus
2:21-40	Jesus presented in the Temple
2:41-52	The boy Jesus at the Temple
3:1-20	John the Baptist prepares the way
3:21-38	The baptism and genealogy of Jesus
4:1-13	The temptation of Jesus
4:14-30	Jesus rejected at Nazareth
4:31-44	Jesus drives out an evil spirit and heals many
5:1-11	The calling of the first disciples
5:12-26	The healing of a man with leprosy and a paralytic
5:27-39	The calling of Levi
6:1-11	Lord of the Sabbath
6:12-19	The twelve apostles
6:20-49	The teaching of the Lord
7:1-10	The faith of the centurion
7:11-17	Jesus raises a widow's son
7:18-35	Jesus and John the Baptist
7:36-50	Jesus anointed by a sinful woman
8:1-15	The parable of the sower
8:16-25	The parable of the lamp and the calming of the storm
8:26-39	The healing of a demon-possessed man
8:40-56	A dead girl and a sick woman
9:1-9	Jesus sends out the Twelve
9:10-17	Jesus feeds the five thousand
9:18-27	Peter's confession of Christ
9:28-36	The transfiguration
9:37-45	The healing of a boy with an evil spirit
9:46-50	Who will be the greatest?
9:51-62	The cost of following Jesus
10:1-24	Jesus sends out the Seventy-two
10:25-37	The parable of the Good Samaritan
10:38-42	At the home of Mary and Martha
11:1-13	Jesus' teaching on prayer
11:14-28	Jesus and Beelzebub
11:29-36	The sign of Jonah
11:37-54	Six woes
12:1-12	Warnings and encouragements
12:13-21	The parable of the rich fool
12:22-34	Do not worry
12:35-48	Watchfulness
12:49-59	Not peace but division
13:1-9	Repent or perish
13:10-17	A crippled woman healed on the Sabbath
13:18-30	The narrow door
13:31-35	Jesus' sorrow for Jerusalem
14:1-14	Jesus at a Pharisee's house
14:15-24	The parable of the great banquet
14:25-35	The cost of being a disciple
15:1-10	The parables of the lost sheep and the lost coin
15:11-32	The parable of the lost son
16:1-18	The parable of the unjust steward
16:19-31	The rich man and Lazarus
17:1-10	Sin, faith and duty
17:11-19	Ten healed of leprosy
17:20-37	The coming of the kingdom of God
18:1-8	The parable of the persistent widow
18:9-14	The parable of the Pharisee and the tax-collector
18:15-30	The rich ruler
18:31-42	Jesus again predicts his death
19:1-10	Zacchaeus the tax-collector
19:11-27	The parable of the ten minas
19:28-48	The triumphal entry
20:1-8	The authority of Jesus questioned
20:9-19	The parable of the tenants
20:20-26	Paying taxes to Caesar
20:27-40	The resurrection and marriage
20:41-47	Whose son is the Christ?
21:1-4	The widow's gift
21:5-38	Signs of the end of the age
22:1-6	Judas agrees to betray Jesus
22:7-38	The Last Supper
22:39-53	Jesus arrested
22:54-62	Peter disowns Jesus
22:63-71	Jesus before the high priest
23:1-25	Jesus before Pilate and Herod
23:27-43	The crucifixion
23:44-49	Jesus' death
23:50-56	Jesus' burial
24:1-12	The resurrection
24:13-35	On the road to Emmaus
24:36-53	Jesus appears to the disciples

EM Blaiklock
Luke
Commentary

1:1-25 The birth of John the Baptist foretold

The introduction to Luke's Gospel is remarkable for being written in the style of the best Greek historians. Luke was aware that he was undertaking a task of enormous historical importance. He devoted everything he could to it – polish, care and an orderly mind.

The story opens on a note of beauty and tragedy. 'In the time of Herod king of Judea'; in his last days, in fact, when Herod's cruel and cynically evil life was speeding to its end in madness and blood. But there was still a remnant of good, godly people in Israel. An amazing experience came to two of them (see Exodus 30:7,8). All the members of the tribe of Aaron were priests, who took it in turn to make the daily sacrifice and to call a blessing upon the gathered crowds at the Temple.

Zechariah For Zechariah, this was a rare privilege, a high point in his life. When the great day came he went with a heart prepared, conscious of the solemnity of the occasion. God met him in the place of duty and at the hour of worship. Zechariah brought his childlessness to the altar and found the burden of it lifted there.

So Luke's story begins with a humble priest, unknown and unrecognized by the proud Sadducees who had taken over the high priest's office for their private advantage. Nor would the Pharisees have noticed his humble service. They prided themselves on knowing the law, that cluttered mass of regulations by which they tried to

An artist's impression of the altar of incense at the Temple.

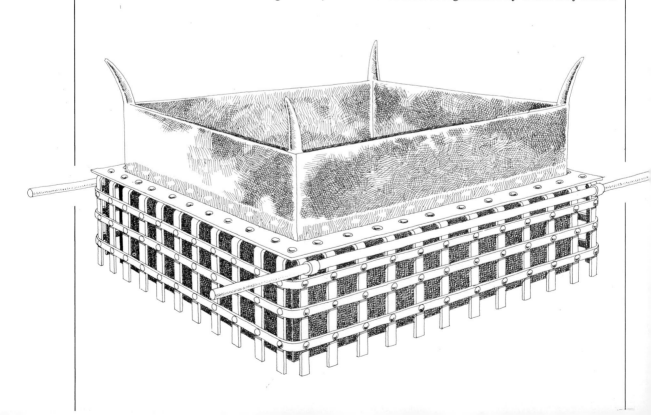

organize life. But among the many, as throughout Israel's history, God had his few. From them was to come the new movement of his grace. God's poor gave to the world Mary, the human mother of God's Son.

Prophecy was about to be fulfilled. The closing words of Hebrew scripture (Malachi 4:5,6) promised the return of the fiery prophet Elijah. Jesus himself pointed out (Matthew 11:14) that this saying was fulfilled in the fiery preacher John (John 5:35).

Zechariah's response to the angel of the Lord shows us more of this good man. Voiceless and overwhelmed, he nevertheless completed his tour of duty. He gave the people the formal blessing and needed no words to convey a message that made them marvel.

1:26-45 The birth of Jesus foretold

Reading this passage along with Matthew 1:18-25 makes it obvious that the New Testament claims that the birth of Jesus was miraculous. John implies the same (John 1:14). We should also remember that Luke was a careful and painstaking historian. While Paul was imprisoned in Caesarea (Acts 24,25) Luke had two years to follow up his researches and to question witnesses. This account clearly contains what the apostles believed and what Mary stated.

In the account of Mary's visit to Elizabeth (verses 39-45) we find a vivid picture of Mary. She was chosen for her faithfulness, not doubting for a moment God's promises (verse 45). When God trusts one of his servants with a job it is rarely easy, it is always glorious.

Virgin birth The virgin birth is of deep significance. God demonstrated in this way a link with humanity and a distinction from humanity. In other words, the Messiah was one with the humans he came to save, but unique in his heavenly origin. Strong support for his unique way in to the human state is given by the fact that the human life which followed was like no other.

It is true that the genealogies include Joseph as father. Mary, too, speaks of Joseph as the 'father' of the twelve-year-old boy. And to the people of Nazareth he was 'the son of Joseph the carpenter'. But this was simply to place Jesus in his social context. Mary's marriage to Joseph validated Jesus' descent from David, and Joseph was his

Betrothal

In the Near East, betrothal was almost as binding as marriage. First marriages were always arranged marriages. Once betrothed, the woman was sometimes called the 'wife', and was bound to be faithful.

In more old-fashioned areas, customs were so strict that it was not permitted for the young betrothed couple even to meet before their wedding night.

Normally, the wedding ceremony came within a year of betrothal.

If the contract of betrothal was broken, for example by the bride losing her virginity, the husband could sign a deed of divorce. This would be handed to the bride or her representatives in the presence of witnesses who could be trusted to be discreet. In this way publicity could be avoided. At the same time, the husband would pay a previously agreed sum due on divorce. Joseph was anxious to dissolve the marriage quietly in this way.

Mary's Well, Nazareth, the source of which is now inside the Greek orthodox church of Saint Gabriel. This was probably the sole source of water for Nazareth in Jesus' time, which means that the town must have been very small.

Luke

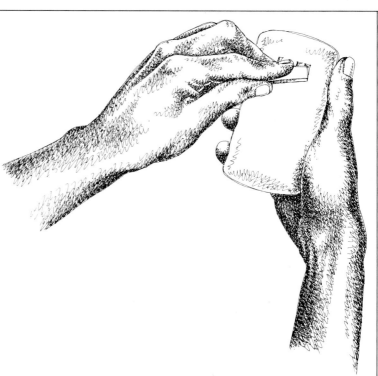

**Luke
1**

There is no reason to question the tradition that Luke wrote the Gospel bearing his name, and also Acts. Luke had every opportunity to obtain first-hand information (Luke 1:1-4) since it is clear from Acts that he travelled extensively with Paul. We can follow some of his travels by noting the passages in Acts where he writes 'we' (Acts 16:10-16; 20:5-15; 21:1-18; 27:1-28:16). In Philemon he is one of Paul's fellow-workers; and in 2 Timothy 4:11 is Paul's only companion. In Colossians 4:14 he is called 'our dear friend . . . the doctor'. In his writings, he often uses precise medical terms, and has an excellent Greek style.

guardian. It should also be noticed (verse 26) that Nazareth was the original home of Mary, not her adopted home, as might be assumed (Matthew 2:23).

1:46-56 Mary's song

Mary was moved by the news to sing. Her hymn was modelled on the poetry of the Old Testament. Study carefully Hannah's hymn of praise (1 Samuel 2) and follow the theme of God's poor in Isaiah. The *Magnificat*, as this song is called from its first word in the Latin version, answers those who claim there is a gulf between Christ and the common man. It is also a reproach to those who from time to time through the ages have tried to restrict the gospel to the rich and to the clever.

Mary's joy had to break into praise. Her words form the first psalm of the New Testament, revealing a mind soaked in the Old Testament. Wonder breaks on her that God should use a humble woman to carry out his purposes. But the truth is that it is the humble alone whom God *can* use. Those who are preoccupied with their own importance are useless in his service. The proud and the mighty are an offence to him. Only those who hunger and thirst for righteousness have the promise of satisfaction.

Mary spoke as one of the common people of the land (verses 51,52). Israel was a land of shocking poverty, overcrowded, pressing hard on its limited resources of food and water. It was as ravaged by hunger and want as much of the third world is today. And yet it was among the masses that deep currents of faithful worship ran. From Elijah to Amos God had spoken through the simple people of the countryside.

In verse 48 is shown Mary's expectation that down the centuries she would be regarded as favoured above all women. Gabriel and Elizabeth voiced similar views. Mary's devotion, humility and self-surrender are marks of her worth. Notice God's care for her, and his help in her time of testing. Mary's authority lies behind this account.

1:57-80 The birth of John the Baptist

John means 'God's gift' or 'God is gracious', the name marking the humble thanks of a devoted couple for the privilege of bringing a new

Angel

The Greek word for angel really means 'messenger'. It usually refers in the Bible to a quite separately created order of heavenly beings.

The angels are spiritual beings (Hebrews 1:7) specially created for particular tasks before the creation of the world (Job 38:7). They appear to be endowed with free will.

Their first task was to act as 'courtiers' in God's heavenly palace. They guarded the way into his presence (Genesis 3:24), attended him (Isaiah 6:1-4) and perhaps even shared in his work of creation (Job 38:7). They also share in his law-giving (Acts 7:53; Galatians 3:19; Hebrews 2:2) and final judgement (Matthew 16:27; 2 Thessalonians 1:7-10).

The angels also act as God's agents to benefit humanity. Sometimes they bring more practical assistance – the expression 'guardian angel' describes the watchful care they exercise over God's people (Matthew 18:10; Hebrews 1:13,14). It was an angel, for instance, who came to Hagar's assistance (Genesis 16:7-14), sustained Elijah after his great ordeal on Mount Carmel (I Kings 19:1-8), warned Joseph to escape into Egypt (Matthew 2:13), came to the rescue of Peter (Acts 12:7) and stood by Paul at some of the most critical moments in his life (Acts 27:23).

The angels were particularly in evidence at Jesus' birth (Luke 2:8-14), his temptation (Matthew 4:11), his agony in the garden (Luke 22:43) and at his resurrection (Matthew 28:1-8).

We are told little about what angels look like. References to their appearance and clothing (Matthew 28:2,3; Luke 2:9; Acts 1:10) suggest a king of majestic beauty, which may have been reflected in the face of the martyr Stephen (Acts 6:15). Nor does there seem to be a fixed pattern in their appearances. God himself was occasionally revealed to people in angelic form (Genesis 18; Joshua 5:13-15) or when the being was clearly some sort of visitor from another realm (Matthew 28:2). At other times they seem not to have been distinguishable from ordinary people (Genesis 19:1-3; Hebrews 13:2), or to have made themselves known simply by a voice (Genesis 22:11).

Angel

'The Annunciation' by Duccio.

life into the world. After the virgin's hymn came that of the priest. He pondered the great prophecies of the Jews and the solemn poetry of the Old Testament.

Zechariah had high ambitions for his son, but they were interwoven with his zeal for God. Thinking of the old saying of Malachi 4:5, the priest understood that his son was to be the forerunner of the Messiah. He probably understood as little as his son did after him the true nature of the Messiah's ministry. A full, clear understanding of what God is doing in life is not needed to carry out faithfully the task required of his servants.

John, the chapter concludes, was 'in the desert' until his tremendous ministry commenced. The Qumran community, by the Dead Sea, was just one of many groups living in the wilderness (see for example Isaiah 40:3; Hebrews 11:9).

2:1-20 The birth of Jesus

A tattered piece of papyrus found in Egypt contains the sort of notice that Joseph the carpenter must have read in Nazareth. It commanded everyone living away from their place of birth to report back to their home-town authorities for the census. Before the torn document breaks off, it speaks of feeding arrangements for crowded towns and villages. The papyrus dates from a century later than the census conducted by the Roman diplomat Quirinius (or Cyrenius), which probably took place in the autumn of 5 BC. (The men who in AD 525 calculated the chronology of Christianity made a slight error in their dating.)

Bethlehem At this time of stress and waiting, Joseph had to take his wife to Bethlehem. He did not realize that, in fulfilling the normal, bothersome duties of daily life, he was also fulfilling God's plan.

Verse 8 shows that the birth did not take place in winter. December 25th was chosen to celebrate Christmas in the 4th century, replacing an earlier pagan festival. For 'the glory of the Lord' (verse 9) compare Exodus 24:16 and Numbers 14:10.

It is significant that an edict of the occupying power brought prophecy to fulfilment, and placed Bethlehem in the story of Christ's

'There were shepherds living out in the fields near by, keeping watch over their flocks at night . . .' (Luke 2:8). A shepherd tends his sheep outside modern Bethlehem.

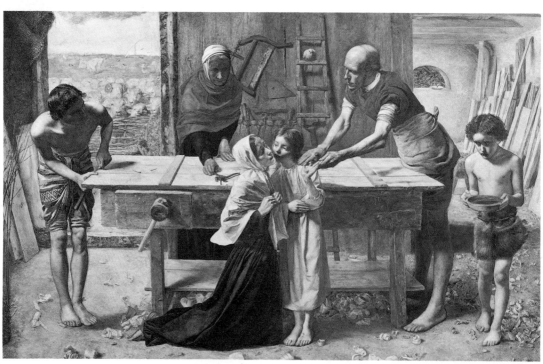

'Christ in the House of His Parents' (The Carpenter's Shop) by Sir John Everett Millais, painted 1849-50.

Joseph

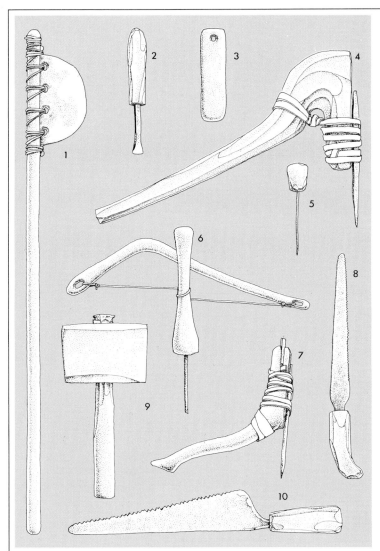

Joseph, the husband of Mary, is not mentioned in Mark, and is only mentioned indirectly in John. Matthew 1:18 and Luke 1:27,35 both record that Jesus was conceived by the Holy Spirit when Joseph was betrothed to Mary, but before he had intercourse with her. Joseph acted as a father towards Jesus, taking him to Jerusalem for the purification, and to Egypt to escape death. He returned to Nazareth, where he settled, taking Jesus to Jerusalem each year for the Passover.

Joseph had almost certainly died by the time of Jesus' ministry. Jesus told John to look after his mother, Mary, when he was on the cross. The brothers of Jesus, mentioned in Matthew 12:46, Mark 3:31 and Luke 8:19 were presumably the subsequent children of Mary and Joseph.

Luke 2

A carpenter's tools
1 Axe
2 Chisel
3 Hone for sharpening tools
4 Adze
5 Bradawl
6 Bow-drill
7 Adze
8 Small handsaw
9 Mallet
10 Saw

birth. In this busy town, full of unusual crowds, in conditions lacking all comfort and privacy, Jesus was born. It was shepherds from David's ancient pastures who first learned of his birth. Shepherding is frequently used in the picture-language of the Bible, yet the proud Pharisees despised the shepherds, since their calling made it impossible for them to carry out the complicated series of ceremonial washings. But God simply by-passed the obstacle which these lawyers had made of his law. It has been claimed that the flocks of Bethlehem were Temple sheep, grazed on the old royal estates as unblemished lambs ready for sacrifice.

2:21-40 Jesus presented in the Temple
The law laid down set obligations, but in its mercy brought these requirements within the reach of the poor (see Exodus 13:12; Numbers 8:17; Leviticus 12:8). The consecration of the firstborn child was in sharp contrast to the foul practices of child sacrifice of many pagan cults.

Three requirements of the law were here fulfilled in the baby and his mother. Mary's offering was the offering of the poor. God had by-passed the pomp and circumstance of mankind, and entered history through a poor family. Many rich men offered lambs on the very day that the mother of Jesus brought the second turtle-dove which the law allowed for the poor.

For Joseph and Mary, Jerusalem lay on their route home. They

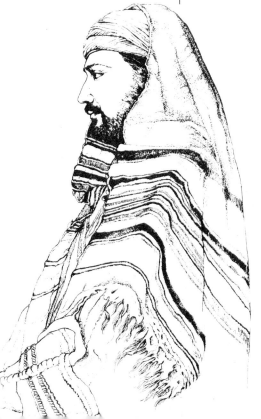

'The Finding of the Saviour in the Temple' by William Holman Hunt, painted in 1854.

would have travelled north, and first seen the city and the Temple from the Mount of Olives, as they brought the child to the Temple.

Anna and Simeon Although the Sadducees and Pharisees had corrupted religion by commercialization and invented regulations, some faithful Jews remained. One of these, Simeon, penetrated God's secret. Notice his quotation of Isaiah 42:6,7, which places him in the tradition of John the Baptist. Simeon's insight stemmed from his knowledge of the Bible. Another of the faithful enters the story: Anna, an aged woman who had given her life to prayer, and whose insight was similar to Simeon's (verse 36).

Simeon and Anna had kept the faith intact and uncorrupted in a day of corruption and unfaithfulness. Simeon clung on to a promise, and in the moment of its fulfilment became the last of the Messianic prophets (verses 30,31,32,34). His words are like a short solemn saying from the prophet Isaiah. The challenge of Jesus' presence tumbles pride; the proud are humbled.

2:41-52 The boy Jesus at the Temple
Here is a revealing picture of the family from Nazareth, travelling to Jerusalem and remaining for the full period of the Festival. There is probably a strong reason for this visit. A Jewish boy was regarded as becoming responsible at the age of twelve. He became a 'son of the law' and adopted a more adult form of dress.

At this time the boy Jesus became fully aware that he was God's Son, the promised Christ. The Sanhedrin Council met in the Temple at the time of the Passover to discuss matters of theology and law. The boy sat at the feet of the great teachers 'listening to them and asking them questions' (verse 46). Questions were also put to him, for they 'were amazed at his understanding and his answers' (verse 47). It was in effect a school scene, for this was the traditional style of Jewish education.

'My Father' When they discovered that Jesus was missing, Joseph and Mary had to abandon the caravan travelling back to Galilee, which helped ensure their safety, and hurry back to the Temple. A new dignity had come upon Jesus, and there was now a part of him they could not understand. Mary speaks to Jesus of 'Your father', meaning Joseph. Jesus replies, 'My Father'. In this delicate shift, Jesus announced the new relationship. The knowledge of who he was had come to him. Yet, without impatience, self-assertion or even independence, he continued to follow an unobtrusive path of obedience for a further eighteen years.

Luke saw no contradiction between the two uses of the word 'Father' (verses 48,49). In civil law and everyday life, Joseph was the father; but equally for Jesus, the Temple was 'my Father's house'.

3:1-20 John the Baptist prepares the way
The first verses provide more evidence of Luke as the careful and precise historian. They list the contemporary rulers, from the Roman Emperor Tiberius to the high priest Caiaphas. These powerful figures formed the backdrop to the great religious revival led by John. It is likely that John had spent years of preparation, perhaps among the sects of the desert.

All four Gospels link the ministry of John with that of Jesus. John was the forerunner, the man of the desert, the Elijah of the New Testament. Study of the Dead Sea Scrolls and the desert community of Qumran has told us much more about the ascetic sects. This community saw only corruption in the city, and apostasy among the religious leaders. It was in the desert that John discovered his faith and calling. But the city was aware of this desert preacher; Jerusalem

'The axe is already at the root of the trees, and every tree that does not produce good fruit will be cut down and thrown into the fire' (Luke 3:9).

Nazareth

Nazareth

Nazareth nestles among hills and looks down on the plain of Esdraelon.

Nazareth was a small town in Galilee, about fifteen miles west of the Lake of Galilee and twenty miles east of the Mediterranean, where Joseph and Mary lived and where Jesus was brought up from early childhood. Jesus was therefore commonly known as 'Jesus of Nazareth' or 'Jesus the Nazarene'. It was probably because of their association with him that his followers, in turn, came to be called Nazarenes.

Nazareth does not appear to have been a place of any significance in antiquity. It is nowhere mentioned in the Old Testament or in pre-Christian Jewish literature.

Nathanael's question, 'Nazareth! Can anything good come from there?' (John 1:46), suggests that it enjoyed no great reputation among its neighbours. In the narrative of Jesus' public ministry Nazareth does not appear in a very favourable light. Mark and Matthew relate that, when Jesus visited the place soon after the beginning of his Galilean ministry, his fellow-townsmen gave him no credence and therefore did not witness any of his mighty works, apart from the healing of a few sick people (Mark 6:1-6; Matthew 13:53-58). Luke adds a summary of his sabbath-day address in the synagogue, where he took as his text the opening words of Isaiah 61. Jesus explained that his present ministry was to proclaim 'the acceptable year of the Lord', implying that he himself was the Spirit-anointed speaker of the passage which he read. The address aroused so much hostility among his hearers that they tried to throw him over 'the brow of the hill on which the town was built' (Luke 4:29) – which is still pointed out as the Mount of Precipitation.

Nazareth is now a city of over 20,000 population, inhabited mainly by Arab Christians. The one place in Nazareth which can with confidence be associated with Jesus' family is Mary's Well, from which water has been drawn from time immemorial.

Here then in Nazareth Jesus grew up, with four younger brothers and an unknown number of sisters. It is precarious to try to fill in the detail of those 'hidden years'. But from the high ground above the town a boy such as Jesus, interested in the Old Testament writings, could look down on many scenes which figured in the earlier history of his people. To the south stretched the plain of Esdraelon (the valley of Jezreel), which had witnessed a succession of great battles, including Barak's victory over Sisera and good King Josiah's fatal defeat at Megiddo. Beyond the plain of Esdraelon, slightly to the left, was Mount Gilboa, where King Saul had fallen in battle against the Philistines. To the east rose Mount Tabor, 1843 feet high, later to be the traditional (but doubtful) site of the Transfiguration. South-west of Tabor lies the small town of Nain, where Jesus was to restore a widow's son to life as he was being carried out of the town to be buried (Luke 7:11-17). Two or three miles beyond Nain was Shunem, where Elisha's generous hostess had lived (2 Kings 4:8). About nine miles north-east of Nazareth was

Cana (if it is to be identified with the modern Khirbet Qana), the home of Nathanael (John 21:2), where Jesus was to perform 'the first of his miraculous signs' by turning water into wine (John 2:1-11).

Nazareth lay off the beaten track, but the road from the lake of Galilee to Ptolemais (Acco) ran a few miles to the north, while the great 'Way of the Sea' from Damascus and farther north passed by not far to the south, leading to the Mediterranean coast and so south to Egypt.

Along it, in both directions, moved trading caravans and detachments of soldiers. Galilee at that time was part of the tetrarchy of Herod Antipas, and not a Roman province (as Judea was); so any Roman soldiers seen in Galilee would be seconded to his service. But Herod Antipas ruled by grace of the Romans, and the Roman presence was never far from people's thoughts, even in Galilee. When Jesus was about nine years old, everyone was talking about the rebellion in Judea led by Judas, a Galilean from Gamala, east of the lake. Judas and his followers raised the standard of revolt in AD6 against Roman control of Judea and the obligation on its inhabitants to pay tribute to the emperor. The rising was crushed, and Judas perished.

John the Baptist may have been influenced by the desert communities such as the Qumran sect, with their Dead Sea headquarters. It was in these caves that some of the famous Dead Sea scrolls were discovered.

'He will baptise you with the Holy Spirit and with fire. His winnowing fork is in his hand to clear his threshing floor and to gather the wheat into his barn, but he will burn up the chaff with unquenchable fire' (Luke 3:16,17).

went out to hear him. John did not look for the crowds; they searched *him* out: proud Pharisees, soldiers, hated tax-collectors, common people all followed him.

John's preaching John's preaching place was the wide river valley of the lower Jordan, near Jericho. John knew that his preaching ful-filled prophecy, and, using the splendid poetry of Isaiah, he pictured himself as a king's herald. There was a fiery note to his preaching which has the mark of the Old Testament rather than the New. He used a word-picture from the scrub-fire of the Jordan desert: the hid-den vipers of the undergrowth darted to safety from its running flames (verse 7). John denounced the Pharisees and Sadducees (see also Matthew 3:7), attacked Jewish nationalism and pride, and demanded repentance. Israel's largest forest, the Jordan jungle, gave John the picture of the axe. Baptism had been confined to con-verts to Judaism, but it was a familiar picture of purification (see Ezekiel 36:25; Zechariah 13:1).

John's call to repentance was very practical. Not only did he show what it required in the lives of particular groups (verses 12-14) but he also attacked sin in high places (verse 19). Herod was living with Herodias, the ambitious, scheming woman who had been married to his brother Philip (not Philip the Tetrarch). When Herod was in Rome, Herodias trapped Philip and fled with him. She was in due course to ruin Herod's life.

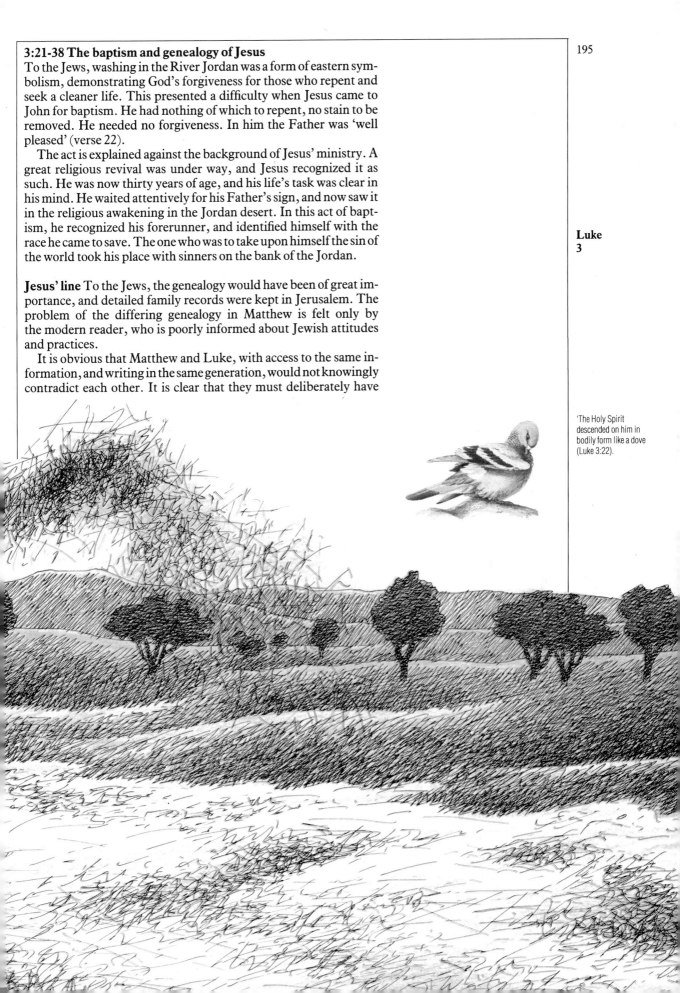

3:21-38 The baptism and genealogy of Jesus

To the Jews, washing in the River Jordan was a form of eastern symbolism, demonstrating God's forgiveness for those who repent and seek a cleaner life. This presented a difficulty when Jesus came to John for baptism. He had nothing of which to repent, no stain to be removed. He needed no forgiveness. In him the Father was 'well pleased' (verse 22).

The act is explained against the background of Jesus' ministry. A great religious revival was under way, and Jesus recognized it as such. He was now thirty years of age, and his life's task was clear in his mind. He waited attentively for his Father's sign, and now saw it in the religious awakening in the Jordan desert. In this act of baptism, he recognized his forerunner, and identified himself with the race he came to save. The one who was to take upon himself the sin of the world took his place with sinners on the bank of the Jordan.

Jesus' line To the Jews, the genealogy would have been of great importance, and detailed family records were kept in Jerusalem. The problem of the differing genealogy in Matthew is felt only by the modern reader, who is poorly informed about Jewish attitudes and practices.

It is obvious that Matthew and Luke, with access to the same information, and writing in the same generation, would not knowingly contradict each other. It is clear that they must deliberately have

'The Holy Spirit descended on him in bodily form like a dove (Luke 3:22).

Costume The costume of the ordinary worker or peasant in Palestine in the time of Jesus consisted of five items of clothing. (Most of these people were not strictly orthodox Jews in either eating or dress.) They would wear a long cotton shirt, a leather or cloth girdle around the waist, a head-dress, shoes or sandals and a cloak made of either goats or camel-hair or some kind of coarse sack-cloth. In most cases the head-dress would be similar to that worn by the Bedouin today; a piece of cloth square, folded diagonally and placed over the head to protect the eyes, cheeks and neck from the direct heat of the sun, and kept in place by a cord ring.

There were two different types of cloak: a heavy, sleeveless cloak worn as protection from the cold and rain, and also used as a bed-cover; and a long-sleeved over-coat, rather like a cassock. The latter was often worn by officials, priests, the rich and the better-educated, while the former was better suited to the needs of country people such as shepherds.

Similarly the under-garment could vary from a simple night-shirt like garment with sleeves to a waist-cloth wrapped tightly round the loins. The latter was ideal for outdoor labourers, boatmen and fishermen. Sometimes the longer

under-garment would be provided with baggy leg-openings, which were often left to trail to show that their wearer was a person of leisure rather than a labourer.

Women's dress was almost interchangeable with men's. The main differences were that women's clothing was usually brighter and more elaborate, and the head-dress consisted mainly of a large veil. Most women wore a white veil, but the veil of a widow was black.

Sandals came in several different styles, but normally consisted of flat soles made of leather, wood or dried grass, with loops attached through which a leather thong was threaded to strap them onto the foot. Since the feet got very dirty wearing sandals, foot-washing was a very important part of greeting visitors into the home.

In addition to these basic items of clothing the orthodox Jew would also wear the head-scarf or 'tallith' which marked him out as a member of the Jewish people.

The most distinctive costume of the Roman citizen was, of course, the toga, which was forbidden to foreigners. It was compulsory for Roman officials to wear the toga on state occasions, although it was often discarded in the country. It was a large, heavy woollen wrap, and sported a purple stripe on its border in the case of free-born Romans. Sometimes a dark toga was worn as a sign of mourning.

1 A peasant wearing a long cotton 'shirt' and sackcloth cloak.
2 A peasant wearing a long-sleeved 'overcoat' and cloth head-dress.
3 A woman wearing a long-sleeved and patterned coat and white head-dress.
4 An orthodox Jew wearing the fringed head-scarf or 'tallith'.
5 A Roman citizen wearing the heavy woollen toga, prohibited to foreigners.
6 Leather-thonged sandals.

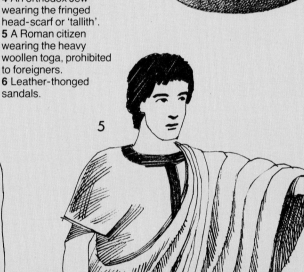

6

4

5

This scale model attempts to give an impression of Herod's Temple as it would have appeared in the time of Jesus. It is located in the grounds of the Holyland Hotel in Jerusalem.

followed different lines of approach. Matthew, while making it clear that Jesus was not Joseph's son, gives Joseph's line because he was Jesus' legal father. But it was also necessary to show that Mary had married within the tribe, in keeping with the laws found at the end of the book of Numbers. Luke almost certainly gives the genealogy of Mary. Joseph, not Mary, is given as the direct descendant of Eli, because Joseph authenticated Mary's inheritance by the laws of Numbers (Numbers 27:1-11; 36:1-13). Matthew takes the line back to David; Jesus was *King*. Luke takes it back to Adam; Jesus was the *Son of Man*, the saviour of the world, not of the Jews only.

4:1-13 The temptation of Jesus

Behind the palms, cypress and jacaranda of the modern town of Jericho, a mile back from the arid mound which covers the remains of a dozen ancient fortresses on the old historic site, stands a harsh, bare mountain on the edge of the Judean desert. This is the traditional site of Jesus' temptation.

Hebrews 4:15 suggests that this was not Jesus' only temptation. This was an assault on Jesus as Messiah, rather than as man. He repudiated the Jewish idea of the Messiah (verses 5-8). The quotation (verses 10,11) is from Psalm 91:11,12, which was regarded as addressed to the Messiah.

The subtlety of the temptations lay in the way they corrupted what was harmless or good. There was nothing wrong in a desire for food. The sin lay in satisfying hunger at the devil's time and in the devil's way. Similarly, there was nothing wrong in wishing to rule men well, and to rule over the warring nations to bring peace. Nor was there evil in a desire to be accepted for what he was, the Holy One of God, and to launch his ministry with convincing power. The sin lay in taking power from the devil, in presenting himself to people according to the devil's suggestions. All the devil demanded was that legitimate desires be channelled through him.

Temptation is not sin. The body's appetites are not evil. There is nothing wrong about wanting to be accepted by people, or to achieve power, position or authority. Sin comes in when the body is satisfied in other than God's way, popularity won by compromise with evil, and social status by loyalty to the devil.

4:14-30 Jesus rejected at Nazareth

Luke begins his story of Jesus' ministry at this point, but much had already happened to bring him fame. The timing is uncertain, but events recorded up to Mark 6, Matthew 13 and John 4 had probably already taken place. Verse 23 shows that Luke was aware of this.

Isaiah was an appropriate book for Jesus to read from. Since the preaching of John the Baptist, Isaiah had been in people's minds. The passage he read was Isaiah 61:1,2, with a phrase from Isaiah 58:6. So Jesus took up the theme of John the Baptist, with one important difference. John had spoken of judgement; Jesus emphasized that the day of God's grace postponed the final retribution.

Jesus' method was dramatic. The passage should be read in Isaiah, from which it is clear that he broke off his reading in mid-verse. He can only have meant that 'the day of vengeance of our God' was not yet. Jesus could not have chosen a more effective way of impressing upon everyone that a new age of God's grace was opening, and that no violent crusade of liberation against the enemies of Israel was in preparation.

The incident here is probably the one described in Mark 6:1-6 and Matthew 13:53-58. The phrase 'The scroll . . . was handed to him' (verse 17) in the Greek means literally 'was further handed to him', that is after the reading of the law. The quotation from Isaiah (verse 18) is a free version based on the Greek translation of the Old Testament (the *Septuagint*).

Luke 4

'All the people in the synagogue were furious . . . They got up, drove him out of the town, and took him to the brow of the hill on which the town was built, in order to throw him down the cliff' (Luke 4:28,29). The Mount of Precipitation shown here is probably the hill mentioned by Luke.

The Synagogue

In the synagogue's large assembly room there was a seven-branched lampstand, or Menorah, and a lamp of eternity. Prayers, readings from Scripture and praise were the most important elements of worship.

The sacred scrolls of the law were kept in a cupboard – probably portable. Women and children were admitted only to the synagogue gallery.

In larger synagogues, there was an extension with small rooms around an open courtyard. These could be used for guests or for class-rooms.

A council of ten elders chose the head of the synagogue.

Synagogue In Jesus' time there was at least one synagogue in almost every village or town. The synagogue reminded the Jew of the Temple in Jerusalem and the worship carried on there.

Services were held in the synagogue on the sabbath and during the great Jewish festivals. The synagogue was also open for prayer three times daily.

An artist's reconstruction of the second-century synagogue at Capernaum.

Remains of the synagogue at Capernaum. About sixty-five feet long, and built of specially-obtained white limestone, the synagogue was evidently of ornate design. It is probable that a centurion of the Roman Tenth Legion contributed to its construction, since the emblem of this legion is to be found carved in the stonework.

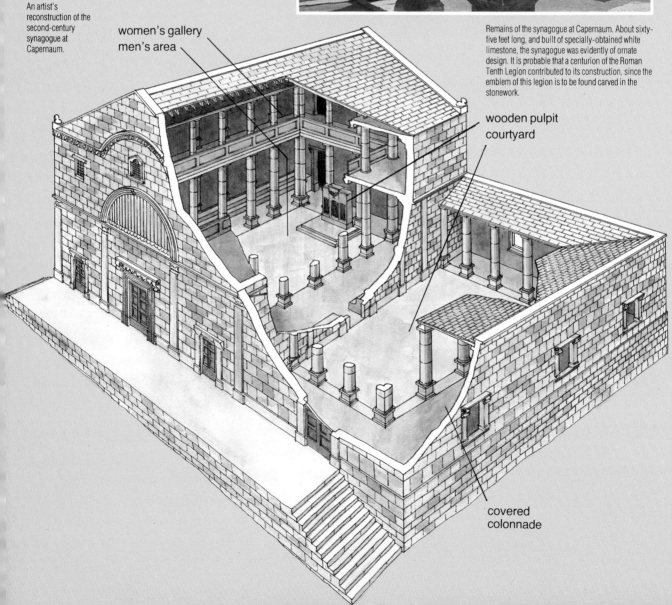

women's gallery
men's area

wooden pulpit
courtyard

covered
colonnade

Blasphemy Luke is often a very ironic writer. He described how the people of Nazareth were at first charmed by the words of Jesus, then realized that he was only 'Joseph's son' (verse 22). It is clear why Luke, Paul's associate, who shared the great apostle's vision of a world-wide gospel, chose to highlight this incident at the beginning of his story. Here, early in the ministry of Jesus, was the Jewish response to the good news, a response which was to be repeated throughout Paul's ministry. The mention of Zarepath and of Naaman suggest the appeal to the Gentiles. This prospect repelled nationalistic Jews.

With his words in verse 23, Jesus refused to demonstrate his power idly. The unbelief of the people of Nazareth prevented his doing such acts among them (Matthew 13:58).

Jesus' reference to the faith of the Gentiles provoked the Jews to take Jesus to a hilltop. Nazareth lies in a hollow in a ridge of hills, and the Mount of Precipitation is the likely site, with its steep drop to the Plain of Esdraelon. Throwing a man down the cliff (verse 29) was a form of stoning, the Jewish punishment for blasphemy.

4:31-44 Jesus drives out an evil spirit and heals many
The 'demon-possession' cannot be lightly dismissed. There are evil phenomena which are not completely explained by modern psychology. Even if some of the 'demon-possessed' of the New Testament were actually suffering forms of recognizable mental illness, Jesus could cure them only on the level of their own knowledge and their faith. 'Us' (verse 34) implies multiple personality.

The impression of the narrative is of Jesus' unwearying activity. Jesus was no cushioned and protected teacher, carefully insulated from the public. He returned to the synagogue to discover a new task waiting for him. He gave himself in public, he gave himself in private. The Sabbath ended at sunset (verse 40), but Jesus continued his ministry of healing.

5:1-11 The calling of the first disciple
This section displays several marks of Luke's authorship. He calls Gennesaret a 'lake' – his less-travelled fellow Gospel-writers call it a 'sea'. He gives prominence to the call of Peter, the apostle in whom

'One day as Jesus was standing by the Lake . . . he saw at the water's edge two boats, left there by the fishermen, who were washing their nets' (Luke 5:12).

Demons

the Gentile world was particularly interested. And in verse 12 Luke uses a medical term ('covered with leprosy').

The low shore of the lake, where the first disciples were called, runs south from Capernaum towards Tiberias in a wavy line. Fishing was the chief industry of Galilee; Jesus taught in the work-place, among the comings and goings along the line of little bays.

Peter obeyed Jesus' order, though he did not understand it (verse 5). But in the great catch of fish he recognized the glory of the Lord. His first reaction was like that of the prophet Isaiah (Isaiah 6:5): an overwhelming sense of his unworthiness, inadequacy and sin (verse 8). It was like Peter to speak the first words to come into his mind. Jesus draws near the repentant sinner, he does not leave him. The one who touched the suffering leper was not likely to shun the repentant fisherman. Peter's prayer was unanswered, but his heart's desire was met.

5:12-26 The healing of a man with leprosy and a paralytic

In the story of the man with leprosy, Jesus both disregarded, and conformed to, the requirements of the law. He touched the man with leprosy, an action which was prohibited. But he ordered the cleansed man to show himself to the priests (Leviticus 14). The reason for Jesus' request (verse 14) is found in Mark 1:45. He wanted to avoid a mass-movement and a wave of emotional enthusiasm.

The gathering of religious leaders (verse 17) was part of the pattern mentioned by Mark; it was the wrongly-based or hostile interest which Jesus was trying to avoid. Jesus' healing of the paralytic demonstrates that he recognized the link between a troubled soul and a broken body; but the experts had come to criticize. The friends who were anxious to help their needy associate were determined to bring him to Jesus, trusting him to do everything else necessary.

In the parallel passages (Matthew 9:2-8; Mark 2:1-12) the minor differences in words and details reflect the fact that more words were spoken than are reported, and that what was said was expressed in Aramaic, the local dialect.

Luke's theme, carefully unfolded in set order, is Jesus' self-revelation. Messiah had demonstrated his mastery over sickness, demons and nature and now showed his authority to forgive sin.

Luke 5

It seems from the Gospels that one of Satan's most vigorous ways of opposing the person and work of Christ was to use his agents to 'possess' people. One of the ways in which Jesus most unmistakably showed his divine power was by casting out these demons (Luke 11:20), and proclaiming 'freedom for the prisoners' (Luke 4:18).

These agents or demons may have been separate beings, or manifestations of the devil himself. They did not produce normal types of physical sickness, but such things as dumbness (Luke 11:14), epilepsy (Mark 9:17-29) and even a type of insanity (Luke 8:26-36).

The power Jesus showed in casting out these demons was also delegated to his disciples (Luke 9:1).

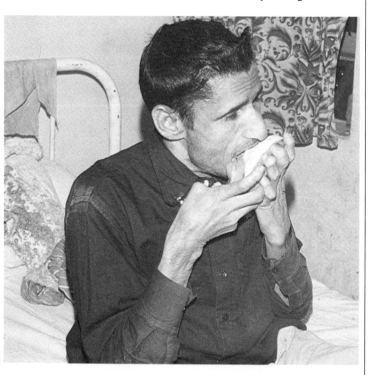

Leprosy is still a dangerous disease in many parts of the world.

5:27-39 The calling of Levi

Levi is known as 'Matthew' in other parts of the New Testament.

There were many opportunities for bribery, extortion and every sort of corrupt and cruel practice in the ancient method of tax-collection. The men who pursued this despised way of earning a livelihood were outcasts of the community, subject to savage jibes and bitter reproaches. There were many tax-collectors in Capernaum, for the town was the customs-post for traffic up the lake.

Jewish writings are full of scorn and loathing for these cynical and wealthy tax-collectors, who were regarded as collaborators with the occupying power. Christ must have recognized the self-hatred and the longing for a clean start which no one else could see in the tax-collector. Matthew left everything, and responded to the call. Unlike the rest of those chosen, he abandoned for ever his calling and his possessions. Fishing was an honourable pursuit, and could be taken up again without criticism. But when Matthew left his tax-office he knew he could never return. To follow Christ can mean completely rejecting the former way of life.

Privacy was a rare privilege at this time. Matthew's dinner party was undoubtedly watched by critics, whose carping question elicited Jesus' ironical remark. Jesus certainly did not mean that there are righteous people who have no need to repent, still less that his critics themselves were such people.

'The bridegroom will be taken' (verse 35) is the first indication that Jesus was expecting a violent end. In the following verses (33-39) he goes onto the offensive. He attacked his enemies at their foundations. Their whole order was outmoded; it was to pass away. Christianity was no mere patch on an aged garment.

6:1-11 Lord of the Sabbath

The two incidents in this section illustrate Jesus' clash with the legalists over Sabbath regulations. His point in both instances is that in the Old Testament the Sabbath was a positive institution. The Scribes and Pharisees had turned it into a burden and often a cruel system.

According to the humane provisions of the law (Deuteronomy 23:25) it was lawful to eat someone else's corn in this way. But the Pharisees, elaborating the simple laws of Sabbath-keeping, listed manual stripping of an ear of corn and the removal of the husk as reaping and threshing.

Similarly, an ox or ass which fell into a pit on the Sabbath could, if injured, be pulled out and slaughtered. The Pharisees, in their system of escape clauses which allowed the initiated to elude their own heavy rules, had decided that you could lift out the beast if you said you were going to destroy it, but then, if you found it was in fact uninjured, you could free it. Jesus was making the point that his critics would twist their laws for an animal, but not for a man. They had laid down that medical aid could be given on the Sabbath only in a case of life and death.

A test case Jesus cut through this clutter of legalism. In their enthusiasm for the law, the Pharisees had forgotten the true meaning of the law, and lost the mercy, love and goodness which the law was intended to foster. The man with the withered hand was to them not a pathetically needy sufferer, but a test-case on Sabbath observance. When Jesus healed him, they were furious. The rules they had laid down were broken. Their position as self-appointed interpreters of the mind of God was challenged. Pride was rebuffed by Jesus' quiet authority, and erupted in anger.

In this incident, Luke takes his theme one stage further. The Son of Man is also Lord of the Sabbath.

Galilee is an area of hill-country about sixty miles by thirty, with the plain of Esdraelon to the south, the Mediterranean to the west and the River Jordan to the east. Well-watered by west winds, it is for the most part green and fertile.

Jesus in the four Gospels

It is clear that the Gospel-writers were not setting out to produce biographies of Christ in the modern sense. They all concentrated most of their attention on the last three years of his life, when he took up his public ministry. However Matthew and Luke do also tell us about his birth and the events surrounding his early years. Luke even adds details about Jesus' youth, but these two writers also fall silent for the intervening years. All four Gospel-writers commence their detailed accounts with the beginning of Jesus' mission in his thirtieth year.

Matthew and Luke report on Jesus' birth and early years, but fall silent concerning his teens and twenties.

Mark and John only commence their accounts with the opening of Jesus' public ministry. Matthew and Luke re-open their accounts here too.

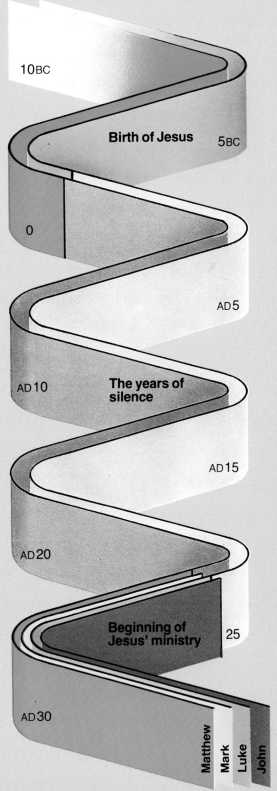

Jesus in the four Gospels

10BC

Birth of Jesus 5BC

0

AD 5

AD 10 The years of silence

AD 15

AD 20

Beginning of Jesus' ministry 25

AD 30

Matthew Mark Luke John

Languages

The New Testament was written in Greek. When the books of the New Testament were compiled Greek was the universal language of the Roman Empire. The language of New Testament Greek was the common language of the day; Greek as it was spoken in daily conversation rather than literary Greek.

The normal language spoken by the Jews of Palestine in Jesus' day was Aramaic. A few Aramaic phrases are found in our New Testament; see for example Mark 5:41; Mark 7:34; Mark 15:34; 1 Corinthians 16:22; Mark 14:36; Romans 8:15; Galatians 4:6.

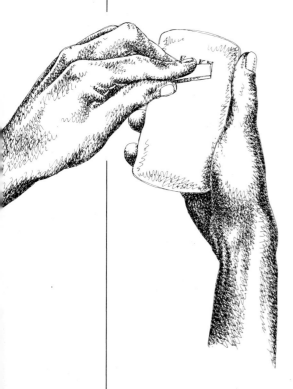

6:12-19 The twelve apostles

Tired out by the conflict with the Pharisees, Jesus withdrew for a period of fellowship with his Father before choosing his apostles. These close disciples are also listed in Matthew 10:2-4; Mark 3:16-19 and Acts 1:13. Nathanael (John 1:45) is Bartholomew, a surname meaning 'the son of Ptolemy'. Matthew is Levi, and Judas, the son of James, is Thaddeus. Peter is always mentioned first, and Judas from Kerioth (Iscariot) last.

The twelve were called apostles, 'special messengers' or 'envoys'. The word means 'one sent' and implies a goal, a purpose and a specific task to undertake. These were the twelve men Jesus chose to alter the course of history.

6:20-49 The teaching of the Lord

This sermon repeats some of the material recorded in Matthew 5-7. Luke concentrates on the most challenging and astounding parts of the Sermon on the Mount. The Beatitudes turn human experience on its head. They reveal blessings in poverty, pain and persecution. Indeed, if poverty leads to dependence on God, and pain to the Man of Sorrows, and if persecution is the fruit of being loyal to Christ, these are better than what the world offers as good.

Although the material is similar, this is not the Sermon on the Mount of Matthew. Luke is clear (verse 17) that 'he went down with them and stood on a level place'. There are also slight variations in the wording. For instance, the poor and the hungry are more fully defined in Matthew. But no Eastern listener would mistake the shorter description. They are 'the poor in spirit' and 'the hungry for righteousness'. Jesus was not promising a social and material utopia, although his message came to those scorned and rejected by society.

The Dead Sea scrolls have thrown new light on the meaning of the 'poor in spirit'. They are the tender-hearted. In one of the scrolls they are contrasted with the hard of heart. There is no blessing for those who lack pity and mercy.

The picture-language of the Bible sometimes loses its force outside its own time and place. Israel was a crisis-torn country, experiencing great hardship in its towns and villages, and the pressure of an occupying army on its population. It was also a hot country, where real thirst was commonly felt.

In verse 22, the words 'hate . . . exclude . . . insult . . . reject' are the four stages by which a Jew was excommunicated from the community of the synagogue. The word for 'have received' (verse 24) is that used to receipt a bill in the Greek of this time.

Eastern language In interpreting a section such as verses 30-35 certain principles must be observed. First, realize that Eastern writers use poetry, with images and illustrations woven in pictures into the text. Matthew's parallel passage tells the Christian to give his coat, too, to the person who demands his cloak; to turn the other cheek to his assailant; to go the second mile. The whole keynote of this teaching is selfless generosity; total self-control under persecution; absolute compassion and Christ-like love.

Secondly, remember that scripture must be balanced against scripture. The Christian who strips himself in spectacular or impulsively emotional giving may be falling short in other areas.

Jesus judged the Pharisees (Matthew 23), and judgement is committed to the church and its leaders (1 Corinthians 5:2-5). But Jesus was in a position to judge in a way not open to men. What he condemned (verse 37) was the judging attitude which overlooks personal shortcomings every bit as serious as those condemned in others; absurd self-righteousness which condemns without knowing another's temptation or weaknesses and which loses all love in criticism.

'Can a blind man lead a blind man? Will they not both fall into a pit?' (Luke 6:39).

'Why do you look at the speck of sawdust in your brother's eye and pay no attention to the plank in your own eye?' (Luke 6:41).

Three parables

Three parables close the sermon. The first is the parable of the blind (verses 39-42) – primarily the corrupt priesthood and religious leaders. 'Plank' should be taken as a typical piece of Eastern exaggeration. The 'speck' was a scrap of chaff blown from the threshing floor – a common autumn hazard. The point of the second illustration (verses 43-45) is that a change in nature is needed if a tree is to change its fruit. This parable looks forward to John 3.

The parable of the wise and foolish builders (verses 46-49) pictures two contrasting ways of living. The dry valleys of the Middle East (the 'wadis' of Arabia) were highways of trade. But they are liable to occasional disastrous flooding. Going with the crowd, intent on gain, one man risked danger and built on the sandy floor. The other man, more concerned about security, built on the 'crag' (verse 48, literally translated). His position was lonely, less convenient for trade, buffeted by the winds, but ultimately safe. The Greek 'dug down deep' (verse 48) emphasizes the tedious persistence involved. This whole section underlines that behaviour depends on character.

7:1-10 The faith of the centurion

This centurion was a Roman on special duty, attached to the administration of Herod Antipas. It is noteworthy that all five Roman officers mentioned in the New Testament were men of high integrity. Palestine was a turbulent province. Rome was trying to

It seems that a centurion contributed to the building of this later synagogue at Capernaum, as did the centurion of Jesus' time: 'This man deserves to have you do this, because he loves our nation and has built our synagogue' (Luke 7:45).

Nein, probably the Nain of Jesus' time, where he raised a widow's only son from the dead. This village is about six miles south-east of Nazareth.

After the healing in Capernaum, Jesus went to Nain, which was probably in the valley of Esdraelon, to the south of Galilee

hold it with a garrison of 3,000 men, which, as the final disaster of the Great Rebellion was to show, was totally inadequate. For this reason, Rome cultivated the Herodian royal family, the Jewish priesthood and the aristocracy. For the same reason, the officers selected for duty in Palestine were men of strength and character.

It is not strange to find an officer of this calibre attracted to Judaism. The Jews' lofty view of God and stern standards of moral conduct appealed to many pagans who found the religions of Greece and Rome unsatisfying.

The centurion The centurion was also a man of insight. He could see past the Jewish religious leaders, limited by their legalism and suspicious of Jesus. He recognized the worth and wonder of Jesus, and came to find him courteously and with faith. Inevitably he conceived of God in the forms and terms of his soldier's profession.

'The elders of the Jews' (verse 3) are the leaders of the local synagogue, who administered it under the 'ruler' (Luke 8:41). When Luke wrote his Gospel, much of the career of Paul was already over, and Peter's dramatic meeting with Cornelius, the centurion of Caesarea, was more than twenty years behind. The door was open to the Gentiles, but there were those in the church, the heirs of the Pharisees, who still resisted the giving of the gospel to the world. Luke was pleased to tell the story of a Gentile's faith, for it revealed in Jesus' own experience and strategy what Paul had incorporated into his own world-wide ministry.

7:11-17 Jesus raises a widow's son
Nain lies ten miles south-east of Nazareth, across the eastern extension of the Plain of Esdraelon. A few miles south-west lies Shunem, where Elisha similarly brought back to life an only son (2 Kings 4). At the same distance in the opposite direction lies Endor, scene of the doomed King Saul's grim encounter with the dead. The village is called Nain today, and there are rock-cut tombs nearby which may have been the destination for the sad procession which Jesus met emerging from the gate.

It was a sad sight. An utterly desolate woman, her husband gone, her only son dead. Christ is here called 'the Lord' for the first time

(verse 13). The setting is significant. Luke was writing some thirty years after the incident took place, and is using the term which had become normal in the young church.

7:18-35 Jesus and John the Baptist

Tormented and in prison, John fell prey to doubt. He had expected a conquering Messiah who would cleanse the land of evil and give back to the people their former liberty. He would burn away wickedness and oppression. Even after recognizing the Messiah in his own relative (John 1:31-33) John's old preoccupations persisted. Surely the Messiah would soon 'reveal himself' and 'restore the kingdom to Israel' (Acts 1:6).

However Jesus gave John no special revelation. He returned an answer which responded in no way to John's hopes. John was still looking for a conquering Messiah able to drive the alien into the sea, in the power of God. The commonest experience of prayer is that God's answer rarely meets our specifications.

Jesus aimed to reveal himself through his actions, and still called for faith. He reminded John of the other foreshadowings of himself in the great prophet Isaiah whom he loved (Isaiah 35:5,6; 61:1). But when the messengers had left, Jesus praised John (verses 23-28). He was the greatest of the prophets, because he closed the line of the prophets, and saw with his own eyes the fulfilment of all the prophecies concerning the Messiah.

'What did you go out into the desert to see? A reed swayed by the wind?' (Luke 7:24).

Weddings

A wedding was a great event in a Jewish family. The celebrations could last as long as seven days.

The wedding began with a solemn procession of the bridegroom, his friends and his relatives to the bride's home. This took place at night, and everyone carried torches.

At the bride's home, the bride, dressed and adorned with jewels, was waiting together with her maids. A few bridesmaids would light the entrance with oil-lamps. They would hear the onlookers' cries as the bridegroom approached.

The groom called for his bride, and she went back to his house, in a festive, singing procession. A colourful wedding feast followed. One of the groom's closest friends was responsible for the arrangements at the feast.

Festivities reached their climax with the actual wedding ceremony. The couple stood or sat under a canopy of palm branches and embroidered fabric. Finally, they were escorted to their bridal chamber.

Opposition grows The record of the Gospels is darkened by the lengthening shadow of the religious leaders' attitude (verse 30). They rejected John. The great movement of the Spirit which God began through him took no account of established religion. John the Baptist indeed had nothing but fierce scorn for the religious establishment (Matthew 3:7-12). Jesus mingled with the people he had come to influence, meeting sinners where they were to be found. But like John he paid no undue reverence to the religious leaders. With savagery they turned upon him, reviling him for associating with the outcasts of society.

Jesus whimsically referred to a children's game, with its accompanying song. It is not clear what the game was, but weddings and funerals seem both to have been rejected. Time tells, Jesus concluded; for foolishness and wisdom find expression in action and history. People ultimately see clearly who is wise and who is foolish.

7:36-50 Jesus anointed by a sinful woman
Jesus had eaten with the tax-collectors at Capernaum. He now ate with a Pharisee, who treated his guest rudely. He no doubt had an eye to the comments of his critical friends. People from the streets outside would freely enter the public rooms of larger houses in Palestine, and so it was that the woman in this incident came in and attended to Jesus' needs.

This incident is not the same as that recorded in Matthew 26:7-13, Mark 14:3-9 or John 12:1-8. Simon the cleansed leper is not Simon the Pharisee. In Luke, the incident apparently takes place in Galilee, and the woman is not known by name. In the other Gospels she is Mary of Bethany.

Two debtors The simple human story of the woman in the Pharisee's house was the occasion for Jesus' parable about the two debtors. Simon saw the point and rightly, if rather disdainfully, answered that gratitude in human affairs is usually in proportion to the benefit received. Simon, too, claimed forgiveness for his sins. The whole Jewish ritual to which he subscribed had atonement and reconciliation as its purpose. But for Simon forgiveness was part of a legal transaction between man and God.

The broken woman, on the other hand, had found something in Jesus which convicted her and brought her to his feet for cleansing. That a man could so remodel and redeem, could so care and pity, filled her with love which overflowed in deeply-felt thanks. Jesus brought God to her in such a way that she saw his mercy and his willingness to save. So it was her faith which saved her (verse 50). The implication of verse 47 is not justification by works; she was not forgiven because of her love – her love was evidence of the forgiveness she had received.

8:1-15 The parable of the sower
In the first century Galilee was much more densely populated than it is today. To cover Galilee with a preaching mission was a heavy task. The work of the women (verses 2,3) is mentioned only in Luke; women are more prominent throughout his Gospel. There is also a glimpse of how Jesus and the Twelve were cared for (verse 3).

Joanna, the wife of Chuza, is mentioned only once more in the New Testament (Luke 24:10). Her presence reveals the early links Jesus' followers had with Herod's court (Luke 9:9; 23:8; Acts 13:1). Susanna does not appear again at all. Mary of Magdala appears prominently in the narratives of the resurrection. The strange phrase about the seven demons indicates that there was a battle for Mary's soul, whatever else it may mean.

The first mission in Galilee was finished. Perhaps its results were less sweeping than the disciples had expected. Possibly it had less

dynamic impact than the mission of John. To meet the disciples'
questions Jesus gave this parable.

Jesus' use of teaching by parable now became more frequent, not
to hide the truth (verse 10 does not mean this) but to separate those
willing to learn and follow from the merely curious and the seekers
for personal advantage and reward.

The seed Some of the seed was trodden to death under passing feet.
Secure and affluent, content with society as it is, many people see
Christ as irrelevant because they possess everything they want.
Some of the seed fell where the moist earth lay thin and warm on a bed
of barren rock. In such soil the seed quickly germinates, only to
wither in the slightest drought.

So with God's Word. Some harden their hearts; some appear to
respond but fail to follow up the implications; some who might have
produced a rich and healthy crop are too busy with less important
matters; and some allow the deep good roots to strike down into the
heart and produce a rich harvest.

Some of the seed fell among thorns. There are those who, like
Pilate, cannot escape the evil crop which they have allowed to grow
up. Some of the seed sprouted, proved fertile, and fulfilled God's
purpose. It varied in fruitfulness. Some was more productive, some
less. The place of sowing, good or bad, is passive. The human field
determines its own destiny. People are free to choose. Hearing is an
urgent business; each person must attend to it.

'But the seed on good soil stands for those with a noble
and good heart, who hear the word, retain it, and by
persevering produce a crop.' (Luke 8:15).

'He told this parable: "A farmer went out to sow his
seed . . ." ' (Luke 7:4, 5).

The quotation from Isaiah 6:9 comes six times in the New Testament: Matthew 13:14,15; Mark 4:12; John 12:40; Acts 28:26,27; Romans 11:8 and here.

8:16-25 The parable of the lamp and the calming of the storm

Ancient lamps were small and feeble, giving little light from their tiny wicks of flax or tow. To place them where they would give most light was only common sense.

Jesus' brothers and sisters (verse 19) are mentioned several times in the Gospels (Matthew 12:46; 13:55,56; Mark 3:32; 6:3; John 2:12) and he himself is called the 'first-born'. There can be no doubt that they were the children of Mary. The story that they were the children of Joseph by an earlier marriage, or even Jesus' cousins, was invented by Jerome and other later writers.

Before seeing harshness in Jesus' attitudes towards his family, remember the briefness and the purpose of the story. There are only fifty-six words in the Greek original. The visitors were not necessarily rejected nor dismissed unkindly. Jesus did however use the occasion to speak to the brotherhood and close relationship of all believers. Those who are one in Christ can be more closely linked than blood relatives, who do not share their faith.

Sudden storms sometimes whip Galilee into a fury. The calming of the storm continues Luke's theme; Jesus Christ is also Lord of the elements.

8:26-39 The healing of a demon-possessed man

Gadara lay across the lake, somewhere on the eastern shore where the hills rise steeply near the Yarmuk Gorge. There were graves of the Roman Tenth Legion in Gadara, indicating a continued Roman presence there. This possibly explains the name the man had taken.

Jesus had to prove to the man that he had been healed; this cost two thousand swine. The people of Gadara, preoccupied with swine, urged Jesus to leave. They were in the presence of Christ, and preferred pigs. He went, but left behind the first apostle to the Gentiles, the healed lunatic. The area was called the Decapolis, and by one estimate roughly one million Gentiles lived in its ten towns. In this area there was no need for secrecy (verse 30). It was a predominantly Greek region, rather than Jewish; hence the presence of swine, which were unclean for the Jews.

The 'abyss' (verse 31) is the resting place of wicked spirits (Romans 10:7; Jude 6; Revelation 20:3).

8:40-56 A dead girl and a sick woman

Jesus' progress towards Jairus' house must have been slow because of the crowds which 'almost crushed him' (verse 42), a strong verb in Greek. Then came the fatal interruption. The sick woman secretly touched Jesus' garment. God met her at the level of her faith, and she was healed. Quite apart from her illness, a literal interpretation of Leviticus 15 would have made her a permanent outcast. The severity of the Pharisees would no doubt strengthen the prohibitions against her. The word 'stopped' or 'staunched' (verse 44) is a medical term, typical of Luke.

Next came the message that the child was dead. The cruel delay which had ended fatally must have been hard for Jairus to bear. But as with the family at Bethany (John 11:4,6) Jesus deliberately delayed. He wanted to give Jairus not less, but more than he asked; not a child restored but one brought back from the dead. Luke notes the significant detail again; 'only one daughter' (verse 42).

In the room where Jairus' daughter was lying Jesus allowed only the reverent. The scornful are not allowed to see God's mysteries. Jesus' touch could have given life to the little girl in any place. The scornful were excluded because they were not worthy of God's

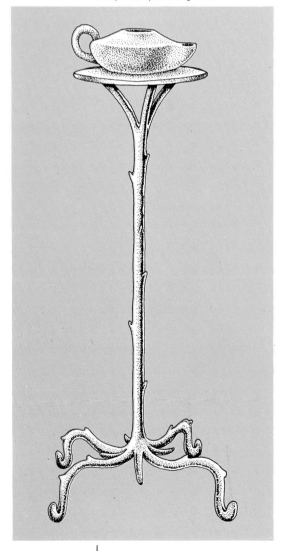

Lamps were found in every home in Palestine. They were pottery bowls filled with olive oil, and with one or more wicks. Sometimes they were placed on a special lampstand to spread their light better.

revelation. God reveals himself to the faithful and humble. Jairus was both of these. And as a leader of orthodox Jews, he must have been well aware that the authorities were turning against Jesus.

9:1-9 Jesus sends out the Twelve

The mission of the Twelve was designed to train them for their lifelong task of evangelism without Christ visibly at their side. The directions laid down here are still applicable in general, though not in detail. To abandon all provision for the journey was practicable in the small area which they were called on to travel through. It formed an object lesson in speed and in complete dependence on God.

The message was simple: the kingdom of God—God's rule in life and the acknowledgment of him as Lord. Good deeds and the relief of suffering were to accompany the preaching. To 'shake the dust off'(verse 5) was the action of a rabbi after travelling in Gentile territory.

Jesus' own progress through Galilee, and the consolidating mission of his closer followers, caused in the north something like the stir which John's preaching in the lower Jordan valley had created in Judea (verses 7-9). Herod Antipas was worried. Mark tells us that he had been impressed by John's witness (Mark 6:20); but Herodias ruined his life. Unable to break free from a vicious entanglement, he had descended to the crime which now preyed on his mind and left him 'perplexed'. Luke must have had informants at Herod's palace.

9:10-17 Jesus feeds the five thousand

Bethsaida Julias is across the Jordan a mile north-east of the lake. It is in a quiet area, where Jesus tried to find rest for his weary followers. But the eager crowds followed and Jesus met their needs.

This miracle is reported by all four Gospel-writers, and it is instructive to compare their accounts (Matthew 14:13-21; Mark 6:30-44; John 6:1-13). There is no difficulty provided Christ was who he claimed to be. If he was less than he claimed, Christian doctrine falls apart.

A divine principle of action is to be found in this incident. God seems to demand some point of entry into the world, something surrendered, some scrap of experience, a widow's mite, a handful of

Tiberias was founded between AD18 and AD22. Herod Antipas named it after the new Roman Emperor, and in time the name also became attached to the lake. The town was totally populated by Gentiles, and we have no record of Jesus having visited it.

Bradd

Bread was the most important food item for the Israelites. The women made bread every day. Round barley loaves were commonest, but bread was also made from wheat. Early in the morning the women started to grind the flour, using a mortar and pestle or some sort of hand-mill.

The coarse-textured flour was mixed with water and salt and worked into a dough. Sometimes leftovers of old dough, called 'leaven', were used to make the new dough rise (Matthew 13:33). But if they were in a hurry, the women would make unleavened bread.

The dough was shaped into thin rounds of bread. The simplest way of baking the loaves was to put them on hot ashes or heated stones, or on a griddle over the fire.

A simple oven was made from an upturned clay dish or shallow bowl. This was put on top of the fire with its rim resting on a few stones. The loaves were placed on top of the dish.

bread and fish, a sorrow, a pain, a joy. Given completely to God, the small gift becomes miraculous in his hands. What God blesses, he infinitely multiplies (verse 16). The blessing was probably the Jewish grace: 'Blessed are you, O Lord our God, King of the universe, who brings forth bread from the earth'.

Note in the middle of this creativity Jesus' care for the fragments. The Jew on a journey carried a rush-woven basket to avoid buying bread from Gentiles. The disciples were equipped in the same way, and each of the Twelve collected up food for the following day.

9:18-27 Peter's confession of Christ

If Matthew and Mark are compared, it will be seen that there is a gap in Luke's narrative at this point. This passage corresponds with Matthew 16:13-28 and Mark 8:27-9:1. The events of almost two chapters in the two other Gospels are omitted. It is a mark of Luke's style of writing that he liked room to expand when the subject seemed particularly important, and that he gained space by heavy pruning elsewhere. There was also, of course, the simple consideration of the practicable length of a roll of papyrus.

Luke refers to Jesus praying in six places where the other Gospels make no comment (Luke 3:21; 5:16; 6:12; 9:18; 11:1). All of these come before momentous words or actions. 'The Christ' (verse 20) (in the Greek 'christos') is the Hebrew 'Messiah' or 'anointed'. This is the title given to the chosen Servant of God foretold in the Old Testament. The Greek word for 'rejected' (verse 22) implies examination

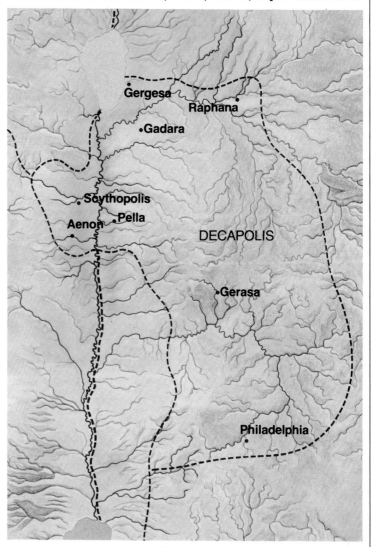

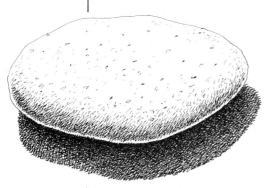

and rejection. The three classes of people mentioned (verse 22) were those who formed the Sanhedrin.

The kingdom Peter understood little when he delighted his master with his confession. He was thinking in terms of a conquering Messiah and an earthly kingdom. But Jesus overlooked all this. The disciples had the love he wanted to see and the will to understand. Jesus promised that those who were there would see the first beginnings of a kingdom they had not dreamed of.

The longer treatments in the other Gospels make it clear that these events climaxed weeks of fellowship and instruction in the Decapolis. Jesus had been striving to prepare his followers for what was going to happen in Jerusalem. They had recognized him as the Christ; but the implications were not to be what they expected. Three interpretations of verse 27 have been suggested: it could refer to the resurrection, the transfiguration or the fall of Jerusalem in AD 70 which swept away the remnants of the old order.

9:28-36 The transfiguration

The transfiguration was the prelude to Jesus' return to Jerusalem, the Passion week, his death and resurrection. So, in the truest sense, came the 'kingdom of God'. Not the summing up of all things, but the completion of God's revelation of himself in Christ.

Severe testing and temptation lay ahead. As a climax to weeks of spiritual preparation in the villages round Caesarea Philippi Jesus chose to strengthen three of his men for the testing which lay in front of them, and the tense weeks when their leadership was to count for so much. Hence the night journey up Mount Hermon, the beautiful 9,000-foot mountain fourteen miles north of Caesarea Philippi.

A new exodus They would be tempted to doubt whether a crucified man could possibly be the Coming One. Hence the strange scene on the mountain, which showed Jesus first as the climax of Old Testament history. Moses was the great law-giver, Elijah the first of the prophets. Both were linked with the Messiah in prophecy (Deuteronomy 18:15-19; Malachi 3:1; 4:5,6). There are other Old Testament parallels: the cloud indicating the presence of God

The snows of Mount Hermon, which is probably the site of Jesus' Transfiguration, feed the River Jordan. It is easily the highest mountain in the area.

If the Transfiguration took place on Hermon, the healing which follows probably took place near Caesarea Philippi. This beautiful site lies at the foot of Hermon, and was named Caesarea in honour of the Roman Emperor.

(Exodus 40:34,35) – the cloud of Sinai and the cloud of Mount Carmel. Moses led the children of Israel at the Exodus; the conversation on the mountain concerned 'the exodus which he was to accomplish at Jerusalem'. Secondly, the vision of John the Baptist was confirmed, and Jesus was shown to be God's beloved Son.

Luke's eight days (verse 28) is on the inclusive Roman reckoning; Matthew and Mark both say six days.

Difficult times lay ahead. The privileged disciples were to need all the strengthening that the memory of this experience could give in the days which led up to Golgotha. There is always work to be done following the moment of special revelation. We must look for the task of service which almost inevitably follows God's unveiling of himself to us.

9:37-45 The healing of a boy with an evil spirit
Mark tells this story a little more fully. It seems that the nine men who had not shared the journey up Mount Hermon were in the middle of a curious crowd which included some of the religious leaders of Caesarea Philippi. The area was strongly Gentile, but also included a large Jewish population who watched Jesus' activities with critical or interested gaze.

The epileptic boy, like the blind man at the gate (John 9:2) posed a theological problem for the disciples; a case for display of dire need and an object for sacrificial love. This accounts for their helplessness. Jesus once more pointed forward to his betrayal (verses 44-46).

9:46-50 Who will be the greatest?
Conscious that a climax was approaching, and still not grasping the spiritual nature of 'the kingdom', the Twelve were beginning to bicker about precedence. The choice of three of their number for the experience on Mount Hermon may have underlined tensions within the group. Their reasoning (verse 46) may have been a reaction to Jesus' prediction (verse 44); they were wondering who would take over from him their leadership.

The child placed in the middle of the disciples, a picture of open-eyed and wondering trust, offers a pattern of simplicity of faith. If verses 49,50 follow chronologically (which may not be the case) they show how little John had listened to the instruction about childlike simplicity. His narrow sectarianism provoked Jesus' statement (verse 50) a rebuke to all intolerance. The contrary remark, recorded two chapters later (Luke 11:23) is not a repudiation or an afterthought, but a principle applying to a different situation.

9:51-62 The cost of following Jesus

At this point Luke includes a selection of material not found in the other Gospels. In his usual way, he has shortened his accounts on each side to make room for it. From Luke 9:51 to 19:44 there is an account of Jesus' words and actions as he moved forward on his last journey up to Jerusalem: first in Galilee, then down the Jordan valley, and finally up from Jericho. Luke has concentrated much material here, and we need not always assume it comes in strict chronological order.

The boorishness of the Samaritans may have been caused by disappointment (verses 51-53). Jesus' sternness may have made them unenthusiastic to keep him. Jesus now had Jerusalem and the cross firmly in view.

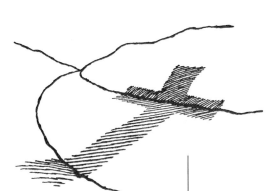

Counting the cost As previously, a demonstration of intolerant behaviour produced a valuable saying by Jesus (verses 54-56). On a sudden impulse a scribe (Matthew 8:19) promised to follow Jesus. He had failed to count the cost, though we are not told the result when he did come to count it (verses 57,58).

The man of verses 59,60 would certainly not have been there if his father was lying dead at home. The demands of an Eastern funeral would have preoccupied him. He must mean 'Let me wait, like Abraham at Haran, until my father dies, and I can follow without offending him'.

The ploughman The man of verses 61,62 had a divided mind. He lacked stability. The good ploughman fixes his eyes steadily on a far point, grips the plough firmly, throws all his energy into the activity, and neither wavers nor stops till the furrow is cut to its end as clean and straight as he knows how. So are those people who Jesus wants to follow him.

'Jesus replied, "No-one who puts his hand to the plough and looks back is fit for service in the kingdom of God" ' (Luke 9:62).

'Woe to you, Korazin! Woe to you, Bethsaida! For if the miracles that were performed in you had been performed in Tyre and Sidon, they would have repented long ago' (Luke 10:13). Bethsaida and Korazin today lie in ruins.

10:1-24 Jesus sends out the Seventy-two

Some of the old manuscripts have 'seventy' rather than 'seventy-two', which suggests a comparison is being made with the mission of the Twelve. If the Twelve represented the missionary role of Israel's twelve tribes, so the Seventy perhaps suggested the seventy members of the Sanhedrin, the highest Jewish religious assembly. They were supposed to prepare the land for the coming of the Messiah.

It has also been pointed out that the Jews thought of the Gentiles as seventy nations. Jerusalem Jews had neglected the area of TransJordan. It was through this strip of territory, with its part-Gentile population, that the Seventy were to go if they went 'ahead of him'.

The detailed instructions given were suited to the urgency of a short pioneer mission, and are not to be applied generally to Christian work. Time was short, and Jesus prohibited detailed preparations. He told them not to waste time in social activities. Greetings here do not mean the courtesy when friend meets friend, but the endless formalities of Eastern hospitality. Since the area to be crossed contained many non-Jews, Jesus also ordered that no Jewish over-sensitivity about eating requirements be allowed to cause awkwardness or spoil the visitors' witness (verse 7).

The lakeside towns had been uniquely favoured. Jesus had lived in Capernaum and was familiar in many of the communities. To have lived in the light of the truth and yet to have neglected it is a heavy responsibility indeed.

The return The Seventy returned jubilant from their mission. Jesus' remark about the fall of Satan was designed to check the growth of pride. It is phrased in the style of Jewish apocalyptic poetry. The devil fell by pride, and minds taught in such picture-language would see immediately the point of the warning. Success in their preaching-mission could so easily lead to arrogance.

Jesus' comments on the report of the Seventy contain important words. The mysterious phrase in verse 18 probably means that the defeat of evil was sure, once ordinary people learned to preach the message of Christ. This is what the mission of the Seventy had triumphantly demonstrated. Success in preaching, and the perilous approval of men, is no cause for personal pride or self-congratulation (verse 20). Christ cannot use people without humility.

Snakes and scorpions In a similar vein and unlikely to be taken literally by Eastern people, is Jesus' remark about snakes and scorpions. These are symbols for cunning, vicious enemies.

Next, Jesus simply told his followers to take thought humbly of their privilege – not their power.

Verse 22; John undoubtedly takes up this theme more fully, but here in Luke, where it is an integral part of the text, these words witness to the Son's oneness with the Father.

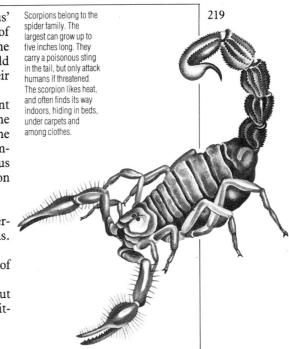

Scorpions belong to the spider family. The largest can grow up to five inches long. They carry a poisonous sting in the tail, but only attack humans if threatened. The scorpion likes heat, and often finds its way indoors, hiding in beds, under carpets and among clothes.

10:25-37 The parable of the Good Samaritan

From Jerusalem, 2,600 feet above sea-level, down to Jericho is the great rift valley. It was a place for bandits and highwaymen, with boulders on the barren hillside to hide the waiting thieves and desert to conceal their flight.

The Samaritan belonged to a race despised by the Jews. When Assyria overran and depopulated the northern kingdom of Israel, their cruel policy of transporting the population cleared the land of its inhabitants. To keep the provinces from complete social and economic collapse, the Assyrian king re-populated Samaria with aliens (2 Kings 17:24-41). Instead of regarding the newcomers as objects for Jewish evangelism, the people of Judah, which remained independent until Nebuchadnezzar took Jerusalem a century later, turned away in contempt, and the bitter racial division between Samaritans and Jews began.

The priest in the story feared ceremonial defilement if the still figure lying by the road proved to be dead. The Levite was perhaps afraid of a trap set by brigands. Modern men might similarly avoid involvement in some inner-city situation of assault or mugging. There is no pointer that the victim was a good man. The Samaritan did everything that the other passers-by failed to do. As a visitor from the hated north, he lacked the Jews' knowledge of the Old Testament scriptures. Samaria only knew the books of Moses; ironically it is Leviticus 19:18 which commands us to love our neighbour. As ever, the Jewish legalists had a way of avoiding this duty. They redefined 'neighbour' to suit their interest. Jesus' reply once more cut through the clutter of their nonsense with clear common sense.

10:38-42 At the home of Mary and Martha

John 10:22 suggests that Jesus visited Jerusalem briefly during the last months of his life, sometime before the historic journey up from Jericho to the cross. This was no doubt the occasion of his visit to Bethany and the incident vividly described here.

John, writing later, reminded Christians that Jesus loved Martha (John 11:5). Jesus' rebuke to Martha was kindly and affectionate; but Martha was at fault for losing control of the situation. She was 'distracted' and rebuked her master. 'Don't you care that my sister

The olive tree, which has a thick, gnarled trunk, can grow to a great age. It has a large crown of leaves, and can give welcome shelter from the sun.

'Christ conversing with Mary and Martha' a pen-and-wash drawing by Rembrandt.

has left me to serve by myself? Tell her to lend me a hand'. The Greek text here is very vivid. There is need of only one thing, and Mary has chosen the good part which shall not be taken away from her'.

The reference to 'what is better' may be to the dish of honour, such as the one placed in front of Benjamin at Joseph's banquet (Genesis 43:34). Briefly, Jesus' meaning was that we can be deprived of food and comfort without real harm. But we cannot safely go without fellowship with our Lord.

11:1-13 Jesus' teaching on prayer

Jesus' teaching on prayer was that it consists of simply speaking to 'our Father in heaven'. He would never have called God 'Father' if he had not intended those who heard him to take the word for what it means. God is infinitely wise, infinitely loving, and can be approached as an earthly father may by an anxious child.

The prayer which Jesus gave was never intended as a hasty gabble of words. It consists of a series of headings by which a time of prayer may be guided. The prayer calls for pauses in which the worship or the request is related to the whole of life, its different needs and its personal problems.

'Hallowed' means treated as holy; 'name' includes character. 'Daily' means here 'for the coming day'; this is a morning prayer. Most of this prayer has parallels in writings of the rabbis; it is not new words but a new spirit which is significant.

Persistence By the everyday story of the individual who knocked up his neighbour at midnight (verses 5-10) Jesus did not mean that God, like the weary neighbour, could be brought to a different frame of mind by repeated requests. What he did mean was that people are not put off by delays or a first refusal, if their desire is deep enough, or their confidence firm enough in someone else's ability to give. God's children should be no less persistent with their father, while at the same time examining their prayers and seeking his purpose in delay.

The words of verses 11-13 reinforce the earlier argument that the fatherhood of God is no mockery. The round desert stones of Palestine looked similar to loaves of bread. 'Though you are evil' (verse 13) means sinful by disposition.

Joy

In the Gospels we find that the birth of Jesus (Matthew 2:10; Luke 2:10) and his resurrection (Matthew 28:8) were occasions of special joy. Joy was perhaps one of the most precious gifts Jesus bestowed on his followers (John 16:22). They were to discover it in the fact that their names were written in heaven (Luke 10:20), in suffering persecution for his sake (Luke 6:23), in answered prayer (John 16:24) and in service well done (Matthew 25:21).

'Which of you fathers, if your son asks for a fish, will give him a snake instead?' (Luke 11:11).

11:14-28 Jesus and Beelzebub

Notice how the accounts in Matthew 12 and Mark 3 supplement each other and Luke's account (especially the strong words of Matthew 12:31,32). The people who saw Jesus' healing touch on disturbed minds were unable to deny the evidence of their senses. But they preferred an evil explanation for it to an explanation based on faith. The tense of the verb (verse 14) is significant; it suggests that the cure was not in this case instantaneous. 'Beelzebub' is used for the devil in the New Testament. It is possibly derived from Baal-zebub – 'Lord of the high place' – a Canaanite god.

The briefness of the account (verses 24-28) sometimes blurs the line of thought. It deals with the possibility of being neutral. What of the person who is cleansed of the evil in his life, but does not fill the vacuum with Christ? Old sin will return, the defeated invaders of the soul will sweep back in force. Verses 24-26 had a particular application for the Jews, who had known the blessings of the Old Covenant; they were now being called on to accept the Messiah, following John the Baptist.

11:29-36 The sign of Jonah

Two historic instances illustrate the point made in the earlier discussion of faith. The choice is often decided by the moral attitude of the person involved. Men set on evil asked in vain to be convinced. The 'sign of Jonah' was given in Nineveh, the stronghold of the cruel

'A house divided against itself will fall' (Luke 11:17).

Assyrians. The Queen of Sheba, similarly from an alien civilization, came with an open mind, seeking conviction. She found it.

The reference to Jonah (verse 30) is filled out in Matthew 12:40, which also connects with the hint contained in the future tense here. 'One greater than Solomon' (verse 31) is neuter in the Greek; the *New English Bible* translates it 'what is here is greater than . . .'

Verses 33-36 look like a fragment of the Sermon on the Mount. Jesus' teaching, like all good teaching, was often repeated, and this period of his ministry was one of tough teaching, preaching and controversy. The light was certainly not concealed.

The strange saying about the eye (verse 34) covers another truth. There were many blind people in Palestine; Bartimaeus was waiting down in Jericho. The sun was blazing in the Jordan valley, but Bartimaeus saw nothing. If light is to flood the mind, the eye must receive and interpret the situation outside. God's grace is the waiting illumination of the sun; and the eye is the faith which receives. Salvation is at the point where grace and faith meet.

11:37-54 Six woes

The washing which Jesus missed out (verse 38) was not a simple act of cleanliness. It was the ceremonial of the Pharisees, a ritual act demanded and regulated to the last detail by the complex laws which they had invented. The amount of water was specified, including the movements by which it was poured from fingertip to wrist, and the way in which the hand was to be rubbed in the other hand.

The story does not suggest that Jesus went with unclean hands to his host's table. It demonstrates once more his contempt for the idle and vexatious formalities into which the Pharisees had distorted true religion.

The regulations covering the cleanness and uncleanness of tableware were equally detailed. This was all part of the clutter of nonsense which Jesus contemptuously dismissed. Jesus' denunciation shows that Pharisaism had much to say about rules and regulations, but little positive about the duties of mercy and love. Yet the Pharisees began well. Thanks to them, in the stern days of exile the law was kept by the children of Israel. But human institutions can become an end in themselves, lose their true meaning and die.

Jericho lay deep in the Rift Valley, about seventeen miles east-north-east of Jerusalem. A very ancient settlement, Herod the Great had built himself a winter palace here with elaborate gardens. The city's famous plantations of palms and balsam trees earned rich profits.

'Woe to you Pharisees, because you give God a tenth of your mint, rue and all other kinds of garden herbs, but you neglect justice and the love of God!' (Luke 11:42). The herb rue is still found in Israel.

'Woe to you, because you build tombs for the prophets, and it was your forefathers who killed them' (Luke 11:47). Probably Jesus was referring to tombs like these of the patriarchs in pronouncing this 'woe' against the Pharisees.

Pharisaism The Pharisees were laymen, fanatically concerned with details of the law. The lawyers were professionals, the 'scribes' linked with the Pharisees in their excessive legalism. It is difficult to draw a sharp line between the two groups. Verse 46 forms the core of Jesus' charge. The lawyers had made the simple and positive law of Moses into a complicated web of regulations too difficult for ordinary people to follow. But they had also made it possible for those who knew how to evade their own burdensome obligations.

Many examples can be quoted from writings of the rabbis. The Sabbath day's journey offers one illustration. It was limited to one thousand yards; but this was of little use. You could extend the distance by extending the limits of 'home', for instance by putting a rope across the end of your street. The journey could then be measured from that point. Or, if greater licence still were needed, a parcel of food, hidden on Friday at the end of the permitted distance, formed a second 'home'. You could begin measuring again from that point and proceed for a further Sabbath day's journey.

'Shed' (verse 50) has the force 'being constantly poured out'. The incidents in verse 51 span the whole of Old Testament history. The scribes and Pharisees honoured the tombs of the prophets who had denounced legalism (Isaiah 1:11-15), but their ancestors had persecuted the very same prophets. The 'key' (verse 52) was the law teacher's badge of office, his work being to open the scriptures to others (Isaiah 22:22).

Warnings and encouragements It is difficult to say whether Luke has concentrated a number of sayings at this point, or whether this is a summary of one address. Teaching was repetitive, and the same illustration or word-picture could well have been used with more than one point.

The disciples were told to avoid the deceitfulness of the Pharisees, the concealing of an unholy life behind an outer show of complicated holiness. They acted a part, which is the literal meaning of hypocrisy. But 'play-acting' can also describe the Christian who covers up his real convictions and tries to hide his faith. If conviction is real and faith genuine such deceit is pointless (verse 2). Therefore speak out boldly about the truth (verse 3).

The reason for such hesitation is fear of men (verse 4) which ought to come second to reverence for God (verse 5). 'Hell' is 'Gehenna' in the Greek; the valley of the sons of Hinnom, outside Jerusalem, where fires burned continually to consume rubbish (see Jeremiah 7:31). The name was used as a word-picture for a place of punishment after death.

Trust and denial Sellers of small birds still stand by the roadside in modern Lebanon. The birds were sold two for a penny, said Matthew; five for twopence, said Luke. So cheap were the little birds that an extra one was thrown in for the bigger sale. But even such a trivial death does not escape God's knowledge. Those who trust such a God should value above all God's honour (verse 8). To deny him is to forfeit his acceptance (verse 9).

Denial can be a form of rejection. This thought must have led in the full account to the solemn matter which Matthew and Mark treat more fully, the 'sin against the Holy Spirit'. It is obvious that this must mean the ultimate, deliberate and final rejection of Christ as Saviour; the wilful and conscious repressing of the movement of God's convicting Spirit in the heart and conscience. It means wilfully crediting to the activity of the devil what is clearly the activity of the grace of God. To deny God can end in such disaster (verse 10).

Jesus accuses the Pharisees of this 'sin against the Holy Spirit'. It can only be the sin of someone who utterly quenches the voice of God's spirit so that he can no longer hear it. Such a sinner loses all

'Are not five sparrows sold for two pennies? Yet not one of them is forgotten by God' (Luke 12:6).

'And Jesus told this parable. ''The ground of a certain rich man produced a good crop. He thought to himself, 'What shall I do? I have no place to store my crops' '' ' (Luke 12:16, 17). Parts of Galilee offer very rich farming country.

realization of sin. He cannot be forgiven because he cannot repent. He cannot repent because he has no concern, no remaining consciousness of sin or of God. He has no fear because his heart is dead to every notion of eternity or of coming judgement. So it follows that no one who in a dark hour of the soul fears that he may have 'committed the unpardonable sin' can possibly have committed it.

12:13-21 The parable of the rich fool

The stern rebuke to the man who brought his problem of injustice to Jesus might be looked at in its context. There is no reason why such difficulties should not be brought reverently to him. But it seems clear from the drift of the highly-compressed account that the man interrupted a serious talk about dependence on God. Deaf to the words which he might have heard to his eternal profit, he blundered in with his financial problem. All he could think about in the presence of Jesus was money. Hence Jesus' rebuke.

And hence the parable about the fool who could not see that there lay anything beyond material things. There is nothing to indicate that he was a bad man in other respects. In difficult farming country he had built up great prosperity and, unlike some rich people, he saw that riches are intended for use and enjoyment. He owed no one anything, and his wealth had been fairly gained. But his fault is clear. In a land plagued with poverty, inequality and suffering, he had no thought of sharing. It was 'my barns', 'my grain' and 'my goods'.

In fact he had no thought except for himself. Life, for him, was

Threshing in Israel today. In Jesus' time, the wheat was taken to a threshing-floor bound in sheaves. The threshing took place outdoors, since there was no rain in summer. The wheat was spread out upon the ground, and oxen were used to tread the grains out of the ears of wheat. Sometimes they pulled a heavy sledge round the threshing-floor. The sledge would be made of wood, with stones or iron spikes underneath to separate the grains.

'Don't be afraid; you are worth more than many sparrows' (Luke 12:7).

'eat, drink and be happy'; happiness a state limited to self, to eating and drinking. He had three faults: he imagined that he was in full control; he mistook his body for his soul; and he confused means and ends. This is the essence of materialism.

12:22-34 Do not worry

This thought runs on from the parable just told, and some teaching from the Sermon on the Mount is introduced. Life is more than food and more than mere physical needs. All such matters must be kept in proportion by the Christian. Verse 33 seems to be a drastic statement; but it must be remembered that, in line with Eastern literary custom, the Bible speaks in poetry as readily as in prose. So it must be expected that paradoxes and striking statements will occur. Also, scripture must be balanced against scripture. The disciple John had a home, and the family at Bethany had a house and the means with which to entertain Jesus.

Jesus' remark has to be seen in its context. He began by commenting on the rich fool who thought that the sole purpose of life was food and drink. He passed from this to the preoccupation with the needs of daily living, which exclude and quench higher and more vital concerns. For the rich farmer, acquiring goods was his lifelong aim. Jesus urges us, his listeners, to cast care aside. Does worry achieve anything? Worry is unreasonable (verses 22-24). 'Worry' (verse 29) in the Greek describes the tossing of a ship, literally 'raised between heaven and earth'.

Luke 12

'If this is how God clothes the grass of the field . . . how much more will he clothe you' (Luke 12:28).

The prophets and the Messiah

Amos indicates that the Messiah will come from David's line and 'will restore David's fallen tent', re-establishing his rule in a new way (Amos 9:11-15).

Hosea explains that in future the house of David will become very important (Hosea 3:5).

Isaiah describes the Messiah as a person with divine characteristics. The book of Isaiah also speaks of him as the Suffering Servant of the Lord (Isaiah 9:2-7; 11:1-10; 32:1-5; 53).

Micah mentions that the ruler, the Messiah, will come from Bethlehem, the city of David (Micah 5:2).

Joel and Habakkuk have several descriptions of the time when the Messiah will come (Joel 2:1; 3:18; Habakkuk 3:13).

Jeremiah speaks of the Messiah, the King of the house of David, who will 'reign wisely and do what is just and right in the land' (Jeremiah 23:5-8).

Ezekiel describes the future Messiah as a true shepherd, who will take his flock to good pastures. This shepherd will come from the family of David (Ezekiel 34:11-16; 23).

Daniel speaks of the Messiah as the Son of Man. When he comes, an eternal kingdom will begin, which will never be destroyed (Daniel 7:13,14).

'Jesus said to the crowd: "When you see a cloud rising in the west, immediately you say 'It's going to rain,' and it does ... How is it that you don't know how to interpret this present time?" '
(Luke 12:54,56)

12:35-48 Watchfulness

Teaching about the Lord's return haunts the Bible. Notice how frequently it comes in both the teaching of Jesus and in that of his apostles. No time is specified, and the manner of his coming is not clear. It is stated, not for speculation, but as a matter which prompts zeal and calls for urgency and dedication. Like servants alert for the return home of their master, so the followers of Jesus must be ready for his coming.

The insistent warning of these words is that we should take care to be prepared for the reckoning of God. The warning may be applied more widely than to the need to be ready for his coming. That great day will come at a time we do not know, and nothing in life matters more than that we should be found, like devoted and expectant servants, busy with our master's work. We should be awaiting his coming with eagerness and joy.

For his coming, see also 1 Corinthians 4:12; James 4:17; 2 Peter 2:21. Notice how Jesus frequently answered one question by putting another (verse 41).

God never hardens the heart of anyone who is willing to respond. But if we choose to remain blind, and persistently turn away from the truth, he lets us become immune to it (verse 40).

12:49-59 Not peace but division

These words (verses 49-53) must also be taken in their context. It is a fact that Jesus brought peace between man and God, and peace between man and man for those who applied his teaching and lived in its light. It is also a fact that he sets man at odds with man. A binding and demanding loyalty can challenge old loyalties. Fire (verse 49) both burns and purifies. On the picture of baptism see Mark 10:8.

The next section (verses 54-59) was addressed to the crowds who were alert enough to the signs of the weather, but who shut their eyes to the signs of the times. Hence the description used: 'hypocrites'. They were pretending with the blindness of obstinacy and pride.

A litigious man Like a man doggedly determined to push a bad or hopeless case to the final judgement of the law-court (verses 57,58) instead of seeking just and reasonable settlement out of court, the

people were blundering on towards the disaster which lay ahead. The picture in the little parable is of a man obstinately going to court with a bad case to plead. The last verse of the chapter takes it for granted that the defendant will lose; this point is the whole reason for the story. So stands man with God.

The signs of the coming Great Rebellion of AD 66-70 multiply in the New Testament. This warning is among them. Wilfully blind, the Jews refused to listen to reason, and beat themselves to destruction against the iron might of Rome. Among the few who survived in liberty were Christians who listened to warnings such as these.

The 'last penny' (verse 59) was the Jewish *lepton*, the smallest coin in circulation.

13:1-9 Repent or perish

Mention of Pilate's massacre in Galilee and the disaster of the Siloam tower flow on from the words about judgement which closed the previous chapter. People were no doubt suggesting that the victims of the two catastrophes were under some special judgement of God. Not so, Jesus replied. Man is exposed to the chances of life, and God does not always intervene to protect the innocent from disaster.

The mention of the atrocity at the altar (verse 1) gives a glimpse of Pilate's tough-handed government. It may refer to the men who caused a riot when Pilate used money taken from the Temple treasury to build a new aqueduct into Jerusalem.

The fig tree Hosea 9:10 and Joel 1:7 are probably the key to the word-pictures of verses 6-9. Jesus had used the word 'perish' (verses 3,5) and this parable answers the unspoken question: How can a chosen people perish?

Fig trees were often planted in spare corners of vineyards. It would be natural to expect signs of fruit after three years. The truth which Jesus was trying to emphasize was that national privilege carried with it national responsibility. To those taught to think in the word-pictures of the Old Testament, it was plain that Israel was the fig tree. Israel, it was suggested, would only stand as long as she fulfilled the historic purpose for which she came into being.

'From now on there will be five in one family divided against each other, three against two and two against three' (Luke 12:53).

13:10-17 A crippled woman healed on the Sabbath

This story has all the marks of direct reporting. It is the last instance in Luke of Jesus' appearing in a synagogue. The places of assembly were closing to his teaching as the opposition of the Pharisees grew.

The leader of the synagogue stands out vividly in this brief account. In line with common Jewish practice, he was chairman of a board of ten men who were in charge of the local synagogue. He did not dare to confront his visitor directly. He rebuked him indirectly (verse 14) with an exhortation to the congregation about Sabbath-keeping. It was Pharisaical play-acting of the first order, and earned Jesus' prompt retort.

The detailed regulations in the Talmud for the care of livestock on the Sabbath laid down that water could be drawn for an ox or an ass on the seventh day, but that it should not be brought to the animal's mouth. Men who reduced religion to such an absurdity could look with indifference on both human affliction and human deliverance. Hence the confusion among Jesus' enemies and the joy of those who had found the religion of their leaders so burdensome.

13:18-30 The narrow door

The grain of mustard seed (verse 19) was the smallest kind of seed sown by the farmers of Israel, yet grew to become the largest of their

Jesus was now moving down the Jordan valley. He was never to come this way again. Evidently he was still inside the boundaries of Herod's territories (Luke 13:31).

seed crops. It was a picture of history. Twelve men were chosen from obscure towns of Galilee to stage an assault on the world. Those who have found their release and joy and fulfilment in Jesus are 'a great multitude that no one could count' (Revelation 7:9).

Yeast (verse 21) is used elsewhere as a symbol of corruption (see Luke 12:1; 1 Corinthians 5:6-8). But here it follows on the previous parable and carries a similar meaning. There is no need to expect the same word or image always to be interpreted in the same way. The picture here is surely of the secret working of a principle of life hidden within a lifeless mass. So the gospel works in society and in the human personality.

The theme of verses 22-30 is urgency. Jesus was moving down the Jordan valley for the last time, and the cross was in clear view. Opportunities came and went. Some people who saw that many passed on their way and few came to a live faith asked whether only a few would be saved. The question was rejected as irrelevant by Jesus. There was only one urgent need – to take advantage of the hour's opportunity to meet the challenge of the moment. The Jewish nation was failing at this point, and others were grasping their privilege. 'Make every effort' (verse 24) is the same word as 'fight' (1 Timothy 6:12).

13:31-35 Jesus' sorrow for Jerusalem

Jesus must still have been inside the boundaries of Herod's territories, which included north Galilee and Perea. It is impossible to say whether the Pharisees' warning amounted to sincere concern or

'What is the kingdom of God like? . . . It is like a mustard seed . . . ' (Luke 13:18, 19).

Jesus warned again of the desolation that was to come upon Jerusalem. Masada, a stronghold near the Dead Sea, is a reminder of the Jews' heroic but vain resistance against the might of pagan Rome.

was merely a ploy to get rid of Jesus and drive him into Judea. Some of the Pharisees did not deserve the evil reputation which the majority had earned; think for example of Nicodemus and Gamaliel.

The sad remark about Jerusalem (verse 33) leads Luke to record here the lament over the city which was delivered by Jesus from the summit of the Mount of Olives some weeks later. It must be remembered that a tidy and ordered account with a clear historical and geographical sequence was not necessarily Luke's first aim. His primary purpose was simply to record.

14:1-14 Jesus at a Pharisee's house

The strict Jew ate three times on the Sabbath. The meal here was probably the midday meal. 'He was being carefully watched' (verse 1) – the Greek implies close scrutiny with a suspicious motive. The guests would be invited as a religious duty. Jesus again uses the devastating argument based on the laws about the care of animals, which contained elements of mercy and compassion (compare Luke 13:15 and John 5:17). The Pharisees gave to the beasts what they denied to suffering men.

There is a touch of irony in this table-talk. The gathering was crowded, and competition for the important places among the guests embarrassingly evident. Jesus lay down some simple rules for such occasions, with a serious rebuke to pride beneath them. Verse 12 literally means 'do not always invite your friends'.

The Christian lives in the spotlight of attention, for he is striving to be different. People hate difference. The answer must be simplicity and humility. Hence the story about the presumptuous and the humble guests. Let there be no boasting, no self-righteousness, no loud or arrogant words, no pride in virtue or obtrusive piety, no brash claims to holiness. Quiet strength, calm uprightness, the simple carrying out of duty, courtesy, reserve, dignity, friendliness and taking part without compromise are the appropriate characteristics of the Christian.

14:15-24 The parable of the great banquet

In ancient times a feast was announced and invitations did not carry the date. You accepted the personal inconvenience in accepting the

Jesus called Herod a 'fox' because the animal is known for its cruelty and cunning.

In rich Jewish homes guests at a banquet reclined on couches on three sides of the table.

invitation. For those who accepted, the honour of the invitation and the pleasure of the banquet outweighed all grounds for hesitating or refusing. When the time came for the banquet, the call went out and the guests gathered. It was the height of rudeness to excuse yourself with last-minute problems.

This parable was a picture of history. The Jews had a legend of a great feast when the Messiah came. The invitations had been out since the beginning of the nation of Israel. And now the hour had come. It was a banquet of richer food than any ordinary meal, but the guests were busy, rude, preoccupied. Those they despised filled the empty places at table.

Excuses It was the hope of every Pharisee to earn the reward of sitting at the banquet of the righteous (verse 15). Israel had received the first invitation through the prophets (verses 16,17). The second invitation had been given by John and Jesus himself. The first man's claim to have business which could not be delayed was insincere (verse 18). No one would buy a farm without inspecting it beforehand. Similarly, the second man was set on seeing his new team working (verse 19). The third man had the law behind him (verse 20). A regulation of Moses released a newly-wed man from military service for a year. Rebel man shirks, but shirks in vain, the responsibility for his withholding.

In verse 23, the compulsion is not the compulsion of force but of loving earnestness (see the same word in Matthew 14:22; Mark 6:45). 'You' (verse 24) means the disciples.

14:25-35 The cost of being a disciple
No verses could illustrate more strikingly the need for Western readers to realize that they are reading the poetic language of the East. Purposeful exaggeration (hyperbole) is a recognized figure of speech. The words cannot be taken literally; the one who told his followers to love their enemies would not call them in fact to hate their own families. The expression simply set out absolute priorities. Its use in this context flows from the third excuse in the story of the ungrateful guests. Loyalty to Christ is so demanding that it takes priority over all other claims of life, however natural or legitimate.

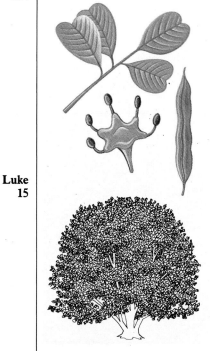

The carob tree was very common in Palestine. Its fruits are long pods which are used as animal fodder. In the parable of the prodigal son, the pods were fed to pigs.

'This fellow began to build and was not able to finish' (Luke 14:30).

Christianity is a hard and costly business (verses 27-30). It is like taking on a building project, an illustration taken up by Paul (1 Corinthians 3:10-15). It demands dogged perseverance and persistence to the very end. It is also a battle, another figure of speech taken up by Paul (Ephesians 6:11-17).

Those who do count the cost, and are ready to pay it, are like salt (verses 34,35); they preserve the mass from corruption. It is said that the rock salt of Israel lost its sharpness and usefulness by a form of chemical breakdown in its places of storage. It became useless except as a type of gravel. Notice that on his way to Jerusalem, Jesus, considered by the crowds to be a potential Messiah, was increasingly thronged (verse 25); but clearly he discouraged any mass movement.

15:1-10 The parables of the lost sheep and the lost coin

The key word for this chapter is 'lost'. The sheep was lost, the coin was lost, the son was lost; but all were found.

The sheep is a foolish animal, helpless when confronted by bold and fierce enemies. It needs protection with the shepherd's restraining crook and with the defensive staff. Sheep go blindly in crowds, are liable to stampede, and fatally prone to wander. 'All we like sheep have gone astray . . .'

From the beginning of the Bible to the end, the shepherd's calling and the shepherd's flock formed an important word-picture. Moses was trained in the desert for leading the flock of God. Jesus is the

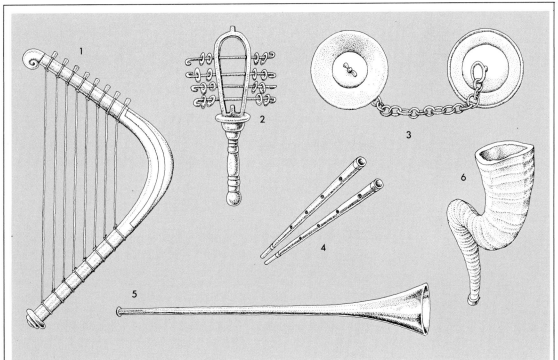

shepherd of Psalm 23, and he claimed the title in John 10:11. The shepherd's care is the notable part of the parable. To the Eastern shepherd, sheep were individuals, not a nameless flock.

The lost coin (verse 8), a silver *denarius*, was the equivalent of a working man's daily wage. Dark Eastern houses and their rush floors would have made the search difficult. The nine silver coins remaining were no joy to the woman while one was lost. The point of the story is again God's care for the individual. It is wrong to press too much meaning into the details of the parable. The chief and central point is that the woman made an eager search for the lost silver on the rush floor. Jesus is trying to show above all that he came to seek and to save that which was lost.

15:11-32 The parable of the lost son

On leaving home, the prodigal son did not necessarily travel a long distance. He was able to return home, half-starved, when famine came. 'A distant country' is not necessarily remote geographically. The rebellious son was as alienated and distant in heart and mind while he was still in his father's house. He merely translated an attitude of mind into a geographical fact when he laid hands prematurely on what he might later have enjoyed in fullness and in peace.

Famine was common in first-century Israel. The son's motives for returning were low, but he had enough faith to go back. When faith reaches out, grace more than meets it.

'To feed pigs' (verse 15) would be particularly repulsive to a Jew. 'Hired men' (verse 19) had lower status even than slaves; they could be dismissed at will. The robe is a mark of honour, the ring a mark of authority, and the sandals a mark of sonship (verse 22).

This story is also the parable of the unforgiving brother who had fulfilled the letter of the law meticulously, and felt he had earned much from his father. But it was a purely legal relationship: service rendered without love and with no understanding of his father's heart. 'This son of yours', he said (verse 30), repudiating his brother despite his father's pleas (verse 28). By contrast the father displayed the same love to both sons. Notice the rebuke (verse 32) 'this brother of yours'. The parable ends without a word of the future. The Pharisees are left free to make their own ending.

Musical instruments of Jesus' time.
1 Harp
2 Sistrum
3 Cymbals
4 Double oboe
5 Metal trumpet
6 Ram's horn trumpet

A full-grown olive tree may give as much as eighty litres of olive oil in a year. Olive oil was used in cooking, as fuel for oil-lamps and to treat skin wounds.

16:1-18 The parable of the shrewd manager

The story of the shrewd manager illustrates well the basic principle for interpreting parables. The parable must not be pushed beyond its specific purpose. In other words, a parable is not an allegory. In an allegory, every part has its symbolic meaning. Here the 'master' (verse 3) was simply the manager's employer, not Jesus.

It is important to note that there is no commendation for the rascal who falsified his master's accounts, for the rogues who were foolish enough to let themselves get involved in his dishonesty and become the victims of possible blackmail, or for the master who praised the unjust manager (verse 8), cynically praising a bit of fraudulent practice as clever, no doubt, as some of his own business deals. It is a picture of corruption, and papyrus records surviving from this time preserve the names of several similar tricksters.

The parable explained This parable may have arisen out of conversation about contemporary events. Several lessons emerge. First the manager was ingenious and enterprising in his attempts to ensure his own safety and comfort. It would be a good thing if men were as eager and inventive in securing the blessings of God. Second, money had no place when it came to true friendship. Certainly worldly rogues will use money to win friends. Yet there are those who should know better who seek money for its own sake. Jolting his listeners and his disciples (verse 1) with the strange story, Jesus was asking them why they were not equally inventive in a better cause.

Earthly wealth is a loan on trust which may be withdrawn at short notice. Heavenly possessions do not diminish or fail. The Christian is expected to manage well and honestly in getting money, using it sensibly, generously and usefully. He must not love it, trust it, or use it for evil ends.

Verses 14-18 form a highly compressed account of a clash with the Pharisees (verse 16; compare Galatians 3:24; Matthew 11:12). The words on divorce (verse 18) were no doubt provoked by the legalism of the Pharisees. The liberal school of the rabbi Hillel allowed divorce on the most trivial grounds. The stricter school of the rabbi Shammai was not the target of Jesus' reproach here.

16:19-31 The rich man and Lazarus

The parable of the rich man and Lazarus must be interpreted in the way already emphasized. It was designed to teach that now is the time and place of opportunity, and that the signs of earthly prosperity, social standing and wealth are no indication of a person's standing before God. The rabbis regarded riches as a special mark of God's favour. Obviously the details of the picture are figurative. 'Abraham's side', 'the great chasm' and 'this fire' are all apocalyptic images, not intended to teach physical realities. But this does not strip the story of its meaning. Heaven is not to be earned by charity, but the rich man's callous disregard for the needy indicated his hard heart. Love awoke too late (verse 28).

Misery had not turned the poor man to God. Poverty is no more a way to heaven than riches. The grace of God alone could bring him salvation. Like his brothers, the man had God's word. So there comes the sad prophecy. Those who did not heed God's word failed also to heed the one who returned from the dead.

'Hell' (Old Testament 'Sheol') in Jewish belief is the resting place of all the dead. But in the New Testament it is the place where unbelievers wait for final judgement.

17:1-10 Sin, faith and duty

These crowded chapters, in which Luke presents material from the final teachings of Jesus, sometimes read like notes taken by hearers or disciples. Indeed, this is what they may well have been. Luke packed this section of his book with all the sayings he could find, and the connecting thread is not always obvious. However it is there more often than not.

First comes his teaching about the awfulness of sin. Let those who make someone else an accomplice in their wrongdoing remember that God records and punishes. Retribution awaits those who spread their wickedness (verses 1,2). We should ignore the artificial interruption of the new chapter, and see the rich man as one who caused a 'little one' to sin. Better by far had he been drowned before the years piled a weight of guilt on him.

Forgiveness The rabbis in their arithmetical teaching about goodness gave top marks to the person who forgave someone else three times. Jesus swept aside such mean thinking (verses 3,4). Verse 4 can be compared with Matthew 18:21.

The language of the discussion between Jesus and the Twelve is distinctly Eastern (verses 5,6). Rooting up a tree (the mulberry had deep roots) and planting it in the sea is simply impossible. It was intended to underline the great power of faith; its reality rather than its size is what counts.

The difficult little parable (verses 7-10) can only properly be understood if the principles of interpreting outlined earlier are strictly applied. Notice first that this is a picture taken from life. It is not a picture of God, nor of God's way with men. It merely stresses that the servant of God must be prepared to serve doggedly, to expect no special rewards, and to realize that his performance is nothing more than what he owes. The lesson is humility. Surely we should give to God without grumbling what man gives to man without complaint. In approaching God for new blessings, we should never forget to return thanks for blessings already granted. If we stop and think how many of our prayers have been answered, and how seldom we have gone back to give thanks, we will be overwhelmed with shame.

17:11-19 Ten healed of leprosy
The geography here is difficult. This section may have been displaced, and perhaps ought to have come earlier in Luke. In Luke

In the Old Testament we learn that God's forgiveness springs from his love; but if man is to enjoy it he must be willing to repent and forsake his evil ways (Exodus 34:6,7; Isaiah 55:7). We see the measure and scope of God's forgiveness in the imagery used. For example, we are told that our sins have been put out of sight (Isaiah 38:17; Micah 7:19), out of reach (Psalm 103:12), out of mind (Jeremiah 31:34) and out of account (Psalm 103:10).

In the New Testament, the Greek word most frequently used for forgiveness has the meaning to send away or release. It is the removing of a burden and a stain which brings relief to the sinner, and makes possible the renewal of friendship.

Perhaps the most perfect picture in the New Testament is found in the story of the Prodigal Son (Luke 15). The young man in the story was not only received back but restored.

However, forgiveness is costly. The New Testament continually reminds us that it has only been made possible for us through the death of Christ on the cross (Matthew 26:28; Ephesians 1:7).

God's forgiveness of us has no limits (Matthew 18:21-35). It is closely linked with our own readiness to forgive those who offend us (Matthew 18:23-35). The person who holds back his forgiveness from someone has not properly repented, and to that extent does not qualify for God's forgiveness of himself (Luke 6:37; Colossians 3:13).

Ploughing in Israel today. In biblical times, ploughing took place after the autumn rains had softened the soil. A simple wooden plough was used to turn the top-soil. It would be pulled by a pair of oxen yoked together.

Jesus was now leading his followers through the lower Jordan Valley on their way from Galilee in the north to Jerusalem in the south. The Samaritans would not let him pass through their lands, so Jesus went down the east bank of the River Jordan.

9:51,52 and 13:22 we are told that these events took place on the journey from Galilee via the Jordan valley to Jerusalem. The Samaritans had been hostile and denied Jesus passage through their territory (see Luke 9:51-53). He therefore passed out of Galilee through Bethshan, crossed the Jordan and journeyed down the east bank almost as far as the Dead Sea. He re-crossed the Jordan at Jericho, near the place where he had been baptized.

Somewhere along the road a band of men suffering from leprosy met him and were healed. Of the whole group, one returned and thanked Jesus. He found not only cleansing for his body but salvation for his soul. The Samaritan would have gone to his priests at Gerizim (verse 14). The wording (verse 18) suggests a mixed group of lepers. The healed man's return (verse 19) sealed the link which his cure had forged between Jesus and him.

17:20-37 The coming of the kingdom of God

This highly-compressed section can only be understood if taken with Matthew's fuller account of Jesus' teaching about the last things (Matthew 24). Jesus answered the Pharisees negatively (verse 20) and positively (verse 21). Verse 20 is a hard saying, but must mean that no one can predict the coming of the Lord as we can predict the movements of the sky. Meticulous observation fixes sunrise and sunset and the phases of the moon. It will not fix and date the second coming. Compare John 1:26.

But trouble is coming (verse 22) which will make Christians long for God's decisive intervention, and at the same time expose careless and thoughtless people to false Messiahs, such as Theudas (see Acts 5:36) and Bar-Kochba.

The climax of all things will come suddenly upon a world totally preoccupied with material things (verse 26). God's judgement is like the lightning (verse 24), with the results described (verses 31-36). 'Preserve' (verse 33) in the Greek means 'bring to new birth'. It is judgement which is apparently in view in verse 31, with its specific warning. This verse seems to warn about the catastrophe which was to come in the years AD 66-70. The mob had called down judgement on themselves (Matthew 27:25). The Christians of Jerusalem remembered the warnings and escaped to the Decapolis when the

Roman army surrounded Jerusalem. The eagles (verse 37) may be the legionary standards. The end of the age will be God's intervention. Christians should watch, work and sit loose to the visible, material world.

18:1-8 The parable of the persistent widow

Here is another of the forceful stories which Luke discovered and preserved for us. It once again illustrates the need to keep the central meaning in view when interpreting the parables, and to note the details that have no theological significance. The story is obviously rooted in everyday life. Here is a godless and arrogant petty magistrate from Galilee denying a widow her just rights. The widow was chosen as the victim of callous disregard because widows were the weakest and most helpless people in that society. The judge (verse 2) broke both great commandments. The reference to faith (verse 8) shows that this parable is not concerned with God allowing himself to be bullied into answering prayer. He is encouraging us to hold on by faith in difficult times.

The widow was a dogged woman who worked upon one simple conviction. The magistrate's duty was to dispense justice impartially to everyone. She was determined to hold him to that duty, and so came daily to the court. Preoccupied with the more profitable law cases (contemporary papyruses show that the most profitable were those based on bribery and corruption) the judge adjourned the widow's case until she finally persuaded him to act.

'In a certain town there was a judge who neither feared God nor cared about men' (Luke 18:2).

The heavenly Father God is no unjust judge. But for other reasons he appears to delay and to leave his children to suffer the world's injustices. If a village woman in a local court can be sufficiently convinced that action will ultimately be taken, against all discouragement, how much more should Christians persevere in faithful requests to God. At least they can be sure that the delay which seems so often to meet them is not due to selfishness and corruption, but to wisdom and God's good will.

If dogged determination can make a bad man good, how much more should a Christian expect what is best for him from a holy and loving God. In his own good time God will answer his children's prayer, not perhaps in the form they expect, but in wisdom, love and perfect goodness. We should ask no more.

18:9-14 The parable of the Pharisee and the tax-collector

The final perversion of prayer is self-congratulation. The Pharisee's God was too small. Like the people mentioned in Psalm 50:21 he had made himself a God in his own image.

The picture is vividly drawn from life. The Pharisee 'takes his stand' (verse 11, literally) no doubt in a prominent position. He then made sure his words could be heard by everyone. He was clearly guilty of the enormous irreverence of advertising his own presence in a holy place.

His prayer was for himself and about himself. It did not reach the ear of God. He prayed aloud for everyone to hear. This was a common practice in the ancient world. The Roman poet Horace gives us a picture of a similar hypocrite making a similar prayer in the temple of Apollo.

True prayer Pride is always wrong. In the holy place it approaches blasphemy. With a contemptuously curled lip, the Pharisee even dared draw attention to the wretched tax-collector. The watching crowd was expected to look from the richly-robed figure of the Pharisee looking up to God down to the bent and downcast form of the broken man seeking forgiveness.

The tax-collector came with the first requirement needed for for-

Humility

The humble person is one who is not self-important or self-assertive. On the other hand, he does not put on a show of false modesty to impress people (Colossians 2:23). He has a quiet and sober estimate of himself in relation to God and his fellow men (Romans 12:3).

Throughout the Bible, humility, meekness and lowliness are commanded (Micah 6:8; 1 Peter 5:5,6), praised (Proverbs 16:19) and rewarded (Proverbs 15:33; 1 Peter 5:6). Only the humble person can fully enjoy God's help (James 4:6), guidance (Psalm 25:9) and rest of heart and mind (Matthew 11:28-30).

Perhaps the chief reason for humility is that it is at the very heart of the Godhead. We see it in God's personal interest and involvement in his creation (Psalm 113:5-9). We see it in his willingness to live with the believer (Isaiah 57:15). We see it above all when he came to visit and redeem his people (Luke 1:68), becoming truly man, a servant, and finally accepting the death of a criminal on a cross (Philippians 2:5-8).

In his earthly life, Jesus was 'humble in heart' (Matthew 11:29), never seeking his own glory (John 8:50). When Paul wanted to teach his readers humility he appealed to the example of Jesus (2 Corinthians 10:1).

giveness, 'a broken and contrite heart' (Psalm 51:17). God despises the arrogance and sham of the self-satisfied hypocrite. The tax-collector heard what the Pharisee said about him. He made no response. He simply cried out 'God be merciful to me, *the* sinner' (verse 13, correctly translated); that is, the sinner of whom the Pharisee spoke.

According to the law, only one fast-day per week was necessary (verse 12); the extra fast was practised by tradition by the Pharisees.

18:15-30 The rich ruler
The value of humility is the connecting link with the previous section. At this point Luke's account re-joins those of Matthew and Mark. In comparison with Mark (Mark 10:13-16) Luke tones down the rebuke to the Twelve here. This is typical of Luke's gentler approach. He was not as free to speak as Matthew or John, who were apostles themselves, or as Mark, who probably wrote under the direction of Peter.

In general the Jews tended to be very strict in their attitudes towards children. In comparison, Jesus is notably less severe, as he was with women too. A papyrus letter dating from about the time of Jesus' birth throws more light on the harsh contemporary attitudes towards children. It is a loving note from a Greek workman in Egypt to his wife in Alexandria, who was expecting a child while her husband was away. 'If it is a girl, throw it out', he finishes casually. This was common practice in the brutal pagan world. Unwanted children were left to die wretchedly on the city rubbish tip, or were picked up by slave masters.

Humility The theme of humility continues into the following story (verses 18-23). 'Good teacher', cries the young man, with no idea of the true meaning of the word 'good'. Jesus is not repudiating goodness by his reply, but trying to bring the young man face to face with the truth. The young man's answer ought to have been: 'I call you good because you are the Son of the Living God, the Messiah'. But when Jesus failed to get a true answer from him, he challenged him with the commandments. The young man in turn made a naive claim to perfection. He certainly had not understood the commandments

The camel was used in Jesus' time both for riding and for carrying burdens. A loaded camel usually covers about thirty miles per day.

as Jesus explained them in the Sermon on the Mount. Jesus followed up the weakness exposed, in a similar way to that in John 4:16. Unable to meet up to such a test of self-denial, the young man went sadly away. It is interesting to notice Jesus' different answer to him from his answer to the case of the lawyer in Luke 10:25-28.

Jesus looked sadly after the retreating figure. Like so many, he was pleasant, upright, generous, and a useful member of the community – but unwilling to follow Jesus. The ruling passion of his life was money. This was the chief preoccupation. Jesus would not have recommended such a drastic course had this not been so.

Jesus' severity Jesus' attitude must have been unusually severe, for it puzzled the Twelve, especially when he added the strange saying about the camel and the needle. People have spent much ingenuity in trying to explain this saying. Some suggest that a gate into Jerusalem was so small that it was known as the 'Needle's Eye'. A camel could only pass through it if its load was removed. But there is in fact no evidence that such a gate ever existed. The simplest – and likeliest – explanation is the picturesque exaggeration of Eastern language, a phenomenon we have already met several times.

'Entering the kingdom' (verse 24) means the same as 'inheriting eternal life' (verse 18) and 'being saved' (verse 26). The literal meaning of verse 28 is 'we have abandoned our homes'.

18:31-43 Jesus again predicts his death
The group was now approaching Jericho. To the left was the great salt sea. They were travelling through the green river valley, flat-floored and covered with farming land, of the Jordan 'jungle'. The oasis of Jordan was a green splash in the middle of the plain.

They were doggedly following the road to the cross. It is clear from the other Gospels that Jesus had spent a great deal of time training his men to meet what was to come. But they had understood little of what he had to say (Luke 9:22,44; 13:33). Jesus always spoke of the crucifixion in the same breath as the resurrection (verse 33).

The last journey There is something awesome about this last journey up to Jerusalem. It is a truly brave man who goes into danger with full foresight, who faces its agonies from far off, completely understanding what is to come, and still goes on. Jesus anticipated the cross, but moved towards it calmly and deliberately. And more than this, he did not move forward in tense silence and with stern self-control, but continued to instruct as he went. It was quite common for a rabbi to teach his followers as he walked along, and this was the situation of which the blind man became aware.

The blind man healed The healing of the blind man (a contrast to the blindness of the disciples?) took place as the group entered Jericho. Mark speaks of blind Bartimaeus and Matthew of two blind men who were healed as Jesus left the town. These are separate incidents rather than confused reporting of the same event. If the three accounts are read exactly as they are put down, it is clear that three (or possibly four) men were healed, one of whom was called Bartimaeus. Incidents took place on both sides of the town. It is quite likely that the news of the first healing spread through the town and provoked further requests for healing. Others see a confusion between old Jericho, the mound which covers the Canaanitish city-fort, where the excavations may be seen today, and New Jericho, Herod's foundation. But it is simply the brevity of Scripture which causes misunderstanding.

The verb 'he shouted all the more' (verse 39) underlines the more intense emotion than that used in verse 38. Luke makes a special point of recording the form of words glorifying to God (doxology) in verse 43.

Zacchaeus the tax-collector lived in Jericho. He climbed one of the sycamore-fig trees so that he could see Jesus.

Jericho

The old road from Jerusalem to Jericho followed the course of the Wadi Qilt. This was the site of the robbery featured in the story of the Good Samaritan. Close to old Jericho, Herod built a new city on both sides of the wadi.

Jericho

Jericho plays a notable part in the gospel narrative of Jesus' last journey to Jerusalem. It is here that he gave blind Bartimaeus the power to see, here too that he invited himself to be a guest in the house of Zacchaeus, the chief tax-collector of the district (Luke 18:35-19:10).

No doubt Jesus had visited Jericho on several earlier occasions. The traditional site of his baptism in the Jordan is about five miles to the east; Mount Quarantana, the traditional place of his forty days' fast and temptation, rises to the north-west (due west of Tell es-Sultan). The old road down from Jerusalem (2,500 feet above Mediterranean sea-level) to Jericho (820 feet below), descending well over 3,500 feet in some fifteen miles, follows the course of the Wadi Qilt; this road was the scene of the 'mugging' which features in the parable of the Good Samaritan. The courtyard of the Inn of the Good Samaritan marks the supposed site of the place where the injured man was lodged and tended (Luke 10:30-35).

Jerusalem

The Jericho that Jesus knew lay nearly two miles south of the Old Testament Jericho. The site of Old Testament Jericho – the city destroyed by Joshua and rebuilt 400 years later by Hiel the Bethelite (1 Kings 16:34) – is marked by the mound called Tell es-

Sultan, near Elisha's fountain ('Ain es-Sultan), the perennial spring whose plentiful water-supply of 1,000 gallons a minute irrigates the whole surrounding countryside and makes it a place of palm-trees, gardens and plantations.

New Testament Jericho,
represented by the ruins called Tulul Abu el-'Alayiq, had its beginnings in the period following the return from the Babylonian exile. The Hellenistic rulers erected a fortress here to guard the road from the Jordan to Jerusalem. Bacchides, a general of the Seleucid kingdom who waged war with Judas Maccabaeus, added further fortifications about 160BC, and the early Hasmonaean rulers continued these operations.

The importance of Jericho economically as well as strategically was, if anything, enhanced under the Roman occupation, from 63BC onwards. The presence of a chief tax-collector in Jericho in the time of Jesus is not at all surprising: the city commanded the main road from Transjordan into Judea. Herod the Great (37-4BC) constructed a series of fortresses around the area to protect it, and augmented its water-supply by a system of aqueducts bringing water from other sources than Elisha's fountain (always the principal source). He built a new city on both sides of the Wadi Qilt,

after the style of contemporary Italian cities. Herodian Jericho, in fact, resembled a more extensive Pompeii. It contained public buildings, amphitheatre, hippodrome, gymnasium or palaestra (wrestling arena), parks, gardens, pools and villas, and (most impressive of all) a luxuriously-appointed winter palace. It was here that Herod died in 4BC.

Jericho suffered damage by fire in the disorders which broke out

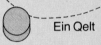
Ein Qelt

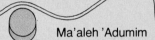
Ma'aleh 'Adumim

after Herod's death, but was soon restored by his son Archelaus. It was taken, but not destroyed, by Vespasian in AD68, when, as commander-in-chief of the Roman forces in Judea, he was engaged in suppressing the Jewish revolt.

A new city was founded in Byzantine times about a mile to the east of it; it is on the site of the Byzantine city that modern Jericho stands – still, like its Old Testament predecessor, 'the City of Palms' (Deuteronomy 34:3).

'Ein Nueima

Ancient Jericho

Modern Jericho

Hasmonean
Winter Palace

Herodian
Winter Palace

Birket Mousa

Wadi Qelt

A monastery has been built in a remote part of Wadi Qilt.

River Jordan

A refugee village stands in the valley floor, with the so-called 'Mount of Temptation' rising behind it.

DEAD SEA

Qumran

Scale

0   5 kilometres   5 miles

Today Jericho lies on the green valley floor of the Jordan.

Jericho, with its fresh-water spring, is sometimes known as the 'city of palm trees'.

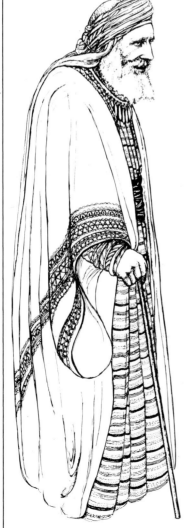

The costume of a rich merchant.

19:1-10 Zacchaeus the tax-collector

Much trade passed through Jericho, which lay on the highway between the fording-places of the River Jordan and Judea, an important east-west commercial route. At such a place there were many customs duties to be collected, and many collaborating tax-collectors to do the job.

Zacchaeus' eagerness to see Jesus indicates his longing for something better than the despised calling of tax-collector with its temptations, corruption and stigma of being a traitor.

Something had already happened to Zacchaeus, or he would not have been alone in the hostile crowd, and made himself ridiculously prominent up the tree by the roadside. As with the blind beggar, Jesus met need where he found it, without a moment's concern for the prejudice and hostility of the crowd. Zacchaeus tried to show himself worthy of such friendship. He immediately cleansed his life of the very things that had corrupted it. His immediate response to Jesus' words made him a 'son of Abraham' spiritually as well as physically (see Romans 4:16).

In climbing the tree to try to see Jesus, Zacchaeus was showing that he wanted a glimpse of another world, a world of peace with God and a heart at peace. He did not realize how close such a world could be to the uproar of daily living.

This story may well have been first written in Aramaic. There are many phrases which suggest Aramaic origins.

19:11-27 The parable of the ten minas

When Herod I died, his will divided his kingdom between his sons. Judea went to Archelaus, and this was why Joseph and Mary, returning from Egypt, did not go back to Bethlehem, but went north to Nazareth, which was ruled by Herod Antipas (Matthew 2:22,23).

Archelaus was every bit as cruel as his father, but lacked his diplomatic skills. He started his rule in Judea with the bloody suppression of riots in Jerusalem. A widespread Jewish uprising called for the intervention of Varus, the governor of the province of Syria. It was during this period of tension that Joseph and Mary were returning from Egypt; the disturbances in the country were reason enough for them to move to Nazareth and comparative safety.

The first servant said, 'Sir, your mina has earned ten more'. The second said, 'Your mina has earned five more'. Another servant said, 'Sir, here is your mina; I have kept it laid away in a piece of cloth.'

Meanwhile it was vital for Archelaus to get his own authority confirmed by the Emperor Augustus in Rome. To do this, he hurried off to the capital of the Empire before reports from Palestine, and particularly official despatches from Varus, gave a poor view of his rule in Judea. Archelaus found that his appointment was opposed in Rome by Jewish envoys and by Herod Antipas in person. Against the odds, Augustus did confirm Archelaus as ruler of Judea, but refused him the title of king.

Archelaus and the parable Archelaus was, then, the nobleman who went abroad to be 'appointed king'. It was quite natural for Jesus to base a parable on this incident while in Jericho, since it was from this city that Archelaus set out on his journey. He had a large palace here, and the sight of its white marble and terraces may well have prompted Jesus' story.

The parable illustrates once more the necessity of not reading meaning into every last detail. There could hardly be a greater contrast between Jesus leaving behind his disciples with responsibilities and the villain from the Herod family.

The parable is not another version of the parable told in Matthew 25:14-30. We must not imagine that Jesus taught each lesson once only, and in the same way. The differences between these two stories and their teaching are significant. For instance, the 'wicked' servant is not in this case thrown out.

The reason for the parable is given in verse 11. There was excitement among the Twelve. Mark's account of the incidents during the journey up to Jerusalem reveals the eager mood of expectation. The 'kingdom' was near – though they still saw it as a matter of an earthly Messiah who would triumph by force of arms and distribute the prizes of victory.

The parable first hints at a long delay before the king returns. The ruler went to 'a distant country'. The servants of the ruler had one job to do during his absence. It was to test their faithfulness and their ability that he gave each of them a modest sum of money. They were to show how fit they were to serve him, and whether they were concerned to do his work.

Perhaps Archelaus did something like this, and when he returned

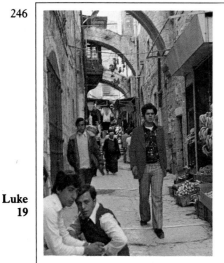

A narrow street in the old city of Jerusalem.

'They . . . threw their cloaks on the colt and put Jesus on it' (Luke 19:35).

from Rome bitterly frustrated over Augustus' failure to make him king, he may have meted out savage reprisals.

The parable also teaches that the day of reckoning is inevitably coming. Archelaus returned. The coming of God's judgement is even more certain. God's servants are called to long and hard service. Faithfulness in small things will open up the possibilities of wider opportunities. Every one will give an account of his services before the judgement seat of Christ (see also 1 Corinthians 3:12-15; 2 Corinthians 5:10).

19:28-48 The triumphal entry

The long climb up from Jericho reaches its highest point on the Mount of Olives. It approaches the summit by way of a long, high ridge on which the village of Bethany still stands today. The mountains of Moab lie behind, towering above the Dead Sea. In the opposite direction, still screened by the Mount of Olives, lies the Holy City, Jerusalem. The ancient road ran right over its summit, to give approaching travellers a magnificent view of the city.

In using a donkey for his entry into the city he was deliberately setting out to fulfil a prophecy of Zechariah (Zechariah 9:9). It was on a donkey that an ancient ruler rode when coming on a mission of peace. A horse, by contrast, was an animal of war. Jesus was offering himself to Jerusalem as the Prince of Peace, not as a Messiah of war. The cheering crowds, however, saw him as someone who would lead them to victory over the occupying forces. Spreading their cloaks in front of him was a form of royal honour (see 2 Kings 9:13). But Jesus was offering himself on his own terms. He offered a peace that passes all understanding. He would not let those who wanted to follow him imagine that they would gain material advantages, that they would be protected from all harm.

The Mount of Olives The whole of Jerusalem can be seen from the summit of the Mount of Olives. Here, forty years later, the Roman legions had their camp. On this vantage point their commander, Titus, built his headquarters. The slopes below were covered with Roman siege machines and giant caterpults. The city was destined to lie in ashes, with multitudes of dead buried beneath the rubble. When Jesus, seeing what was to come, wept over it (verse 41), there still remained a choice between the growing powers of hate and the acceptance of Jesus. The choice of Barabbas – and the violence, self-assertion and hatred he stood for – was to lead to this destruction. To have chosen Christ would have meant salvation.

From Mark 11:11,15, it appears that Jesus crossed the Kidron valley, entered Jerusalem, and went straight to the Temple. He looked to see what the state of affairs there was. The old abuses had crept back to the holy place since the time when he had driven out the traders and money-changers (John 2:13-17). He then left the city to spend the night in Bethany, returning next morning to cleanse the Temple again.

It was the Sadducee priests who permitted the market that took place in the Court of the Gentiles. They were reluctant to move against Jesus because of the popular support he was clearly receiving from the crowds. It took them several days to plan how to get rid of Jesus. They waited till the mob was disillusioned with Jesus, who gave no sign of meeting their demands for a violent liberator.

20:1-8 The authority of Jesus questioned

Mark 11:12,20,27 suggests that this day of questions was the Tuesday of Holy Week. Each of the main religious groups put a question which reflected their particular concern. The Pharisees asked about authority (verses 1-8); the Herodian party asked about political responsibility (verses 21-26); and the Sadducees asked a question concerning speculative theology (verses 27-38).

The group from the Sanhedrin 'came up to him' (verse 1). This is the same verb as is used in Luke 10:40 for Martha's sudden, exasperated approach to Jesus. They came on him suddenly; they came and stood over him: both meanings are in the verb. The same word is used again in Luke referring to the coming of judgement (see Luke 21:35).

The authorities' dilemma is clear. What authority did Jesus have to take over the court of the Temple for his teaching? They were still searching round for a charge to pin on Jesus when he counterattacked with a devastating question. 'John's baptism – was it from heaven or from men?' They could only answer 'We don't know . . .' (verses 3,7). The authorities' dilemma about John was desperate. If they had admitted the truth, that John spoke as God moved him, they would have had their answer to the question on Jesus' authority. For John the Baptist bore witness to the truth and pointed to Jesus' being the Messiah.

20:9-19 The parable of the tenants

This parable is closer to being a full allegory than most of the other parables in the New Testament. The religious leaders had no doubt in their minds who Jesus was aiming the parable towards. The picture of the vineyard as standing for God's people is frequently found in the Bible; see for example Psalm 80:8-16; Isaiah 5:1-7. But history

Luke 20

Wine-making was a vital part of Israel's agriculture. Both the climate and the soil favoured the cultivation of vines. Vineyards with terraces were often constructed on the hillsides, where they would catch the most sunlight.

is woven bitingly into Jesus' story. The people entrusted with looking after the vineyard saw it as their own private property, to be treated as they pleased. Neither Israel, nor Israel's rulers, held a prerogative here. From history the parable passes to prophecy (verses 14,15). Verse 17 quotes from Psalm 118:22, a song which is supposed to have been sung when the walls of Jerusalem were completed in 444 BC. Jesus now showed the true meaning of these words. The early Christians remembered this (see Acts 4:11; 1 Peter 2:7; Romans 9:33).

20:20-26 Paying taxes to Caesar

Since AD 6 the country had been under the rule of procurators. A procurator was a minor governor, directly responsible to Caesar. The silver *denarius*, bearing Ceasar's image, was minted for taxation purposes. Jewish coins bore farming symbols. The legal fiction was that coins stamped with the Emperor belonged to the Emperor, who, in receiving tribute, was simply recovering what belonged to him. It was a subtle point, used by some legally-minded Jews to make the payment of taxes to the foreign power more acceptable, and to license the use of a type of 'graven image' forbidden by Jewish law. Taxation and the use of the embossed coins were burning issues of the day and the trap set in this way was deadly. It would have been fatal for Jesus to answer either way.

Jesus' reply set a lasting principle. Those who knew the Old Testament would realize that man, too, carries an image – the image of God, in whose likeness he was created. To Caesar, and even more so to God, should be paid what is owed.

20:27-40 The resurrection and marriage

The Sadducees were a worldly sect who controlled the priesthood. They also formed the core of the Jewish group who collaborated with Rome. They accepted only the five books of Moses as binding on them, and so among the teachings they rejected was the resurrection.

The Sadducees' question was an attempt to make both the teacher and his teaching look ridiculous. But Jesus answered their absurd question with dignity. A future life cannot be crudely seen as a material continuation of the present form of life. It is another level of existence, altogether different, but completely blessed (1 Corinthians 2:9). The Sadducees applied the limited faculties of the senses and human reason to spiritual questions, reached absurd answers, and rejected truth. Later Pharisees used the argument of verse 37.

20:41-47 Whose son is the Christ?

Jesus' use of scripture was one that his enemies and his questioners were familiar with. Jesus could usefully use the prophecies of the Old Testament, which clearly showed that the Messiah would come of David's line, to prove to the Jews who he claimed to be. The verses he quotes can bear a Messianic meaning and a local significance at the same time. He could argue from such passages as 2 Samuel 7:8-29; Isaiah 9:5-7; Micah 5:2 and Psalm 110:1. Jesus was teaching in the tradition of Jewish interpretation of the Old Testament. He defeated his critics, using their own teaching and their way of interpreting the Jewish scriptures.

21:1-4 The widow's gift

Weary with these arguments, Jesus sat down in the courtyard of the Temple, with his eyes downcast. Perhaps he buried his head in his hands as he prayed for his strength to be renewed. Then he looked up (verse 1). The normal comings and goings of the Temple continued around him, and in full view were the 'trumpets': offering-boxes shaped like upturned horns.

Rich men were ostentatiously throwing their gifts into the trum-

Two dilepton coins from the period of the Jewish Revolt of AD 66-70.

A Roman legionary eagle. The legion was a Roman military unit consisting of about 5,000 men.

pets. Among them came a poor woman with two tiny coins. As it turned out, she gave more than everyone else. The Temple authorities laid down that two gifts were necessary, hence two coins (verse 2). The coins the woman put in were *leptons*: 128 *leptons* made one *denarius*.

21:5-38 Signs of the end of the age

Jesus and his disciples were inside the Temple. The 'beautiful stones' were its marble walls. The gifts included a table from Ptolemy of Egypt, a chain from Agrippa and a golden vine from Herod. The Roman historian Tacitus called the Temple 'a shrine of enormous wealth'. It was shocking to be told that this Temple was shortly to be destroyed. But a greater than the Temple had been rejected; judgement was inevitable.

Jesus' prophetic words described the grim happenings which would follow his rejection. They telescoped the centuries, as prophecy often does. But they looked first to the two generations of judgement which followed Jesus' rejection, leading up to the destruction of Jerusalem after the Great Rebellion. There was an earthquake in Phrygia in AD 61; Mount Vesuvius in Italy erupted in AD 63; there was famine across the civilized world in the 50s and 60s; there was war in Parthia and in Palestine; following the death of Nero, there were four emperors in the space of the one year, AD 69 (verses 10,11).

The Western Wall, or Wailing Wall, is the only surviving fragment of the stone sheathing constructed by Herod the Great for his splendid Temple. Jesus said: 'As for what you see here, the time will come when not one stone will be left on another; every one of them will be thrown down' (Luke 21:6).

Judas Iscariot

The betrayer's name 'Iscariot' was also carried by his father (John 6:71), and probably means 'man of Kerioth'. It is one of the mysteries of the Bible why Jesus chose him as an apostle (Mark 3:19) knowing he would finally betray him (John 6:64). Judas was money-minded and helped himself to cash from the common purse (John 12:6). The bribe of thirty shekels was too tempting for him (Matthew 26:14-16), and he arranged the arrest of Jesus at a time and place that ensured minimum publicity.

Bringing together Matthew 27:3-10 and Acts 1:18, 19, we can trace the story of his death. He had negotiated with a potter to buy his field with the blood money, but, realizing the enormity of his deed, flung back the money to the authorities and went to hang himself in the potter's field. The authorities then bought the land themselves as a cemetery for foreigners.

Warnings The warning of verse 8 forms the core of this section. There was to be persecution; but delusion was a far greater danger. Those who pay attention to Jesus' words will not readily be led astray by heresy, folly and exhibitionism.

Verses 12-17 were all fulfilled in the history of the early church as recorded in the book of Acts. These special directions were given to the persecuted to meet their immediate needs, as uneducated men were often called on to defend themselves in front of learned and prominent public figures.

When the Great Rebellion broke out in AD 66 (verses 20-24) the local Roman garrison was unable to deal with it. The main forces of the Roman army were concentrated in Syria, since the Romans regarded the Parthians as the major military threat. As a result the Jews achieved initial success until the Syrian legions could bring their force to bear. The Emperor Vespasian soon led the re-conquest in a typically Roman style of orderliness and finality.

Jerusalem itself was left until the surrounding countryside had been thoroughly subdued; hence the warning of verse 21. The city could appear deceptively to be a place of refuge from the ravaging Romans for the rural population. But ultimately all those trapped in the city were slaughtered or taken away as slaves. One million Jews died, and 97,000 were transported for slavery. Many Christians managed to escape to Pella.

The last times Verses 25-28 refer mainly to the 'last times' at the end of the day of grace, the 'time of the Gentiles' (see Romans 11:25). The last words of verse 25 indicate this clearly. Jesus was using apocalyptic language, with its recognizable poetic word-pictures. The meaning of such language was much clearer to the Jews, familiar with such phraseology, than to us. But the restless sea stands for the rise and fall of nations in more than one language. The heavenly bodies stand for world rulers (for example, Genesis 37:9).

The section following (verses 29-36) seems to deal mainly with the fall of Jerusalem. The word 'generation' (verse 32) illustrates the two levels of meaning in the poetic language used here. It can mean those living at a given time, and also 'race'. It is true that some of those living saw the destruction of Palestine, but Jesus was also prophesying that the Jewish race will still be living at the winding up of history, at the end of the age.

22:1-6 Judas agrees to betray Jesus

Judas was 'one of the Twelve'. The story shows that simply to belong to a group may have little significance. It is sympathy, love and fellowship which bind a man to his friends. Judas had long been alienated. His betrayal laid the way open for the successful attack from outside. The church can fall only by betrayal from inside, with the decay of standards.

Verse 3 stands as one of the most terrible statements in the Bible. Good and evil come about through human actions. The devil entered Judas and used him for his own purposes. This became possible because Judas opened the way.

The Feast of Unleavened Bread (verse 1) lasted from 14 to 21 Nisan; 15 Nisan was the Day of Passover. The 'officers' (verse 4) were the Captain of the Temple and his force of Jewish soldiers. They were 'delighted' (verse 5), since the crowds of Jews gathered in Jerusalem for the Passover formed a mighty force, which deterred them from arresting Jesus in daylight.

22:7-38 The Last Supper

It was common practice for rabbis at Passover time to gather their disciples in an upper room for confidential discussions about the true religion. In the event, Jesus held the conversation elsewhere. John tells us that he made a sudden decision to leave, and the solemn words of John 15 and 16 were probably spoken in the courtyard of the Temple. Jesus had several reasons for this move. Perhaps he wanted to win more time before the betrayal took place. But it also seems likely that he felt that the upper room where the Last Supper had taken place had been contaminated by Judas and by the disciples' quarrel about precedence.

The house (verse 11) was probably the same as the one mentioned in Acts 12:12, the home of Mark's mother. Jesus was aware that Judas was plotting, and tried to conceal the location for the Last Supper as long as he could. It was quite easy for Peter and John to pick out their host (verse 10) among the crowds of pilgrims; it was most unusual for a man to be seen carrying a water-pitcher. It was women who carried pitchers; men used water-skins.

The order of events at the Last Supper (verses 15-23) is described in Matthew, and with some differences in Mark. But the variations are not of significance. An early Syrian manuscript of Luke is different again, and may represent an ancient tradition. This manuscript reads: 'And he took bread and gave thanks over it, and broke and gave to them, saying, this is my body which I give for you; this do in remembrance of me. And after they had supped he took the cup and gave thanks over it, and said, take this and share it among yourselves. This is my blood, the New Testament. For I say unto you that henceforth I will not drink of this fruit, until the kingdom of God shall come'. It is also a fact that several cups of wine were drunk at the Passover Feast. If a full and detailed account of the Last Supper had survived the details of the various accounts we have would doubtless be totally integrated.

The Passover It was a time of solemn fulfilment. The symbol of the Passover lamb was very relevant to Jesus' last hours and to the coming sacrifice of the Lamb of God. The Passover Feast was the most colourful of all the Jewish religious ceremonies. It demonstrated in its dramatic ritual the whole concept of a substitutionary sacrifice and God's saving power. It was now about to be replaced by a Christian ceremony which speaks graphically of God appearing in human form, and of life poured out in sacrifice.

Passover is the most important Jewish festival. It is celebrated to recall the Exodus of the Israelites from Egypt in the time of the Pharaohs. Families would normally celebrate the Passover together in their homes. There was a detailed pattern to be followed, with readings from the Psalms and the book of Exodus interspersed by the breaking of bread and drinking of four special cups of wine.

Gethsemane is still today noted for its many ancient olive trees, with their gnarled trunks. Once there was a garden stretching up the slopes of the Mount of Olives, but like Jerusalem itself, this was almost entirely destroyed by the Romans.

The hand of the traitor was on the table with Jesus. This stirred the others, who were embarrassed by the divisions which appeared. The dissensions among the apostles, which had occurred during the journey from Jericho (Matthew 20:24-28; Mark 9:33-37; 10:41-45) now broke out again (verse 24). Perhaps this time the cause was their positions at the table.

There was quite a range of ages among the Twelve, as verse 26 shows. Peter was the oldest. He was a married man with his own home (see Luke 4:38) when he first joined Jesus as a disciple; and he called himself an 'elder' in the sixth decade of the century (1 Peter 5:1). John, who lived on until the death of the Emperor Domitian in AD 96, was probably the youngest of the apostles.

Verse 30 is expressed in apocalyptic language, which the Twelve should not have taken too literally. Verse 31 refers back to the opening of the book of Job. Peter, like Job in the Old Testament, was to pass through a period of darkness and testing to emerge toughened and better able to help his fellow believers. Notice the use of his name 'Simon', the name of his frailty.

The reference to the sword (verse 36) is again in apocalyptic language. Since later the same night Jesus rejected one of the knives produced in answer to his words here, he obviously cannot have meant his words to be taken literally. As with the parable, he was trying to stimulate a greater spiritual understanding in his followers. But once again success was limited (verse 38). Jesus was in effect attempting to call the Twelve to courage for their time of testing.

22:39-53 Jesus arrested

A remnant of the Garden of Gethsemane still lies across the Kidron valley on the lower slopes of the Mount of Olives. Two or three trees of great age stand there, with short trunks gnarled, twisted and eroded by the passing centuries. The hill was stripped of all vegetation during the two great rebellions, but olive trees are extraordinarily tenacious. They will spring up again from old roots when all the visible parts are burnt and destroyed.

That Jesus, knowing what lay ahead, should shrink from his task is not strange. The divine and the human were perfectly blended in him. His perfect under standing led to suffering which imperfect

'The Agony in the Garden' by Bellini.

minds could never imagine (Hebrews 5:7-9). Haematidrosis (the rupturing of tiny blood vessels into the sweat-glands) is a reported medical phenomenon. It reveals extreme stress in a mind under great pressure.

The kiss was the traditional way for a disciple to greet his rabbi. Only John reveals that it was Peter who resorted to violence (verse 50). When he wrote, nearly forty years later, it was safe to reveal Peter's name. The impetuous apostle had by then been dead a number of years. John was also familiar with the high priest's house, and thus knew the name of the injured man (John 18:10). It was typical of Peter to turn to action in a moment of bewilderment or stress; this characteristic appears a number of times in the Gospels.

22:54-62 Peter disowns Jesus

Luke spares the apostles wherever he can. Matthew and John were both numbered among the Twelve, and Mark wrote under the direction of Peter. Here Luke misses out Peter's outburst of foul language (Mark 14:71). John explains how Peter came to be in the high priest's house (John 18:15-18).

It is obvious that Peter himself was the source for the stories of his disowning of Jesus. It begins with Mark, Peter's friend, and is recorded in faithful detail in all four Gospels. It is also clear that Peter told the historians to say nothing in his defence. He wanted his repentance to be complete. The person who makes any sort of excuse takes away from his complete contriteness.

Peter's testing There is much about Peter to be admired even in this hour of his failure. After all, when the others had fled, he had found his way, with John, to the high priest's palace. While John was known there, Peter's gate-crashing was more obvious and more hazardous. He faced these dangers; but the pressures were more than he could stand. He was brave, but it had been a long, tense and wearing night.

By the coal fire in this hostile, unfamilar place the air seemed full of menace. Peter was unused to such company. He was unnerved by the subtle, sarcastic wit of city people. When the test came, his nerve failed. Sometimes the 'way of escape' promised for temptation lies in

High Priest

The High Priest was the leader and the head of the priesthood in Israel. He was responsible for the services in the Temple and for the Temple building itself. Certain special sacrifices had to be made by the High Priest, who alone could enter the Holy of Holies (Leviticus 16; Hebrews 9:7). He also presided over the Sanhedrin.

The first High Priest in Israel was Aaron, who was consecrated by Moses. From then on the office was handed on to the eldest son, who remained in office for life. When the Romans came to power, they deposed and appointed High Priests quite often, so that several people could call themselves 'High Priest' at any one time.

During the Passover when Jesus was crucified, it was Caiaphas who was High Priest. He was the son-in-law of Annas, one of the earlier High Priests who still had considerable influence (John 18:13). Caiaphas held office between AD 18-36.

avoiding the place where we know testing is likely to overwhelm us.

Luke is now reaching the length of account which the largest papyrus roll could conveniently accommodate. He still had incidents such as the story of the walk to Emmaus which could not be shortened without loss. Possibly it is for this reason that sections such as this appear slightly sketchy and telescoped in length.

22:63-71 Jesus before the high priest

Luke mentions five trials of Jesus. If we compare this first trial with Mark 14:53-64 we may conclude that the Sanhedrin met with Annas to draw up their charges against Jesus. They were not supposed to meet by night; hence their morning's business consisted of the formality of rubber-stamping what had been agreed the previous night.

Even so, the court's proceedings were irregular. Witnesses for the defence ought first to have been called and solemnly warned to speak from their own knowledge of events. The court should not have sat on a Jewish feast day. Sentences of condemnation were by law supposed to be held over for a period of twenty-four hours.

In verse 69 Jesus is again using apocalyptic language, which would recall the words of Psalm 110:1. He was referring to the resurrection. The 'glorifying' of the Son of Man began with the crucifixion (John 13:31). The title 'Son of Man' was recognized as one of the names of the Messiah (Daniel 7:13) and taken as such by Jesus' listeners. Hence the direct question of verse 70. Mark expresses this same reply as 'I am'. This is enough to indicate that the form of words of verse 70 is agreement. (See also Acts 2:33-35; Romans 8:34; Hebrews 1:3,4; 1 Peter 3:22; Revelation 3:21.) The Jewish leaders clearly understood that Jesus was claiming to be Messiah.

23:1-25 Jesus before Pilate and Herod

Pilate, as a Roman procurator, was directly responsible to the Emperor Tiberius himself. His arrogance and heavy-handed official behaviour had left him dangerously vulnerable to threats of complaint to Caesar. It was vital to Rome to maintain peace in Palestine, which was a strategic communications route between the valleys of the Nile and the Euphrates. Palestine linked the important Roman provinces of Egypt and Syria.

Undoubtedly Pilate had orders to cultivate the collaborators – especially the Sadducee priests. He was also ordered to handle the rank and file carefully, and to maintain wise relations with the petty kings of the area. He had done none of these things, and his failure was known to Tiberius. Pilate could not risk more complaints to Caesar. Thus it was the best course for Jesus' enemies to present him as a subversive agitator.

Notice how the charge developed (Mark 14:57,58, 61-64). Despite this, Pilate actually acquitted Jesus (verse 4). He could have stood by his own conclusions. But he was frightened by the violence of the mob, and realized with relief that he could shirk his responsibility by trying to get Herod, the tetrarch of Galilee, to take over the case from him.

Herod was in Jerusalem for the Feast. He had once listened to John the Baptist, and was fascinated to see this prophet from Galilee. But Herod was too good a diplomat to get caught by Pilate's trickery. Jesus was Pilate's responsibility.

The 'elegant robe' in which Jesus was dressed was a white holiday robe which added to the mockery. (For this whole section see also 1 Peter 2:21-23.)

Luke is the only one of the four Gospel-writers who tells of the visit to Herod. He had some first-hand source of information (see Luke 8:3) from which he obtained details such as these and those of Acts 12:20 and 13:1.

Jesus had nothing to say to Herod, the puppet-ruler of Galilee. He

Gordon's Calvary in Jerusalem is put forward by some as the site of Jesus' crucifixion. They claim that the rock formation resembles a skull, and hence a connection with 'Golgotha' (Matthew 27:33), 'the place of the skull'. However the traditional site, the Church of the Holy Sepulchre, is much more likely.

'But they kept shouting "Crucify him! Crucify him!" '
(Luke 23:20).

presented a mere curious spectacle to this corrupt ruler who was guilty of murder and adultery. When Jesus' enemies could get no word out of him, they 'ridiculed and mocked him' (verse 11).

Pilate and the priests The struggle between Pilate and the priests was extremely dramatic, and Luke tells it in his most vivid style. In the book of Acts, Luke is eager to show that Roman magistrates, as well as experienced local rulers, found nothing subversive about Christianity. His treatment of Jesus' trial is an early example of this later preoccupation of Luke.

Pilate underlined the double acquittal, and ought to have freed his prisoner with a safe-conduct. His cowardice now becomes clearly visible (verse 16). There was no reason to scourge Jesus (this was the punishment meant) if he was indeed innocent. Scourging in itself was a savage sentence which often resulted in death.

When they saw that Pilate was hesitating, the priests shrewdly and ruthlessly pressed home their advantage and whipped up renewed chanting. The shouts of 'Crucify! Crucify!' drove Pilate to re-open the case. His correct course at this point would have been to dismiss the accusers, call out the garrison and clear the mob. This would have out-manoeuvred the priests.

Barabbas It was quite illogical for the priests who had brought Jesus before Pilate charged with subversion and a breach of the peace to call for the release of the terrorist Barabbas. It is significant that at the last moment at which the Jewish nation could have chosen the way of peace, they called for the freedom of a man of violence. 'Barabbas' means 'son of a rabbi'.

Who then crucified Jesus? Was it Caiaphas and the priests, eager to retain their easy life, their comfort, and to avoid at all costs getting involved in a popular movement that might embarrass them with Rome? Was it Pilate, tight in the grip of his past administrative errors, determined at all costs to protect his career, and to avoid any danger of another complaint about him to Caesar? Was it Herod, corrupt and guilty, refusing to lift a finger to save a man from Galilee? Was it the mob, ready to applaud when they thought they might benefit from the King of Israel, but who bawled for his blood when he called for sacrifice? Was it the soldiers who obeyed orders and drove the nails into Jesus' flesh?

23:27-43 The crucifixion

Simon of Cyrene may have come to Jerusalem for the Passover (verse 26). Acts 6:9 shows that the Jews of Cyrene had a synagogue of their own in the city. Some scholars have suggested that the place of crucifixion may have been the skull-shaped hill north of the city, not far from the Damascus Gate. This is known today as 'Gordon's Calvary' after the English soldier General Charles Gordon. However the traditional site, underneath the Church of the Holy Sepulchre, has more solidly-based archaeological support.

At Calvary the issues of eternity found their climax. Notice the restraint of Luke's account. He passes over the physical horrors of the crucifixion. At this very moment when 'God was in Christ reconciling the world to himself' (2 Corinthians 5:19) the treatment of Jesus by the Roman soldiers, by the religious leaders and the inflamed crowd all demonstrated man's rebellion against God. Jesus asked forgiveness (verse 34) not so much for the soldiers as for the world as a whole.

Luke gives plenty of attention to women in his account (verses 27-32). Their presence in his story illustrates Luke's sources, and throws interesting light on the make-up of the early church. The women may have come to offer Jesus drugs (Proverbs 31:6).

The rich were able to afford special tombs, with a stairway leading down through the rock to an underground burial chamber. A slab of stone was placed against the door, with a boulder to secure it. Sometimes a huge circular stone was rolled across the doorway in special grooves.

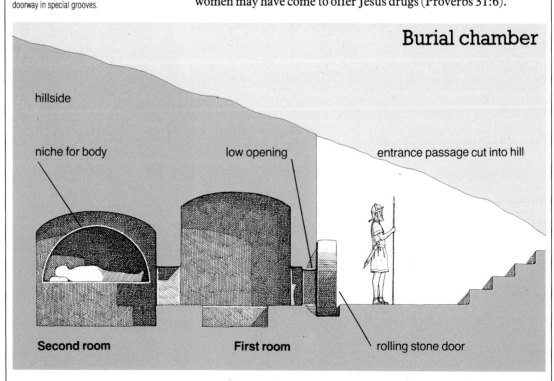

Burial chamber

hillside

niche for body

low opening

entrance passage cut into hill

Second room

First room

rolling stone door

The inscription The different versions of the inscription over the cross (verse 38) are a result of its being written in three different languages. If Matthew's version is translated back into Latin, Luke's into Greek, and John's into Aramaic, lines of roughly equal length result.

There is of course no clash between Luke's account of the two criminals and that of Mark (verses 39-45). Both criminals at first spoilt their last hours with abuse and blasphemy (Mark 15:32). One of them watched Jesus' behaviour, heard what he said, and found a saviour despite his unimaginable pain. He received immediate and complete forgiveness. He cried for pardon, and received what he craved. There could be no more graphic demonstration that salvation is of grace (Ephesians 2:8). 'Paradise' (verse 43) means a garden, the resting place of the spirits of the blessed, awaiting the resurrection.

23:44-49 Jesus' death

The tearing of the veil in the Temple (verse 45) was a deeply significant sign for the Jews. The writer of the letter to the Hebrews made much of it in his masterly explanation of the Christian significance of the Jewish rituals. He related the torn curtain to Jesus (Hebrews 9:3-8;11,12; 10:9-22). The curtain indicated separation between man and God. Now it was destroyed. No priest or mediator other than Christ can come between man and God. Access to God has become the right of everyone.

The darkened sun (verse 44) was a sign to the Gentiles, as the torn curtain was to the Jews. The sun was not darkened by an eclipse, since an eclipse cannot take place at full moon. This was a supernatural phenomenon.

The story of Jesus' death is told at greater length by the other Gospel-writers. Perhaps Luke found it too painful to dwell upon. He heard the story from the women who had followed Jesus (verse 49).

The terrible solemnity of this moment seems to have quietened the crowds. Mass psychology tells us that crowds are liable to sudden changes of mood. This is demonstrated by the changes of the crowd in Jerusalem from Palm Sunday to Calvary. It was now finished. Salvation had been won for all who chose to repent and follow Christ.

'When they came to the place called The Scull, there they crucified him, along with the criminals – one on his right, the other on his left' (Luke 23:33).

'The curtain of the temple was torn in two' (Luke 23:45).

Funerals

When a Jewish person died, the funeral took place as soon as possible. The body was washed, anointed with oil and wrapped in a linen shroud. The hands and feet were wound in bandages, and the face covered with a cloth. Often myrrh and aloes were put in the shroud to give it a fresh and pleasant smell.

The body was carried to the grave on a bier or in an open coffin. Mourners followed, with music, weeping and laments. Professional women-weepers were hired for the occasion.

To show their grief, relatives would fast, tear open their mantles at the neck, put ashes on their heads, dress in coarse sack-cloth, shave off their hair and beards, and tear themselves with their nails till they drew blood.

Poor people used natural caves for tombs as well as holes dug in the ground.

23:50-56 Jesus' burial

Joseph was a member of the Sanhedrin. We do not know if he openly opposed the condemnation of Jesus in the council (verse 53). He now went with great courage to Pilate and begged to have the body of Jesus. If he had not done so, it would have been thrown out for the dogs and vultures to devour. Joseph gave Jesus a decent, reverent and honourable burial. The women were also present at the burial, which possibly explains the fuller account of these events in Luke than in the other Gospels.

But Luke was not merely thinking of narrative here. The resurrection was the first main feature of the Christian gospel, as the earliest preaching shows. Faced with the empty tomb, sceptics would most readily argue that Jesus had not really died. Luke was a medical man, and took considerable care over this aspect of the question. Joseph and those who helped him had no doubt that they were burying a dead man. The great stone was rolled in front of the grave entrance, and the garden emptied. Then guards came to watch the tomb.

24:1-12 The resurrection

Luke chose to record the resurrection appearances of Jesus that were associated with Jerusalem. There is no reason why he should not have been selective in composing his Gospel in this way. Some critics have emphasized discrepancies in Luke's account when compared with the other Gospels, but these differences amount to little of importance. For instance Luke mentions two men in the tomb, while

The Garden Tomb in Jerusalem, close to Gordon's Calvary, claimed by some to be the authentic site of the burial of Jesus. The tomb lies in the lower part of a tranquil garden.

'Now that same day two of them were going to a village called Emmaus, about seven miles from Jerusalem' (Luke 24:13). A view of the road near Emmaus.

Luke
24

Mark mentions only one (Mark 16:5). But Mark seems to have been writing in a great hurry. He therefore only mentioned the visitor who actually spoke.

Luke's informants are again in evidence. Joanna (Luke 8:3) probably gave him many of the details we find in this story, just as she gave him the details for Luke 23:8-12. When Luke was searching Palestine for the surviving witnesses of the resurrection twenty years later the apostles had gone abroad. It was the women who remained and could give him the information he needed.

Paul's account Another of Luke's sources was his travelling companion Paul, who at the time of writing the Gospel was probably in prison at Caesarea, though probably accessible to his friends. The first account of the resurrection is probably Paul's version in 1 Corinthians 15:1-7. (His letter was written before Mark's Gospel.)

Just as Mark missed out one angel, so Luke misses out one apostle (verse 12). Doubtless he had heard Peter describe the event. The story is told in greater detail in John 20:3-10. The Greek word translated as 'nonsense' (verse 11) is a medical word meaning delirious babbling.

If Jesus did not rise from the dead, the body must have been stolen by men. This is what the Pharisees alleged. But how could these scattered and broken men possibly envisage such a fraud? And would they have faced everything they did in life to maintain a lie? Who else would have removed Jesus' body without stating the truth? Joseph? Pilate? Caiaphas?

24:13-35 On the road to Emmaus

This beautifully told story is found only in Luke. The two disciples (they were not apostles) lived at Emmaus, perhaps modern Kalonich, north-west of Jerusalem. Walking home in animated conversation they hardly noticed the stranger join them.

Their reply to the stranger's question rings with the hopelessness of the disciples following the crushing events of Calvary. Their broken spirit contrasts strongly with the triumph and jubilation of the days which followed. Only a cataclysmic event could have transformed such shattered men. They must have been

Ascension

totally convinced about the central fact of the resurrection faith. The experience of the Emmaus road was no delusion. It transformed dejected men. The clear and specific report of events in verses 22-24 show these to have been no gullible enthusiasts. They admit only what they have seen with their own eyes.

Jesus called the disciples 'foolish' (verse 25). The risen Saviour proceeded to unravel for them the thread of his own foretelling from the Old Testament. The truth dawned on them as he broke the bread. Perhaps it was only then that they saw the torn and ravaged hands. Perhaps he was revealed by a familar gesture. Forgetting their tiredness, they hurried back the seven miles to Jerusalem to find the Eleven. They, too, were full of strange, thrilling news.

The appearance of the risen Christ to Peter, mentioned here and in 1 Corinthians 15:5, is never given in detail in the New Testament. Perhaps the words of the interview were too painful and private for common knowledge.

The words and this entire incident bear the hallmark of truth. This is not fiction. Prose fiction was in any case hardly practised at this time.

24:36-53 Jesus appears to the disciples

There can be no doubt whatsoever that the New Testament teaches that Jesus rose physically from the dead. The witnesses were adamant that they were not merely communicating with a spirit. He ate food in their presence. Verse 39 forms part of their witness.

The witnesses to this first appearance of Christ to the apostles themselves are Luke, John (John 20:19-23) and Paul (1 Corinthians 15:5). In Luke the account is linked with the Emmaus story. In John it comes as a separate episode. Only Luke mentions the fish and the honey-comb, but John mentions Jesus' eating with them on the beach in a resurrection story set in Galilee and told only by him.

The Gospel-writers took the greatest care to establish the fact that the body in which Jesus appeared was a real body, not a fantasm or spirit manifestation. It was the body of the cross and the tomb, still bearing the marks of suffering. On the other hand, it belonged to a different order of existence. Something about this body prevented people immediately recognizing him.

Luke 24

The account of Jesus' ascension is found in Luke 24:51 and Acts 1:4-11. Jesus spoke of it when he was on earth (John 6:62), and also said he would be returning to his Father (John 14:1-4).

Some people claim it cannot have taken place since it assumes an out-of-date idea of heaven as 'up there'. But Jesus was trying to show ordinary people that he was making a final and miraculous departure from earth. The best way was to go 'up'.

In any event, if heaven means anything, it is somewhere away from this earth, outside space-time. It is quite reasonable and logical to think of it as upwards.

The idea of 'going up' suggests promotion to a higher state. It is a symbol of glory, just as 'coming down' was a symbol of grace. We are told that Jesus now sits at God's right hand (Hebrews 1:3), suggesting he has been given a place of honour.

'The Supper at Emmaus' by Caravaggio.

261

Luke
24

'When he had led them out to the vicinity of Bethany, he lifted up his hands and blessed them. While he was blessing them, he left them and was taken up into heaven' (Luke 24:50,51). The traditional site of Jesus' ascension on the Mount of Olives.

The conclusion Luke concludes his Gospel very briefly. He was already planning his second volume – the book of Acts. He intended to enlarge on some of the events between the resurrection and the ascension in that work. He treats the time of teaching (verses 44-48) very rapidly, as he does the appearance of the risen Christ in Galilee.

The 'great joy' of the group who came back from Bethany now became historic fact. The church was born out of it. Tremendous conviction gave power and coherence to what had been a feeble scattered band of people. Jesus' earthly ministry apparently ended in defeat. The powers of evil and of destruction seemed to have won. There was an air of broken hopelessness (verse 21). But now doubts were dispelled, despair quenched, and fear cast out; defeat was turned to victory.

The ascension The ascension is necessary to finish off the story. Jesus had revealed himself as truly risen from the dead. He had eaten with them, Thomas had touched him and believed. But the earthly ministry of the Son of God was over. It would obviously be painful and confusing to them if he simply stopped appearing to his disciples. Some clear break with earth was needed, as well as a confirming that he had gone to his Father. This is the clue to the meaning of the ascension.

The disciples were told to wait at Jerusalem until they received a gift of power. They had no clear idea of what this meant; this is often the case when God delays.

Tradition has it that Jesus ascended from a point on the brow of this hill just outside Jerusalem. A church has long stood over the site.

Contents

	Page
People	
John	271
Nicodemus	315
Thomas	339
Places	
Bethany	307
Words	
Word	268
Life	270
Regeneration	275
Authority	283
Temptation	284
Love	285
Exodus	286
Miracles	288, 89
Incarnation	292
Trinity	305
Glory	312
Revelation	317
Counsellor	318
Truth	320
Prayer	324
Death	337
Life	
The land Jesus knew	266, 67
Measures	278
Samaritans	280
Scribes	281
Nazirite	322

John

Introduction to John

John Introduction

This Gospel was traditionally believed to have been written by John, the son of Zebedee, who is thought to have lived at Ephesus until about the end of the first century AD. Because John is nowhere mentioned by name (there is only a reference to the sons of Zebedee in John 21:2), and because the Baptist is simply referred to as 'John', there seems little doubt that the Gospel-writer intends the readers to suppose that the 'beloved disciple' is the apostle John. It seems likely, then, that John was the real author of the Gospel, even if he did not necessarily pen or dictate every word of it. While some scholars suggest that chapter 21 was added later as a sort of postscript, possibly after he died, others believe that this chapter, too, is largely the work of John. In either case, even if the date of publication is late, the material in the Gospel, coming from an eyewitness,

will have as much historical value as that in the other Gospels.

The purpose of John's Gospel is similar to that of any Gospel. It is to present a selection of the deeds of Jesus in such a way that people will put their faith in Him as the Son of God and find eternal life, and that believers will be built up in the faith (John 20:31). It was written in the first place for Greek-speaking Jews who lived outside Palestine, but its message has been embraced by people of every race in every age.

The relationship of this Gospel to Matthew, Mark and Luke presents a large number of problems, few of which are dealt with here. Some scholars have held that John knew Mark's Gospel and adapted it for his own purposes. Others have suggested that he is independent of Mark, which is probably based on the preaching of Peter, and that any resemblances can be traced back to

Peter and John being eyewitnesses of the same events. All the Gospel-writers were interested in the facts and in their interpretation, and though John makes the interpretation more obvious, he is not necessarily less interested in the facts. Archaeological discovery has done a certain amount to confirm that a number of details found only in John fit well into the background of the times. It is often difficult to know when John intends things to be taken symbolically, and imagination must not be allowed to run riot. But the discovery of a symbolic meaning for something does not automatically mean that it was not also an historical fact.

There are seven 'signs' in the Gospel which present in dramatic form the challenge of the person and work of Christ. And there are seven 'I am' sayings which are evangelistic appeals. In the Gospel many people recognize Jesus partially, but only the confession of Thomas after the resurrection, 'My Lord and my God!' (John 20:28), is adequate.

One of the features of the Gospel is irony. Men say and do all sorts of things with deeper significance than they realize. God's own people put God's own Son to death. The Jews, who are mentioned frequently, seem to be the Jewish leaders, the people who live in the promised land, and have a vested interest in the old order of things. The supreme paradox is the way in which the shameful death on the cross reveals the glory of the Father and the Son.

Outline to John's Gospel

1:1-51	**The Prelude**	10:22-42	The unbelief of the Jews
1:1-5	The Word became flesh	11:1-16	The death of Lazarus
1:6-8	A man sent from God	11:17-37	Jesus comforts the sisters
1:9-13	The true light	11:38-44	Jesus raises Lazarus from the dead
1:14-18	Full of grace and truth		
1:19-28	John the Baptist denies being the Christ	11:45-57	The plot to kill Jesus
		12:1-11	Jesus anointed at Bethany
1:29-34	Jesus the Lamb of God	12:12-19	The triumphal entry
1:35-42	Jesus' first disciples	12:20-36	Jesus predicts his death
1:43-51	Jesus calls Philip and Nathanael	12:37-50	The Jews continue in their unbelief
2:1-12:50	**The Book of Signs**		
2:1-11	Jesus changes water into wine	**13:1-19:42**	**The Book of the Passion**
2:12-25	Jesus clears the Temple	13:1-17	Jesus washes his disciples' feet
3:1-15	Jesus teaches Nicodemus	13:18-30	Jesus predicts his betrayal
3:16-21	Jesus summarizes the gospel	13:31-38	Jesus predicts Peter's denial
3:22-30	Jesus and John the Baptist	14:1-4	Jesus comforts his disciples
3:31-36	He who comes from heaven	14:5-14	Jesus the way to the Father
4:1-26	Jesus meets a Samaritan woman	14:15-31	Jesus promises the Holy Spirit
4:27-38	The disciples rejoin Jesus	15:1-17	The vine and the branches
4:39-42	Many Samaritans believe	15:18-27	The world hates the disciples
4:43-54	Jesus heals the official's son	16:1-16	The work of the Holy Spirit
5:1-15	The healing at the pool	16:17-24	Grief turned to joy
5:19-30	Life through the Son	16:25-33	Parting words to the disciples
5:31-47	Witnesses to Jesus	17:1-5	Jesus prays for himself
6:1-15	Jesus feeds the five thousand	17:6-19	Jesus prays for his disciples
6:16-24	Jesus walks on the water	17:20-26	Jesus prays for all believers
6:25-59	Jesus the bread of life	18:1-11	Jesus arrested
6:60-71	Many disciples desert Jesus	18:12-14	Jesus taken to Annas
7:1-13	Jesus goes to the Feast of Tabernacles	18:15-18	Peter's first denial
		18:19-27	The high priest questions Jesus
7:14-24	Jesus teaches at the feast	18:28-40	Jesus before Pilate
7:25-36	Is Jesus the Christ?	19:1-16	Jesus sentenced to be crucified
7:37-44	Streams of living water	19:17-27	The crucifixion
7:45-52	Unbelief of the Jewish leaders	19:28-37	The death of Jesus
7:53-8:11	The woman caught in adultery	19:38-42	The burial of Jesus
8:12-20	Jesus the Light of the World	**20:1-21:25**	**The Resurrection and Epilogue**
8:21-30	Where I go you cannot come	20:1-10	The empty tomb
8:31-47	Abraham's children and the devil's children	20:10-18	Jesus appears to Mary of Magdala
8:48-59	Jesus' claims about himself	20:19-23	Jesus appears to his disciples
9:1-12	Jesus heals a man born blind	20:24-31	Jesus appears to Thomas
9:13-34	The healing investigated	21:1-14	Jesus and the miraculous catch of fish
9:35-41	Spiritual blindness		
10:1-21	Jesus the Good Shepherd	21:15-25	Feed my sheep

The land Jesus knew

The land
During the time of Jesus Palestine was divided into a number of different administrative areas.

Judea was the name of the large territory ruled by Herod the Great. It was also the name for the area immediately surrounding Jerusalem, and after the Jewish Exile was used as the title for the Jewish state. Yet another use of the name was for the Wilderness of Judea, the arid, mountainous region lying between Jerusalem and the Dead Sea.

While Herod's son Archelaus succeeded him as ruler of Judea, Herod Antipas took over the area called Perea, east of the river Jordan. Perea is not mentioned by name in the Bible, but its name means 'the other side', and it is referred to by the words 'across the Jordan' (Mark 10:1; John 10:40).

Decapolis was the name of a league, probably originally consisting of ten cities, east of the river Jordan. The league was probably formed largely by

Greek settlers around 70-80 BC. It consisted of the ten cities of Damascus, Raphana, Kanatha, Dion, Hippos, Gadara, Pella, Gerasa, Philadelphia (modern Amman) and Scythopolis.

Galilee was the name of the most northerly province of Palestine, ruled in the time of Jesus by Herod Antipas. When the Romans destroyed Jerusalem in AD 70, many Jews fled to Galilee for refuge.

Right
The shore of the Sea of Galilee
Far right
The hills near Bethlehem
Below
Cliffs rise steeply from the east shores of the Sea of Galilee
Below right
The rich hillside of Galilee, west of the Sea of Galilee.

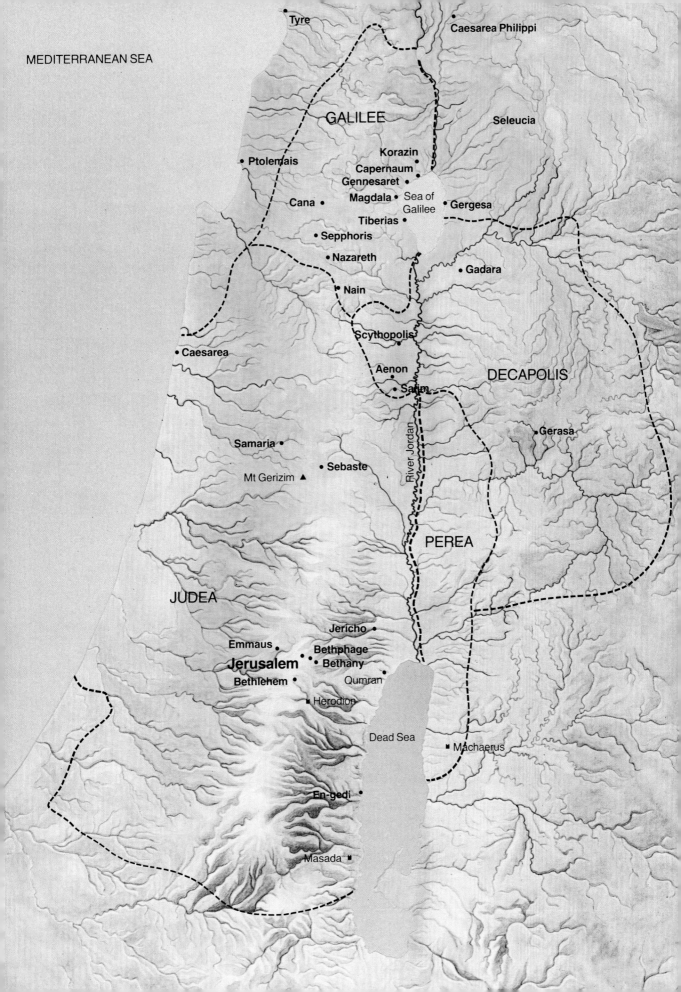

MEDITERRANEAN SEA

• Tyre

• Caesarea Philippi

GALILEE

Seleucia

• Ptolemais

• Korazin

Capernaum
Gennesaret •

• Cana

Magdala

Sea of
Galilee

• Gergesa

Tiberias

• Sepphoris

• Nazareth

• Gadara

• Nain

Scythopolis

DECAPOLIS

• Caesarea

Aenon

Salim

River Jordan

Samaria •

• Gerasa

Mt Gerizim ▲

• Sebaste

PEREA

JUDEA

Jericho •

Emmaus •

Bethphage

Jerusalem

• Bethany

Bethlehem •

Qumran •

Herodion ▪

Dead Sea

• Machaerus

• En-gedi

Masada ▪

Word

A E Cundall (with R E Nixon)

John
Commentary

There are several different senses in which this word is used in the Bible.

1 It is used to describe God's decree by which the world first came into being (Psalm 33:6-9).

2 Mainly in the Old Testament, it was a special personal communication from God to man, which he was often required to pass on to others. We frequently read that 'the word of the Lord' came to one of his servants (Jeremiah 1:4). When this occurred, it had a special authority and urgency (Jeremiah 2:5).

3 One very specialized use comes in John's writings, where Jesus is spoken of as the 'Word' (John 1:1). This difficult concept expresses the means by which the transcendent God can reveal himself to his creatures. The Thought or Wisdom or Idea behind the universe embodies itself in a Word – a meaningful saying.

4 'The word' is also used to mean the gospel. (see for example Acts 20:32; 13:26; 2 Corinthians 5:19).

5 Finally 'the word' is often used for the written record of God's revelation – that is as much of the Bible as existed at the particular time. In the Psalms (particularly Psalm 119) it frequently occurs, and means the same as God's laws, statutes and judgements. In the New Testament we discover it is indestructible (1 Peter 24:25) and that it can be a sword for the Christian in his fight against temptation (Ephesians 6:17). It is also pictured as a looking-glass (James 1:23-25) and as food to nourish the Christian in his spiritual life. He is to receive it, study it and obey it (Matthew 4:4).

1:1-5 The Word became flesh

The Prologue (verses 1-18) gives a preview of some of the great themes of the Gospel and sets the earthly ministry of Jesus in its heavenly perspective.

The resurrection was the great event which confirmed his divine sonship (Acts 2:36, Romans 1:4). But a voice had declared it before that at his transfiguration (Mark 9:7), and even earlier at his baptism (Mark 1:11). Matthew and Luke show that he was divine from his birth and his conception (Matthew 1:20-23, Luke 1:35; 2:10). Yet all these events were but stages in the revelation of an eternal truth.

In the beginning 'In the beginning was the Word' – long before he took human flesh in the person in Jesus. Mark's 'beginning' (Mark 1:1) is the beginning of Jesus' ministry, culminating in his death and resurrection. But John's 'beginning' is the beginning of everything. If God *created* 'in the beginning' (Genesis 1:1), then the uncreated Son *was* 'in the beginning'.

'The Word'; this would mean something to Greek readers, for whom 'Word' (*logos*) meant 'reason'. For Jews 'the Word' was the revelation of God's character, expressed in increasingly personal terms in the Old Testament. 'The Word was with God', that is, in personal relationship with him. 'God' has the definite article, marking this out as referring to the first person of the Trinity. 'The Word was God'; here there is no article since the Word is not said to be the same person as God, but to have the nature of God.

This is the starting point for the Gospel-writer; but in the Gospel story he shows how people failed to recognize the full deity of Jesus until Thomas' confession of faith (John 20:28), which is in some ways the climax of this Gospel.

After telling us again that the Word has always existed with God (verse 2), the Gospel-writer goes on to describe his work in creation (compare Colossians 1:16-20, Hebrews 1:1-4). Through his work everything came into being – not just material things but life itself. So we meet two of the great themes of the Gospel – life and light. The light shines on (present tense). The darkness made an attempt to master it but failed decisively (past tense). In this fact lies salvation.

1:6-8 A man sent from God

The first paragraph has seen the Word and his work in God's perspective. In the second paragraph we come to earth with a bump, for the great philosophical truths have been brought into focus in human history! The drama has been played out with human actors; 'There came a man who was sent from God; his name was John'.

The Gospel begins with John the Baptist as does Mark (Mark 1:1-11), whereas Matthew and Luke give additional material about the birth of Jesus. Here, at the start of the apostolic proclamation, John is seen as the forerunner (Mark 1:2), and as the link between the old and the new covenants (Matthew 11:13; Luke 16:16). In John

'In the beginning was the Word, and the Word was with God, and the Word was God . . . Through him all things were made, without him nothing was made that has been made' (John 1:1,3).

In biblical times, after the harvest had been threshed, winnowing took place.

especially, he is the witness to the incarnation rather as the apostles were to the resurrection (compare John 1:15,32,34; 3:26). He was sent from God with his authority, as a prophet. Jesus, too, was sent from God (John 4:34; 5:37), but unlike John he *was* God. John was the lamp (John 5:35), but not the light itself.

1:9-13 The true light

The significance of Jesus Christ is world-wide. He was the genuine light in contrast to the many false lights that seemed to shine, and he came to give light to every man. His sphere of activity had to be the world – made through him (verse 3) and loved by God (John 3:16), but refusing to acknowledge him. So in this Gospel 'the world' often comes to mean human society organized apart from God.

The rejection by the world of its maker is brought into sharper focus in the rejection by God's people of their Messiah. His own people were the Jews, and again and again in this Gospel the emphasis is on their being Judeans, living in the promised land. But God's purposes are not frustrated. The Gospel is addressed to the whole world, and all who receive Jesus in faith are given authority to become members of God's family. Their birth, like that of Jesus, is not natural but supernatural. The two verbs, 'received' and 'believed' (verse 12), do not indicate two separate actions, but two aspects of a person's response to the gospel.

1:14-18 Full of grace and truth

Whatever the Greek philosophers might have said about the cosmic operations of the Word, they could never have said that it 'became flesh'. This is the startling claim of John. The eternal Word became flesh; that is he became man in all his weakness, sharing our nature, living and visible in our midst. It was not God taking over a human being, nor the Word ceasing to be God in order to become man. Somehow, in the most profound mystery of all time, he remained God and yet became man. One who was with God (verse 1) dwelt among us as in a tent, for his permanent residence was not here (compare 2 Corinthians 5:1).

He was no ordinary man, for he was full of grace (which shows the generosity of the action of God) and truth (which shows the reality of it). These two characteristics had been demonstrated in part in the Old Testament; now they are displayed perfectly. Christ fulfils the redemption and the revelation of God. His glory is the outshining of God's nature. This had been seen in the divine presence in the Tabernacle (Exodus 40:34) and in the Temple (1 Kings 8:11). Such men as Moses (Exodus 33:22) and Isaiah (Isaiah 6:3) had caught glimpses of it. But its fullness was reserved for the future (Isaiah 60:1). Here it is shown as God's presence incarnate among men (compare John 3:18; John 5:16,18).

The evidence of John is re-emphasized in order to show that though Christ 'came' after him as far as his birth and ministry were concerned, he 'was' before him (verse 1). The fullness of grace was for all to receive as they received him (verse 12). Grace was unlimited. John is concerned to show the superiority of the new over the old, even though that too was given by God. No one ever yet saw God, not even Moses (Exodus 33:20). Now Jesus had explained him by who he was and what he did. One day we shall see him as he is (1 John 3:2).

In verse 14 'we have seen' may mean the apostolic church as a whole, but suggests eyewitnesses. His glory was seen especially in his signs (John 2:11; 11:4,40). There is no account in John of the transfiguration .

1:19-28 John the Baptist denies being the Christ
One of the most important themes of this Gospel is the evidence that Jesus is the Son of God. Here is the evidence of John, whose ministry had the essential purpose of bearing witness to him (compare verses 7,8 and 15). He was the last of the prophets, but while they had spoken in general terms of the Messiah, it was John the Baptist who was to identify him.

John's evidence was, in the first place, negative (verses 19-21). His ministry and unusual appearance and habits had aroused curiosity. What did it all mean? Who was he? He explained in shorter and shorter sentences that he was neither Messiah nor Elijah reincarnated, nor the prophet promised by Moses and said to be like Moses (Deuteronomy 18:15). In answer to repeated questioning he claimed the role of the forerunner (verses 22,23) as depicted in Isaiah 40. The emphasis is not on his person but on his message. He insisted on directing attention away from himself (compare John 3:30).

The supplementary question inevitably followed. Why, then, was he baptizing, for a ministry of baptism was generally thought to be the preparation for the messianic age (verse 24 onwards). He replied that his baptism was only an outward symbol, and his own dignity was nothing compared with the person who was coming (verse 26 onwards).

1:29-34 Jesus the Lamb of God
The Gospel does not mention the baptism of Jesus, so the Gospel-writer may have assumed that it was well-known to his readers. Compare also the omission of the transfiguration and the inauguration of the Lord's Supper. He does, however, record John's reference to the descent of the Spirit on Jesus to commission him for his work, and John's description of his own baptism as a foreshadowing of the baptism with the Holy Spirit.

The title which John applied to Jesus, 'the Lamb of God', is of considerable importance. It may combine ideas of the lamb of the sin-offering, the Passover lamb (compare John 19:36) and the suffering servant of Isaiah 53. He deals not just with individual sins but with the sin of the whole world. John's solemn declaration of verse 29, probably coming immediately after Christ's temptation (Matthew 4:1-11), would underline vividly his renunciation of any short cut to success. Christ's ministry began under the shadow of the

John 1

In John 1:4 we read 'In him (Jesus) was life'. He is the source of spiritual life; it is only through faith in him that we may possess and enjoy it (John 3:36; 17:3). Life of this sort is not merely everlasting, stretching on into eternity, but on a new level or dimension, which we can start enjoying here and now. Man is regarded as spiritually dead until he is 'quickened' into new life through faith in Christ and by the working of the Holy Spirit (Ephesians 2:1; Romans 8:11).

A pair of leather sandals from Jesus' time.

cross. But the promise of John's statement must not be eclipsed by this note of foreboding. The cross, finally, was a place of triumph.

1:35-42 Jesus' first disciples

The evidence which John the Baptist gave, that Jesus was the Son of God and the Lamb of God, led to two of his own disciples' leaving him and following Jesus. This was a literal following which also became a spiritual following in due course (compare John 8:12; 12:26; 21:19,22). But it was not to be simply on second-hand evidence. Jesus invited them to come and see for themselves and to stay with him. (For a spiritual *coming* to Jesus compare John 3:21; 6:35; for a spiritual *seeing* compare John 14:9; for a spiritual *staying* compare John 15:4-10.) Notice that John was concerned not to attach disciples to *himself* but to Jesus. He could even rejoice in their transferred allegiance (John 3:29-31); a sure indication of his spiritual greatness.

Their conviction was infectious. Andrew's first thought was to share his new experiences with his brother. Finding him was perhaps as great a service to the church as ever any man did. Andrew is described as 'one of the two' (verse 40). The most natural assumption is that the other was John, the Gospel-writer.

1:43-51 Jesus calls Philip and Nathanael

The phrase 'the next day' (verses 29,35 and 43) suggests different days in a week of momentous events. Andrew had found Simon for Jesus, now Jesus himself found Philip, and Philip in turn found Nathanael – the Israelite without any touch of the guileful Jacob (Genesis 32:28). Nathanael is probably the same as Bartholomew (Mark 3:18).

To every misconception about Jesus' true origin, that his true home was Nazareth or that his real father was Joseph, there came the answer of experience; 'come and see'. It seems likely that the preliminary meetings with the apostles recorded here were the reason for their immediate response to Jesus' call (Mark 1: 16-20).

Son of Man The titles ascribed to Jesus in this passage are probably rather an outburst of exalted hope than a rooted conviction of faith.

John 2

John was linked with Peter in making the arrangements for the Last Supper (Luke 22:8-13). John is not mentioned by name in the fourth Gospel, but is probably the anonymous disciple of John 1:35-40; 18: 15, and the 'disciple Jesus loved' (John 13:23). He was given the care of Jesus' mother (John 19:26,27) and ran with Peter to the empty tomb (John 20:3-8).

John was in the Upper Room at Pentecost (Acts 1:13,14) and soon afterwards arrested with Peter for preaching Jesus as Messiah. He and Peter were sent as representatives of the Jerusalem church to acknowledge the Samaritans as full members of Christ by laying on hands (Acts 8:14-17).

Little more is said in the Bible about his movements, but there is a strong tradition that he lived and died at Ephesus. He is credited with the fourth Gospel, the three letters bearing his name, and the book of Revelation.

'We have found the one Moses wrote about in the Law . . .' (John 1:45).

The Galilee hills near Cana. The village lies a few miles north-east of Nazareth.

But 'Rabbi' (verse 38), 'Messiah' (verse 41), 'the one Moses wrote about . . . and . . . the prophets' (verse 45), 'Son of God . . . King of Israel' (verse 49) all have to be understood in the light of the preconceptions of the time. Jesus preferred the cryptic title 'Son of Man' (verse 51). Only after he rose from the dead did true Christian faith come. Only then could Jesus be seen as Jacob's ladder (Genesis 28:10-17), as the house of God (compare John 2:19-22) and the gate of heaven (compare John 10:7,9; John 14:6).

2:1-11 Jesus changes water into wine

Jesus, having gained some disciples, was now invited with them to a wedding. Cana is probably the modern Khirbet Qana, eight or nine miles north of Nazareth. The presence of Jesus' mother there suggests that some friend or relative of his family was being married. The wedding celebrations might last several days, and it seems as if Jesus and his disciples did not arrive until near the end. It may be that the presence of a number of extra guests put a strain on the resources, and the wine ran out. Jesus' mother, (she is never named in this Gospel, compare John 6:42 and 19:25-27) mentioned the need to him as a simple statement of fact. The seeming rebuff was not one of disrespect but, nevertheless, a clear indication that he would not be pressurized into action. His power was not to be controlled by a mere mother-son relationship.

The six stone jars were used to provide water for the washing of hands and of vessels. Jesus' command to fill them was put into effect completely. Then the miracle occurred. It is not clear whether all the water in the pots was turned into wine, or only what was drawn out.

Miracles and signs The miracles recorded in John are described as 'signs'. That is, they have a deeper significance than just the action itself. Here, the old flat water of Judaism was turned into the sparkling new wine of the gospel. This had been kept 'until now'. Christ came as the heavenly bridegroom (John 3:29; compare Mark 2:19-22) who by his presence enriched the social occasions of life and pointed forward to the marriage feast of the kingdom (Matthew 22:1-14). His glory is revealed at other times in this Gospel (John 11:4,40) and the purpose was to bring those to faith in him who had

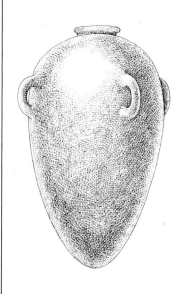

A stone wine-jar of the time of Jesus.

eyes to see. The majority were ignorant about what had happened; the servants knew and expressed wonder, but the disciples both saw and believed.

'Christ driving the Traders from the Temple' by El Greco (1541-1614).

2:12-25 Jesus clears the Temple

Jesus now went up to Jerusalem where John shows that he presented the challenge of his person and work to the Jewish leaders. He had just demonstrated, by his sign at Cana, the superiority of the new religion over the old. Here he made a symbolic purification of Jewish worship as an indication of the coming of the messianic age. The Lord of the Temple came suddenly into his Temple (Malachi 3:1-3). He found at the very heart of Judaism, in the very place where the Lord had chosen to reveal himself, commercial exploitation and corruption. This allowed for a kind of 'instant religion' where everything was on hand, convenient for the 'worshipper' no doubt, but governed mainly by the profit motive.

Zechariah's prophecy The prophecy of Zechariah 14, which had spoken of the Lord's reign over all the earth and the pilgrimage of all nations to Jerusalem to worship him, ended with the words, 'And on that day there will no longer be a merchant in the house of the Lord Almighty'. The zeal of Jesus for God's house and honour was such that he was prepared to use strong methods to drive out those who were profiteering from the need of the people to have animals and birds for sacrifice.

The timing of the cleansing of the Temple creates a problem, as the other Gospels place it just before Jesus' death. The Gospel-writers were not bound to write in a strict chronological order. It may be that John put it here as an incident symbolizing the nature of Christ's mission; or that the others for conciseness put it in the one visit to Jerusalem which they record. But there are sufficient differences of detail to allow the possibility that there were two separate Temple cleansings.

The Jews demanded a sign to prove that Jesus had the right to take this action, and he gave them an answer which they misunderstood (compare Mark 14:58). The Temple, as the symbol of God's presence with his people, was 'redundant', as the Word had become

'Unless a man is born again, he cannot see the kingdom of God' (John 3:3).

'Just as Moses lifted up the snake in the desert, so the Son of Man must be lifted up, that everyone who believes may have eternal life in him' (John 3:14,15).

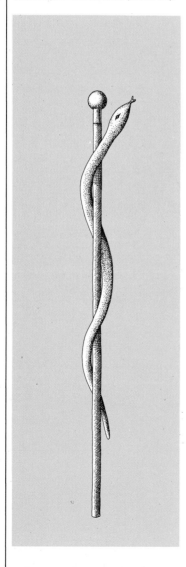

flesh and was living among men (John 1:4). It was doomed to destruction in due course, paradoxically through their possessive attitude to it (John 11:48; compare Luke 13:35: '*your* house'). But the new temple of Christ's body had to go through death to resurrection before it could be a spiritual temple and body of believers (1 Corinthians 3:16; 12:27).

3:1-15 Jesus teaches Nicodemus

If the Messiah brought a new beginning for the nation and its religion, he also brought one for the individual and his religion. Nicodemus was a member of the Sanhedrin, the Jewish council. He was probably both a theologian and a diplomat. He came by night, anonymously. His questions show an inability to understand the spiritual significance of the gospel. Eventually he is 'faded out' of the scene and Jesus is left talking to a baffled Judaism, and to puzzled and uncommitted religious men as a whole.

Nicodemus' approach was cautious. He not only came by night, so as not to commit himself (compare this with Joseph of Arimathea, John 19:38 onwards), but his opening gambit was also non-committal. He recognized in a general way Jesus as a rabbi, doing signs and sent, in some sense, by God.

When Jesus answered him, he was answering the thoughts rather than the words. He called directly for a radical response, a completely new start. Without a new birth a man cannot even see the kingdom of God, cannot begin to understand what it is all about. Nicodemus probably took Jesus literally, as others did mistakenly (compare John 6:42,52; 8:33). But perhaps he did see that it is figurative, and protested that a new spiritual start is impossible.

Born of water and the Spirit Jesus said a man must be born with water, and the reference in the first instance was perhaps to the baptism of John as an external rite standing for repentance (compare John 1:26, 31-34). From there the extension may be made to Christian baptism, which in its turn must be linked with the internal experience of new life in the Spirit. Two worlds are shown to us in this Gospel – flesh and spirit, the earthly and the heavenly (compare John 8:23). Even a man's religion may be on the level of 'flesh' – human effort. But spiritual life needs spiritual birth. The Spirit is like the wind, free, powerful, unseen, unpredictable. But its results may be observed. The power of the Spirit goes far beyond the physical realm, to every sphere of life.

This new analogy of the wind and the Spirit which Jesus introduced baffled Nicodemus further. 'How can this be?' he asked, not so much, it seems, wanting to know how to take the step of faith himself, as unable to comprehend what it is all about. Jesus expressed surprise that someone appointed as a theological teacher of God's chosen people should be so out of his depth. The idea of birth by water and the spirit was foreshadowed in the Old Testament (especially in such passages as Ezekiel 36:25-28).

The bronze snake Jesus spoke not only from scripture but also from experience. On the basis of both he gave his testimony. But Nicodemus and those like him did not receive it. An earthly analogy was meant to clarify the heavenly reality. It would be impossible to speak directly of unseen heavenly things to those who cannot understand what they see. The Son of Man is the interpreter of heavenly things. His origin is heavenly, he has a foot in both camps, and bridges the gap between heaven and earth in his own person (compare John 1:51; 1 Corinthians 15:47). Man could never ascend to meet God. God had to descend to meet man.

Not only was the incarnation necessary to reveal the life of heaven to men, the atonement was also. The bronze snake on the pole was a

The idea of national (Ezekiel 36:25-27) and personal (Isaiah 57:15) renewal is found in the Old Testament, but is more prominent in the New Testament. However, the word 'regeneration' itself only appears in Matthew 19:28 and Titus 3:5 (in some translations).

It is in John's Gospel that the start of this new life is described for us. We are to be 'born again' in a spiritual sense, through God's initiative and the working of the Holy Spirit (John 3:3-8). This new birth is the entry to God's kingdom and brings us into a new relationship with him as members of his family (John 1:12).

Paul carries this teaching further. He shows that in Christ we are 'a new creation' (2 Corinthians 5:17), not just morally reformed, but regenerated. This 'new man' (Ephesians 4:24) with new tastes and ambitions begins to walk in newness of life (Romans 6:4).

Finally, in John's first letter we find this new life spelt out in more detail. It entails a new mind; for we believe that Jesus Christ is God (I John 5:1); a new moral outlook on sin and righteousness (I John 2:29; 3:9); a new social outlook (I John 4:7); and a new practical outlook when faced with the sinful pressures of the world (I John 5:4, 18).

'I tell you the truth, unless a man is born again, he cannot see the kingdom of God' (John 3:3).

symbol of healing (Numbers 21:4-9). The Son of Man was likewise to be lifted up (in a double sense – compare Genesis 40:12 onwards and 18-22; John 8:28; 12:34; 18:32). As the one lifted up was not a bronze snake but the living and dying Son of Man, so the benefits were far greater. Here was no temporary cure, but eternal life as the result of faith.

3:16-21 Jesus summarizes the gospel

Here is an important paragraph which summarizes some of the main themes of the Gospel. It shows the purpose and effect of the mission of the Son, and the reason why it did not meet with a full response.

It is not certain whether verses 16-21 are a continuation of the words of Jesus, or a comment by the Gospel-writer. As punctuation marks were not used in the New Testament manuscripts, it is a matter for individual interpretation according to the context. A similar problem is found in verses 31-36.

God so loved the world Verse 16 asserts that the love of God was the motive force behind the incarnation and death of Christ. It was a love great enough to embrace the whole world, a world which was made through the Son but which did not recognize him (John 1:10), and even hated him (John 7:7). It was a love shown not just in sentiment but in giving. God's gift was the greatest that could ever be made – his only Son (compare Genesis 22:2,16). It was a love which required commitment in return. The resulting relationship could be described as eternal life, the life of the age to come experienced in the present time.

Salvation Light inevitably casts shadows. Though the purpose of the Son's mission was salvation (rescue and health), the effect of it was often judgement. It can even be said that in one sense its purpose was judgement (John 9:39). This was not something arbitrarily imposed, but it resulted naturally from a refusal to be exposed and to face realities. It was something which, like the offer of eternal life, was taking place already. It was even then showing up what is genuine and what is shoddy and mean. Light and the process of discrimination are inseparable.

'Now John . . . was baptising at Aenon near Salim, because there was plenty of water, and people were constantly coming to be baptised' (John 3:23). The Jordan Valley near Salim.

3:22-30 Jesus and John the Baptist

The ebb and flow of Christ's ministry can be seen in the movement between Jerusalem, Judea and Galilee. Jesus had made his first challenge to Jerusalem and been misinterpreted. Now he went to Judea (verse 22), before returning to Galilee (John 4:3). In the Jordan valley he began a ministry of baptism parallel to that of John. This was not performed by Jesus himself but by his disciples (John 4:2), though it was done with his authority.

The ministry of Jesus was inevitably controversial (verses 25,26), and there were occasions where controversy occurred amongst those who should have been his supporters. The Jew mentioned (verse 25) is unknown, and it has been suggested that there could have been a slip in copying an abbreviation for 'Jesus'. The issue at stake here, so common amongst religious people, was one of jealousy. It seemed to John's disciples that he should take precedence over Jesus, whose growing popularity they probably resented (compare John 12:19 and the attitude of the Pharisees).

The 'best man' But John explains (verses 27-30) his role as 'best man'. His precedence was one of service and preparation (John 1:30 onwards). He never claimed to be the Christ (John 1:20). His privilege was to make arrangements for uniting the Messiah with his bride, Israel.

3:31-36 He who comes from heaven

This may well be another comment from the Gospel-writer rather than a continuation of John the Baptist's explanation. It underlines the fact that John's ministry was essentially on a human and earthly level. But Jesus had a heavenly origin, spoke the truth of God and imparted the Spirit of God. Man's response is decisive for life or for wrath, God's implacable hostility to sin. This heavenly otherness of God and Christ is denoted in this Gospel by the use of the words 'from above' (verse 31), in pictorial language, 'up there'.

4:1-26 Jesus meets a Samaritan woman

Jesus was anxious not to provoke a major clash with the Pharisees until 'his hour had come'. He therefore left Judea, having made his

Mount Gerizim, which the Samaritans believed to be the right place to worship God.

challenge, and went back to Galilee. Geographical necessity took him through Samaria, for this was the shortest route home, though Galilean pilgrims often took a long way round to avoid it.

This gave Jesus the opportunity to present to the sectarian Samaritans the true way to worship God. In his own human weariness and thirst he was able to offer them true satisfaction for all their needs. The town called Sychar (verse 5) is probably the modern Ashar near Mount Ebal, where 'Jacob's well' may still be seen.

This story illustrates vividly, and at some length, the way in which Jesus dealt with individuals (compare John 9:1-41; 11:1-44). Jesus met a Samaritan woman on the level of felt and shared human need. He began by asking her a favour which caused considerable surprise. There was a barrier of race and of sex. This would normally have prevented anything but a superior and scornful attitude by a Jewish rabbi to a Samaritan woman who may have been an outcast in her own community.

Living water The surprising thing did not, however, lie in this encounter but in the fact of his identity and the spiritual offer which he was making. But talk of living water was understood by her on the literal level only (compare John 6:52; see also Jeremiah 2:13; Zechariah 14:8; Ezekiel 47:9). How could a tired stranger be greater than Jacob, the ancestor of the race? (compare this with the reference to Abraham in John 8:53).

Jesus had to open up a completely new dimension. The rabbis sometimes used 'water' as a metaphor for the law, sometimes for the spirit. Jesus spoke of the water of eternal life which satisfies people at the deepest spiritual level (John 6:35).

True worship But before the woman could receive the living water, Jesus told her to go and call her husband. She had probably come to draw water just for herself, but the water of life was to be for others too (verse 16). The mention of her husband brought a denial that she had one. Jesus showed that he knew all about her marital and extra-marital relationships. 'Five husbands' (verse 18) may refer to the five peoples with heathen 'baals' ('baal' meant 'husband') who were the ancestors of the Samaritans (2 Kings 17:24-33). If this is so, it

Measures in New Testament times

Measures

The cubit was about the equivalent of 17½″ (45cm). The fathom was approximately 6′ (185cm). The stadion was 629′ in length (192m) and the Roman mile slightly less than one English mile.

The cubit was measured from the elbow to the finger-tip, while the long cubit was a hands-width longer at about 20½″ (520mm). The span was measured on the outstretched hand from the thumb to the little finger. The span equalled three hand-breadths – or half a cubit.

The Sabbath's day's journey, which was the maximum distance allowed under Jewish law, was 2,000 cubits.

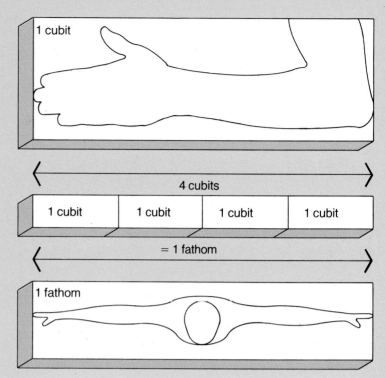

1 cubit

4 cubits

| 1 cubit | 1 cubit | 1 cubit | 1 cubit |

= 1 fathom

1 fathom

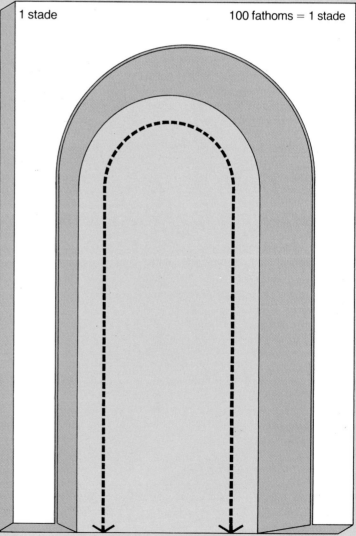

1 stade   100 fathoms = 1 stade

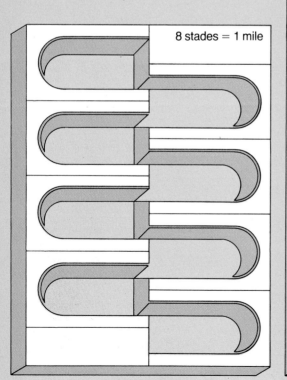

8 stades = 1 mile

explains why the woman asked about the right place to worship.

But in any case her reaction was natural; someone with such insight must be a prophet. He could therefore solve the great denominational dispute; was Mount Gerizim or Mount Zion the correct place to worship? Jesus showed that both were but temporary local symbols. When God's hour comes, worship will be universal and its location irrelevant. He was not saying, however, that all religions are the same. God's saving actions had been among Jews. The Jewish people, as a cradle for the Messiah, were the means of salvation for the world.

God's nature is spiritual not local. Men's worship must therefore be not in Jewish letter but in spirit, that aspect of man which answers to God and is made alive by the Holy Spirit, and not in Samaritan falsehood but in truth. As she did not understand, the woman wanted to push off the challenge until later, when the Messiah came. Back came the startling reply, 'I who speak to you am he'.

4:27-38 The disciples rejoin Jesus
The private personal conversation which Jesus had with the woman had to come to an end with the arrival of the disciples. They were still at the stage of being surprised at his attitude to women, but had become aware that they were in no position to question his actions. The woman left her waterpot and went off to spread the news of her meeting with someone who was so remarkable that he might even be the Messiah.

If the woman had made a discovery after misunderstanding, the disciples continued to misunderstand. They were rightly concerned about Jesus' physical welfare, but could not appreciate his spiritual metaphor. He was sustained by doing his Father's will (John 5:30; 6:38), and completing his work (John 5:36; 17:4; 19:28-30).

In the natural world there may have been four months between the end of sowing and the beginning of harvest. In the spiritual world sowing and reaping may seem almost simultaneous. As far as the presentation of the gospel to the Samaritans was concerned, John the Baptist and his disciples had done their part, Jesus and his disciples were now doing theirs, and in due course Philip and the others were to do theirs (Acts 8:5-25).

'I tell you, open your eyes ad look at the fields! They are ripe for harvest. Even now the reaper draws his wages, even now he harvests the crop for eternal life, so that the sower and the reaper may be glad together' (John 4:35,36).

Samaritans

John 4

When the Assyrians conquered the city of Samaria in 722 BC, a large part of the population was taken away and strangers settled in Samaria (2 Kings 17). There was intermarriage between the Israelites who had been allowed to stay in the country and the foreign settlers (Ezra 6:21). Their descendants were called Samaritans.

At first the Samaritans' worship of Israel's God was mingled with the foreigners' worship of their gods (2 Kings 17:33; Ezra 4:2). But later this worship was purified from these non-Israelite practices, and the Samaritans built a temple on Mount Gerizim, where the ritual of the Pentateuch was followed. Although this temple was destroyed in the time of the Maccabees, the Samaritans continued to worship on Mount Gerizim without a temple.

In Jesus' day, the Samaritans regarded themselves as part of Israel. Their scripture was the Pentateuch. Samaria became a province of the Roman Empire, but the Jews wanted nothing to do with the Samaritans, partly because it was the ancestors of the Samaritans who had opposed the rebuilding of Jerusalem. The Jews tried to avoid travelling through Samaria, and a Jew would not sit down to eat with a Samaritan. At times, Samaritans were regarded as worse and more ungodly than Gentiles (John 8:48).

4:39-42 Many Samaritans believe

Despite the unbelief of the Jews (John 1:11), knowing all that they did of God (John 4:22), we see the Samaritans believing in Jesus. This was not yet a full Christian faith. In the first instance, it was based upon what the woman had said about a man who had some sort of supernatural knowledge of her life.

Nevertheless this was testimony – part of the unfolding of the whole testimony to Christ in this Gospel. The testimony of God (John 5:37), or of Christ himself (John 3:32), or of his deeds (John 5:36), or of some other person (John 1:7) is one of the bases of faith in this Gospel.

The Samaritans gave Jesus an invitation to stay with them. There is no hint that a stay in Samaria was in Christ's original plan, but he was sufficiently flexible to meet an obvious need. So the Samaritans moved on from accepting testimony at second-hand to experiencing Jesus at first-hand. The Jews, who were in one sense the source of salvation (John 4:22), were preceded by the Samaritans in the confession of the Messiah as the Saviour of the world.

4:43-54 Jesus heals the official's son

Samaria was a stop on the road to Galilee (John 4:3), and Jesus continued his journey. Here too he was to have more honour than in Jerusalem. In fact, the Galileans welcomed him because they had seen for themselves his signs in Jerusalem (John 2:23). Here is the

The scribes were a professional group in Israel. It was their task to study the law, to teach it and to explain it (Ezra 7:6; Matthew 23:2). The scribes were also called lawyers, teachers of the law or rabbis. Jesus criticized them for adding to the law (Matthew 23; Mark 7:1-23).

The scribes were not allowed to ask payment when they did their work of interpreting the law. Therefore a scribe had to earn his living in some other way.

The scribes were employed by other parties, particularly the Pharisees, but also the Sadducees.

irony of faith and unbelief. The Samaritans believed without a sign, the Galileans with a sign, and the Judeans, his own people, not at all, despite a sign.

However, Jesus returned not only to Galilee but more especially to Cana, the scene of his first sign. The general pattern of his movement is repeated; departure to Galilee (John 1:43; 4:43), arrival at Cana (John 2:1; 4:46), going up to Jerusalem for a festival (John 2:13; 5:1).

Here at Cana he performed another sign. This showed his power, even at a distance, to heal and rescue from the gates of death. Many commentators have suggested that this account is a different version of the story of the healing of the centurion's servant found in the other Gospels (Matthew 8:5-13; Luke 7:1-10). There seem, however, to be enough differences in detail between the two to make it more likely that this was another, though similar, event.

Your son will live The official in question was probably an officer at the court of Herod Antipas. It is not clear whether he was a Jew or a Gentile. He must have known of Jesus' reputation as a miracle-worker, so he left his sick son at Capernaum and came to ask for Jesus' help in his desperate plight. Jesus' reply seemed off-putting (compare John 2:4). He addressed not only the official but others like him ('you people', in verse 48), deploring their dependence on spectacular miracles before they believed. But the man's urgent need showed that there was faith of a kind in the power of Christ to help. It was an appeal from the heart which did not go unheeded. Jesus confidently assured him that his son would live.

The man took the step of faith by believing Jesus' word and acting on it. Confirmation of his faith was provided by his servants, with their news of the boy's recovery. The discovery that the healing was instantaneous and simultaneous with Jesus' words brought the man and his household to faith. As in the first sign (John 2:11), individual faith and obedience were matched by Christ's response, and they led to belief.

5:1-15 The healing at the pool

The word which had recently given life in Galilee now gave healing in Jerusalem. There the emphasis had been on the rescue from the jaws of death, here there is the return of lost powers. Once again water played a prominent part. At Cana water was turned into wine (John 2:1-11). At Sychar water was unable to satisfy true human thirst (John 4:13 onwards). Now at Jerusalem water could not make a man's paralyzed limbs function again. As 'water' was one of the terms used by the rabbis to describe the law, there is possibly an implied contrast between the impotence of the law and the life-giving power of the word of Christ.

The Pool of Bethesda was a shrine for sick people who wished to be cured. Presumably having despaired of healing by any other means they came in the superstitious hope that they might be able to benefit from the mysterious powers of the pool. Some manuscripts include

'Get up! Pick up your mat and walk!' (John 5:8).

The Pool of Bethesda in Jerusalem. Recent excavations have revealed that before AD70 a rectangular pool existed on this site. There was a colonnade on each side, and a fifth across the middle.

as verses 3b and 4 a statement that an angel of the Lord went into the pool and troubled the water, and the first person in after that was cured. This is, no doubt, simply a deduction from the authentic text and describes what was believed to happen.

Jesus came to this scene of helplessness and superstition and, as always, his eye picked out an individual in special need of help. He altogether removed the idea of healing from the realm of chance and put it in the realm of will. This man proved his real desire to be healed by his obedience to Jesus' startling command to get up, pick up his mat and walk.

Bethesda Though manuscripts differ as to whether the name of the pool was Bethzatha, Bethesda or Bethsaida, the actual site seems to have been discovered just north of the Temple.

But there was one snag about this miracle, forgotten no doubt by the man in his joy. It was the Sabbath. If Jesus had really come to give new life in a way that the old order could not, then he was bound to clash with the guardians of the old order concerning their religious institutions. He had tried to show them the true significance of the Temple (John 2:13-22). Now he had to reveal to them the true meaning of the Sabbath.

In one sense, there was no urgency about this miracle; one extra day could hardly have made much difference. And it may be that its performance on the Sabbath (compare Matthew 12:9-15; Luke 13:10-17; 14:1-6) was a direct challenge to the Jews. The Sabbath, intended for man's benefit and enjoyment, had been hedged about with petty restrictions, many enforceable by death.

The Jews attack The healed cripple was the first object of the Jews' attack. To carry his bed on the Sabbath was against the law (Jeremiah 17:21). He had the feeling that the man who gave him healing also had authority in other matters, and defended himself by referring to Jesus' command. Naturally enough they wished to know who it was who gave such illegal orders.

But Jesus had not been ready to reveal himself and had slipped away. However, not wanting to leave the man in ignorance, Jesus found him and gave him a solemn warning (verse 14). This does not mean that the man's physical illness was the direct result of his own sin (compare John 9:3). Rather, that spiritual warnings are to be taken from physical evils (compare Luke 13:1-5). What the man made of this warning we do not know, but he dutifully gave the authorities the information for which they had asked. This attitude to the Sabbath became a main cause of the persistent hostility of the Jews towards Jesus.

5:19-30 Life through the Son
The real issues had now been revealed. They concerned the relationship of Jesus to the Father and his right to act as God alone can in giving life and judging men. Jesus spoke (in verses 19-24) of his authority in the first instance as far as his incarnate nature was concerned. It came from the close relationship of love which exists between Father and Son. There is in a way little to marvel about in the healing of a cripple. They could begin to marvel when they saw the Son raising the dead and giving them life, for that was the work of God alone (compare 2 Kings 5:7). God the Father who is judge of all the earth (Genesis 18:25; Psalm 94:2) in fact delegates his office as judge to his Son. With these prerogatives there logically follows a title to divine honour, a denial of which shows failure to honour the Father. To hear the Son's words and to believe the Father gives life on an eternal plane, by-passing the terrors of judgement.

Having stated the general principles Jesus now showed (verses 25-29) that these would be given concrete expression in the future

Authority

This word is mainly of interest when it applies to Christ in the New Testament. Although he refused to tell his critics where his authority came from, he made it clear that it derived directly from God (John 17:2, Matthew 28:18), who is the only source of all authority and power.

Jesus revealed his authority in several ways. It was seen in his teaching, which distinguished him from the religious leaders of his day (Mark 1:22). He showed it in the way he forgave people their sins (Mark 2:5-7); to claim to forgive sins was to make himself equal to God.

Jesus' authority was also seen in his miracles (Mark 1:27,28), in the way he controlled the pattern of his life (John 10:17,18) and in the fact that God committed to him the judgement of mankind (John 5:27; Acts 17:31).

But Jesus delegated his authority, in the first instance to his followers (Luke 9:1; 10:17; Matthew 28:20). It was in his name and with his authority that they went into the world to preach the gospel (Acts 1:8). They rested on the commission they had received from Christ himself (John 20:21), believing that their commands and advice had his stamp of authority (I Corinthians 14:37).

This authority was also invested in the Bible. The Old Testament looks forward to his coming (John 5:39) while the New Testament looks back on his life and ministry, seeing it as the pattern and yardstick of Christian belief and practice (2 Timothy 3:16).

Temptation

John 5

Temptation includes the idea of testing or proving. Although temptation is carried out by the devil, it is allowed by God for our good. That is why Christians are actually told to rejoice in temptation (James 1:2) as well as to endure it (James 1:12).

Sometimes there will be a direct personal confrontation, as between Eve and the serpent (Genesis 3), and between Jesus and the devil (Matthew 4:1-11). On other occasions temptation will come through a third person. It was in this way that Adam fell, and Jesus recognized the voice of the devil in the suggestion of one of his closest friends (Matthew 16:22, 23).

On yet other occasions the temptation comes from inside, from our own evil desires (James 1:13-15).

It is important to remember that temptation is not sin. Otherwise Jesus himself would not have been tempted (Hebrews 4:15). But giving way to temptation is sin. Temptation itself can do us good, strengthening us and perhaps preparing us for greater responsibilities (1 Peter 1:6,7). God will never allow temptation to become greater than we can stand. He will always provide a way of escape (1 Corinthians 10:13).

and even in the present. 'A time is coming and has now come' is a characteristic phrase of Jesus in this Gospel, and shows the way in which divine and human time-scales overlap in the ministry of Jesus. Those who believe receive spiritual life now, those who are physically dead will come into the fullness of the resurrection.

5:31-47 Witnesses to Jesus

Such a claim to authority cannot be accepted without evidence. There follows, therefore, a presentation by Jesus of the evidence upon which he based it. Again he stated that it was derived authority, and added that the unselfish nature of his motives reinforced his claim to the truth (verse 30). A man's own evidence was not sufficient, and the law did not allow it without corroboration (Deuteronomy 19:15). But Jesus had another witness of whose testimony he was sure ('another' in verse 32 refers to the Father).

On the human level, there was the evidence of John the Baptist (verses 33-35). His mission was described in similar terms to those used before (John 1:6-8). He was a lamp which was kindled and shone temporarily, but he was not the light itself (John 1:8). His evidence could have led to salvation, but it was not the real evidence which mattered in the case.

The real evidence was that the Son was doing the works of his Father (verses 36-38). This was supported by the Father's witness, both in scripture and in experience. This was unavailable to the Jews, because they could not see or hear him directly, and they did not accept his Son, who gave perfect expression to him. So there came about the extraordinary situation that those who possessed, read and professed to trust in the scriptures were unable to recognize the one to whom the scriptures were referring (verses 39,40).

Spiritual blindness The Jews were blinded by prejudice towards Christ. In his attack on them he had shown that they had no personal knowledge of God (verse 37b). Of course no man could expect to see God physically, but he *was* revealed in the scriptures and through Christ, and here the Jews had a massive blind-spot. They were motivated by a preference for human approval over divine approval (compare John 11:42 onwards). The irony is that those who

Love

In the Old Testament the Hebrew word for 'love' covers all our English meanings of the word – sexual, social and spiritual. It was translated into Greek as *agape*, a word which scarcely appears in Classical Greek. Because it had few pagan overtones, New Testament writers used it for Christian, distinguishing it from sexual love (*eros*) and friendliness (*philia*).

God's love

Because 'God is love' (1 John 4:8), he must from the very beginning have had an object for his love. This object was Jesus, who spoke of the love which his Father had for him 'before the creation of the world' (John 17:24). At the outset of his ministry on earth, Jesus was acclaimed by God as 'my Son, whom I love' (Matthew 3:17). God reserved for him a special kind of love worthy of their unique relationship (Ephesians 1:6). Throughout his life God's love for him was, if possible, deepened by his perfect obedience to his Father's will (John 10:17).

God's love for mankind is implied in his creation of mankind. It is fully expressed for the first time in Deuteronomy 4:37-40, where it is applied to his specially chosen people. Throughout the Bible God's love for man is always regarded as consistent with his discipline (Hebrews 12:5-8)) and even with his anger.

As the Old Testament goes on, we find God's love compared with a father's love (Psalm 103:13; Malachi 3:17), a mother's love (Isaiah 49:15; 66:13), and a husband's love (Hosea 2:19-3:1). Perhaps the most remarkable part of this love is that it is still given to the wayward and unfaithful (Jeremiah 31:3).

When we reach the New Testament, God's love finds its fullest and deepest expression in the gift of his Son to be the Saviour of the world (John 3:16; Romans 5:8; 1 John 4:10), and in his adoption of us into his family (1 John 3:1).

But chiefly God's love in the New Testament is continued and fulfilled in the life and work of Jesus himself; 'As the Father has loved me, so have I loved you' (John 15:9). This love was seen all through his earthly ministry (Matthew 9:36; Luke 7:13) and reached its climax in his death on the cross (Galatians 2:20). It still continues to surround and protect all those who belong to him by faith (Romans 8:35). Not only this, but his love for us is to be the example of our love for others (Ephesians 5:2; John 13:34) and the inspiration of our service for him (2 Corinthians 5:14).

Human love

Man's love for God is derived, not original. It is only because he first loved us that we are capable of loving him in return (1 John 4:19). From the earliest days love is put before man as his most important duty to God (Deuteronomy 6:5). Because it is commanded, it is primarily a matter of the will rather than of the feelings. Throughout the Bible we find that obedience is the result and the proof of love (Deuteronomy 10:12; John 14:15; 15:14; 1 John 5:3).

No one can truthfully say he loves God if at the same time he hates his fellow man (1 John 4:20). Love towards other people is one of the hall-marks of the true Christian (John 13:35). It is a love which must be shown not only to friends (John 15:13), but to the ordinary people we call neighbours (Mark 12:31), and even towards enemies (Matthew 5:44). But perhaps it is reserved in a special way for those with whom we share our faith in Christ (John 13:35). This love for fellow-Christians will show itself in service (Galatians 5:13), generosity (1 Peter 3:8,9), suffering (2 Corinthians 12:15) and humility (Romans 12:10). For a complete study of it we should turn to 1 Corinthians 13.

Exodus

John 6

The word 'Exodus' means simply 'going out', a departure. But the 'going out' of the children of Israel from Egypt was the key event in the history of Old Testament Israel. Through Moses God led the Hebrew slaves out of Egypt and started to mould them into the nation of Israel. All future generations looked back to it, and annual festivals such as the Passover commemorated it.

There are seven 'I am' sayings in John's Gospel. They are similar to parables in their purpose.

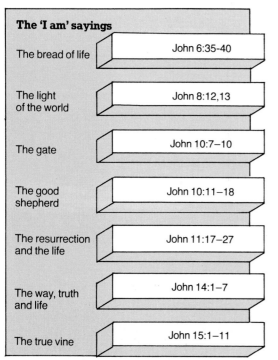

The 'I am' sayings	
The bread of life	John 6:35-40
The light of the world	John 8:12,13
The gate	John 10:7–10
The good shepherd	John 10:11–18
The resurrection and the life	John 11:17–27
The way, truth and life	John 14:1–7
The true vine	John 15:1–11

professed that they were Moses' disciples (John 9:28) were going to have Moses in the witness box testifying for Jesus and against them (verses 45-47).

6:1-15 Jesus feeds the five thousand

We have seen Christ as the provider for human need (John 2: 1-11), and the giver of life (John 4:46-54). Now, in providing again for human need, he demonstrated that he was not only the giver but also the gift of life. He was the bread which alone could sustain men's souls. He revealed this truth through a miracle in which, as at the wedding at Cana, he brought into focus in a single dramatic act what God was always doing.

The Passover setting of this miracle (the only miracle recorded in all four Gospels) and the discourse which follows it, are of considerable importance. Under the old covenant the great act of redemption was the Exodus from Egypt. This had associated with it the feeding of the people with manna in the wilderness, which was a sign to the people and a temporary provision for their need. As a continual remembrance of this redemption, the annual festival of the Passover was held, in which each succeeding generation identified itself with those whom the Lord had brought out of Egypt. So under the new covenant the great act of redemption is the cross and resurrection of Christ. This has the Lord's Supper as its permanent festival of remembrance. But it also has a temporary sign parallel to the feeding with manna, namely, this feeding miracle. Both old and new covenants point forward to the final messianic banquet.

Reactions to Jesus Notice in this incident the various reactions to Christ. Philip calculated human need in terms of cash, and in the unlikely event of their having such an amount, it would only blunt the edge of the crowd's hunger (verse 7). Yet he was in the presence of the Son of God, with all his unlimited resources. Andrew was more hopeful. He noted the scanty, inadequate provision, but appears to have left the question open, as does Ezekiel (Ezekiel 37:3).

The crowd, seeing possibly the fulfilment of Moses' prophecy (Deuteronomy 18:15-19), were about to respond (verse 15). But all they sought was a Messiah of their own devising who would fill their

'Jesus Walks on the Water' an etching by Rembrandt.

empty stomachs (verse 26). Their possible military formation (described in Mark 6:39,40) suggests that there might have been an attempt at a messianic uprising as it was Passover time. Jesus will have none of it (verse 15). Note how resolutely Christ dealt with this temptation to short-circuit Calvary (verse 15; compare Matthew 14:22 onwards). When his hour finally came, men *did* come and take him by force (John 18:12) and made him king (John 19:1-22).

6:16-24 Jesus walks on the water
The disciples had presumably been given instructions by Jesus in order to avoid the attention of the crowd. They set off across the lake for Capernaum, obviously expecting him to join them somehow (verses 16,17). And now, after the feeding of the five thousand, Jesus again demonstrated that he was Lord over nature by walking on the surface of the Sea of Galilee. The phrase 'on the water' (verse 19) could mean in the Greek simply 'on the seashore'. The story in Mark 6:45-51, and the general context here, make it most unlikely that this is what was intended. It shows the power of Christ to help and guide even in the face of adverse natural conditions (compare Mark 6:45-51). His presence banished fear and guaranteed arrival at their destination. Jesus' 'It is I' greeting may mean this, or simply 'I am' or 'I am he'. In view of the 'I am' sayings in this Gospel, and such a claim as is found in John 8:58, it is probable that there are intended to be overtones of divinity.

Verses 22-24 give a rather complicated explanation of how the crowds on the east shore of the lake discovered that Jesus and his disciples had gone over to the west shore, and how they followed across as soon as there was transport available for them. They were sufficiently impressed by what he had done to be anxious to search for him, though their motives were materialistic.

6:25-59 Jesus the bread of life
There now follows a long discourse of Jesus with the Jews about the meaning of the sign he had performed. This is similar to the discourse concerning the light of the world and related themes (John 8:12-59) which precedes the healing of the blind man (John 9). In each of these dialogues there is an 'I am' saying of Jesus, and a failure

The Lake of Galilee was also known as the Lake of Tiberias. Like the city of Tiberias on its shore, the name was derived from the Roman Emperor. Herod Antipas built the city as the capital of the province he ruled.

A barley loaf

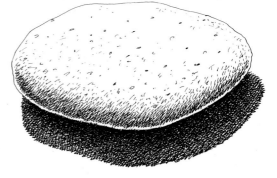

Miracles

by the Jews to understand his meaning.

A query as to when he had come across the lake was met by a rebuke to those who had found him, on the grounds that they wanted him for the wrong reason – merely as a supplier of bread for the hungry. He had already rejected this as an adequate programme for the Messiah (Matthew 4:2-4). Like water (John 4:13,14), food is a sign of spiritual nourishment. It must be worked for, yet paradoxically it is the gift of God. Work of this kind is therefore not an external striving but faith in the Son.

Bread from heaven The people wanted a further sign. Their ancestors had been fed with manna in the wilderness, and a repetition of this was expected to be one of the marks of the coming of the Messiah. Jesus reminded them that the source of the manna was not Moses but God, and that the manna was not the genuine bread from heaven. This was to be sought, not in anything temporary and corruptible, but in something of heavenly origin which could bring life to the whole world. This offer sounded so good to Christ's listeners that they wanted to have it always available to themselves (compare John 4:15). The mystery was still hidden from them.

The Jews had been looking on Jesus as one who claimed to give food. Now came the startling assertion that he was the food itself! His claim to be the bread of life is the first of the seven 'I am' sayings in this Gospel (compare John 8:12; 10:9,11; 11:25; 14:6; 15:1). Each of them is a statement about the person of Christ coupled with a consequent promise of what he offers to the believer. The emphatic 'I am' may carry overtones of the presence of God (compare with Exodus 3:13,14).

The problem of unbelief The offer to faith revealed as ever the problem of unbelief. Men could see without believing, for true faith depended not on physical sight but on the gift of God. The identity of will between Father and Son is such that those given by the Father will be received by the Son and brought to eternal life in the present and resurrection at the end. The twofold reference to 'the last day' (verses 39,40), would remind the Jews of the Old Testament concept of the 'day of the Lord' (see for instance Amos 5:18), when God's

---

John 6

Miracles are often regarded as contrary to nature, but it would be better to say that they are contrary to what we know about the laws of nature.

The Bible records many such miracles, and though perhaps in some instances there may have been a natural explanation (for example Joshua 3:16) the supernatural alone can account for the prediction, timing and occurrence of the particular event.

The greatest of all the miracles was, of course, the resurrection of Jesus from the dead. 'If God can do this, then he can do anything.'

The Bible seems to suggest four reasons why the miracles were performed:

1 To reveal God's power (Psalm 145:3-6). It was through his 'marvellous deeds' that God distinguished himself from the 'local gods' and revealed himself as the one, true living God.

2 To benefit God's people. From the very earliest days and right through the New Testament this was the case. There were miracles at critical periods of history: the Exodus, the entry into Canaan, and during the time of Elijah and Elisha, when true religion was in decline. In the New Testament we find miracles accompanying the birth and resurrection of Jesus. On a humbler level, too, miracles brought a personal or a social benefit – relieving pain and suffering, saving life, casting out demons and so on.

3 To strengthen believers' faith. Miracles were rarely performed to convince sceptics. The reason may have been that there were false wonder-workers in the world (Deuteronomy 13:2,3; Matthew 7:22; 24:24), and miracles of themselves did not guarantee that the

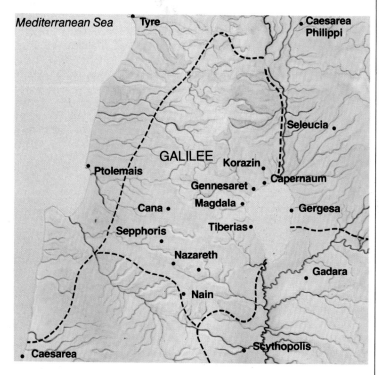

purposes would be consummated. Christ's claim that this was in his control was a further assertion of his deity.

A claim such as this could hardly fail to be disputed. The most obvious objection to it was that this was a local young man of known parentage (verse 42). As so often in this Gospel, they thought they knew his origin, but they saw it only from the human side (compare John 7:27,41; Mark 6:3). It was a preposterous thing for him to say! But Jesus stood his ground concerning his Father's calling people to him. Living experience of the Father leads to faith in the son.

The living bread Then Jesus repeated some of what he had said before in a slightly different way in order to reinforce his message (verses 47-51). Faith is the way to life, to be enjoyed in the present (compare John 3:15). Jesus alone in his person could give true spiritual food of a permanent kind. But the bread had to be given, in death, for the life of the world. And the bread was his flesh.

There was inevitably misunderstanding not only of his person but also of his offer. It was taken as a literal promise of his giving his flesh for them to eat, which sounded very much like cannibalism. In reply Jesus made no attempt to soften the language which he used. Rather, he strengthened it. He described it as the true food and drink, essential for life and resurrection and the means of union with him. He claimed that those who 'eat' him would have his life in them as he has the Father's life in him. The language was supposed to be strong and startling. The metaphors eating and drinking clearly point to that act

spoken word was authentic. But miracles did serve to strengthen the faith of those who already believed (Exodus 14:31) or were inclined to do so. It was after the miracle at Cana, for example, that we read 'his disciples believed on him' (John 2:11).

4 To teach a hidden lesson. This was particularly true of the miracles of Jesus which were often called 'signs' (John 2:11). This means that there was an inner spiritual meaning that he wanted people to understand. For example the turning of the water into wine was followed by Jesus' teaching about the new birth (John 3). The last of his great miracles, the raising of Lazarus (John 11), foreshadowed his own resurrection from the dead.

The teaching about the bread of life was given by Jesus in the synagogue at Capernaum. These ruins are part of a later synagogue at Capernaum.

The Feast of Booths was a harvest thanksgiving festival connected with the fruit harvest. During the feast, people moved out of their homes into simple huts built from leafy branches and decorated with leaves.

by which one 'comes' and 'believes' in Christ (John 6:35), and through which one is made one with him. His flesh and blood alone provide spiritual nourishment. This is clearly demonstrated in the Lord's Supper, but the sacrament is not the source of this experience, nor is it the only place where this spiritual truth is realized.

6:60-71 Many disciples desert Jesus

Jesus' ministry had already for some time been causing controversy with 'the Jews'. Now dissension came to the disciples as well. There were clearly a good number of people who followed Jesus in some way or other during his ministry, for he was able to send out seventy on a mission as his representatives (Luke 10:1). Amongst those associated with him were some whose commitment was very loose, or who had badly mistaken ideas of what sort of ministry the Messiah would have.

Possibly we can hardly understand the 'cultural shock' on men with the traditional Jewish background of allegiance to the law, good works and religious observances. Instead, Jesus claimed their complete spiritual loyalty. The harshness of his statements shocked them because of their materialism, and maybe also because of his implication that life came through death.

To their objections Jesus made a twofold reply. On the one hand, the return of the Son of Man to heaven, after his death and resurrection, would show them the true meaning of what he was talking about. On the other hand, they had left the Spirit out of account. The Spirit gave life, and the word he spoke was the living interpretation of this figure. But because they did not believe it was lost on them.

Faith and unbelief We are now faced clearly with the issue of faith and unbelief amongst his disciples. Jesus clearly knew who would be faithful, and that true faith was the gift of the Father. Some separated themselves from him at this stage. But disloyalty and unbelief had gone further. The Twelve, and this is the first time Jesus used the expression 'the Twelve' in order to emphasize the fact of their being the chosen inner circle, were now challenged about their position. Simon confessed him on their behalf as the Holy One of God. But even then Jesus had to describe one of them as 'a devil'.

7:1-13 Jesus goes to the Feast of Tabernacles

The clouds of conflict increasingly overshadowed the ministry. Jesus still continued with his offer of life for his own people and for the world. His own people had decided upon his death. Jesus paused for a while in Galilee. When the Feast of Tabernacles came round, his brothers (presumably they were sons of Mary and Joseph born after Jesus) showed that they were most anxious that he should go and reveal himself in Judea.

This was one of the great festivals, at which there would be pilgrims from all over the world. It was held in September or October, and was a thanksgiving for the harvest (Exodus 23:16), and for the provision which God had made for the people when he led them through the wilderness (Leviticus 23:39-43). To commemorate this, the pilgrims erected tents or booths all over Jerusalem and lived in them for eight days. But Jesus' brothers, who had still not come to faith in him, were arguing with purely human plans. Galilee, to them, was an unimportant back-water; Judea was where he ought to be if he was to gain acceptance. Let him be venturesome and dazzle men with an open display of power! Jesus was concerned about God's strategy. The thing that really mattered was whether his hour had come.

A narrow street in the old city of Jerusalem.

Jerusalem In the end, after a delay in Galilee, Jesus went up to Jerusalem, not publicly, as he did for the final Passover when the issues had to come to a head, but privately. The people had expected that he would come, and there was a great deal of excited discussion about him. This was largely at a superficial level which failed to wrestle with the challenge of his claims. Clearly, at this juncture there was much uncertainty, influenced by official hostility which muzzled discussion (verses 12,13). Both opinions expressed were rather vague. The discourses which follow show Jesus presenting himself to God's people as life and light for themselves and the world, and his being rejected (John 1:4,5, 9-13).

Galilee viewed from the surrounding hills.

Incarnation

Although this word does not actually appear in the Bible, it was coined to express what is stated time and time again in the New Testament, namely that in Jesus Christ, God 'appeared in a body' (1 Timothy 3:16).

Nowhere in the Bible is this stated more clearly or simply than in John 1:14: 'The Word became flesh and lived for a while among us'. Jesus Christ was revealed to us in human form. Just as thoughts, if they are to be communicated, have to be clothed in words and deeds, so God, who is pure Spirit (John 4:24), can only be known by his fallen creatures if he himself is revealed in human form (John 14:8,9; Philippians 2:8).

We must not think of God as merely masquerading as man, but all the time immune to the trials and troubles which surround us. He shared our human nature. He was tempted, just as we are (Hebrews 4:15), he wept (John 11:35), he rejoiced (John 16:33), he suffered (Matthew 16:21) and he died (Philippians 2:8).

It was supremely for our salvation that God became incarnate. It was necessary in order to take away sin that Jesus should die as a perfect man, a substitutionary sacrifice (2 Corinthians 5:18-21; Hebrews 2:14-17; 9:26-28).

7:14-24 Jesus teaches at the feast

This Gospel shows that the festivals were the most significant occasions, and the Temple the most significant place, for Jesus to present his challenge to Judaism (John 2:13-22; 5:1; 10:22-39; 12:12-36). So about the middle of this feast he went to the Temple and taught. (Compare his sudden coming into the Temple with Malachi 3:1.) His ability to engage in argument with the rabbis was a considerable surprise, for he was without formal education in their discipline. (The same charge was later made against Peter and John; see Acts 4:13.)

Spiritual blindness What should have impressed them was not the style of his discourses, but their content. Intellectually they had to acknowledge his skill; spiritually they were blind to his authority. Jesus' authority should have been accepted as God's authority because his motive was clearly God's glory. They could not accept it unless they were willing to obey God's will. In this controversy Christ appeared as the one person completely sure of himself, his origin and his mission. Notice the practical test which he offered (see verse 17).

Whose authority? The question of authority can be pinned down more specifically. Those who claimed to accept the authority of the law of Moses did not even keep it themselves. They made a great issue of Jesus' breaking the Sabbath by his healing of the cripple, while they themselves practised circumcision on the Sabbath. If a ritual operation might legally be performed on one part of a man's body on the Sabbath, how much more might a man's whole body be healed. There had to be some conflict of laws, and it should have been clear to all but petty legalists which was the more important. Moreover their lawlessness was such that they wished to kill him. No wonder that he had to impress upon them the need for just, rather than superficial, judgements.

7:25-36 Is Jesus the Christ?

From the more superficial questions which had been raised, the discussion passed to the question of who Jesus really was. Some knew him only as a wanted man. When they found him teaching without being arrested, they wondered if the authorities had decided that he was after all the Messiah. This solution, however, seemed to be ruled out by the fact that they knew his origin. Jesus retorted that it was precisely what they did not know. His true origin was from his Father, and it was for that reason that he came with the authority of his Father.

The Jewish leaders decided that after all they had to try to arrest him. But Jesus was protected by the fact that it was not yet his hour. Many of the people were sufficiently impressed by the number of his miracles to believe that he was after all the Christ. What more could be expected of the Messiah (verse 31)? Their estimate of Christ was shallow, with little understanding of his person and nature. But it was at least a movement towards truth.

The authorities accordingly made another attempt to arrest him. But they could not stop his ministry. For Jesus was confident not only of his origin but also of his destination and of his time. His destination was one that was out of reach of the unbelieving Jews. They thought that the barrier was a geographical one and failed to see that it was a spiritual one.

The term 'Greeks' here (verse 35) need not mean the Gentiles. It could be a word used by the 'Jews' (Palestinian Jews) about the Jews of the Dispersion (compare John 12:20). It was inconceivable that the Messiah would go where they (the Jews who actually lived in the promised land) could not find him.

'On the last and greatest day of the Feast, Jesus stood and said in a loud voice, "If a man is thirsty, let him come to me and drink. Whoever believes in me, as the Scripture has said, streams of living water will flow from within him"' (John 7:37,38).

7:37-44 Streams of living water

It was only on the last day of the feast, probably the eighth rather than the seventh day, at the climax of the festival, that Jesus was ready to make an astonishing offer to his people and to the world. On this occasion, water from Siloam's pool was solemnly offered in the Temple. Probably this was an ancient rite invoking God's help in bringing the refreshing 'former rains' to end the long summer drought. Jesus seized this opportunity. Any thirsty soul was invited to find deep and lasting refreshment through faith in him. The punctuation of the saying of Jesus (verse 37) is uncertain. It is probably better to make of it two parallel invitations, and then refer the quotation to Jesus himself rather than to the believer. The scripture may be Zechariah 14:8, which was part of the reading appointed for the Feast of Tabernacles. It was no longer Jerusalem but Christ who was the source of blessing.

But the blessing which Jesus offered was to be made available through the Holy Spirit, who had not yet been given in a new way to believers (verse 39). The Spirit had been active in the world from the beginning, but was not to be given to the believer in the Christian sense until Pentecost. The phrase is literally 'the Spirit was not'. The third person of the Trinity had to wait for his full personal revelation, as did the second person.

As usual there was a mixed reaction. For some this offer marked him as the promised prophet (Deuteronomy 18:15; John 1:21;

6:14). For others it showed him to be the Christ. Those who knew their scriptures knew that the Christ had to come from Bethlehem (his birth at Bethlehem is not mentioned in this Gospel). So there was a division among them, with one party relying on scripture and one on experience. (Divisions are also mentioned in John 9:16 and 10:19.) Again a desire to arrest him failed.

7:45-52 Unbelief of the Jewish leaders

The Temple police now found that there was something about him and his teaching which marked him off as unique. But ignorant men can soon be crushed, without any need of reasoned argument, by an appeal to superior office and knowledge. When Nicodemus, who first came timidly to Jesus by night, now dared to raise his voice as 'one of their own number' in protest in the name of the very law which they professed to uphold, he too was scornfully dismissed as having baseless provincial sympathies. Galilee of all places!

7:53-8:11 The woman caught in adultery

This story may not originally belong here, nor indeed anywhere in John's Gospel. This is clear both by the evidence of the manuscripts and by its style. It was possibly inserted by a copyist at this point as an illustration of the principle in John 8:15. Some manuscripts put it elsewhere in John, others after Luke 21:38. There is no reason, however, to doubt that it is a genuine story about our Lord's ministry.

There is a close parallel between the story and that of the tribute

'The Woman caught in Adultery' by Veronese.

money (Mark 12:13-17). Each of them represented an attempt to force Jesus into a position where he made a pronouncement which would put him out of favour with either the Romans or the Jews. His accusers, hypocritically pretending to be scandalized by this woman's conduct, were in fact using her not as a person, but as a political pawn.

Stoning In this case to recommend stoning would be to usurp the power of the Roman authorities. They alone were allowed to carry out death sentences. To do otherwise would be to contravene the law of Moses, which ordered stoning in such circumstances. Though the word 'adultery' is used, only for extra-marital sex by a betrothed virgin was stoning laid down as the punishment (Deuteronomy 22:23,4). The same punishment was laid down for the man, but the woman seems to have been an easier victim for his accusers' scheme. It may be that when Jesus wrote on the ground with his finger (verse 6) he was writing the sentence as the Roman judge would do, and that the words were what he then spoke to them.

Jesus' answer The answer which Jesus gave was a model. He transgressed neither Roman nor Jewish authority. Instead he turned an attempt to trap him into a penetrating moral challenge to those who were prepared to play politics with human sin and misery. His point was well enough made both with them and with her. The men, convinced of their hypocrisy, soon made their exit. In the end, all knew themselves to be sinners and the one who had committed the greatest sin in letter, and probably the smallest in spirit, left with Christ's word of advice and exhortation. Jesus did not condemn her; the witnesses having left, he was in no position to pass judgement according to the law. By implication he offered her forgiveness, but did not excuse her conduct. For she was to go and not sin again.

8:12-20 Jesus the Light of the World

The scene continued in the Temple at the Feast of Tabernacles. This festival commemorated, amongst other things, the pillar of fire which had been given as light to the Israelites in the wilderness (Exodus 13:21,22). One of its most impressive ceremonies was the

In the Temple at Jerusalem there was a seven-branched lampstand called the Menorah. An oil lamp was placed on top of each branch. The Menorah was always kept alight to remind the people of God's presence.

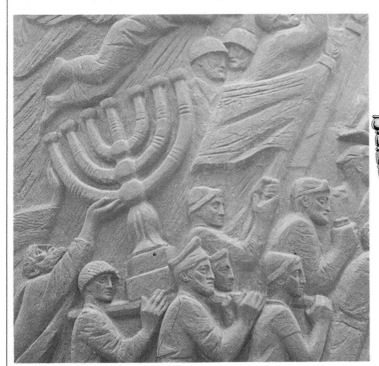

lighting of the golden candelabrum. The light was said to be so brilliant as to illuminate every courtyard in Jerusalem. It was a festival of light. And the law was also held to be light (Psalm 119:105; Proverbs 6:23).

But neither ceremonial nor even scripture is the true light. It was God who was the light of his people (Psalm 27:1). Jesus therefore came to direct men's attention away from the symbols to the reality – God's own presence personally in their midst. It was the destiny of the Servant of the Lord to be a light to the nations (Isaiah 49:6). The 'light of life' (verse 12) is given not to those who simply gaze in admiration, but to those who follow.

An argument about evidence Jesus' great claim to be the light of the world was challenged on the ground that it was testimony in his own case. Jesus replied that there was a validity about such evidence in this instance because he had a knowledge of his origin and destination which they did not share. The argument concerning evidence was very similar to that in John 5:31-39.

The question of judgement (verse 15 onwards) is one of the most paradoxical themes in the Gospel. It was not Jesus' purpose to judge men (John 3:17; 12:47), and yet it was (John 3:18; 12:48; 5:22; 9:39). The Pharisees' idea of judgement was governed by purely human rules. He had in fact the testimony of his Father to support him, a fact which they could not understand because they did not know him.

8:21-30 Where I go, you cannot come

The long discourse which follows to the end of the chapter is connected with themes which have already been introduced. Here are discussed Jesus' origin, his destination, his parentage and his identity. The contrast is made between what he claimed to be, and in fact was, and what the Jews were, despite their claims.

Jesus spoke first of going away. His destination was somewhere that they could not reach (compare John 7:33-36). Their tragedy was that death would overtake them before their sin had been forgiven. The probable allusion to death was picked up by the Jews, but they suspected that he was planning suicide. Jesus again pointed out the contrast between himself and them. There are two worlds, one above and one below. His origin, unlike theirs, was from the one above.

'Christ preaching the forgiveness of sins' by Rembrandt.

Lifting up To a direct question about his identity, Jesus replied that he had been telling them all along, if only they had been able to exercise spiritual discernment. His authority was a derived authority. As they could not understand this, Jesus went on to speak of the 'lifting up' of the Son of Man which would authenticate his message.

The words 'lifted up' (compare John 3:14; 12:32,34) already had a double sense in the Old Testament, where the heads of Pharoah's chief butler and chief baker were 'lifted up' in exaltation and in death (Genesis 40:20 onwards). Here it obviously marks an important shift in Christ's relationship with the world (compare John 3:14). Later on, Christ made clear that this expression referred to his cross (John 12:32-34). In all circumstances, Jesus enjoyed his Father's presence and lived a life completely in line with his will. Such claims as he made, though baffling to many, led others in some measure to believe in him.

8:31-47 Abraham's children and the devil's children

The debate moved on from the question of authority to that of freedom. The basis for the proper enjoyment of this most treasured human possession is discipleship and truth. But few concepts are so much misunderstood as freedom. National pride revolted against the suggestion that they were in need of liberation. Was not the fact of their ancestry sufficient guarantee of their freedom?

The assertion of their descent from Abraham gave Jesus an opportunity to discuss the real issues of their ancestry and his. Despite periods of foreign domination, such as the Roman occupation at this time, they had always thought themselves to be truly free as Abraham's sons. (For reliance upon their descent from him compare also Matthew 3:9; Luke 3:8.) It is similar to their reliance on being Moses' disciples (John 9:28). But whatever their physical ancestry, their rejection of his offer of true liberty shows their failure to enter into that liberty and their consequent enslavement by sin. The position of servants and sons in a household (as verse 35), and their relationship with God are often contrasted in the New Testament (see Hebrews 3:2-6; Galatians 4:1-6).

Like Abraham To be Abraham's children in the true sense required moral conformity to Abraham, and this they clearly did not have. They must spiritually have had another father. Oh yes, they agreed about that. Their father in that sense was, of course, God. No, said Jesus. If that were true they would recognize God's message which he had come to proclaim. Their complete failure to do so marked them off as children of the devil, with all his hatred and falsehood. They could find no fault in him, yet they did not believe him. Their attitude showed quite plainly that they did not belong to God.

8:48-59 Jesus' claims about himself

People with weak arguments often shout louder. There was something of this in the attitude of Christ's adversaries who, unable to combat his teaching, resorted to slander and invective. They could not understand Jesus' claims or accept them in so far as they did understand them. They therefore accused Jesus of being a demon-possessed Samaritan. In their eyes, to be a Samaritan was one step worse than being a Galilean. The Samaritan's ancestry was mixed (2 Kings 17:24), and this may be a further charge of illegitimacy (compare John 8:41).

Jesus was accused of having a demon (John 7:20; 10:20) but it is only here that he refutes the charge. He would not let them get away with such slanderous suggestions. The fact is that he was honouring the Father in doing his work, and it was God who would make the truth plain. Obedience to his word is a passport through death.

The Pharisee could be distinguished by his dress.

The Pool of Siloam is probably the pool also known as Shelah, or the King's Pool. It was supplied by an aqueduct known as Shiloah.

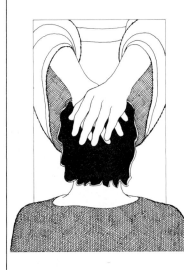

Greater than Abraham Such an assertion settled the question of demon-possession as far as the Jews were concerned. Abraham, the great ancestor of the race, had to die. How could a man such as this promise immortality? 'Are you greater than. . .?' The woman of Samaria asked the same question about Jacob, and the answer given was indirect, as it is here (verse 53 onwards).

Jesus had to remind them again that what he did and said was not simply his own whim. His mission was inspired and authenticated by his Father. It would have been false for him to say less than the truth of his relationship with God.

Abraham had rejoiced to see his day. Jewish tradition held that Abraham saw the whole history of his descendants and the messianic age. Yet even before Abraham was born, Christ was there in his eternal being. Abraham not only died but was born; Christ *is* eternally. Here, as the reaction shows (verses 58,59), there must be a claim to deity (compare Exodus 3:14). This was sheer blasphemy and an attempt was made to stone him for it. But again, for the moment, he escaped. By hiding himself, Christ was in effect passing judgement on them. They had rejected him and thereby stood condemned (compare John 3:18).

9:1-12 Jesus heals a man born blind

While the sign of the feeding of the five thousand preceded the discourse about the bread of life, the sign of the healing of the blind

A blind beggar sits by the roadside trying to attract attention.

The costume of a Levite priest.

man succeeds the discourse about the light of the world. John does not record many miracles compared with the other Gospels. But when he does, it is usually with full detail and careful explanation, to illustrate a divine truth. It was one of the marks of the Messiah that he would open the eyes of the blind (Isaiah 35:5; 61:1,2; Luke 4:18; 7:21,22). Here Jesus is shown in action demonstrating the truth of his claim that he is the Messiah and the light of the world.

As Jesus was going along, perhaps from the Temple on the last day of the festival, he noticed a man who was blind from birth. He had never been able to see; this illustrates man's spiritual condition. This pitiful condition was assumed by the disciples to be a punishment for sin; as the man was born blind, the possibilities were that he had committed some sin before birth (Genesis 25:22; Psalm 51:5), or that he had sinned in a previous existence. If neither of these explanations seemed satisfactory, then it was assumed that his parents' sin was the reason (Exodus 20:5).

Such speculation failed to take into account the fact that, while there is a connection between human sin and human suffering as a whole, there is not necessarily a direct connection between a man's suffering and his own sin. This was pointed out in the book of Job. Jesus did not deny that either party were sinners, but asserted that this was not the point at issue. In any event he looked, not to the past but to the future, and saw it as an opportunity to glorify God (compare Luke 13:1-5).

Jesus had only limited time to work in his role as the light of the world. He therefore anointed the man's eyes (this was an ancient remedy, but its use on the Sabbath was specifically forbidden by Jewish tradition) and sent him off to wash. The mention of the name of the pool meaning 'sent' suggests a symbolic meaning. The name was due to the water being sent from another pool. Jesus, the source of living water, was also 'sent' (John 3:17;4:34). When the man returned with his vision restored, so incredulous were those who had known him that they questioned his identity.

9:13-34 The healing investigated

The acquaintances of the man were baffled by the whole business, so they took him to the Pharisees to investigate further the issues raised by the incident. In particular, there was the fact that the cure had taken place on the Sabbath. The cripple of John 5:9 was also healed on the Sabbath, and the two stories have much in common. But at this more advanced stage of Christ's ministry, this man was much nearer to a full faith in Jesus and gave a far more spirited defence of his own experience.

The Pharisees asked the man what happened and he gave a straightforward, factual reply. There was a division amongst them. On one side were those who knew the religious traditions, and on the other those who could see the evidence which lay in front of them (compare John 7:40-43; 10:19-21). They decided therefore to ask what the man himself thought. He replied bravely, but inadequately, that he thought Jesus was a prophet.

The Jews then reverted to the position his neighbours had taken. This was a case of mistaken identity. Sensibly they asked his parents to tell them. They were perfectly prepared to vouch for his being their son and his having been born blind. But the method of his cure they would not state. Maybe they had no first-hand evidence themselves. But in any event they were afraid of reprisals. For if they were led into a statement that Jesus was the Messiah, they were in danger of being excommunicated. They therefore transferred the responsibility for that part of the answer to their son. The age of legal responsibility was thirteen (verse 21). But the idea may have been simply that he was old enough to tell his own story without his parents' intervention.

A second investigation The religious leaders then decided to examine the man a second time, and on this occasion they were in a tougher mood. He had to make a clean breast of what had actually happened. They clearly could not believe his story, for they knew that Jesus was a sinner. The man would not be browbeaten. He was not very concerned with technicalities which were beyond his understanding. He knew one thing with full conviction; the reality of his change from a state of blindness to one of sight. They inquired again how it happened.

'Jesus said, "For judgment I have come into this world, so that the blind will see and those who see will become blind" ' (John 9:39).

Now it was the turn of the man to be tough with them. He had already stated the facts quite clearly. They had taken no notice then. There was no point in repeating the facts unless they too wished to become disciples of Jesus. The crushing retort followed. They are disciples of Moses, someone to whom God had undoubtedly spoken (compare 'We are Abraham's descendants', John 8:33). He is a disciple of someone utterly unknown (verse 29). Ironically, ignorance of his origin was now their ground for rejection of Christ, just as supposed knowledge of it was before.

Yet the man would not abandon his defence of his experience. His eyes had been opened, there was no doubt about that. And if they had to force him into theology, into his own simple theology he would go: God does not answer the prayers of sinners. No one has ever heard of the healing of a man *born* blind. Such an extraordinary miracle therefore proves that Jesus is not a sinner but is from God.

But as the man born blind moved steadily into clearer sight, the Pharisees plunged into deeper darkness. There was no attempt to answer the man. Assessing of evidence gave way to prejudice. Living experience was rejected by the dead hand of tradition; 'How dare you lecture us!'

9:35-41 Spiritual blindness

Until now in this chapter the whole discussion has been concerned with the physical healing of a blind man and the identity of a person who was able to perform it. Now Jesus drew out the further lesson of his spiritual mission to the world and to individual people. Not even a miracle was sufficient, by itself, to create faith. A personal meeting

The shepherd's job involved a number of different tasks. He would call the flock together in the morning; take the animals to good pastures; find springs or brooks where the animals could drink water; walk in front of or behind the flock when it was to move, and generally protect the sheep.

301

John
10

with Christ was required.

Jesus had disappeared from the scene (John 9:12), but kept an interest in the man. On hearing that he had been thrown out by the Jews, Jesus found him (compare John 5:13,14). He now asked him the direct question whether he believed in the Son of Man. (Some manuscripts read 'Son of God', but 'Son of Man' is more likely to be correct.) The man was baffled as to who such a person might be, and Jesus had to explain that it was he himself (compare John 4:26). The man gave him his trust and his reverence up to the limit of his understanding. His words (verse 38) may not yet have acquired their full Christian content; 'Lord' may be only 'Sir' and 'worshipped' need only mean 'bowed before'.

A hard saying Jesus then uttered one of his hard sayings. His purpose in coming into the world was judgement. There had been a perversion of the judicial process. He would set things right by giving sight to the blind and blindness to the seeing. All the Gospels refer to the saying about blinding in Isaiah 6:9,10. Though salvation was the primary purpose of Christ's coming (John 3:17), judgement was its inevitable result, and so could be said in one sense to be its purpose. Some of the Pharisees were disturbed enough by the whole affair to ask whether they too were in some measure blind. Jesus replied that the really incurable blindness was that which has convinced its victims that it is in fact sight.

10:1-21 Jesus the Good Shepherd

Chapter divisions in the Bible can be misleading. While in a sense the story of the man born blind is rounded off at the end of John 9, there is no evidence that the Gospel-writer intended a break there. The blind man and the Pharisees are mentioned again in John 10. While the main figure changes from light and darkness to the shepherd and his sheep, the theme of judgement is still prominent. This figure of speech (verse 6) is not the sort of parable usually found in the other Gospels.

First, Jesus distinguished between two kinds of people who go into sheepfolds (probably the enclosed courtyard of a house). There are those who use the gate put there for the purpose, and those who choose some other way in. It is false spiritual claimants who are in view. The shepherd is known to the gatekeeper and the sheep. Because of the shepherd's personal knowledge of the sheep, they are willing to follow him wherever he leads. They would do the opposite for strangers

This parable was lost on the Pharisees. They were unable to apply the teaching of Ezekiel 34, about the true and false shepherds of Israel, to their own situation.

The gate and the shepherd Jesus therefore had to be more explicit. He identified himself with first the gate and then the shepherd in two further 'I am' sayings. Other claimants to spiritual authority over the people of God had a destructive purpose in coming. The purpose of his coming was to bring life; life in far fuller measure than they had ever had before. For the people listening to Christ, the picture of a shepherd calling his sheep one by one, by name, was familiar (verses 3,27). It is a vivid illustration of the fact that God knows and cares for people as individuals.

Next (verses 11-18) comes the specific identification of Jesus with the shepherd. The figure of the shepherd was applied frequently to God in the Old Testament, and also to such leaders as Moses and King David. It is not by itself necessarily a messianic title. The proof that Jesus is the good shepherd is shown not by any outward office or

The sheep 'will never follow a stranger; in fact, they will run away from him because they do not recognise a stranger's voice' (John 10:5).

external display of strength but by the fact of his sacrificial love for the sheep.

There is a clear contrast between Jesus and those whose supposed work of shepherding was done not for love but for financial or other reward. When it comes to the crunch, they do not really care about the sheep. Jesus, on the other hand, has such a knowledge of his sheep and such a love for them, that he is prepared to lay down his life for them. There is no need to try to identify the 'wolf' (verse 12) precisely. The point at issue in these verses is the different attitude of the true and false shepherds. The point so far as Christian ministry is concerned is well made in 1 Peter 5:2-4.

Other sheep But not all Christ's sheep were to be found within the fold of Palestinian Judaism. He would unite his flock, which was scattered all over the world. The 'other sheep' (verse 16) might in the first instance be the Jews of the Dispersion. But the thought of the Gentiles lies in the background.

The secret of all this is not that Jesus would accept a martyr's death which he could not avoid. It is rather that he laid his life down voluntarily and with a specific purpose. He laid it down in order to take it up again. This was a fulfilment of his Father's command and a reason for his Father's love. Once again, Jesus' claims brought division and a charge of demon-possession and madness (compare John 7:43; 9:16). Once again a gap opened between those who would consider the evidence and those who had written him off.

10:22-42 The unbelief of the Jews

The visit of Jesus to the Feast of Tabernacles, which occupies a large section of the 'Book of Signs' (John 7:10-10:21), ended in division. This was the inevitable effect of light coming into the world (John 3:19-21). After a further two or three months, he came back to Jerusalem to make his last challenge before the final crisis.

The festival in question was the Feast of Dedication, or 'Hanukkah'. The Temple, which had been desecrated by Antiochus Epiphanes in 168 BC, was re-dedicated by Judas Maccabeus three years later. This was commemorated annually in late December. As this was always a winter festival, the mention of the season (verse 23)

The wolf could present a great hazard to sheep. Wolves often lay concealed near the sheep enclosures awaiting their chance to prey on the flock.

'... but Jesus said to them, "I have shown you many
great miracles from the Father. For which of these do
you stone me?" ' (John 10:32).

is perhaps an eyewitness touch to emphasize the particularly cold weather. The reference to the colonnade seems to be a similar touch. It is of course possible that the visit to the Feast of Tabernacles ended earlier and that the Feast of Dedication began earlier, perhaps at the beginning of John 9.

More about evidence It seems that Jesus did not take the initiative in pressing his claims, but was available to be questioned further about them. The uncertainty and speculation had evidently not abated. He was now pressed to make an unequivocal statement as to whether or not he was the Christ. But an apparently straight answer would be misleading in view of the climate of belief. Jesus pointed them yet again to his deeds as the evidence (compare John 5:36; 10:37,38; 14:11).

What was wrong was not the evidence, but the fact that they did not belong to him. If they had belonged to his sheep, their obedience and discipleship would have been evident, and there would never have been any doubt about their salvation. Yet the fault of unbelief was in them and not in him. There is in this passage as strong a strain of predestination as there is in Paul's letters. The unity of Father and Son meant that if they enjoyed the protection of the Son, they enjoyed the protection of the Father too; 'I and the Father are one'.

Blasphemy This last claim of Jesus was such that for the second time the desire of the Jews to kill him actually got as far as their picking up stones to throw at him (compare John 8:59; 11:8). Jesus again reminded them of the evidence of his deeds. For which of them did he deserve to be stoned? For none of them, they told him, but for blasphemy. The charge of blasphemy was put in its most succinct form; 'You, a mere man, claim to be God' (verse 33). Here is one of the great ironies of this Gospel. The one who was God (John 1:1) had become man (John 1:14).

Jesus answered their objections with a piece of rabbinic argument. If they looked at the scriptures they would see that the name 'gods' could be applied to the judges of Israel, because they were exercising a divinely-appointed function. They accepted the authority of the scriptures, which allowed such a title. Why then object to the application of the title 'Son of God' to one sent by the Father? This would be a most unusual argument for any Christian to invent, because it does not distinguish Christ from other men clearly enough. But Jesus argued with them on their own terms. The proof of it all must once again be his deeds. Again argument gave way to an abortive attempt at arrest (compare John 7:30,44; 8:20).

Jesus then retired briefly before the final conflict. Many people came to see him there. On meeting him, they confirmed that John, though no miracle-worker, had achieved his purpose in giving faithful evidence about Jesus. So they believed in him.

11:1-16 The death of Lazarus
The stage was now set for the greatest of all Jesus' signs, other than the resurrection itself. He had shown mastery over the natural order and over disease. If death had previously had a potential victim snatched from its jaws (John 4:46-54), now it must yield up a man who has been in its realm for four days. Here is the Prince of Life in action as he goes to his death.

The historical character of this story has been more questioned than that of any other in the Gospel. The real problem is not whether Jesus could raise the dead (that was part of the messianic claim; Luke 7:11-17,22), but why such a vivid demonstration of this power was not recorded in the other Gospels. It must be said that the vivid detail speaks strongly for the story's being factual. The simplest possible

Trinity

This word, not actually found in the Bible, was introduced to describe a phenomenon revealed there. It means 'three-in-one', and is applied to God, who seems to reveal himself to us in three distinct yet inseparable ways.

At the time of Jesus, the Jews believed only in one God, unlike the surrounding peoples. An understanding of the three persons of the Trinity grew out of the disciples' encounter with God, which took more than one form. Taught to believe in one God, it became perfectly clear to them that Jesus claimed to be equal with God (John 10:30-38; 14:10,11; 17:21), and that the Holy Spirit, whom he promised to send (John 14:17,18) and whom they later received on the Day of Pentecost (Acts 2:1-4), must also be thought of as God. The New Testament is full of references to a God we might describe as 'threefold' (Matthew 28:19; 2 Corinthians 13:14; Romans 1:1-4).

The Bible seems to indicate different spheres of activity for each person of the Trinity. God the Father is chiefly linked with creation (Genesis 1:1), God the Son with redemption (Galatians 4:4,5) and God the Holy Spirit, who indwells the Christian believer, with sanctification (Romans 8:11). But there is also a good deal of overlapping as, for example, when Jesus is described as indwelling the Christian (Ephesians 3:17) and sharing in the creative work of God the Father (Hebrews 1:2).

There are certain errors which we must avoid. We must not think of a God who simply reveals himself in three different ways. There are three distinct persons, not just one person disguised in three different ways. For example, all three were present at Jesus' baptism (Matthew 3:16,17).

On the other hand we must not separate the persons to the extent that we have three gods. The presence of one means the presence of all (John 14:16, 18, 23). As with so many mysteries in scripture, the truth lies not in the middle, nor at either extreme, but at both extremes at once. There are three distinct and definable persons, and yet there is only one God.

Trinity

'As soon as Jesus was baptised, he went up out of the water . . . he saw the spirit of God descending like a dove. . . . And a voice from heaven said, ''This is my Son, whom I love; with him I am well pleased'' ' (Matthew 3:16, 17).

explanation for its not being mentioned in Mark is that Peter, who was probably the source for Mark's Gospel, was not present; but this is mere speculation.

The last sign This last sign, like the first, took place within a family circle. It is specifically said to show the glory of God and of Christ (John 2:11; 11:4,40). Lazarus and his sisters are the only persons named in a miracle story in this Gospel, apart from the Twelve. They are mentioned also by Luke. Despite the urgent call of Mary and Martha, and his special affection for the family, Jesus delayed visiting the sick Lazarus. He saw God's purpose in the whole incident. Eventually he told the disciples that he was going to Judea again and, despite their protests about the possible dangers there, he insisted that his work must be done at the right time. As they misunderstood his allusions, he had to tell them outright that Lazarus had died and that the purpose of their visit was to raise him. The reason for his delay had been, surprisingly, his love for the family. His absence would be the means of their faith and that of the disciples (verse 15).

But Thomas, seen in the latter chapters of the Gospel as a man of action slightly bewildered by the events around him, could see only death ahead. He urged his fellow disciples to come and face death with Jesus.

11:17-37 Jesus comforts the sisters

Jesus arrived on the scene, not only too late to save Lazarus from dying, but also to find him already buried for four days. (He would have been buried on the day he died). There would have been seven days of solemn mourning, and many people from Jerusalem had come to console the sisters.

The news then came that Jesus was on the way. It was Martha, the active and aggressive sister, who went out to meet him, and apparently rebuked him for his slowness in coming. She and her sister did not have faith like that of the centurion, that a word spoken from a distance would be enough. They expected Jesus to come back with their messenger.

The fact that he did not do so must have seemed to them hard and inexplicable. Even so Martha's faith in him remained, and she knew that he would be able to do something to help.

Martha's confession Jesus told Martha that her brother would rise again. This was taken by her as merely an orthodox statement of belief. She knew that he would in the end. Jesus then spoke to her the fifth of the 'I am' sayings. He is the resurrection and the life – faith in him means in one way the overcoming of death and in another the avoiding of it. The relationship of physical and spiritual life and death had already been foreshadowed (John 5:25-29). When Jesus asked whether she believed this, Martha's reply was a confession of faith in him as Christ and Son of God, without any reference to his claim to raise the dead.

Mary and Martha both said the same, 'if you had been here . . .'. But if he had, their faith would not have been tested, and neither they nor the other people with them would have seen the great sign of eternal life. Here was proof that the hour was not only coming, but had actually arrived. Martha's orthodox faith had to be turned into a living experience through seeing Christ in action.

Martha may at times have been a difficult person to live with (Luke 10:40), but she had a sense of responsibility. She went to Mary, and aware of her sensitive nature she called her quietly, saying that Jesus had asked to see her. She too had to be involved in the amazing event that was to happen.

Mary went off, not, as the Jews supposed, to weep hopelessly for her dead brother, but to meet the Lord of life. 'Teacher' (verse 28)

Bethany

Bethany is best known in the gospel story as the home of Mary, Martha and Lazarus. Luke does not give us the name of the 'village' where Martha (evidently the older sister) received Jesus into her house, but it must have been Bethany, if John's record is allowed to shed light on Luke's. Here Mary sat at Jesus' feet and listened to his teaching while Martha was busily engaged in preparing a meal for the honoured guest (Luke 10:38-42). Here, later, Lazarus their brother fell ill and died, and was raised to life by Jesus (John 11:1-44). Here Jesus was guest of honour at a meal during Holy Week in the home of Simon the leper (Mark 14:3; compare John 12:2), and was anointed with costly nard by a woman whom John identifies as Mary. Later, after he was raised from the dead, Jesus led his disciples out 'to the vicinity of Bethany' and took his leave of them (Luke 24:50, 51;

compare Acts 1:9-12).

Bethany lies on the eastern slope of the Mount of Olives, less than two miles from Jerusalem (John 11:18). The meaning of the name is uncertain: if it is an abbreviation of Beth-Ananiah (the house of Ananiah), it may be the Ananiah of Nehemiah 11:32.

The visitor to Bethany today is shown an opening in the hillside leading into the underground chamber traditionally held to be the tomb of Lazarus.

Bethphage

The old road from Bethany to Jerusalem, crossing the summit of the Mount of Olives, passed by Bethphage (meaning 'the place of figs'). This was the village where the disciples found the donkey ready tethered for Jesus' use and brought it to their master, in accordance with his instructions, so that he might complete his journey to Jerusalem on its back.

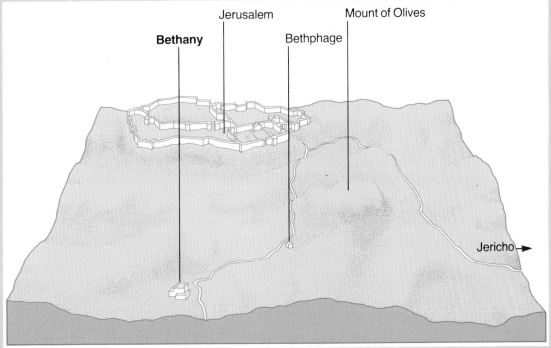

Bethany   Jerusalem   Bethphage   Mount of Olives   Jericho →

The entrance to Lazarus' tomb, Bethany.

may have been the name by which he was known to the family; it is an inadequate description of him at this crisis. Her words to Jesus were the same as Martha's. They both believed that he could have prevented the tragedy, and failed to understand why it was that he had not come when they had called for him.

Jesus weeps Jesus was deeply affected by the sight of mourning which confronted him (verse 33). Compare this being troubled as he faced his death with John 12:27; 13:21. When they took him to the tomb, he too wept. To the Jews this was evidence of his love for Lazarus, and some of them, too, wondered why he did not intervene sooner. But it seems that Jesus' weeping went a good deal deeper than sympathy; there was an anger about it. The Greek for 'deeply moved' (verse 33) has this force. This was probably, at the deepest level, anger against sin and death; perhaps also anger at the unbelief or half-belief of those who could not see that he was able to fulfil his claims to raise the dead. It was his preparation for grappling with the power of death here and on the cross (Hebrews 2:14,15, compare with Hebrews 5:7-9).

11:38-44 Jesus raises Lazarus from the dead
Jesus was inwardly stirred again as he prepared to wrestle with sin and death. He gave the order that the stone be removed. This and the unwinding of the graveclothes needed human co-operation. In his own resurrection no human agency was involved (John 20:1-10). But Martha kept her feet firmly on the ground. This was an impossible command. A putrefying body will give off an appalling stench after four days in a warm climate. Only the firm assurance of Jesus that faith was necessary, and the glory of God the object, caused them to obey.

Jesus then addressed a prayer to his Father (apart from the long prayer of John 17, there is only one other occasion in the Gospel when Jesus is clearly recorded as addressing his Father, John 12:27,28), acknowledging his dependence in this particular action, and thanking him that he had already heard. Jesus added words which emphasize his confidence that his Father always heard his prayers. He said what he did in order that the crowd should see this; not as a

display of wonder-working, but as the most impressive of his signs to show that he was sent by God to do God's work.

Action had been taken, prayer had been offered, now came the word of life. There was no magical formula, but a straightforward command (compare John 5:8 and Mark 5:41). So the dead heard the voice of the Son of God and, hearing, lived and came out from his tomb (John 5:25-29). The bandages were still all over him. Jesus told them to untie them and release him. The liberation he brings is meant to be complete.

11:45-57 The plot to kill Jesus

Surely this supreme and indisputable demonstration of Jesus' power would lead to his acceptance by those who had seen it, and by those who would hear their evidence. Many who had come with Mary believed, but others, no doubt still bewildered, went to tell the Pharisees. They joined together with the chief priests to call a council. The chief priests, who were Sadducees, were thrown into alliance with their rivals, the Pharisees, through common opposition to Jesus. The priests now took the leading role and the Pharisees are only mentioned again in John 12:19,42. They did not now deny that Jesus was doing signs. The evidence was far too strong for that. Nor, however, would they accept what the facts were shrieking at them, that this man was acting with the power of God, for he had been sent by God (compare Mark 3:22).

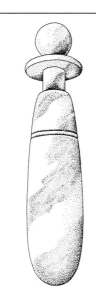

Nard, or spikenard, was an ointment made from a plant from India. It was brought to Israel in sealed alabaster jars to preserve the perfume.

The high priest acts There was no attempt now at theological assessment. They had already made up their minds and they were confirmed in their resolve now that such an obvious threat to their position was developing. There was such a danger of a popular uprising that it would lead to counter-action by the Romans, and that would be the end of both Temple and nation. (Ironically, this was just what the Romans did in AD70.)

It was the high priest, of all people, who with cynical expediency chose the victim for sacrifice. In this masterpiece of dramatic irony he decided that one man should die that the people should live. (The office of high priest did not change annually (verse 49) but he was high priest that memorable year.) And the high priest was unwittingly exercising his power of prophecy, despite his arrogant claim to knowledge. He spoke far more than he could ever know, for that was the purpose of Jesus' mission, which stretched far beyond the confines of Palestine to all God's scattered children (John 3:16). Now the issue was settled and his enemies would relentlessly pursue Jesus to the point of death.

The statement of Caiaphas, and the decision and subsequent action of the Council, illustrate what is frequently stated in scripture: that God can take the evil that men do and weave it into a larger pattern, which is for his glory and the good of other people. Caiaphas acted as a free agent, personally responsible for what he did. God, however, used his action without destroying his freedom, and turned evil into glory.

Jesus knew the situation clearly enough and withdrew to Ephraim. When the Passover came there was widespread speculation as to whether he would come to Jerusalem or not.

12:1-11 Jesus anointed at Bethany
Now there began the momentous events of the last week of the ministry of Jesus. While the ordinary people were divided and the Roman authorities had not yet been asked to show their hand, the Jewish leaders were firmly committed to getting rid of him and well aware that they had to take action at the time of the Passover festival. The story which follows is the same as that recorded in Mark 14:3-9, but different from that in Luke 7:36-38.

Jesus still went calmly on his way and enjoyed a meal with Lazarus and his sisters. The domesticated Martha saw to the arrangements, while Mary, in an act of extravagant devotion, anointed his feet with expensive ointment and wiped them with her hair. Sensitive people, whose capacity for grief and sorrow is great, have the compensation that they can also rise to great heights of love and devotion.

Judas, whose financial ability seems to have made him the treasurer of the band, but whose weakness it would also prove to be, failed to see the point of such seeming waste. Far better to use the money for charity! But his idea of charity seemed to be concerned more with himself than with the poor. Mary had kept the ointment for this significant and unrepeatable moment, in preparation for the burial of Jesus. There would be many other opportunities of helping the poor, many of them inspired in fact by his death for mankind. So the crowds turned out to see him. They were also interested in seeing the unusual phenomenon of a dead man who had come to life again. This living evidence of the truth of his claims was winning supporters for Jesus, so the chief priests decided that he too must be got rid of; a natural reaction from Sadducees, whose disbelief in resurrection was refuted by this man's presence.

12:12-19 The triumphal entry
A great crowd of the Jews had come out to Bethany to see Jesus and Lazarus. Now a great crowd of those who had come as pilgrims to the festival heard that Jesus was coming to Jerusalem, and set out to meet

him. They took with them branches of palm trees, such as had been used to hail Simon Maccabeus after his victory (1 Maccabees 13:51). They greeted him with words from Psalm 118, which was used at the Passover, applying the words to him as the King of Israel. The word 'Hosanna' is a Hebrew word meaning 'save now' and having the general force of 'Hail'. The words of verse 15 are a free rendering of Zechariah 9:9. There is no doubt that they were giving him a messianic welcome into the city. He could not now avoid being king as he had done before in Galilee (John 6:15).

But Jesus would not have messiahship of the sort that they are looking for. He had to come into Jerusalem, yet he did so, not on a royal charger, but on a donkey, the beast of burden symbolizing peace. His interpretation of the incident was based on Zechariah 9:9, and was more far-reaching than theirs. For the passage was in a context of the Messiah's universal reign of peace, and of his liberating mission through the blood of the covenant. No wonder the disciples did not understand this until after the resurrection (compare John 2:22; 14:26). The excitement about the expected Messiah had spread from crowd to crowd.

12:20-36 Jesus predicts his death

The world seemed to have gone after Jesus in the Pharisees' eyes. And so it was, because some of the pilgrims at the festival were Greeks. Whether these were Gentile converts or Greek-speaking Jews is not certain. It is unlikely that they were Gentile worshippers,

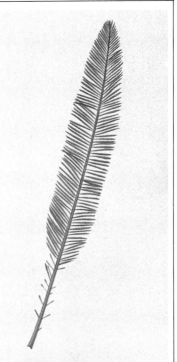

John 12

A palm branch.

'Jesus found a young donkey and sat upon it, as it is written,
"Do not be afraid, O Daughter of Zion;
see, your king is coming, seated on a donkey's colt" '
(John 12:14,15).

Many of the people in Jerusalem for the Feast saw Jesus enter the city in triumph. This is one of the modern gates to the old city of Jerusalem.

Glory

In the New Testament we find that the glory of God is almost always linked with the person and work of Jesus Christ. We are told that 'God is glorified in him' (John 13:31). He was described as 'the radiance of God's glory' (Hebrews 1:3). While no one has ever seen God, we are given 'the knowledge of the glory of God in the face of Christ' (2 Corinthians 4:6).

His glory was perhaps demonstrated supremely at Jesus' transfiguration (Luke 9:28-36), when Peter, James and John were 'eyewitnesses of his majesty' (2 Peter 1:16-18), at his death (John 12:23,24), at his resurrection (Romans 6:4) and at his ascension (Acts 7:55). It was doubtless these occasions that John was thinking of when he later wrote, 'We have seen his glory, the glory of the one and only Son, who came from the Father, full of grace and truth' (John 1:14).

Jesus shares his glory with his followers (John 17:22; 2 Corinthians 3:18). Man was made in 'the image and glory of God' (1 Corinthians 11:7), but through sin has fallen 'short of the glory of God' (Romans 3:23). One purpose of our redemption is that we should be 'conformed to the likeness of his son' (Romans 8:29).

as these would probably not come up to Jerusalem for the festivals.

What was important is that the mission of Jesus was shown to extend beyond the boundaries of Palestinian Judaism. The principles of the Gentile mission were firmly laid in this Gospel, even if the Romans might have been the only Gentiles with whom Jesus ever came into contact. And it was a Galilean with a Greek name, Philip, whom they approached with their request to see Jesus. The Judeans had their chance to see him during his ministry, and these pilgrims seemed to want the same privilege. Jesus was soon to hide himself finally (verse 36).

The hour of glorification We are not told whether their request was granted. But Jesus saw it as an extremely significant occasion. Now was the hour of his glorification. This term 'glorified' covered the whole act of redemption which Jesus was about to perform. It may appear contradictory that the cross was as glorious as any other part of his work. Glory was to come to the Son of Man through death; it was only in death that there lay the possibility of growth. It was only in the death of one man for the people that there lay the hope of the salvation of the whole world. The paradox of redemption also applies to discipleship (verse 25). Only in death does the self discover what it is meant to be.

As Jesus entered into the supreme crisis, not only in his own ministry but in the history of the world, he cried out to his Father for strength and guidance. John does not describe the agony in the Garden of Gethsemane; this passage shows that he was aware of the real spiritual struggle which Jesus had to undergo as he faced death for the sins of the world.

However tempting it might be to try to avoid the horrors that lay ahead of him, Jesus would not do it. He knew it was his hour at last. He knew that the purpose of it all was to glorify his Father's name. It was for this he asked, and a heavenly voice assured him that his prayer had been, and would be, answered. The nature of the heavenly voice is not clear. The crowd heard the sound without distinguishing the words (compare Acts 9:7; 22:9). As usual, they misunderstood; they no more grasped the meaning of the heavenly voice than they had the meaning of the words of Jesus.

St Stephen's Gate into the old city of Jerusalem.

Judgement If this had seemed a strange time to be speaking of glory, it was an equally unusual one to refer to judgement, when it was not judgement of Jesus but judgement of the world and the devil which was meant. (For the cross as a victory over the devil, compare Colossians 2:15.) But paradox cannot be avoided, and it was his exaltation in death that would be the means of life for all. The idea of being 'lifted up' (verse 32) was important because of its double meaning (compare John 8:28; Genesis 40:20), and also because it specified death by crucifixion rather than by stoning or in any other way.

Still people did not understand. Still they did not know who this mysterious Son of Man was. So Jesus could only give them an urgent warning concerning the need to act while the light was there with them in his person. Faith in him would change their whole being. And with that final challenge he went, hidden from them until he appeared as a prisoner about to be put to death.

12:37-50 The Jews continue in their unbelief

The Gospel-writer now gives us a brief summary of the lack of success of Jesus' ministry and the reasons for it. Signs were meant to be an aid to faith, so that men should have life. This is why the writer himself took the trouble to write them down (John 20:31). But for the majority of the people the signs did not have this effect.

All sorts of excuses were made at various stages of the Gospel why men should not believe in Jesus. It was possible to question the evidence in one way or another, or to take the theological position

This large-scale model of the city of Jerusalem in the time of Christ, found in the grounds of the Holyland Hotel, Jerusalem, gives a good overall idea of the appearance of the city. The Temple dominates the entire city, crowded inside its protective walls.

that Jesus could not be a man of God, or simply use their position as religious leaders to crush the suggestion. But it would be wrong to look for the whole cause merely at the human level. The trouble went deeper than that. For this was a fulfilment of prophecy. In Isaiah 53:1, the fact of unbelief had been stated, and when the Suffering Servant of the Lord came, that had to be fulfilled. In Isaiah 6:10, the prophet went further and credited unbelief to the action of God who blinded them. The other Gospels also account for the apparent failure of Jesus' mission by the quotation from Isaiah (see Mark 4:11,12; 8:17,18; Acts 28:26,27).

Eternal life Despite all this, there was no clear-cut rejection of Jesus' claims. There were many secret believers who were anxious not to lose their position in Judaism, especially those of them who were among the authorities. They come under the devastating condemnation that they preferred to be praised by men than by God. However Nicodemus and Joseph became bolder later (John 19:38-42). Perhaps someone like Gamaliel was also a secret believer (Acts 5:34-39).

Jesus' message summarized The 'book of Signs' finally closes with a summary of Jesus' message, as if in a final presentation of it to an unbelieving or half-believing Judaism. Here we have, in concentrated form, themes which have been dealt with at greater length previously. Here there is faith and sight, the Son as the representative of the Father, light, judgement, authority and life. In view of the reference to 'Jesus' hiding himself (John 12:36), there seems little doubt that this section was not supposed to have been spoken by Jesus at this time, but is a summary of his words, made by the writer, in the same way that verses 37-43 are a summary of the response to the works of Jesus.

13:1-17 Jesus washes his disciples' feet

So far Jesus had been putting his claims, by deed and word, before the people of God. Their response had been largely negative. Now the last appeal had been made to the Jews. The rest of the Gospel has been called the 'book of the Passion'. The great sign is that of Jesus' death and resurrection. This was preceded by discourses which

'Jesus washes the feet of his disciples' by Ford Madox Browne.

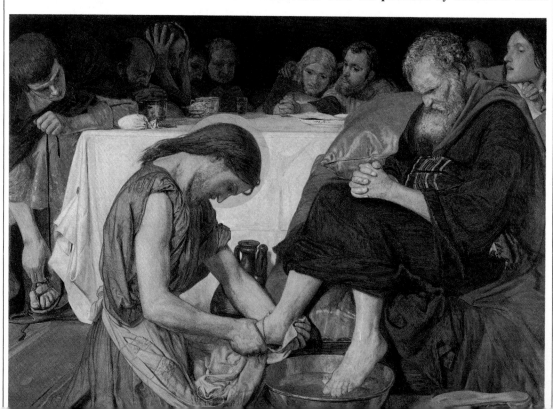

explain it and its consequences. The teaching was now no longer given openly to the world, but privately to his disciples.

The feast of the Passover was the theological setting for what follows. The festival, which commemorated the great act of redemption of the old covenant, was to be the setting of the great act of redemption of the new covenant. The hour, which Jesus or the writer referred to earlier as not yet having arrived (John 2:4; 7:30; 8:20), had now come.

Jesus had to return through death to the Father. His mind was fully assured of his divine origin and destination. The necessary work of the traitor, inspired by the devil (see John 6:70,71; 13:27), was already in hand. It was the member of the Twelve, probably the only Judean and who bore the very name of Judah, who was to betray him. At this point, where so many other emotions might have been present, Jesus' dominant characteristic was love. This was shown in a demonstration of humble service towards his disciples.

The foot-washing also had a symbolic meaning. Peter at first impetuously refused to be washed, and then asked to be washed all over! But Jesus explained that once a man had been made clean all over, this was all that was necessary afterwards. There is a once-for-all cleansing, symbolized by baptism and dependent on the 'baptism' of Christ in his death (Mark 10:38; Luke 12:50). But there is also the need for daily cleansing and forgiveness. The Spirit would enlighten them (verse 7) and show them that they needed to accept service from Christ before they could serve.

Jesus' demonstration Now all the disciples, apart from Judas, had been made clean. Jesus took his clothes again and resumed his place. The whole action suggests that it is, amongst other things, a vivid demonstration of his death, resurrection and exaltation. He laid aside his clothes as he laid down his life (John 10:11,15,17,18); he takes his clothes as he takes his life again (John 10:17,18) and he resumes his place as he returns to his Father (John 6:62; 13:1).

The disciples rightly put him in a place of authority (he is elsewhere called 'teacher' and 'rabbi' but the idea of him as 'Lord' figures predominantly in this Gospel, particularly in chapters 13 and 14). Yet he had done such a menial service for them. Rabbis could expect some such acts from their disciples, and masters could demand them from their slaves. But here the roles were reversed. How much more should the disciples be willing to serve one another! There is not much in any of the Gospels which is specifically referred to as 'an example', therefore all the more importance must be attached to this one.

13:18-30 Jesus predicts his betrayal
There have been a number of allusions in this chapter to the traitor. The scripture had to be fulfilled concerning the betrayal. Jesus' foreknowledge of the fact should have helped the disciples to understand that he was the Messiah (verse 19). Now Jesus, in distress of spirit, confronted the disciples openly with the prospect and solemnly asserted that one of them would betray him.

While John does not record Gethsemane, he emphasizes as much as the other Gospel-writers the tremendous pressure on Jesus as he prepared himself to bear the sin of the world. 'One of us? Surely not! Who on earth could it be?'

Peter was determined to find out. So he asked the beloved disciple, whom we assume to be John, to ask Jesus. Because of his position of closeness to him, 'reclining next to him', John was able to ask Jesus. Jesus told him that it was the person to whom he would give a morsel of bread. So Jesus then handed it to Judas. As such an action showed that the recipient was an honoured guest,

Nicodemus

This prominent member of the Sanhedrin had a Greek name meaning 'conqueror of the people'. He seems to have been a fair-minded Pharisee who, in standing up in the council for fair treatment for Jesus, was jeered at by the opposition for not knowing the scriptures (John 7:45-52). Jesus suggested the same thing to him when he came to him by night to discuss Jesus' claims (John 3). It is likely that Nicodemus became a secret follower of Jesus, and joined another secret follower, Joseph of Arimathea, in preparing the body of Jesus for burial (John 19:38-42).

James

James, the son of Zebedee, was the brother of John (Matthew 4:21). Their mother may have been Salome, possibly the sister of Mary. James and John were called together from their fishing (Matthew 4:21,22), enlisted in the Twelve (Matthew 10:1,2), privileged to be with Jesus at the raising of Jairus' daughter (Mark 5:37), and at his transfiguration (Mark 9:2) and in Gethsemane (Mark 14:33). At an early date, James was martyred by Herod (Acts 12:2, compare Mark 10:39). God did not save him from death, as he saved Peter (Acts 12:3-17).

this was in effect a last appeal to Judas, as well as an indication to John of the identity of the traitor. It seems likely that Judas occupied the place of honour on the left of Jesus, and this is why he was able to give him the piece of bread.

If there had been any chance of change of heart from Judas, it now disappeared, Satan took possession of him. So Jesus bid him do his deed quickly, as the agony of the last struggle grew upon him. Apparently Judas was not suspected by the others, who thought Jesus was simply sending him on an errand. (Verse 29 does not necessarily mean that the Passover had not yet begun, for the feast lasted for seven days.)

In an action full of tragic symbolism, Judas went from the room, from the circle of the disciples, from the presence of the Saviour of the world (compare 1 John 2:18,19). As he turned his back on the Light of the world, it was night!

13:31-38 Jesus predicts Peter's denial

When the Greeks had asked to see him, Jesus said 'The hour has come for the Son of Man to be glorified' (John 12:23). His soul had been troubled as he considered what the 'hour' would mean (John 12:27). At the supper he was troubled again (verse 21), as he contemplated the betrayal. When the traitor had gone out into the night he repeated in similar terms, 'Now is the Son of Man glorified' (verse 31). Each step that brought death nearer brought glory nearer too, for there was glory even in his death. What is glory for the Son of Man is glory also for God, for it is the final result of perfect obedience to his Father's will.

Jesus now spoke, as he would do frequently in this discourse, of the fact that (as he told the Jews in John 7:33; 8:21) he had to leave the disciples very soon and go somewhere they would not be able to penetrate. If he was to be absent physically, his presence would still be known in their midst. It would be demonstrated clearly to all men by the new Christian virtue of love. This was a love that was to spring out of his love for them (John 13:1,15,35).

A new commandment The 'new commandment' (verse 34) was not new in the sense that it had never been commanded before, for the law had told them to love their neighbours as themselves. It was new in the sense that the love of God had been demonstrated by the sending of his Son who had himself loved them right to the end (John 13:1). Their mutual love was to be a reflection of that, which gave it a new dynamic.

Peter inevitably wished to know where Jesus was going, and to follow him even if it meant laying down his life. Fine words and sincerely meant. But he did not know what lay ahead and Jesus, with sounder knowledge of coming events and of human nature, had to tell him sadly that he would deny him three times before morning.

14:1-4 Jesus comforts his disciples

In the face of the disturbed atmosphere among the disciples – his saying that he would leave them and his prediction of Peter's denial – Jesus told them not to be troubled. Such a situation was an occasion for faith in the Father and in the Son. There were many places in heaven (the word 'rooms' in verse 2 means places to stop and remain in, rather than progressive halts on a journey). His departure was in order to make them ready for his disciples. Nor did he intend to leave them for ever, for he would return and take them to himself so that their fellowship might be restored and continue. The main reference here seems to be to the second coming, or to his receiving each disciple at death. But the succeeding passages show a great emphasis on his coming through the resurrection and the Holy Spirit (see John 14:18,28; 16:16,22).

14:5-14 Jesus the way to the Father

When Jesus had asserted (verse 4) that they knew the way where he was going, Thomas protested that as they did not know the destination they could not possibly know the route. This gave Jesus the chance to deliver another of the 'I am' sayings. He himself is the way, the truth and the life; he is the only way to the Father. It is clear that the second and third words explain further what Jesus meant by the first. He is the true way and the living way. 'Life' is a word which occurs with particular frequency in the first twelve chapters of this Gospel; 'truth' occurs an almost equal number of times in chapters 1-12 and chapters 13-21.

Even at this stage of the ministry the disciples were still baffled about many of the leading themes of Jesus' teaching, and they still failed to understand the nature of his relationship with the Father. Their bewilderment about the Father was due to their muddle about who Jesus was. To know him as what he really was would be to know the Father too (see John 8:19).

But if Jesus talked darkly about knowing and seeing the Father, Philip was not satisfied. Philip is mentioned on four occasions in the Gospel, and the overall impression is of a man enthusiastic but uncomprehending. Now he asked for a proper revelation of God such as Moses had (Exodus 24:10); to see him with their own eyes, so that there would no longer be any doubt.

Philip's failure Jesus sadly had to point out to Philip his failure to grasp who he was. The mutual indwelling of Father and Son was a basic thing which the disciples ought to have grasped. To see Jesus is to see the Father (verse 9). The same applies to honouring him (John 5:23), knowing him (John 8:19), believing in him (John 12:44), receiving him (John 13:20) and hating him (John 15:23). This was shown by his teaching, which was not given simply on his own authority. It was also demonstrated by his miracles, which were not the deeds of a mere man.

Having used his doing the works of God as evidence of his relationship to the Father, Jesus, no doubt to their great surprise, went on to say that the disciples would do even greater deeds (greater because more far-reaching in their scope throughout the world and to all

Revelation

God has revealed himself to man in nature, in the Bible and also in Jesus Christ.

It is in Christ that his revelation of his person and his will are perfected. It was as people watched and heard Jesus that they saw God's splendour – his holiness, power and love (John 14:9). Just as light can be properly appreciated only in the form of a rainbow, so Jesus revealed the true qualities of God, who is light unapproachable (1 Timothy 6:16).

No one has ever seen God, but Jesus Christ has embodied him for us (John 1:18; Colossians 2:9). It is only in him that we see 'the radiance of God's glory and the exact representation of his being' (Hebrews 1:2,3; 2 Corinthians 4:6).

But there are divine depths which we shall never be able to know in this life, and for which we shall need eternity to complete the revelation, (1 Corinthians 13:12,13).

John 14

'I am the way and the truth and the life. No-one comes to the Father except through me' John 14:6).

Counsellor

This word is used to describe the work of the Holy Spirit in John's Gospel (John 14:16, 26; 15:26; 16:7). The word can mean an 'encourager' or 'consoler', or 'someone called alongside to help'. Matthew 10:19,20 pictures him at work encouraging, consoling, advising the believer.

men), because of his return to the Father. The glorification of the Father in the Son was not to end with the earthly life of the Son. Through prayer it would be continued. Such prayer would be limited only by the important condition that it should be in his name; that is, in obedience of will and a true desire for the glorification of Father and Son.

14:15-31 Jesus promises the Holy Spirit

Much of what Jesus says in the final discourse can only be understood in the light of the coming of the Holy Spirit. A new coming of the Spirit had been referred to by the Gospel-writer in John 7:39. Now Jesus devoted some time to explaining the personality of the Holy Spirit, the nature of his coming and the work that he would do in the world.

The promise of the Spirit's coming was made in the context of the disciples' loving, and therefore obeying, their master. The coming was to be in answer to the Son's prayer to the Father. The Spirit is described as the 'Counsellor'. The Greek word is *parakletos*, sometimes having the meaning of 'advocate'. Christ is described as the believer's advocate, or paraclete, in 1 John 2:1.

Another counsellor The Spirit is 'another' counsellor (verse 16), because he continues what Christ has done. He was to be there to stand by them and help them. Despite the reality of the coming and the presence of the Spirit, the world at large would not recognize his presence or his existence. But the disciples would know from their own experience.

Jesus now went on to say that the Spirit's coming would be his own coming. As the days of his earthly life came to an end, the world would not be able to see him any longer. His disciples, however, would go on seeing him because his life would be in them through the Spirit. But love and obedience are necessary for the continued enjoyment of the love of Father and Son, and to receive his revelation. There will be no fleeting visit. The man who loves and obeys will have the tremendous privilege of having the Father and Son coming to make their home with him through the Spirit.

The Spirit as teacher Not only was the presence and power of Jesus limited in the incarnation, his teaching also had to be restricted. There were such obvious limitations in the capacity of the disciples to understand. One of the functions of the Holy Spirit was therefore to be teaching them further, and also reminding them of what Jesus had said. With the new help which the Holy Spirit would now give them, and in the new situation after the resurrection, they would be able to grasp his message, and the meaning of his own person and mission, in a new way. (For the teaching role of the Spirit see also John 15:26 and John 16:13,14; for the disciples' understanding later what they could not understand during his ministry see John 2:22; 12:16; 13:7.)

In the midst of so much that was disturbing, Jesus promised them peace. There should be joy also from following that he was returning to the Father and the fulfilment of the blessings which he had promised would come to them through the Holy Spirit. Verse 28 does not imply any inferiority, but only that the Father was the source and origin of everything. He is greater than the Son in the sense that Jesus' mission was one of obedience to his Father's will.

It was necessary for Jesus to let the disciples know where he was going. They could easily have been confused (as in fact they were) by the impending crisis. Satan was about to have his hour. He had no power over Jesus. What was going to happen was done in obedience to the Father's command, and was a demonstration to the world that he loved the Father.

15:1-17 The vine and the branches

Mutual indwelling and mutual love are the keynotes of chapter 14. They are now strikingly illustrated by the figure of the vine and the branches. This is perhaps suggested by the 'fruit of the vine' at the Last Supper, which provides the last of the 'I am' sayings, and is expounded further in this chapter.

Israel was frequently described in the Old Testament as a vine (see Psalm 80:8; Jeremiah 2:21 and Hosea 10:1) or as a vineyard (Isaiah 5:1-7). The metaphor suggests something belonging to God, tended by him and expected to yield fruit in due course. This expectation was not fulfilled (Mark 12:1-9). Israel, however, only prefigured the Messiah, who was the true, genuine, real vine. Christ must not be thought of here simply as an individual; for by faith his people belong to him and are united with him. Consequently they are the branches and he is the vine.

Bearing fruit The main point of the figure now ceases to be the relationship of the vine to the gardener, and becomes the relationship of the vine to the branches. The branches must be fruitful, and become increasingly so. Fruit-bearing is only possible through the close union of vine and branches. When this union occurs things will happen. The fruit is first and foremost the fruit of Christian character (compare Galatians 5:22-24). The close union depends upon love and obedience. Fruitfulness proves discipleship (verse 8) and brings joy to the Father, joy to the disciples.

Next we return once again to the all-important theme of love. The link between love for God and love for one's neighbour is so strong in John's Gospel that it has been stated that love to God and Christ takes second place after love to the brethren. My 'command' (verse 12) being in the singular may perhaps indicate a summary of all the commandments.

But this love is no mere sentiment which can be worked up by a man at will, or which comes irrationally upon him. Its source is the love of God shown in Christ. Only those who have first meditated on, and responded to, this love are able to reflect it in their attitude to others. Jesus' love was proved by laying down his life.

Verse 13 does not imply that Jesus did not die for the whole world;

Jesus did many miracles or signs. They show his power, his love for people and his desire to help them.

John records seven miracles, apart from the death and resurrection of Jesus. He chose particular miracles to help readers see Jesus as the Son of God, and to show the need to trust in him.

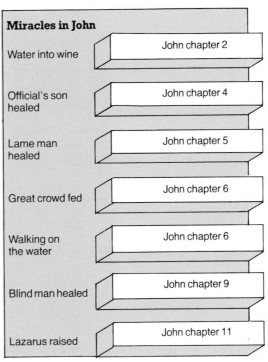

'I am the true vine' (John 15:1).

Miracles in John

Water into wine	John chapter 2
Official's son healed	John chapter 4
Lame man healed	John chapter 5
Great crowd fed	John chapter 6
Walking on the water	John chapter 6
Blind man healed	John chapter 9
Lazarus raised	John chapter 11

When Jesus said 'I am ... the truth' (John 14:6) he meant he was the one authentic answer to all the problems that have vexed people down the centuries. 'The truth of the gospel' (Galatians 2:5) means that it provides the one and only way of man's salvation.

Jesus is 'the true bread' (John 6:32,35) and 'the true vine' (John 15:1), because he alone is the source of satisfaction and life. The Holy Spirit will guide the followers of Jesus into all the truth (John 16:13), because he will teach the difference between good and evil, right and wrong, truth and error.

Remember that truth in the Bible is not just something to believe, but something to obey (Romans 2:8, 10:16). Just as the truth about my physical condition will dictate my diet, exercise and way of life, so the truth about God will determine how I live, and how he must be obeyed.

it is his friends who specifically benefit from it and appreciate it. This way in which Jesus treated his disciples as friends, keeping them informed about what he was doing, was another proof of his love. The contrast is drawn here (verse 15) between friends and servants (compare servants and sons in John 8:35). Friends need to do his will just as much as servants but, because they have a different relationship and a fuller knowledge, it is done on a different footing. His friendship was also shown by the fact that it was he who had chosen them, rather than the reverse. The friends of Jesus were not marked off by natural attractiveness nor even by their own moral choice. His sovereign will initiated and maintained the relationship.

15:18-27 The world hates the disciples

If it was previously impossible to speak of light without mentioning darkness, now it became impossible to mention love without in the end coming on to hatred. Men hated the light (John 3:20) and the 'book of Signs' showed how many of them came consequently to hate the one who was the light of the world. Jesus acknowledged that the world hated him, though it could not hate his unbelieving brothers (John 7:7). But where his disciples were faithful, the hatred would spread to them (compare John 17:14). The reason for the hatred was that he had picked them out from the world, and no one likes a convert taken away from his own side.

The new relationship which Christ offered his disciples was such that it became all the more inevitable that they would stand alongside him and share the world's reaction to him. They had been called friends, but there was still a proverb about servants which fitted their case. 'A servant is not greater than his master' (compare John 13:16).

While the note of warning predominates, that there would be persecution, there is also a note of encouragement. Some, at least, would keep their words. Yet the emphasis seems to be on the adverse reaction, which happens 'because of my name' (verse 21, and see also Matthew 5:11; 10:22; Mark 13:13) through people's failure to know God.

Hatred of the light What is the root cause of sin? The Jews might have been able to make excuses for their sin, had not the light come

Christians have been persecuted for their faith at many points in history.

and shone among them, and had not the words and deeds of Jesus been witnessed by them. Their hatred of the light, their hatred of Jesus, was hatred of the Father. This is a hatred which fulfilled scripture, being without any valid cause fulfils Psalm 35:19 and 69:4.

All this must be seen and understood in the light of the great new fact; the personal coming of the Holy Spirit. He was to be sent by the Son from the Father. In verse 26, there is no reason to suppose that the Spirit does not come from the glorified Son as well as from the Father. He was the Spirit of truth sent to combat the falsehood and unbelief of the world.

It was one of the functions of the Holy Spirit to bear witness to Jesus. It was also the task of an apostle to bear witness to Jesus. They were qualified to do this because they had been with him from the beginning of Christ's ministry (compare Acts 1:21,22). They were consequently able to testify to the truth of the apostolic preaching about him. (The Greek word for this preaching or proclamation of the gospel is *kerygma*.)

16:1-16 The work of the Holy Spirit
Jesus had been aware all along of the presence of a traitor in the apostolic band. But he was also aware of the great weakness in understanding and in character of those who sought to be loyal to him. This teaching, he told them, was to keep them from falling away. There were going to be many temptations for them to do that.

Excommunication from the synagogue (verse 2) could be a powerful pressure on them (compare the threat of expulsion in John 9:22). But things would go much beyond that. The time was coming when religious bigots, no doubt convinced in themselves of the rightness of their attitude, would do their best to kill them, really believing this to be something which was for the service of God. There was a Jewish saying that 'everyone who sheds the blood of the godless is like one who brings an offering'. This was an attitude well-illustrated by Saul of Tarsus, who was convinced he ought to act in the way he did (Acts 26:9-11). Jesus himself was threatened with death on the grounds of God's honour (John 10:31-33) as well as of the welfare of God's people (John 11:50). The reason for the persecution of the Christians will be lack of knowledge of the Father or Son.

'Greater love has no-one than this, that one lay down his life for his friends' (John 15:13).

Nazirite

This name comes from a Hebrew word meaning 'set apart'. The Nazirite was a person set apart to serve God in various ways. He could take a Nazirite vow for his entire life, or for a shorter period. He was not allowed to drink wine or to touch a dead body, and could not cut his hair. When the period of his vow was completed, his hair was cut and burned on the altar (Numbers 6).

The first Nazirite in the Old Testament was Samson (Judges 13:4,5), but they were well-known by the time of Amos (Amos 2:11,12). John the Baptist took Nazirite vows for life (Luke 1:15).

Jesus' departure Jesus emphasized that he was telling them things now which they did not need to know earlier when he had been with them. (Compare John 13:19, where such information would help them to believe in him.) These things had to be said because of his imminent departure. They had not asked where he was going, as they had in John 13 and 14. They had become so involved in their own sorrow at his going that they had not pursued the question further on this occasion.

Paradoxical as it may have seemed to them, it was for their benefit that he went. Ironically, Caiaphas had seen the advantage of Jesus' 'going away'; it is the same Greek word in John 11:50; 18:14. Without Jesus' departure the arrival of the Holy Spirit would be impossible. In view of what had already been said about the Holy Spirit, they should have realized how, along with all the Christians who followed them, they would be better off. So long as their love for Christ, their knowledge of him and their joy in him, were linked to his physical life alone, they were vulnerable.

Conviction by the Spirit The first task of the Spirit is the conviction of the world of sin, righteousness and judgement. This would be an exposure of the attitudes of the world in such a way as to touch the conscience of men. As the world cannot receive the Paraclete (John 14:17), this would, presumably, normally be achieved through the witness of the apostles (John 15:26,27).

It is interesting to note the substance of these charges. The charge of sin was connected not with wrong actions, but with unbelief. The people of Israel had long ago been condemned for stifling the national conscience. God had given them prophets and Nazirites to remind them of his truth by their words and by their deeds. But they made the Nazirites drink wine and told the prophets not to prophesy (Amos 2:11,12). God's people had done the same again in refusing to accept the words and deeds of Jesus (John 15:22-24).

The Spirit would show them also that they had the wrong idea of righteousness. True righteousness was God's vindication of the righteous life of Jesus, through the resurrection and the ascension. Likewise with judgement. Despite all that was to follow, they could not judge Jesus. It was the devil and those who followed him who were judging and condemning themselves in the death of Christ.

Taught by the Spirit In addition, there was the teaching role of the Spirit. He would guide them into all the truth about Jesus. This does not mean that the Holy Spirit guided the apostles or the church into the fullness of truth about everything. It was a specific promise to those whose business it was to record, interpret and pass on the once-for-all events connected with Christ's ministry, death and resurrection. 'The things that are to come' (verse 13) may mean specifically the cross and resurrection rather than a general reference to things in the future. It would be the Spirit's function to pass on to them all that Jesus wished to reveal, and so to bring glory to him.

16:17-24 Grief turned to joy
Jesus now told his disciples about their not seeing him and then their seeing him again. This would be in a little while. The disciples were puzzled and did not know what he meant.

The question is whether the two references to 'a little while' refer to different periods of time. Some have suggested that within a few hours they would not see him because of his death. Then a few hours later they would see him again because of the resurrection. More

'A woman giving birth to a child has pain because her time has come; but when her baby is born she forgets the anguish because of her joy that a child is born into the world' (John 16:21).

probably, both instances of the phrase refer to the brief period between the cross and resurrection, which was a time of not seeing, but being about to see Jesus again. The seeing may not be altogether unconnected with the seeing of Christ in the end (1 John 3:2). Seeing him after the resurrection gives a foretaste of the final vision.

A short parable Because of their difficulty in understanding, Jesus gave them a short parable. The time would be one of sorrow for them and of joy for the world. But their sorrow would be turned into joy. It was like the anguish of childbirth, a time of crisis which soon turns into joy with the advent of new life.

This is not merely an illustration of any sorrow giving way to joy. In the Old Testament, the messianic age was expected to be like childbirth, delivering God's people from their afflictions (Isaiah 26:16-20). So their brief, temporary sorrow would turn into deep, permanent joy. Then they would start to ask the Father things in his name. There would be direct access to the Father because of Christ's effective work of reconciliation. If they asked, they would receive, and their joy would be full.

16:25-33 Parting words to the disciples

The circumstances of Christ's ministry and the degree of understanding which the disciples had achieved were such that Jesus had to use a great deal of figurative language. The time would soon come when he would speak plainly of the Father. Not, of course, that it is possible to speak of God's truth without some use of human metaphor. But the possession of the Holy Spirit, and the new degree of understanding which would come to the disciples, would make much more direct teaching possible.

Jesus returned to the subject of prayer. After his exaltation, prayer would be made in his name. It would depend on his opening up of the way to the Father. But there would be no idea of the Son having to plead with an unwilling Father for the needs of his disciples. This would be unnecessary, because of the Father's love for them. Their own love, and faith in, Jesus were tokens that they were recipients of the Father's love. There was this close connection between attitudes

Prayer

In the Bible, prayer includes adoration (Revelation 1:12-18), confession (Psalm 51), praise (Psalm 103), thanksgiving (Luke 17:11-19), petition (2 Samuel 7:18-25), intercession (Genesis 18:23-33) and communion (Luke 10:39). There are also instances of sudden prayer at a moment of crisis (Nehemiah 2:1-5; Matthew 14:28-33). There were in addition times when one person led a group in prayer (1 Chronicles 16) and when a small group would meet to pray for some special need (Daniel 2:14-18; Acts 12:5; Matthew 18:20).

Prayer is presented in the Bible as one of our first duties. Men 'should always pray and not give up' (Luke 18:1), and it was to encourage us to pray that Jesus gave us a pattern which we call 'The Lord's Prayer' (Luke 11:1-13).

Scripture indicates certain elements which relate to prayer. David didn't expect the Lord to answer him if he lived in disobedience to God (Psalm 66:18). We must steadfastly believe in God's power to give us what we ask (James 1:5,6; 5:15). It must be in the name of Christ because of who he is and what he has done (John 14:14) and according to the will of God (1 John 5:14). If a prayer is not granted, God may have a better plan for us, and answer it in another way (2 Corinthians 12:8,9).

It is the Holy Spirit who gives us the desire to pray, the strength to pray, and who makes our prayer acceptable to God (Romans 8:26,27).

Finally, it is only for the sake of Christ that God can receive our prayers. Without his death on the cross, sinful humans could have no right of access into the presence of a holy God (Ephesians 2:18; Hebrews 9:19-22).

to the Father and the Son because he himself had his origin and destination with the Father, only being in the world for a time.

The disciples now professed to see the plain truth. Perhaps verse 28 is, in very summary form, the plain truth which Jesus told them. They said that they understood his supernatural knowledge and therefore his divine origin. But Jesus warned them that such a belief would be tested soon. For they were about to be scattered and to desert him. In the face of the assault of the world he offered them peace and the confidence that he had already won the victory. (Compare 1 Corinthians 15:57 and Colossians 2:15 for the cross and resurrection as victory over the powers of the world.) This would be a proof of his claims.

17:1-5 Jesus prays for himself
After his final conversation with the disciples, Jesus now turned to speak to his Father. This is often called the 'High-Priestly Prayer'. Jesus, the great High Priest, devoted himself to his death, through which he would atone for the sin of the world (compare John 1:29).

Yet there is a good deal more to the prayer than just this theme. It deals with some of the great doctrines of the gospel; the relationship of Father and Son (verses 1-5); the relationship of the Son to the disciples and of the disciples to the world (verses 6-19), and the relationship of the Son to later generations of believers and their relationship to the world (verses 20-26).

The Western Wall, Jerusalem, for centuries known as the Wailing Wall. The only surviving part of the great Temple built by Herod the Great. Jewish worshippers come here to pray.

The hour towards which the clock of destiny had been ticking throughout his ministry had now come. In the mind and will of Jesus his work was already finished (verse 4). He had accepted the cross and taken it upon himself as the full and perfect expression of love. Complete obedience to the Father's will characterized his ministry, and was sealed in his death (John 19:30). So now Jesus asked the Father that it might be an occasion for the glory of both Father and Son (John 13:31,32).

The object of the Son's mission was to give eternal life in the knowledge of the Father and Son. Verse 3 contains the only attempt in this Gospel at a definition of one of its leading concepts – eternal life. It is shown to be a personal relationship with God based on the historical mission of the Son, to know whom is to know God. This mission had been accomplished, and so had given glory to the Father. As it had been accomplished, Jesus asked that he might now return to his Father and to the glory which he had before the incarnation, and which had been his from the beginning, even before the creation of the world.

17:6-19 Jesus prays for his disciples

The mission of Christ was partly to make the name or character of the Father known to his disciples. The manifestation of the name or character of God was necessary for a true knowledge of him, which was not mere religious emotion. They belonged to the Father and

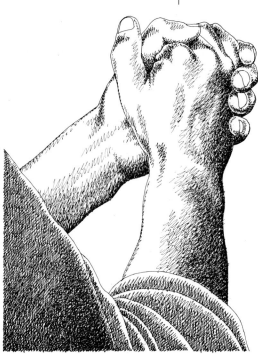

'I pray also . . . that all of them may be one, Father, just as you are in me and I am in you' (John 17:20,21).

An olive tree, distinctive with its gnarled trunk.

were given to the Son and they had been faithful. Now they also had knowledge of the divine origin and authority of Jesus.

Having described something of what he had done for the disciples, Jesus now turned to praying for them. He clearly distinguished them from the world, for they belonged in a special way to the Father and the Son. This does not mean that 'the world' is not still the object of God's love for whose sake the Son came (John 3:16). In the writings of John 'the world' means, not the created order as such, nor the gifts of God in nature and human life. It means human life and society lived in disregard of God and under the power of evil.

Unity In God's strategy, the outreach to the world is always through the disciples. Because Jesus was leaving the world, their position as his representatives was of special importance. So he prayed that his Father would keep them united and faithful. The unity of the disciples should be such as the unity of the Father and the Son. He also prayed that they might have joy such as he had, and would have, through his return to the Father.

By passing on to them of the Word of God he effectively called them out of the world. Their true allegiance was now elsewhere, and they would therefore incur the hatred of the world. But he did not pray for their withdrawal from a hostile world; rather for them to be kept safe in the world from the attacks of the evil one. Just as Jesus himself had a heavenly origin and destination, so in a sense the disciples had too. But just as he had a mission to the world, so had they. And his consecration of himself was also a consecration of them for service. This latter depended both on the truth of God's word (maybe a reference to Jesus himself; see John 1:1 and 14:6), and on Christ's own consecration of himself. It was not merely a human effort at self-improvement.

17:20-26 Jesus prays for all believers
If the prayer had earlier been confined to the disciples as against the world (verse 9), now it was extended to future generations of believers. The faith which they would have is expected to come through the word, the apostolic preaching. The prayer, for what would in due course become a very diverse company, was for unity.

But the reference is to a unity of will and purpose, rather than one of organization. The dynamic relationship of Father and Son is the pattern, and its origin is in their unity. It would be sustained by a continuing relationship to them. Its object would be that the world should believe in the mission of the Son from the Father.

Even the glory which belonged to God is in some way passed on to the disciples to assist the perfection of unity and the demonstration to the world that they are the recipients of God's love. So he prayed that they might see his true glory. The disciples could not fully follow yet (verse 24 and see John 13:33,36) but there would be a foretaste of his glory before the full enjoyment of it. Because Jesus has known the Father and they have known the mission of the Son, he has made the Father's name known to them and will continue to make it known. This revelation of the Father's character was to further their experience of the Father's love of the Son and deepen the Son's unity with them.

18:1-11 Jesus arrested

After three chapters of teaching and one of prayer, we come back to action. But the Passion narrative in John, which we now begin to read, is different in emphasis from those of the other Gospels. Glory dominates. Even in the darkest moments there was triumph and victory. Jesus had warned his disciples about what was to happen, so that they would believe in him (John 13:19). He had summoned them to rise and go out to the conflict (John 14:31). He had set the

The Golden Gate, Jerusalem, seen from the Garden of Gethsemane outside the city walls. The gate originally opened from the Temple area onto the Kidron Valley. It has been suggested that it was through this gate that Jesus entered the city when he came in triumph.

coming affliction in the context of the whole plan of God, and consecrated himself and his disciples for this affliction.

Now he went out across the Kidron valley to a garden. John alone describes it as such and does not name it as Gethsemane. Perhaps we are meant to see a conflict between Satan (John 13:27) and the Son of Man, the second Adam.

The Betrayer Judas, having been identified and sent off to do his deed quickly, had gone out into the night (John 13:21-30). With the inner knowledge that he had from having belonged to the Twelve, Judas took a band of Roman troops and Jewish Temple police. He thus combined the religious and the secular authorities, and went to find Jesus.

Because of his foreknowledge of what was to happen, Jesus took the initiative in coming forward and asking them whom they were seeking. To the reply 'Jesus of Nazareth' (his human title) he responded, identifying himself in terms which probably carried overtones of his deity, 'I am he' (compare John 6:20; 8:24,58). This is supported by their immediate reaction of withdrawing and falling to the ground. This verse shows Jesus in command, willingly laying down his life (see John 10:18).

When the question and answer were repeated, Jesus told them to let the disciples go. The impetuous Peter drew his sword and cut off the right ear of the high priest's slave. But Jesus rebuked this attempt to frustrate his drinking the bitter cup given to him by his Father.

18:12-14 Jesus taken to Annas

Despite the willingness which Jesus had shown to be arrested, civil and religious authorities combined to seize and bind him. They took him first to Annas, father-in-law of Caiaphas the high priest. Annas was high priest from AD 6-15. Other references to him in the New Testament are in Luke and Acts, both in connection with Caiaphas (Luke 3:2; Acts 4:6). He may have been the power behind the throne. Caiaphas (also mentioned in Matthew 26:3,57) succeeded him after his deposition by the Romans and held the office until AD 36. The Gospel-writer reminds his readers of Caiaphas' attitude of cynical expediency to the execution of Jesus (John 11:49-52).

An artist's impression of Jerusalem in the time of Christ.

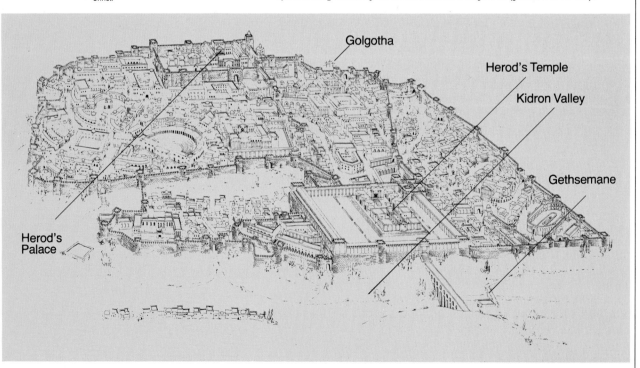

Golgotha

Herod's Temple

Kidron Valley

Gethsemane

Herod's Palace

18:15-18 Peter's first denial

While Jesus went alone as the prisoner, Simon Peter and another disciple followed. (It is natural to assume that this was the 'beloved disciple', but this is not certain.) This disciple was known to the high priest, so he managed to get into the court. Peter had stopped outside and had to be brought in by him. To a question from a maid as to whether he was one of Jesus' disciples Peter, the 'man of rock', denied it. He then stood with the servants and officers trying to keep warm round a fire. He had denied the true light, and stood with the enemies of his master in the dark and in the cold.

18:19-27 The high priest questions Jesus

The high priest began his examination of Jesus, not by asking him the basic questions about his origin and authority, but more peripheral ones about his disciples and his teaching. Questions were put to Jesus, but hardly pursued. The decisions had already been taken in secret without giving him a fair trial (see John 7:45-52).

Jesus' response Jesus had nothing to add to what he had already said in his public ministry. While he gave special teaching to his disciples at the Last Supper, his ministry was an open one. His teaching had been done openly and to the world, though not in the way which his brothers had expected (John 7:3-4). His message had been proclaimed in synagogue and Temple, places of public gathering. (There is only one reference in this Gospel to his teaching in the synagogue. The main challenge to the Jews in their religious setting was made in the Temple.) There was no point in repeating his message – his audience could tell them perfectly well. The blind man had questioned the need to repeat his evidence. And there was no possibility here of their wishing to become his disciples.

'Pilate answered, "... As for me, I find no basis for a charge against him"' (John 19:6).

Where argument fails, violence often takes over. An officer struck him, but Jesus reminded them that the point at issue was the truth of his teaching. Such a point is not solved in this way. Annas then sent him, bound, to Caiaphas.

The scene switches back to Peter. Those with whom he had identified himself asked him if he in fact belonged with the prisoner. For the second time he denied that he was a disciple. One of Malchus' relations then asked suspiciously whether he saw Peter in the garden with Jesus. There was no glory here, only shame. For the third time Peter denied, and, as Jesus predicted, the cock crowed.

18:28-40 Jesus before Pilate

Jesus was sent from the religious leaders to the Roman governor; from the prejudiced judgement of his own people to the bewildered judgement of the world. With a supreme example of hypocrisy, they refused to run the risk of ritual defilement (which would come by going into the house of a Gentile from which the leavened bread had not been removed) by entering Pilate's headquarters, though they were in the midst of defiling themselves morally (Isaiah 59:3). In an amazingly ironic situation they were preparing to eat the Passover without realizing that they were putting to death the true Passover Lamb. In his redemptive death the real significance of the festival was found.

Pilate and the people To Pilate's tactful visit to them outside the Praetorium, and to his question about the charge which they brought, there was no reasoned answer. If he had not been a criminal, they would not have brought him. Pilate wished them to judge him by their own law (which in fact was against them in their opposition to Jesus, John 5:45-47). They said it was not lawful for them to put any man to death. But they had determined that Jesus should die, and die on a cross.

John
19

There is an inner stage as well as an outer. Inside the Praetorium, Pilate confronted Jesus. He asked him the question that mattered, as far as the Roman authorities were concerned. Are you the King of the Jews – a revolutionary leader? When Jesus tried to find out whether this was a conclusion Pilate had reached for himself Pilate asked in desperation what on earth he could know about it all. What was this all about?

Jesus put the whole idea of kingship on to a different footing. Kingship, as Pilate knew it, was not the point at issue. It was truth. Outside, Pilate had to face the demands of the Jews; inside he had to face the claims of truth.

So Pilate, with a despairing rhetorical question about truth, went out in the cause of truth to tell the Jews that Jesus was innocent. But he wanted to find a way around the problem, and so made use of the Passover amnesty. He had misjudged public opinion. They called out not for Jesus their 'king', who was no threat to the Roman rule, but for a terrorist called Barabbas.

19:1-16 Jesus sentenced to be crucified

Having failed to get rid of the responsibility for dealing with Jesus by an amnesty, Pilate now had him flogged. This may have been an attempt to get Jesus to give evidence (compare Acts 22:24); or an attempt to placate the Jews so that they would not go on asking for the death penalty (Luke 23:16,22). The soldiers then did their utmost to humiliate this so-called king by mockery. They dressed him up in

Rulers of Palestine after Herod the Great

Ethnarch of Judea	Tetrarch of Galilee	Tetrarch of Iturea
Archelaus	**Herod Antipas**	**Philip**
Archelaus was deposed and banished. Judea became a Roman province administered by prefects appointed by the emperor.	'Herod the tetrarch' imprisoned and executed John the Baptist. He also built the city of Tiberias. He was deposed in AD39.	Philip was a moderate and just ruler. He married Salome, the daughter of Herodias.

4BC

AD6

AD34

AD39

Roman Procurator

It is often claimed that it was here, on a pavement now under the Convent of the Sisters of Zion, that Jesus was brought before Pilate. The pavement formed the courtyard of the Antonia Fortress during the time of Christ.

royal robes and proceeded to call him 'King of the Jews' and strike him. The crown of thorns was probably not so much an instrument of torture as a symbol of mockery. It was probably a 'radiate crown', which was sometimes used as a sign of divinity.

Pilate went out in the name of truth, on the level at which he understood it, and told the Jews that he found no case against Jesus (compare John 18:38). The Jews themselves had been unable to prove any moral charges against him (John 8:46). Jesus then followed, a pitiful sight in his mock array. Pilate offered him to their view, telling them to look at the man. Here is this poor fellow, your deluded and rejected Messianic claimant, is what he meant. But here is 'the Man', the Son of Man, the Second Adam, offering his perfect obedience for the life of the world (Romans 5:15,19; Philippians 2:6-8).

Crucify! The religious leaders saw him, and howled for his crucifixion. Pilate was still concerned enough for the truth not to be willing to order the crucifixion. He had, however, given in sufficiently to the pressure of the Jews to offer them the opportunity of performing it. (The Jews could not actually crucify him so this may have been a taunt by Pilate.) But they continued to call out for Pilate to act. The true charge now came out. It was a charge of blasphemy, which under Jewish law carried the death penalty (Leviticus 24:16). The 'man' had made himself Son of God (compare John 10:33).

Against the apparent hardness and moral unconcern of the 'Jews', Pilate is clearly set as a man trying to make up his mind. On the level at which he understood them, he tried to come to terms with the claims of the truth. So he was afraid. Partly afraid because the title 'Son of God' was one that the Roman emperors claimed and therefore had a smell of treason about it. Partly afraid no doubt because the 'man' showed so many signs of being more than an ordinary man.

Pilate and the prisoner Pilate therefore asked Jesus where he came from. This may be simply a matter concerned with jurisdiction (compare Luke 23:5,6). But it is the all-important theological question (compare John 3:31; 8:23). Jesus did not reply to this direct question (compare John 8:25). Pilate then reminded the prisoner of

בן לך מלך היהודים

REX IVDAEORVM

OBACIΛEYCTШNIOYΔAIШN

The title 'The king of the Jews' was written in Aramaic, Latin and Greek on the cross. It would have appeared something like this.

his authority – power to release and power to crucify. But this was no absolute power. It came from above, not so much from Rome as from God (Romans 13:1-7). Pilate had not realized that Jesus had power to lay down and take up his life (John 10:18). Pilate was, in a way, only doing his job. The real sinner was the one who handed Jesus over. This last phrase could refer either to Judas or to Caiaphas. Each represents Judaism as a whole, with its claim to sight (John 9:41).

Pilate, seeking again to release Jesus, made another attempt to follow the claims of the truth. But the Jews had another weapon – insecurity. In the face of possible action by the political authorities they had acted to preserve their interests (John 11:48-50). Now Pilate was reminded of his interests with the one who had on the earthly level given him power. This was sufficient to sway Pilate finally, for, like most men, he had his price. Ironically, in the end Pilate was removed by Caesar.

Pilate brought Jesus out and sat down on the judgement seat. He then offered him to them again, this time as their king. When they called for his crucifixion, Pilate asked incredulously, 'Shall I crucify your king?'. He received the terrible reply, 'We have no king but Caesar'. So did the people of God abandon their heritage. Nothing remained but to hand over Jesus for execution. The day of preparation might be the day before the Passover, or the day before the Sabbath of Passover week. The 'sixth hour' probably referred to the Roman (and also the modern) time system.

The decisive shout of the priests in verse 15 marked the end of the continual conflict in John's Gospel between light and darkness – the light and truth of Christ, and the darkness of the Jews. It was an ironic end. The Jews rejected their King-Messiah, whom they could not and would not recognize. They declared their allegiance to an Emperor and an army of occupation which they hated.

19:17-27 The crucifixion
The struggle between the two ideas of kingship ended with apparent victory for the rulers of this world. The argument concerning the truth was over. The one who was true was falsely charged and sentenced, the truth only shining out of the narrative unintentionally or ironically. The decision had been made on the human level.

Now came the action. Jesus went out carrying his own cross to Golgotha. It is possible to harmonize this idea with Mark 15:21. John is emphasizing that Jesus went alone to accomplish the world's salvation. Compare also Isaac carrying the wood for his own sacrifice (Genesis 22:6). The derivation of the name 'Golgotha' is uncertain, and its location is not sure. There he was crucified with two others, who were possibly associates of Barabbas in his terrorist activity. So radically was Jesus misunderstood that they numbered the sinless one among the transgressors (Isaiah 53:12). They crucified one whose kingship was not of this world, and who abhorred the use of violence, between two violent criminals.

The inscription There must be a reason why a man should receive the sentence of crucifixion. Pilate, therefore, was to have the last grim laugh. This was 'The King of the Jews'. So the title went up in the three most important languages of the day. Aramaic, rather than Hebrew, was the language of the Jews; Greek and Latin the official languages of the Roman Empire. So far as Pilate was concerned, he was Jesus of Nazareth, a description such as any of his subjects might have. To that was added, in scorn of the whole business, the title of king. Pilate had already used this title five times. But the Jews, who had just declared that they had no king but Caesar, naturally objected. In a sense it was a more limited title than 'the King of Israel', and all the more ironic for the way in which the 'Jews' have been so opposed to him in this Gospel. To show that he was a false messianic pretender would hurt no one as this did. But Pilate stood firm and the title, unwittingly given, remained. So, in the end, they did take him by force to make him king (John 6:15).

To the soldiers Jesus was just another criminal to be dealt with; a political one with no very noticeable difference at the moment. So they carried on and collected the 'benefits' of the job, the prisoner's clothing. His tunic, the undergarment worn next to the body, was like that of the high priest, made out of one piece of cloth, and could not therefore easily be divided. There was no point then in trying to tear it. 'Let's toss for it', they said. And so the soldiers committed themselves to chance by gambling for the tunic. But there is no chance in the ways of God. This was to fulfil the scripture. Through

A simple pole or stake, hammered into the ground, was used to hang up and execute criminals and prisoners of war. The Romans also used a pole with a horizontal piece to execute people guilty of serious crimes. Early tradition claims that it was on this sort of cross that Jesus died.

Christ's crown of thorns may have been constructed out of branches of the spiny burnet.

Hyssop belongs to the same family of plants as the herb marjoram, and has been used for cooking and as a medicine. It can grow up to three feet high.

'When he had received the drink, Jesus said, "It is finished." With that, he bowed his head and gave up his spirit' (John 19:30).

the operation of those who did not know what they were doing, Psalm 22 was fulfilled in the death of Christ!

If the cross created a false fellowship of gamblers trying to gain from the victim and from each other, it also created a true fellowship of believers. Not only was there a group representative of the church gathered around, but from the cross the word was spoken which put Jesus' mother and the 'beloved disciple' into a new relationship with each other.

19:28-37 The death of Jesus

The mission of Jesus had been concerned with accomplishing the work which the Father had given him to do (John 4:34). Here he knew that it had been accomplished, fantastic as this must have seemed to those who stood by. So he cried out, 'I thirst'. They came to meet his thirst on the physical level, so fulfilling the scripture (Psalm 69:21). Hyssop would not be a very suitable plant to hold up a wet sponge. A similar word means 'javelin' which might be a possible translation.

But Jesus' real thirst may have been a spiritual one, for his Father (Psalm 42:2). He who offered the living water, so that men need never thirst again, himself endured the agonies of thirst. He who offered the Spirit and life gave up his own spirit to death. The last cry from the cross (verse 30) was one of triumph not of despair. He could die in peace. No one took his life. He gave it up freely, completing and perfecting his God-given mission.

So the hour had come, the work had been completed, and Jesus died. But that is not after all the end of the matter. For there were religious consequences for the Jews and for the disciples. The Jews had been busy with their Passover observances. While they went through with the removal of a messianic pretender, they did not intend to slip up in their religious observance (compare John 18:28).

The law said that a hanged man's body should not remain all night upon the tree, as that would defile the land (Deuteronomy 21:22,3). The Romans liked to leave the bodies on the crosses as a grim warning to potential troublemakers. But because the next day was the Sabbath of the Passover, the Jews asked for the bodies to be taken away before nightfall.

Physical death The Romans could not, of course, remove the bodies until the victims were dead. In such cases, as an act of mercy, their legs were broken to hasten death. This was done in the case of the two terrorists. When they came to Jesus, they saw that he was dead already, so there was no need to break his legs. One of the soldiers, probably just to check that he really was dead, thrust a lance into his side, and there came out a flow of blood and water.

There was a witness of this, though this does not seem to be 'the beloved disciple'. He gives true evidence for the faith of the readers. It was clearly something of importance. On the one hand, it was a firm explanation of Christ's death, particularly important as there were heretics who denied that Jesus had ever died. On the other hand, water and blood are symbols in this Gospel. Medical evidence for what happened can be cited, but the point is that 'the real death of Jesus was the real life of men'.

Water and blood Probably the two sacraments are in mind (compare 1 John 5:6,8). Water is applied for cleansing and new birth and drunk for satisfaction. The blood of the Son of man must be drunk so that men may live (John 6:53-56). By what the soldiers did not do and by what they did they fulfilled the scripture. Thus they revealed (verse 36) Jesus as the true Passover Lamb (John 1:29; compare Exodus 12:46; Psalm 34:20). They also fulfilled the prophecies contained in Zechariah 12:10, which has bearing on the death of Jesus.

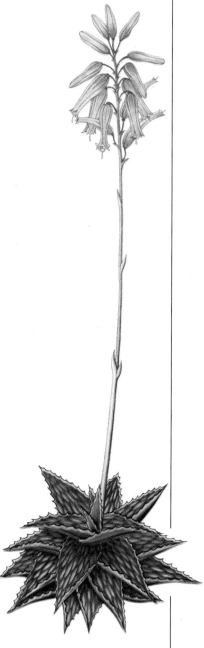

Aloe is a tree from which a pleasant perfume was produced. It was also used as incense. Nicodemus brought a large amount of aloes to bind up with the grave-clothes round Jesus' body.

John 19

The Dome of the Rock seen from the Garden of Gethsemane, Jerusalem.

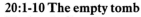

19:38-42 The burial of Jesus

While the fact of the burial of Jesus is mentioned as part of the apostolic preaching by Paul (1 Corinthians 15:3,4), it is referred to very little in the New Testament. As far as Paul is concerned, it is probably only the link between death and resurrection which shows that both really happened. But John records a number of details about the burial which seem to be significant.

Joseph and Nicodemus Joseph of Arimathea, a wealthy man and a member of the Sanhedrin, came and asked Pilate to be allowed to take away the body of Jesus. No doubt due to his influential position he obtained permission. So he did what the Jews wanted, and avoided the defilement of the land. But he was also a secret disciple of Jesus, so that, despite his fear of the Jews, this was an act of courage and was done in order to honour Jesus. Nicodemus, who had not yet been described as a believer, but who was at least an open-minded sympathizer (John 3:1; 7:50-52), joined with him. They took huge quantities of spices (seeming to echo Psalm 45:8) and treated his body according to Jewish burial custom.

It was to a garden that they went with him, for it was here that the Second Adam had to bring life, where the first Adam brought sin and death (1 Corinthians 15:21,22). It was a new tomb, perhaps prepared for the use of Joseph's family, now given to Jesus as no other could be prepared in time. Here, free from corrupting influences, he was laid – the first to lie in the tomb and soon to be the first to rise from the dead to a new sphere of life (1 Corinthians 15:20). Despite the honour paid to Jesus by these two men, outwardly the victory belonged entirely to the Jews and to the forces of darkness. A dangerous pretender had been disposed of by the Romans, Barabbas had been freed, and no one had even broken the law!

20:1-10 The empty tomb

The hand of legalism may seem to have triumphed as the drama had to wait for a day while the Sabbath was observed. But after the Sabbath rest came a new week, and with it a new era in the history of mankind. Mary Magdalene came to the tomb early. It was still in every sense dark (compare Luke 22:53), but dawn was imminent.

Death

Physical death It seems from the Genesis story that man would not have died if he had not sinned (Genesis 2:17). From the moment he sinned, his body came under the same death process as the rest of the animal world.

Spiritual death This is the condition in which people exist who have never come into living personal contact with God through Jesus Christ (I John 5:12; Ephesians 2:1). Life in this new spiritual sense comes through new birth (John 3:3) through faith in Jesus Christ (John 1:11,12).

Eternal death This is not so much a present state as a future event, the final divine penalty for sin (2 Thessalonians 1:8,9). This final state of the unbeliever is spoken of solemnly elsewhere (Matthew 25:41-46), and always in terms of suffering and separation.

She was presumably not alone (see verse 2, 'we do not know'), but is probably mentioned as the leader of the group of women and the one to whom the Lord appeared personally (verses 11-18). It was a forgiven sinner who made the first discovery of the empty tomb and saw the first appearance of the risen Lord. She saw that the stone, such as would normally be placed across the entrance of a tomb to keep it safe, had been taken away. She naturally assumed that someone or other had violated the tomb and taken away the body of Jesus. She probably suspected the enemies of Jesus, but the rifling of tombs was a fairly common crime.

Peter and the 'beloved disciple' With this news she ran off to Peter and the 'beloved disciple'. The two of them ran as fast as they could to the tomb, and the 'beloved disciple', presumably the younger man, got there first. He stooped to look into the tomb from the outside and saw the graveclothes lying there.

When Peter arrived he, as usual, was more impetuous and went into the tomb. He saw the extra details – the different wrappings all lying in place. Lazarus had come out of the tomb with the wrappings still on him (John 11:44). But this was resurrection of a different kind, in which the form of the body seems to have been changed, so that it could slip out of the graveclothes without disturbing them. No one removing the body would have left the wrappings.

The boldness of Peter emboldened the 'beloved disciple' also. He went in and saw the evidence more closely, and believed what had

Mary of Magdala

Mary had been heavily possessed by evil spirits but Jesus had freed her. She joined other women who were meeting the material needs of Jesus and his disciples (Luke 8:1-3). She was present at the crucifixion (Matthew 27:56; Mark 15:40; John 19:25) and noted carefully where Jesus was buried (Matthew 27:61; Mark 15:47).

Early in the morning of Easter Day Mary and other women went to his tomb to add more spices and oils to Jesus' body (Matthew 28:1; Mark 16:1,2; John 20:1). When she saw that the stone had been rolled away, she ran to tell Peter and James that the body had been stolen. Later she met the angels at the tomb, and then the risen Christ, though at first she failed to recognize him. He told her not to cling to him (John 20:1-18).

happened. This is the first true Christian faith in this Gospel, because it is faith in the risen Lord. For an adequate confession we have to wait until verse 28. This had all come as a surprise to them because of their failure to know the scriptural prediction that Jesus should rise from the dead.

20:10-18 Jesus appears to Mary of Magdala

In a sense the 'beloved disciple' had come to Christian faith because he believed in the resurrection. But it was Mary who came to the first full Christian experience because she met the risen Lord. The twin bases of the Easter faith are the fact of the empty tomb and the encounter with the risen Lord. As the Lord had gone, there was no point staying at the tomb as far as the men were concerned. But somehow they had not communicated this to Mary. She remained weeping at the tomb, as it was the place with which her Lord had last been associated. She did not now know where to look for him. Eventually she looked into the tomb and saw two angels. It may be that she needed the evidence of the angels, which was not needed by Peter and the other disciple. When they asked her why she was weeping she answered purely on the human plane. He had been moved and she did not know where they had put him.

Jesus and Mary Turning round, she saw the risen Jesus but did not recognize him. To his question about the reason for her tears, she continued in the same vein, trying to discover where the dead Jesus was. Only the use of her name, no doubt in a familiar voice, made her realize that it was Jesus. Her apparent desire to cling to him was forbidden. She was not to cling to his body in this state because his abiding presence after the ascension would be a spiritual one (John 14:18). He had to ascend to his Father. She had to go and tell his brothers about this. They were now brothers ('my Father and your Father', verse 17) but his relationship to the Father was still unique. So Mary went off to the disciples and told them she had seen the Lord in the garden.

20:19-23 Jesus appears to his disciples

The disciples had now heard of the empty tomb, which some of them at least had seen for themselves. They had also heard of the appearance of Christ to Mary Magdalene. But they had not yet met the risen Lord for themselves. To them the experience of the Easter faith came not at the tomb nor in the garden, but in a room where doors were shut through fear of the Jews (compare John 7:13; 19:38).

It is important to emphasize that this appearance to the disciples was on the first day of the week, the first day of a new era. Jesus passed through closed doors and greeted them with a message of peace, now filled with a new and wonderful meaning for them (compare John 14:27). The emphasis here seems to be more on the power of Jesus in his 'spiritual body' to pass through closed doors and yet be recognized, than on the disciples' fear. But we can see how frightened men were transformed in preparation for their fearless mission to the world. The evidence that he really was Jesus had to come not only from his words, but also from his body. The marks of crucifixion were displayed to them. No wonder the disciples were filled with joy (see John 16:20-22).

The Holy Spirit given Jesus then repeated his word of peace, and commissioned them for mission in his name. It is not certain whether only the Twelve, minus Judas and Thomas, were in the room. If this was so, then they were there as representatives of the church as a whole. Jesus breathed on them and imparted the Holy Spirit to them. Their mission and the gift of the Holy Spirit through which alone they could accomplish it (compare Acts 1:8) were connected with the forgiveness and the retaining of sins.

| 1 Mary of Magdala and the other Mary
John 20; Matthew 28 | 2 Simon Peter
Luke 24:34 | 3 Two from Emmaus
Luke 24 | 4 The disciples except Thomas
John 20 |

| 5 The disciples with Thomas
John 20 | **Jesus' resurrection appearances** | | 6 Seven disciples
John 21 |

| 7 500 plus followers
1 Corinthians 15 | 8 James
1 Corinthians 15 | 9 The disciples
Acts 1 | 10 Paul
Acts 9 |

John 20

Thomas was one of the Twelve (Matthew 10:3). His name means 'twin'. John is the only Gospel-writer to give us substantial information about Thomas. He was prepared to sacrifice his life out of loyalty to Jesus (John 11:16), but refused to accept anyone else's word that Jesus had risen from the dead. When he saw Jesus himself, he was overwhelmed: 'My Lord and my God!' (John 20:28).

Jesus could impart the indwelling Holy Spirit as soon as he had risen. But the full outward manifestation of the gift of the Holy Spirit to the church had to wait until the appearances were over. There was here a new creation (compare Genesis 2:7). The Second Adam is a lifegiving Spirit (1 Corinthians 15:45). The forgiveness or retention of sins (verse 23) is the inevitable result of people's reaction to the gospel. What happened in Jesus' ministry (John 9:39-41) will happen in them through the Holy Spirit (compare John 16:8-11).

20:24-31 Jesus appears to Thomas

For some reason Thomas had not been present when Jesus appeared to the disciples on the evening of Easter Day. As shown earlier (John 11:16; 14:5) Thomas seems to have been loyal, but lacked the perception of faith. When the disciples told him of the resurrection experience in the simplest terms, 'We have seen the Lord', Thomas asked for more detailed evidence by sight and touch before he would be convinced.

A week later came the answer for Thomas. Again Jesus passed through closed doors and again he gave them his greeting of peace. Then he invited Thomas to put the evidence for the resurrection to the test which he had specified. It seems that touch was not necessary; the evidence of sight was sufficient. Thomas cried out in adoring wonder, 'My Lord and my God!'. Paradoxically, it was the doubter who in the end expressed his faith most completely.

The climax of the Gospel The Gospel has reached its climax. An adequate confession of faith had at last been made. Jesus is confessed not only as Lord (compare Romans 10:9; 1 Corinthians 12:13) but also as God (compare John 1:1). Thomas' faith had been based on sight. But Jesus was concerned about those who would believe in later generations and in different places (John 17:20). So he pronounced his last blessing on those who would not have the privilege of sight, but who would exercise the gift of faith.

As the climax has been reached the Gospel-writer rounds off his work. He reminds his readers that the signs recorded are only a selection of all that Jesus did. They are selected for a purpose – to induce faith in Jesus as Christ and Son of God, which will bring life.

21:1-14 Jesus and the miraculous catch of fish

The Gospel proper ends with chapter 20. This chapter is a sort of appendix. Its particular purpose is apparently to explain what Jesus said about the destiny of the 'beloved disciple' (verse 23). It also has importance in showing the manner of Peter's restoration to the service of Christ, and the future which awaited him.

So the relationship between Peter and the 'beloved disciple' is made clear. Both are shown as equal partners with complementary roles – Peter as pastor and evangelist, and the beloved disciple as guarantor of the truth concerning Jesus (verse 25).

There were a number of different appearances to the disciples by

'Jesus said to them, ''Come and have breakfast.'' None of the disciples dared ask him, ''Who are you?'' They knew it was the Lord' (John 21:12).

the risen Lord (see 1 Corinthians 15:3-8). Not all of these are recorded in the Gospels. As always, John has selected one which gets across an important point (John 20:30,31; 21:5). The disciples had evidently gone back to Galilee. They were uncertain of the way in which they were to carry out the commission which Jesus had given the apostles (John 20:21). Seven of them are mentioned. Thomas figures prominently in John, Nathanael is mentioned only by him. This is the only reference to the sons of Zebedee in the Gospel, and it helps us to assume that John was the 'beloved disciple'. But this is not certain; for it could have been one of the two unnamed disciples.

Simon Peter decided to go fishing and the rest followed his lead. Night was the best time for fishing, but a hard night's toil yielded nothing. At daybreak Jesus, unrecognized, asked them from the shore whether they had any fish. When they said they had not, he told them to cast their nets to starboard.

It is not at all certain how far this story is meant to illustrate symbolically 'fishing for men' (compare Luke 5:10,11). The beloved disciple was the very first to discern who the stranger was. But it is Peter who acted first, putting on his clothes and plunging into the lake while the others struggled in with the boat and the catch.

Eventually all the disciples arrived, following Peter. They found that Jesus had already been at work. He had made a fire upon the shore and had cooked some fish and provided some bread. Jesus asked them to bring the fish which they themselves had caught.

'Jesus said, "Throw your net on the right side of the boat and you will find some (fish)." When they did, they were unable to haul the net in because of the large number of fish' (John 21:6).

Peter went back to the boat and hauled the net ashore. In it there were one hundred and fifty-three fish; but the net was not torn. This number has long exercised the ingenuity of commentators on scripture. It may simply be that they counted up, and this happened to be the total. But many have seen it as symbolic. However, the primary meaning of the whole chapter must undoubtedly be sought on the plain, literal level.

Fish for breakfast Jesus then asked them to have breakfast with him. There was about him a special quality which stopped them from asking who he was. In fact, they knew without having to ask, that it was the Lord. It is only after the resurrection that the disciples are recorded as referring to Jesus by this title in the third person. In any event, he could cope with shyness. He took bread and distributed it along with the fish, as he had done to them and the five thousand beside the same lake before (John 6:11). It was in a meal, which must have reminded them of meals which they had shared with him, as well as of the feeding miracle, that he revealed himself. Luke too shows how he 'was recognized by them when he broke the bread' (Luke 24:28-35). While it would be wrong to see this as a celebration of the Lord's Supper, the doctrine of the Lord's Supper should include the idea of eating together with the risen Jesus in the midst of his people.

21:15-25 Feed my sheep

Simon Peter had been the leader of the band of disciples. He had not always believed first (John 20:8), nor perceived first (verse 7), but he had usually acted first. Through being in a prominent position it was he who denied his master three times. He had already hastened ashore to meet Jesus, and it is clear that he wished to put right his denial. First they ate the meal of fellowship and then Jesus took the initiative in restoring Peter.

Three times Peter had denied that he knew Jesus (John 18:15-27), and now three times Jesus asked him if he loved him. It was only in reply to Peter's threefold assurance that he did love him that Jesus gave him the threefold commission to feed his lambs and his sheep.

'Jesus said, "Feed my sheep" ' (John 21:17b).

There seems to be no real distinction between 'lambs' and 'sheep', nor between the words 'feed' and 'tend'.

It was to this pastoral ministry that Peter, in fact, devoted himself (1 Peter 5:1-5). At the third question Peter was upset, but Jesus reminded him, as he had done before, (John 13:6-10) of his need for submission. When he was young he had the independence and opportunities of youth. When he was old, things would happen to him against his will. This was a prediction of a martyr's death (and important early evidence for the crucifixion of Peter). Then he would glorify God as his master had done before him (John 12:23-26). This was to be his destiny; it was for God's glory, it was the way Jesus had gone. So the command came 'Follow me!'

What about the others? It is always interesting to know what is going to happen to other people. Human nature being what it is, we enjoy comparisons with others so that we can exult in our own virtue or grumble about our own misfortunes.

Whatever the motive, Peter wanted to know what was to happen to the 'beloved disciple'. It is not clear why such a long description is given of him (verse 20). It may be to contrast this incident with the other (John 13:21-30), when it seemed of considerable importance to both Peter and the 'beloved disciple' to know who was going to be the traitor. In any case, in answer to Peter's question Jesus replied that it was none of his business. He put it in such a way that he seemed to predict that that disciple would not die before the second coming of Christ. Perhaps this was deliberately expressed as the most different thing that could possibly happen to him, without any implication that it would. The writer wished to make it quite plain (verse 23), that Jesus did not say this but only 'If I want him to remain alive until I return, what is that to you?' It was possibly necessary to state this because the 'beloved disciple' had just died. If this is so, he was the witness behind the Gospel, and the one responsible for writing it.

The book ends with the assertion that it is this disciple who is bearing witness to all this and has written this, and that it is known that his evidence is true. And in a charming concluding sentence, the writer adds that if all the deeds of Jesus were recorded, the world would not be large enough to hold all the books which should be written.

'Jesus did many other things as well. If every one of them were written down, I suppose that even the whole world would not have room for the books that would be written' (John 21:25).

Index

Places

Antonia Fortress 81, *331*
Bethany 83, *84*, 100, 170, 220, 221, 307, *307*
Bethesda *282*, 282, 283
Bethlehem *25*, *27*, *30*, 30, *31*, *188*, 188
Bethphage 83, 307
Bethsaida 128, 149
Caesarea Philippi 66, 146, *146*, 147, 150, *216*
Calvary 81, *179*, *255*
Cana 272, 281
Capernaum 36, 45, *46*, *47*, 118, *126*, 128, 136, 137, *137*, *200*, *208*, *289*
Dead Sea 16, *39*, 52, 53, *153*
Decapolis 266
Egypt 28
Emmaus 259, *259*
Gadara 45, 128, 212
Galilee 16, *36*, *37*, *62*, *65*, *69*, *106*, 116, *117*, *119*, 126-128, *141*, 202, 204, 225, 266, 272
Garden Tomb, Jerusalem *258*
Gerasa 134
Gerizim, Mount *277*
Gethsemane 102, *102*, 172, *172*, *173*, 252, *252*, *327*, *336*
Golden Gate 81
Hermon, Mount *66*, *146*, *150*, 151, 215, *215*
Herodion 50, *72*, *209*
Holy Land (map) *16*, *17*
Holy Sepulchre, Church of the *105*, *179*
Jericho *76*, 82, 158, 198, *223*, *242*, *243*, 243
Jerusalem *20*, *21*, *76*, 77-81, *77-81*, 83, 91, 93, *101*, 159, *161*, 232, *246*, 291, *291*, *311*, *312*, *313*, *325*, *328*
Jordan *116*
Jordan Valley 16, *230*, 238, *238*, *276*
Judea *115*, *157*, 266, *309*
Korazin *50*, 128, *218*
Masada *168*, *231*
Nain 208
Nativity, Church of, Bethlehem *25*
Nazareth 59, *61*, *138*, 138, *185*, *189*, 193, *193*, 199, *199*
Nineveh 56
Olives, Mount of 80, *82*, 85, *92*, 246, *261*
Perea 154
Precipitation, Mount of *199*
Qumran 52, 53, *52*, *53*, 195
Rome *93*, *124*
Samaria *280*, *281*
Siloam, Pool of *298*
Sychar 277
Tabor, Mount *68*
Temple, Herod's 29, *29*, 35, *35*, 84, 92, 96-99, *96-99*, 166, *166*, 176, *184*, 189, *198*, 249, *249*, 273
Tiberias 72, 127, *213*, *287*
Wilderness 35, *35*, 116

Index
Illustrations
in italic

People

³⁴⁶

Index

Abraham 25, 297, 298
Ahaz 26
Anna 190
Annas 102, 328
Archelaus 28, *29*, 244, 245, 266
Augustus 30
Barabbas 255, 256
Caesar 162, 248
Caiaphas 102, 310
Canaanite woman 64
Centurion 43, 207, 208
Constantine 30
David 84
Elijah 32, 68, 69, 105, 115, 215

Eusebius 20
Herod Antipas 61, 72, 140
Herod the Great 27, 28, 29, *29*, 78, 82
Herodias 61, 140
High Priest 254, 310, 329
Isaiah 26, 55, 57, 199
James 157, 316
Joanna 210, 259
John 157, 264, 271
John the Baptist 32, 50, 61, 114, 115, 116, 139, *139*, 184, 186, 188,

191, 194, 209, 270, 276
Jonah 55, 222
Joseph 25, 30, 189, *189*
Joseph of Arimathea 178, 336
Judas 103, 170, 171, 250, *250*, 310, 328
Justin Martyr 30
Lazarus 304, 308
Levi 121, 203, *203*
Luke 182, 186, *186*
Magi 26, 27
Mark 174
Martha 220, 221, 306
Mary, Jesus' mother 25, *25*, 185, 186
Mary 220, 306, 310
Mary of Magdala 337, 338
Matthew 20, 22, 45, 203, *203*
Moses 62, 68, 154, 164, 216
Nathanael 271
Nicodemus 274, 315, 336
Origen 27
Papias 20
Peter 62, 66, 67, 103, 124, 150, 175, 202, 214, 253, 316, 329, 337, 341, 342
Philip 271, 317
Pilate 103, 104, 177, *177*, 254, 255, 329, *329*, 331, 332
Rachel 28, 30
Rich young man 73, 155, 240
Salome 76
Samaritan woman 276, 277, *287*
Simeon 190
Syrian-Phoenician woman 144
Thomas 339
Woman caught in adultery 294, *294*
Zacchaeus 244
Zechariah 184, 185, 188

Jesus' Life

(in chronological order)
Birth 25, 26, 30, 185, 188
Boy at the Temple 190, *190*
Baptism 32, 34, 115, 195
Temptation 34, 35, 36, 117, 198
Ministry begins 36
Family 56, 129, 212
Disciples called 36, 116, 123, 206, 271
Twelve sent out 48, 139, 213
Seventy-two sent out 218

The Miracles: 272, 288
Calming the storm 44, 133, 212
Feeding 5,000 61, 62, 140, 213, 286
Walking on the water 62, 141, 287
Feeding 4,000 64, 148
Water into wine 272
Raising Lazarus 308
Miraculous catch of fish 340

Healing 143
Man with leprosy 42, 119, 202
Centurion's servant 43
Peter's mother-in-law 44, 118, 119
Demoniac 45, 118, 201, 212
Paralytic 45, 121, 202
Jairus's daughter 46, 138, 212
Woman with continual bleeding 46, 135, 212
Two blind men 47, 82
Dumb 47
On Sabbath 54
Canaanite woman's daughter 64
Man with shrivelled hand 122, 204
Deaf-and-dumb 145
Blind 149

Boy with evil spirit 151, 216
Bartimaeus 158
Widow's son 208
Crippled woman 230
Ten lepers 237
Blind man at Jericho 241
Officer's son 281
At Bethesda 283
Man born blind 298, 299

Parables 57, 130, 131
The sower 56, 57, 129, 210, 211
The weeds 58

The enemy 58
The mustard seed 58, 133, 231
The yeast 58, 231
The hidden treasure 59
The net 59
The unforgiving servant 72
The workers in the vineyard 75
The tenants 86, 162, 247
The wedding banquet 87
The thief by night 94
The ten virgins 94
The talents 94
The sheep and the goats 95
The blind 207
Wise and foolish builders 207
The plank 207
Two debtors 210
The lamp 212
Good Samaritan 220
The rich fool 226
Litigious man 229
Great banquet 232
Persistent widow 239
Lost sheep 234
Lost coin 235
Lost son 235

Shrewd manager 236
Rich man and Lazarus 236
Persistent widow 239
Pharisee and tax-collector 239
Ten minas 244

Triumphal entry *15*, 83, 246, 310, 311
Cleansing the Temple 84, 98, 159, 273, *273*
Jesus anointed 170, 210, 310
Jesus arrested 173, 252, 327, 328, 329
Jesus' trial 174, 175, 154-256
Jesus' death 67, 68, 76, 80, 81, 104, 105, 151, 155, 173, 176, 177, 241, 257, 312, 330, 334, *334*
Jesus' burial 106, 178, 258, 336

Index

Adultery 38
After-life 70
Angel 187
Apostles' preaching 11
Ascension 260, 261
Assassins 89
Authority 283, 292
Baal *55*
Baptism 32, *106*, 115, 195, 270
Beelzebub 55, 125, 222
Beatitudes 36, 37, 206
Betrayal 315
Betrothal 185
Blasphemy 102, 175, 201, 304
Bread of Life 287, 288
Brotherly behaviour 71
Chief priests 177
Children 73, 154, 217
Cleanness 62, 142, 144, 223
Commandments 40
Conviction 322
Cost of discipleship 44, 217, 233
Counsellor 318
Cross, taking up 49
Crucifixion 104, 176, 177, 256, *257*
Death 138, 337
Dedication, Feast of 303
Demon possession 118, 202
Devil 35
Disciple 123
Division 228, *229*
Divorce 38, 72, 153
Emmanuel 26
End-time 92, 168, 169, 249, 250
Epiphany 26
Essenes 89
Eternal Life 67, 74, 75, 314
Evidence 296, 304
Exodus 115, 171, 286

348

Faith 11
Family tree 24, *24*, 195
Fasting 40, 46, 121
Forgiveness 45, 72, 237
Fruitfulness 319
Fulfilment 10
Funerals 258
Gehenna 70, 71, 95
Gentiles 144
Giving 39
Glory 152, 312
Good Shepherd 301, 302
Golden Rule 41
Grace 269

Index

Great Commission 106
Greatness 71, 152, 158, 216
Great Rebellion 250
Hades 67, 70
Happiness 37
Hell 153, 225
Hellenists 22
Herald 50
Herodians 88, 89, 164
Holy Spirit 14, 34, 50, 115, 318, 321, 338
Hosanna 83
Humility 240, 315
Hypocrites 90, 225
Incarnation 292
Joy 221, 323
Judgement 32, 41, 51, 94, 95, 313
Judging 71
King of the Jews 22, 29, 330, *332*
Kingdom of God 10, 33, 55, 117, 118, 238
Kingdom of Heaven 32, 33, 36, 58, 59, 71, 73, 87, 94, 215
Lamb of God 270
Last Supper 100, *100*, 170, 250, 251

Law 38, 62, 63, 88
Levite *299*
Life 270
Light 38, 295
Living water 293
Lord 15, 42
Lord's Prayer, the 40
Love 39, 285
Magnificat 186
Mammon 40
Massacre of the boy children 28, 29
Matthew, Gospel of 20-23
Messiah 50, 59, 66, 67, 90, 150, 158, 159, 163, 165, 190, 202, 209, 214, 228, 290, 292, 304, 311
Neighbour 74, 220
New birth 274
Oaths 38
Obedience 35
Palm Sunday 159
Paradise 70
Parties 89
Passover 100, 101, 171, 251, *251*
Persecution 49, 110, 320, *320*
Pharisees 65, 88, 89, 142, 149, 164, *165*, 204, 223, 224, 225, 232, 297, 300
Power 50
Prayer 40, 41, 221, 239, 240, 324, 326, 327
Preparedness 169
Punishment 156
Reconciliation 14
Regeneration 275
Repentance 32, 117, 194, 229
Resurrection 88, 107, 151, 164, 178, 248, 258, 260, 306, 338
Retaliation 39
Revelation 317

Rewards 74
Riches 155
Sabbath 54, 122; 204, 224, 230, 283, 299
Sacrilege 93
Sadducees 65, 88, 89, 164, *165*, 248
Salvation 11, 275
Satan 116, 125
Scribes 89, 90, 121, 166, 281
Self-denial 67
Sermon on the Mount 36-42, 206, 227
Servant 76, 150
Sheol 70
Signs 264, 272
Sin 152
Son of Man 11, 45, 75, 93, 102, 169, 274, 275, 301
Spiritual blindness 284, 292, 300
Swearing 38
Tabernacles, Feast of 291
Temptation 198, 284
Ten Commandments 74
Testing 35, 40
Transfiguration 67, 151, 215
Tradition of men 142
Tribulation 93, 166
Trinity 305
Truth 320
Unbelief 69, 132, 149, 161, 201, 288, 290, 294, 303, 313
Unity 326
Virgin birth 185
Watchfulness 228
Way, the 317
Witness 284
Word 268
Woes 90, 91
Worry 40

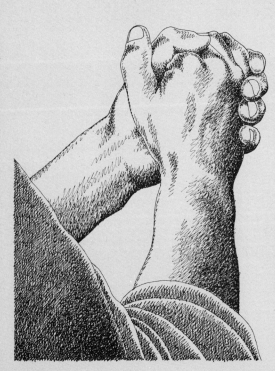

Life and Times

Alabaster bottle *170*
Aloe *335*
Aramaic 67
Ass *83*
Banquet *233*
Bread 214
Bronze snake 274, *274*
Camel *74, 155, 240*
Carob tree *234*
Cinnamon tree *178*
Cock *169*
Colt 158
Costume 196, 197, *196, 197*
Crime 156
Crown of thorns *176*
Cross 333
Cubit 278
Dead Sea Scrolls 52, 53, *53*
Denarius 75
Dog 144
Donkey *311*
Dove *159, 195*
Farming year 112, *112, 113*
Feasting 121
Fig tree 85, *85,* 160, *160,* 229
Fish 71
Fishermen *59,* 117, *201, 341*
Fox *232*
Graffiti *169*
Handmill *71*
Handwashing 104
Harvest 58, *132, 279*
Hen *91*
Homes 120, *120*
Hyssop 333, *333*
Lamp 212
Language 206
Leprosy 42
Locust *115*
Measures in NT 278, *278*
Menorah *295*
Musical instruments *235*
Nard *310*
Nazirite 322
Needle's eye 74

Olive tree *220, 326*
Oxen *51*
Palm branch *311*
Phylactery 90, *90*
Ploughman 217, *217, 237*
Raven *129*
Roman Emperors 167
St Peter's fish *69*
Salt 38, 153
Samaritans 280
Sandals *270*
Sanhedrin 86, 102, 174, 247
Scorpion 219, *219*
Shekel *48*
Shepherd *95, 141, 301, 302, 342*
Snake *221*
Sowing 57
Sparrows 225, *225*
Stoning 295
Synagogue 54, 55, *118, 125,* 136, *136,* 200, *200*

Tallith 197
Talmud 230
Taxes 87, 162, 248
Tax-collector 45, 121, 203, 244
Temple curtain 105, *176, 177,* 257
Temple police 102
Temple tax 69
Terebinth *148*
Threshing *226*
Tithes 91
Tomb *256, 337*
Toga 197, *197*

Index

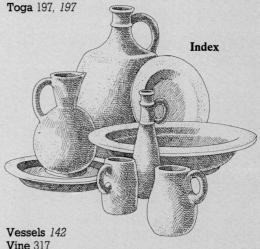

Vessels *142*
Vine 317
Vineyard *75,* 86
Vulture *93*
Water-skin *122*
Weather 65
Weddings 210
Wedding-clothes 87
Weeds 58
Wine-jar *272*
Winemaking 247
Winnowing *32, 194, 269*
Wolf *303*
Zealots 89

Acknowledgements

Illustrators
James Macdonald
Paul Wyart
Kate Pascoe
Pam Stephens
Alan Harris

Photographs
Gordon Gray
Gill Rennie
AN Neilson
N Sharma
Peter Wyart
Tim Dowley
The Bible Society
BBC Hulton Picture Library
The Kobal Collection
The Salvation Army
'The Finding of the Saviour in the
Temple' by courtesy of
Birmingham Museums and Art
Gallery
'Christ Washing Peter's Feet'
The Tate Gallery, London
'The Supper at Emmaus'
'Christ before the High Priest'
'The Agony in the Garden'
'The Adoration of the Kings'
'The Baptism of Christ'
'The Woman caught in Adultery'
'The Crucified Christ'
'Christ blessing Children'
'Christ driving the Traders from
the Temple'
'The Annunciation'
all reproduced by courtesy of
the Trustees, The National
Gallery, London.